THE S. MARK TAPER FOUNDATION

IMPRINT IN JEWISH STUDIES

BY THIS ENDOWMENT

THE S. MARK TAPER FOUNDATION SUPPORTS

THE APPRECIATION AND UNDERSTANDING

OF THE RICHNESS AND DIVERSITY OF

JEWISH LIFE AND CULTURE

*The publisher gratefully acknowledges
the generous contribution to this book
provided by the S. Mark Taper Foundation.*

The Jews of Britain, 1656 to 2000

The Jews of Britain, 1656 to 2000

Todd M. Endelman

UNIVERSITY OF CALIFORNIA PRESS

Berkeley / Los Angeles / London

University of California Press
Berkeley and Los Angeles, California

University of California Press, Ltd.
London, England

© 2002 by the Regents of the University of California

Library of Congress Cataloging-in-Publication Data

Endelman, Todd M.
  The Jews of Britain, 1656 to 2000 / Todd M. Endelman.
    p. cm. — (Jewish communities in the modern world ; 3)
  Includes bibliographical references and index.
    ISBN 0-520-22719-0 (Cloth : alk. paper) — ISBN 0-520-22720-4 (Paper :
  alk. paper)
    1. Jews — Great Britain — History.   2. Great Britain — Ethnic relations.
  I. Title.   II. Series.
  DS135.E5 E485 2002
  941'.004924 — dc21   2001002125

Manufactured in the United States of America
10 09 08 07 06 05 04 03 02
10 9 8 7 6 5 4 3 2 1

For Sue Anne

Contents

Illustrations

Acknowledgments

This book is the culmination of twenty-five years of thinking and writing about Anglo-Jewish history. When I began graduate work in the early 1970s, there was almost no interest in the subject in the academy, even in England. This is no longer true. The writing of Anglo-Jewish history has flourished in the last two decades and has become one of the liveliest areas in modern Jewish history. My own work has benefited from its maturation, and this book is very much in debt to those who championed its cause. Their work stimulated my thinking and caused me repeatedly to temper, if not revise, my views. Indeed, this book would have been much poorer without the ongoing discussion stimulated by their work. In particular, I want to express my gratitude to David Cesarani, Bryan Cheyette, David Feldman, Anne Kershen, Tony Kushner, and William Rubinstein for their contribution to the shape this book took. On numerous trips to England, I have enjoyed their company and their hospitality, as well as that of their families. David Sorkin, who edits this series, and Sheldon Rothblatt, who first taught me how to do history at Berkeley, read the book with their usual care and insight, and I am indebted to them for their comments. I also wish to express my thanks to the Oxford Centre for Hebrew and Jewish Studies and its former president, Bernard Wasserstein, for awarding me a Skirball Visiting Fellowship in 1999. The Lucius N. Littauer Foundation of New York and the Jean and Samuel Frankel Center for Judaic Studies at the University of Michigan funded summer research trips to England. I also wish to acknowledge the help I received from my children, Michael and Flora, who at various times in their college years spent part of their summer vacations searching the pages of the London *Jewish Chronicle* for material for this book. Judy tolerated my absence from Ann Arbor on many occasions and, while I was comfortably at work in English archives and libraries, faced blizzards, power failures, and other crises around the house on her own. For this and countless other things as well, I am, as always, indebted to her.

An earlier version of the introduction to this volume appeared in *Albion* in winter 1995 under the title "Writing English Jewish History." I wish to thank *Albion*'s publisher, the North American Conference on British Studies, and its editor, Michael J. Moore, for giving me permission to reprint it here.

Karl Longstreth, head of the Map Library at the University of Michigan, aided me in the construction of the map of major areas of Jewish settlement in London.

Ann Arbor, Michigan
August 2000

Introduction

Cecil Roth (1899–1970), the preeminent figure in the writing of English Jewish history in the mid-twentieth century, served as president of the Jewish Historical Society of England nine times. In his valedictory presidential address in September 1968 — "Why Anglo-Jewish History?" — Roth defended the enterprise (and the society and himself, by extension) against critics who considered it "petty and unimportant" and believed that "after all that has been written on the subject there is nothing more to be discovered." In his apologia, Roth referred to discoveries made by members of the society that proved that "industrious cultivation of our own modest cabbage patch" contributed to knowledge of both British history and Jewish history in general. In Roth's metaphor, "the inconspicuous inlet of Anglo-Jewish historical research" sometimes branched out into "majestic and . . . unexplored rivers." But, in closing, he confessed that what motivated his choice above all was "the pleasure of the thing" rather than high-minded ideals.[1]

Three decades later the specifics of Roth's defense seem less important than the fact that he felt compelled to defend his choice of research at all. To be sure, until recent times, most works of Jewish history, whatever their focus, served apologetic as well as scholarly ends. Forced since antiquity to justify their survival and their refusal to be absorbed into the societies that hosted them, Jewish intellectuals and publicists, including historians, tended to stress Jewish connections with and contributions to broader national and social units. Beyond this, however, there is a further consideration. Historians of other Jewries (Poland, Germany, Italy, Spain) from Roth's generation felt little need to defend their choice of research vis-à-vis other fields within Jewish history, even when there was an apologetic dimension to their work in other spheres. Why then did Roth feel that the writing of English Jewish history required justification? Roth himself never answered this question, either in his last presidential address or elsewhere, perhaps because he lacked the emotional distance from his subject that would allow him to recognize that this was a question in need of an answer. Still, I suspect that Roth sensed what the problem was, even if he failed to articulate it: the history of the Jews in Britain since their resettlement in the mid-seventeenth century seems to bear little resemblance to the history of the Jews in other European states. It lacks the familiar episodes and movements around which Jewish historians routinely structure their accounts of the past. Instead, it marches to its own drummer, out of step, it would seem, with the experiences of other European Jewries.

To start, Anglo-Jewish history in recent centuries is undramatic, at least in comparison to the travails of Jews in other lands. Show trials, pogroms, accusations of ritual murder, economic boycotts, and other persecutions that punctuated the histories of Central and East European communities were absent, as were political revolutions, like those in France and Russia, that radically and rapidly transformed the circumstances of Jewish life. Political questions that propelled Jews into the national limelight, such as occurred repeatedly in Germany, linking the histories of majority and minority, were also absent in most periods. Those few incidents in British history in which Jews found themselves at the center of political debate—the Jew Bill of 1753, the anti-alien agitation of the late nineteenth and early twentieth centuries, the British mandate for Palestine—were not, in light of tumultuous events elsewhere, critical moments in the life of the British state, shifting and revising its landscape. While the absence of violence and turmoil in their history did not disturb Britain's Jews, who saw it as a mark of their good fortune, the same cannot be said of their historians. For them, the absence of persecution is a problem: it eliminates a familiar framework— Jews as persecuted minority—and a set of related concepts and terms with which to view the history of Britain's Jews. One eminent historian concluded that British Jewish history was so tranquil it did not merit professional attention.[2]

The absence of upheaval also characterizes the internal, cultural history of the community. No new ideological or cultural current in modern Jewish history was launched or nurtured in Britain. The ideological shifts that reoriented modern Jewish consciousness—*haskalah* (the Jewish Enlightenment), Reform Judaism, *Wissenschaft des Judentums* (the critical study of Jewish history and culture), assimilationism, nationalism, and socialism—began and matured in Central and Eastern Europe, where political persecution and material distress bred discontent with conventional practices and values. Historians who chart Jewish modernization in terms of the creation and diffusion of new ideologies, strategies, and programs omit the British Jewish experience as a rule because of its marginal role in this process. Jacob Katz's classic account of the transformation of European Jewry, *Out of the Ghetto,* includes no references to Jewish publicists, ideologues, or activists in Britain. In his treatment, Britain figures largely in terms of its contributions to theories of the secular state and religious toleration. John Locke and John Toland warrant mention but not Jewish brokers or merchants, let alone dealers in secondhand goods.[3]

For historians of the Jewish people, Britain's importance in the nineteenth and twentieth centuries is linked to its role as an imperial power rather than to its treatment of its Jewish citizens or impact on their cultural and intellectual life. In the nineteenth century, Britain's expanding influence in the Levant created a framework in which Western Jewish diplomatic efforts on behalf of persecuted Jews in the Middle East and North Africa could emerge. London Jewish magnates, with Moses Montefiore (1784–1885) in the lead, used their political and economic ties to British statesmen to gain support for intervention in Ottoman affairs, beginning with the notorious Damascus blood libel of 1840 (see chapter 3). Similarly, British interest in the Suez Canal, its lifeline to India, and its long-standing imperial rivalry with France led to the conquest of Palestine and support for Jewish settlement there. As a result, Zionist diplomacy, beginning during World War I, was focused on Whitehall and Westminster, and England's Jews found themselves at the center rather than the margins of efforts to shape the Jewish future.

But, with the above exceptions, events and trends in the British isles have remained marginal to the writing of modern Jewish history, as classroom syllabi and surveys of the field published in the second half of the twentieth century reveal.[4] To some extent, this is a matter of numbers. At its zenith, a few years after the end of World War II, British Jewry numbered not much more than four hundred thousand persons. In contrast, there were over three million Jews in Poland before the Holocaust and over five and one-half million in the United States after the war.[5] At no time, in fact, was Britain home to a substantial percentage of the European Jewish population, which continued to be concentrated in Central and Eastern Europe even after mass migration to the United States. But numbers alone do not explain or justify the marginalization of Britain in modern Jewish historiography, any more than does its geographical location. German Jewry numbered little more than five hundred thousand before the Nazis came to power; French Jewry even less. Moreover, while the total number of Jews in Britain was never high, London was a major center of urban Jewish life from the late eighteenth century. At the time of the French Revolution, more Jews lived in London than in any other European city except Amsterdam. A half century later, it was still one of the largest urban Jewish centers in the West. And, in the wake of the Holocaust, London remained one of the few European capitals whose Jewish community numbered more than one hundred thousand.

Ironically, historians of British Jewry themselves have contributed to the conventional view that their field is peripheral to the modern Jewish experience. Whether written in a celebratory or critical vein, their work has stressed the exceptionalism of Anglo-Jewry—its good fortune, its freedom from mob violence and state discrimination, its uneventful acculturation and integration. Emblematic of this trend is Cecil Roth's tribute to the beneficent influence of English tolerance in the final paragraph of his *History of the Jews in England.* "In this land," he wrote, Jews "have attained a measure of freedom . . . which has been the case in scarcely any other." This was due "in no slight measure to the process of Anglo-Jewish history—a gradual acceptance based on common sense rather than on doctrine, consolidating itself slowly but surely, and never outstripping public opinion."[6] At the same time, historians who take issue with Roth's filiopietistic approach, myself included, have also highlighted the exceptionalism of Anglo-Jewish developments, contrasting in particular the relatively smooth course of emancipation in Britain with its more turbulent, disruptive path in Central European states.[7] One unintentional result of this shared emphasis on the divergent course of Anglo-Jewish history has been to reinforce the notion that it can be more or less ignored when the contours and character of the European Jewish experience as a whole are considered.

Of equal weight in this process of marginalization has been the influence of historians outside the academy. Until the 1970s, the bulk of books and articles on Anglo-Jewry was the work of amateurs, communal dignitaries and functionaries, most of whom were associated with the Jewish Historical Society of England, a nonprofessional body founded in 1893, in part to defend Jews through research that emphasized their rootedness in England and their role in its development. These historians approached their subject in a spirit of uncritical admiration. Their work focused on the establishment of synagogues and charities, the founding of provincial communities, the rise of great merchant and banking clans, the triumph of toleration, and the "contributions" of talented Jews to the larger society. Their version of communal history was Whiggish, apologetic, and triumphalist, emphasizing the harmony between Jewishness and Englishness, while minimizing the discordant aspects of the assimilation process. There was little room in their work for the mass of Jews at any time, whether street traders in the Georgian period or garment workers in the late-Victorian and Edwardian years. Jews who attracted attention for the wrong reasons—criminals, usurers, prizefighters, pawnbrokers, property developers, social climbers, speculators, toffs, and toughs—were also absent, needless to say. In terms of periodization, they focused their attention on personalities and events before 1870, when the great migration from Eastern Europe commenced. In their view, the unanglicized newcomers were the wrong kind of Jews. They believed their presence was a cause of antisemitism, looked forward to their rapid social and cultural regeneration, and hence wrote them out of the historical record. They also tended to treat their subject in isolation from English social and religious history—and from other Jewish histories as well—rarely exploring its comparative dimensions in either context. For all of these reasons, Jewish historians elsewhere took little notice of the work of the amateur school, since it did not address their questions and agendas. The work of those historians, in turn, remained unknown or irrelevant to the practitioners of Anglo-Jewish historiography.[8]

If most Jewish historians have viewed the Jewish experience in Britain as peripheral or irrelevant to major trends in their field, the same is even more true in regard to British historians, though for different reasons. The latter have tended either to ignore Jews altogether or treat them superficially, as victims—of anti-alien laws, social discrimination, or fascist hooliganism—or as success stories, as politicians, bankers, artists, writers, scientists, in short as members of respectable *English* circles. In this context, Jews have no voice of their own as Jews, no internal life of more than parochial interest. This benign neglect should surprise no one: for most of the last three centuries, England has not been a nation of diverse colors, cultures, faiths, and languages, however multidenominational its Christianity. While the toleration it extended to Jews was more generous than in most countries, it was, nonetheless, hostile or indifferent to cultural diversity. It did not respect or value the customs and beliefs of the Jewish religion or endorse the survival of Jewish social or cultural particularism. In this sense, historians, regardless of their political sympathies, have shared mainstream English values. For most of them, the Jewish presence has been almost an absence, or it has been an awkward presence, difficult to fit into conventional models and frameworks, seemingly outside the dominant ways of thinking about English history.

What is striking about this historiographical reluctance to see Jews is how often it has occurred when least expected, that is, when the Jewish dimension of the story is unambiguous. Major accounts of the formation of national identity omit any reference to Jews as foils for the forging of English and British identities, even though the agitation sparked by passage of the Jew Bill in 1753 functioned as a lightning rod for the articulation of nationalist sentiments at the time (see chapter 2).[9] In the realm of social history, accounts of the trade in secondhand clothes in the eighteenth century ignore the increasingly close identification of the trade with Jews and Jewish streets (Houndsditch, Monmouth Street, Petticoat Lane) in this period. This is a breathtaking omission. Jewish old clothes men were a regular feature of the London street scene in the Georgian period, as both visual and written evidence from the period testifies. The link between Jews and old clothes was so fixed in the popular imagination that Victorian political cartoonists regularly drew Benjamin Disraeli (1804–81) as an old clothes man in order to stress his Jewishness.[10]

The sources of this blindness are multiple and complex. At one level, old-fashioned prejudices, both conscious and unconscious, play a role, although not a decisive one. More important, given the liberal tone of the academic establishment, is a sense of awkwardness, even embarrassment, in recognizing the Jewishness of Jews who figured in British history and assigning this Jewishness, however defined, an active or causative role. Unaccustomed to viewing minorities as historical actors in the British context, committed to the tolerant, assimilative powers of English culture, and, above all, wishing to avoid the appearance of being too concerned with Jews (and thus open to charges of intolerance), historians of Britain are content to ignore or minimize the Jewish presence in their work. Before the 1990s, for example, few biographers of Disraeli or historians of Victorian politics acknowledged the prominence of the antisemitism that accompanied his climb up the greasy pole or its role in shaping his own singular sense of Jewishness.[11] Contributing to this reluctance is the often unsettling character of historical writing that addresses relations between dominant and minority groups. In general, such accounts do not reflect well on the former, with their unflattering revelations of narrow-mindedness and intolerance. Colin Richmond remarks that a history of medieval England that includes Jews is disturbing: it depicts England's rulers "without clothes," nakedly and unashamedly despoiling their Jewish subjects, and it reveals its monastic culture to be bigoted and credulous, giving birth to the first accusation of ritual murder in Europe.[12] Beyond their unmasking function, histories that include minorities also reveal the power of myths, fantasies, and fears, the irrational and the unconscious, causal factors that most historians confront with reluctance, if at all, especially when they identify in some way with the societies about which they write.

Whatever the weight of these subjective influences, there are also structural historiographical obstacles to integrating Jews into the writing of British history. These obstacles stem from fundamental questions about how Jews are to be defined within the parameters of historical scholarship on Britain. Are they to be viewed as religious dissenters, as successful nonconformists like Quakers and Unitarians? Or are they to be viewed as marginalized immigrants and aliens, like newcomers from Africa, Asia, and the Caribbean in the decades after World War II, stigmatized and excluded from the mainstream? Or are they, perhaps, to be viewed as ethnics, distinctive by virtue of their origins, customs, and social habits? If so, it must be acknowledged that there is little precedent for including ethnic groups in the telling of English history, since there was little ethnic or national diversity in England before World War II — with the exception of the Irish, of course, who like the Jews were distinctive by virtue of both religion and national origin. Marxist-inspired class categories also fail to encompass the Jewish presence. Were Jews a rising bourgeoisie, a downtrodden proletariat, or, as in the Georgian period, a lumpenproletariat of street vendors and pickpockets?

The truth is that Jews were all of these and thus cannot be fitted comfortably into the standard categories of British historical writing. Efforts to reduce them to one category or another, to privilege their class character, immigrant status, or religious nonconformity, to give them a one-dimensional existence, distort rather than describe their experience. This occurs, for example, when labor historians define Jewish immigrants from Eastern Europe as class-conscious proletarians with attenuated religio-ethnic attachments. Those who define immigrant workers in this way must then rationalize or dismiss behavior that is "inappropriate," that is, does not accord with their class status. They dismiss trade unionists who respect the Sabbath as lumpenproletariat (authentic proletarians reject religion *tout court*) and attribute the embourgeoisement of slum dwellers to an involuntary program of social control imposed from above through charities, clubs, schools, and other welfare schemes.[13] The implication is that Jewish workers would have remained class-conscious proletarians if they had followed their own inclinations.

Rather than continue in this vein, multiplying pitfalls and obstacles, it is time to shift gears and suggest some broad guidelines about how to structure the telling of Anglo-Jewish history. To begin, it must be remembered that the history of the Jews in Britain possesses a dual character, as, indeed, do the histories of all Diaspora Jewries. It is both part of the history of the Jewish people in the West, which encompasses communities in North America and Western and Central Europe, and part of the history of Britain. (In regard to the last century, of course, it is also part of an even more far-flung Jewish history, as events in the former Soviet Union and the Middle East influenced notions of Jewishness and transformed communal agendas.) Anglo-Jewish history cannot be understood without reference to both of these components. To be sure, this dual frame of reference can make for awkwardness at times — Is this British history? Is this Jewish history? — but it does replicate the experience of the subjects of this book, who, however strong their identification with Britain, also felt they belonged to a transnational group as well, the Jewish people, to whom they were linked by blood, belief, sentiment, fate, or some combination thereof.

Yet there is an advantage as well to working with this dual perspective. Awareness of how events in Anglo-Jewish history fit into both frameworks helps to identify what is unique in that history, and thus presumably due to the impact of English circumstances, and what is common to Western Jewries in general, and thus the result of either immanent developments or external conditions found in all Western societies. At the same time, this awareness can also serve to mediate between, or at least place in perspective, opposing interpretations of historical trends. The debate about the place of antisemitism in modern Britain illustrates this virtue. Books and essays published in the 1980s and 1990s discredited the old view, expressed most fully in the work of Cecil Roth, that antisemitism was inconsequential and Anglo-Jewish history an uninterrupted success story.[14] But there are historians who, while rejecting Roth's uncritical perspective, still hold that Britain's record from the eighteenth through the twentieth centuries was, if not unsullied, superior to that of other European states and that this must be explained and its impact on Jewish behavior explored.[15] In this view, rooted in the trans-European perspective of Jewish history, British Jews gained access to non-Jewish circles and at the same time maintained their Jewishness with greater ease than most other European Jews. Critics of this view, whose work examines a more limited period (from the last decades of the nineteenth century to the immediate post–World War II years), do not challenge the notion that Britain was more tolerant than Germany or Hungary or Austria. Rather, they object to the comparison itself, arguing that it is irrelevant, that British prejudices must be weighed in the context of British liberalism, with its professed commitment to toleration and fair play, not in the context of German authoritarianism and illiberalism. And from this perspective, they find the record to be much less spotless than it was once assumed to be. One defender of Roth suggests that these historians resemble the four Yorkshiremen in the famous Monty Python skit who attempt to outdo each other in recounting the deprivations they suffered in childhood.

Leaving aside the ideological differences that add fuel to this debate, what is at stake here is the question of historiographical perspective. Which dimension of Anglo-Jewish history is to be privileged—its English context or its Jewish context? Once this is recognized as the crux of the matter, then questions about the place of antisemitism in English history become more accessible to some kind of resolution. In fact, it can be argued that both contexts are germane in that both generate truths about the experience of Jews in Britain. The former highlights the great limitation of English liberalism, its unwillingness to endorse cultural diversity, while the latter highlights its great strength, its defense of individual freedoms in the face of racial and other organic conceptions of the nation. In other words, historians need to explain why a converted Jew who flaunted his Jewish roots was able to rise to the leadership of the Conservative party in the Victorian period, which would have been unthinkable elsewhere, *and* at the same time why his rise and policies, especially his handling of the Eastern Question (the problems arising from the disintegration of the Ottoman Empire), sparked an explosion of antisemitism directed not just at him but at English Jews in general. Both are significant and both require analysis.

Once it is acknowledged that successes as well as failures warrant explanation, the lack of surface drama in English Jewish history—trials, riots, violence, ideological clashes, cultural ferment—ceases to be troublesome. But there is more to the content of this history than the relative absence of familiar landmarks from other Jewish histories.

One long-term result of the revolution in historical thinking that occurred in the 1960s and 1970s was the legitimization of social history. At its ideological heart was an expansion or democratization of the historical arena, the recognition that the experiences of persons outside intellectual, economic, political, cultural, and religious elites are in themselves interesting and instructive. From this perspective, Anglo-Jewish history is no less dramatic or engaging than its continental counterparts. English Jews, like all Jews in the modern period, faced challenges to their inherited identities, made decisions to embrace, transform, or reject non-Jewish values, and struggled to overcome poverty and enter new spheres of activity. Because English Jews produced no Moses Mendelssohns, Abraham Geigers, Perets Smolenskins, Theodor Herzls, or other ideological trailblazers, it does not follow that their acculturation and integration into state and society occurred spontaneously or in a fit of absentmindedness and thus lacks historiographical importance.[16] In an essay written in the early 1980s, I argued that the career of the London-based "Jew" King (ca. 1753–1824), moneylender, womanizer, scoundrel, and radical, was as important to understanding Jewish acculturation and integration as that of Mendelssohn—perhaps even more so, since parvenus and scoundrels outnumbered philosophers in modern Jewish societies. What I wrote then seems to me no less true now: most Jews did not enter the modern world like a well-disciplined army, tramping faithfully in the footsteps of Mendelssohn and the *maskilim* (followers of the Jewish Enlightenment).[17]

One remarkable feature of Anglo-Jewish scholarship is the strength of its attention to social history. Decades before historians of other Western Jewries took notice of non-elite dimensions of the Jewish experience, Anglo-Jewish historians were addressing themes—urbanization, social mobility, class conflict, for example—that reflected the lives of the Jewish people as a whole rather than their lay and religious leaders alone.[18] The work of the new school of Anglo-Jewish historians, which since its debut in the 1980s has transformed a once somnolent backwater into one of the liveliest, most contentious branches of modern Jewish history, builds on this tradition.[19] It emphasizes the experiences of immigrants, outsiders, women, radicals, critics of the communal establishment, the poor, and the pious—that is, the bulk of English Jews rather than small numbers of notables, intellectuals, and synagogue functionaries. It rejects the view that English Jewish history is to be seen in a

Whiggish glow, its subjects the beneficiaries of an inexorable march toward enlightenment, tolerance, freedom, and prosperity. Instead, it emphasizes disharmonies in the historical record: tensions between Jews and non-Jews and, within the community, between rich and poor, aliens and natives, Reform and Orthodox, workers and masters, nationalists and assimilationists, advocates of religious pluralism and champions of religious centralization and conformity. It takes account, as well, of those who fell away: those who embraced Christianity to advance their social fortunes and careers, those whose Jewish attachments eroded through indifference and neglect, those who were able to find fulfillment only outside the communal pond, those who internalized English attitudes toward Jewishness and felt stigmatized and rebuffed.

The new school also stresses the Englishness of the English Jewish experience, the impress of context and setting on its unfolding, as opposed to what it shares in common with other Jewish histories. In fact, it is difficult to name another corpus of Jewish historical literature written with equal sensitivity to the horizontal dimensions of modern Jewish history. On this score, historians of other Jewries can learn much from Anglo-Jewish historiography, however marginal events in Britain appear to them. The other side of this emphasis on contextualization is the claim that English historians can learn as well from the history of the Jewish minority. This is not as self-serving as it might seem at first. After all, it is now a commonplace that the history of the United States is incomprehensible, not just incomplete, without due attention to its African-American, Hispanic, and other minorities. This awareness is the result of more than sentimental tokenism or political correctness. Historians of the United States recognize that attitudes toward minorities and their actual treatment illuminate the behavior of the white Protestant majority. If true, then why should the case be different in regard to Britain and its minorities, allowing, of course, for the respective importance of minorities in the two countries? As David Feldman argues in the conclusion to his *Englishmen and Jews*, "some of the central issues in modern English history, such as the nature of Victorian liberalism, the growth of the collectivist state, and the history of the working class, can be seen in a new light by closely examining their relation to the Jewish minority."[20]

It would have been impossible to write this history of Britain's Jews without the achievements of this new school. The fruits of their research, as well as their conceptual vocabulary and interpretive insights, inform this book, although they have not been incorporated fully or uncritically.

Given my characterization of Anglo-Jewish history, it should be no surprise that this is a history of English Jews rather than a history of their rabbis or merchant princes, whose impact on communal institutions cannot be denied but whose representativeness can. This means that Moses Montefiore and other luminaries and spokesmen do not receive the attention that earlier histories lavished on them. Nor is this an account of Jewish charitable and religious institutions or the men who created and directed them, although they are not absent by any means. It should be unnecessary to add, as well, that there is little in the chapters that follow about Jewish "contributions" to business, art, literature, or politics, except insofar as they illuminate more general patterns of acculturation, mobility, and integration. My goal has been to paint as broad a canvas as possible, to look for what was representative, to be inclusive rather than exclusive, to account for broad swings and changes, to describe and explain rather than celebrate (or condemn). If I succeed, it is, in part, because I have had firm ground on which to stand.

To avoid confusion, let me explain at the outset two sets of terms whose meanings and parameters require clarification. First, it is conventional to use the term "Anglo-Jewish" to refer to Jews in Britain as a whole, including Jews in Scotland and Wales, even though they were not, in a strict sense, "English" Jews. This usage is too well established to be dropped. Moreover, since the number of Jews who lived in Wales and Scotland was never large, folding them into "Anglo"-Jewry does not distort the overall picture. The history of the Jews in Britain is overwhelmingly the history of Jews who lived in *English* cities, London in particular. The distinction between the terms "British" and "English" in other contexts is unsettled as well. At various times *English* writers used the terms interchangeably. At the start of the twenty-first century, with the devolution of Scotland and Wales, the meanings of "Britishness" and "Englishness" are again much disputed. When I use the term "British," I am referring specifically to the island of Great Britain, its system of government, and its political culture. When I use the term "English," I am referring specifically to the culture and society of the English people, the background against which Anglo-Jewish history unfolded.

Second, Anglo-Jewry evolved a set of unusual terms to refer to its religious leaders. Elsewhere, the religious heads of communities and congregations were ordained rabbis trained in seminaries or *yeshivot* (academies for the study of Jewish law). In Britain, before the mass migration from Eastern Europe, there were few ordained rabbis. In the

Victorian period, "ministers" or "readers" met the liturgical and pastoral needs of anglicized synagogues. They chanted the service, preached English-language sermons, read the weekly Torah portion, and educated the young. Many were graduates of Jews' College, the Anglo-Jewish seminary in London, but had had no advanced training in Jewish law and thus were not ordained rabbis. Britain's Victorian chief rabbis (see chapter 3), wishing to monopolize the title "rabbi," did nothing to encourage the development of a learned rabbinate. (Not until after World War I did Jews' College graduate rabbis with a mastery of Talmud.) The chief rabbis even refused to recognize the rabbinical titles of the few Central European-born and-educated rabbis who occupied British pulpits. This changed only in the mid-twentieth century, when seminary- or yeshivah-educated rabbis began to replace "ministers" and "readers" in even the most anglicized synagogues.

Menasseh ben Israel. Salom Italia's engraving of 1642. Lucien Wolf, *Menasseh ben Israel's Mission to Oliver Cromwell* (London, 1901). Courtesy of the Harlan Hatcher Graduate Library, University of Michigan.

CHAPTER I

The Resettlement (1656–1700)

Edward I expelled the Jews of England in 1290, bringing to an abrupt end the medieval period in English Jewish history. The order of expulsion uprooted a once prosperous community whose origins can be traced to the late eleventh century, when Jewish merchants from northern France crossed the Channel in the wake of the Norman conquest. Although described by Cecil Roth as "the least important, both numerically and culturally," of all medieval western Jewries,[1] the Jews of England nonetheless occupied a prominent position in the life of the country before their decline in the half-century before the expulsion. Jewish merchants and moneylenders performed unpopular economic operations, while the community as a group served as a substantial source of revenue for the crown. The latter function was particularly important. Taxes, extraordinary levies, and outright confiscations transferred much of the profits generated by Jewish moneylending and trade to the royal exchequer. But when the Jews' wealth declined dramatically in the second half of the thirteenth century as a result of new restrictions on moneylending and exorbitant royal imposts, they lost their fiscal utility. This—along with growing religious hostility—paved the way for their expulsion.[2]

At the time of the expulsion, there were about two thousand Jews in England. (Earlier in the century there may have been as many as four to five thousand, but mounting persecution—arbitrary arrests and executions, exorbitant fiscal exactions, pressure to convert, and confiscations of property—as well as civil unrest, had already caused the community to shrink before 1290.)[3] The precise fate of the exiles is unknown.

15

A small number apparently converted to Christianity, some finding refuge in the Domus Conversorum in London, which had been established in 1232 as a hostel for impoverished Jewish applicants for baptism. Some lost their lives in fleeing the country, the victims of unscrupulous ship captains and crews. But the majority probably found refuge in France, where they assimilated completely into the main body of Jews living there, losing all trace of their prior residence in England.

After 1290, Jews were, in theory, prohibited from settling in England. Nonetheless, some persons of Jewish descent, including professing observant Jews, visited England and even lived there for short periods of time in the following centuries. Most were physicians and merchants who left after completing their business. In 1410, for example, the Bolognese Jewish physician Elias Sabot was summoned to treat Henry IV.[4] A handful were drifters, adventurers, and other marginal persons, some of whom found their way to the Domus Conversorum and accepted baptism. At various times there were Jews from France, Flanders, Italy, Germany, Spain, Portugal, and North Africa living in the hostel. The emergence of a modern Jewish community, however, owed nothing to the presence or activities of such individuals, but rather can be traced to events in Spain and Portugal at the close of the medieval period.

In 1492, Isabella and Ferdinand expelled the Jews of Spain. One of their motives was to prevent contact between professing Jews and the large group of baptized Jews and their descendants (known as New Christians or *conversos*)[5] that emerged in the wake of the pogroms of 1391. Many Jews, perhaps more than half, preferred not to leave Spain and embraced Christianity, thus swelling the size of the converso community. Of those who chose exile, a large percentage found refuge across the border in Portugal, but five years later, in 1497, those who had remained there were forced to submit to baptism en masse. Thus, at the end of the fifteenth century, there were several hundred thousand persons of Jewish descent living in the Iberian Peninsula. Some cultivated links to their Jewish past, adhering in secret to remnants of Jewish practice and belief, while others eagerly shed their former identity and became devout Roman Catholics. But whether sincere in their new faith or not, all New Christians faced legal and social obstacles to full integration by virtue of their Jewish descent. Moreover, all conversos risked being accused of secret judaizing and falling into the hands of the Inquisition. For these reasons, many New Christians chose to emigrate to more commercially vibrant lands where there was less risk of prosecution. Those who left the peninsula included both secret judaizers and sincere Christians—as well as persons who were neither and whose religious identity was less clearly fixed.[6]

In these circumstances, several score New Christian merchants settled in London between the 1520s and the end of the century. Most were linked by family and commercial ties to the important New Christian trading colony in Antwerp. (In the 1540s and 1550s, there was also a small converso community of cloth traders in Bristol.) The community in London was not stable and failed to sink permanent roots. This was, in part, because it was a trading colony, a satellite of the larger converso settlement in Antwerp, and, in part, because it was subject to periodic denunciations and prosecutions. In 1541, for example, in the wake of inquisitorial proceedings in Milan that revealed that some New Christian merchants in London lived "in the Hebrew manner," the Spanish authorities pressured the English government to arrest persons suspected of being Jews and to sequester their property. The arrested merchants were able eventually to convince the authorities of their innocence, but much of the community dispersed after this. In Elizabeth's reign, the New Christian colony again grew with the addition of new arrivals. Among them was the physician courtier Roderigo Lopez, who was executed in 1594 for plotting to poison the queen and who, it was once believed, inspired Shakespeare's Shylock in *The Merchant of Venice* (1596). This settlement came to an end in 1609, when, as a result of a quarrel within the group, one party denounced the other as judaizers and the authorities then expelled all Portuguese merchants living in London.[7]

Testimony given in inquisitorial proceedings in Milan, Antwerp, and Lisbon in the 1540s and 1550s leaves no doubt that many of these merchants were indeed secret judaizers. Gaspar Lopes, a former London agent of the Mendes family in Antwerp who turned informer when arrested, testified in Milan in 1540 that Alves Lopes hosted Sabbath services in his London home and that on the day he attended, about twenty "false Christians"—men and women—were there. He also revealed that this New Christian merchant provided aid to conversos seeking temporary refuge in England and Flanders on their way to Turkey and other Ottoman lands, where they could live openly as Jews. The Bristol group also included active judaizers. According to one informer's testimony, the physician and merchant Henrique Nunes hosted festival and Sabbath services and Passover seders in his home, his nephew in London sending him notice every year of when the festivals would occur. His wife Beatriz, the Inquisition was told, baked *matsot* (unleavened

bread for Passover) for the community, gave instruction to new converso arrivals, and avoided eating forbidden foods when traveling back
and forth to London. The same informant also described the reception
and circulation in both London and Bristol converso circles of Samuel
Usque's Portuguese-language *Consolation for the Tribulations of Israel*
(1553), a martyrological work written to strengthen converso faith in
Judaism.[8] It would be an error, however, to infer from this testimony
that "Judaism in England in the first half of the sixteenth century was
in a very robust condition."[9] Not all New Christians were covert Jews.
Moreover, by the late sixteenth and early seventeenth centuries, the
crypto-Judaism of London New Christians was a mere shadow—and
often a distortion—of that which had flourished in Spain and Portugal
before the expulsion. For some, it was little more than a consciousness
of being of Jewish descent.[10]

In the 1630s, merchants of converso origins again began settling in
London, attracted by its growing importance in the international economy and protected by the treaty of 1630 with Spain, exempting Spanish
subjects (which included the Portuguese until 1640) from the laws
against recusants. This colony proved to be more durable than its predecessors, and it is with this group that one can date the beginnings of
the modern Jewish community in Britain. Some of these merchants
came from Catholic lands—France, the Canary Islands, Portugal itself—
where Jewish life was still prohibited and crypto-Judaism actively persecuted. For example, Antonio Fernandez Carvajal (ca. 1590–1659), a
native of Portugal and for many years a resident of the Canary Islands,
fled Rouen when the secret Jewish community there was denounced in
1632 and, along with one or two others, moved to London. There he
became a prominent City merchant and ship owner, trading with the
Levant and the East and West Indies, importing bullion, gunpowder,
and munitions, and acting as grain contractor for Parliament during the
Civil War. Other merchants came from Protestant areas—Amsterdam
and Hamburg, in particular—where Jewish settlement was tolerated and
former conversos did not have to live as nominal Christians. Their motives for migrating were entirely commercial, since they were already
living openly as Jews. Once settled in London, whatever their previous
commitment to Judaism, these Iberian merchants were required to appear as Roman Catholics and to attend mass occasionally in the chapels
of the French, Portuguese, Spanish, and Venetian ambassadors.[11] Nonetheless, it was widely known in Whitehall and the City that some were
crypto-Jews. As James Howell, the royalist spy and pamphleteer, wrote

in 1653 to a friend in Amsterdam, "Touching Judaism, some corners of our city smell as rank of it as yours doth there."[12] Yet, despite this awareness, government and religious authorities did not molest the converso community, probably because they were preoccupied with other matters in the turbulent decades of the 1640s and 1650s.

A dramatic change in the status of this nominally Catholic merchant colony occurred in the winter of 1655–56, as a result of which a permanent, government-tolerated, professing Jewish community emerged. This change was not the result of any single act—it would be easier to explain were it so—but the outcome of a complex of unforeseeable events and long-term currents.[13]

The first Englishmen to propose the readmission of Jews were radical Puritans who eagerly awaited the coming of the millennium and were convinced that Protestant England had an active role to play in bringing it about. A key aspect of their millenarian faith was the conviction that the conversion of the Jews (and, according to some, their return to the Holy Land) had to precede or was in some way linked to the final scheme of redemption. In their vision of the events leading to the end of days, God had assigned England the task of converting the Jews. Having overthrown the yoke of Roman corruption and idolatry and restored Christianity to its uncontaminated original state, the godly English would be able to effect with love and kindness what papal religion had failed to do with its persecutory, blood-stained methods. But for this to occur, the Jews had to be brought into daily contact with the cleansed Christianity of the English—which meant that they had to be readmitted.

Millenarian concern with the conversion of the Jews appeared in England in the last decades of Elizabeth's reign. Initially it was confined to a small number of enthusiasts who expressed interest in the future salvation of the Jews without envisioning a special task for England in this process. In the first decades of the seventeenth century, millenarian views gained a broader audience and, at the same time, increasingly included the notion that England would play a special role in the unfolding of the final days. In the 1640s, with the coming of the Civil War and the breakdown of censorship, church courts, and ecclesiastical control of education, restraints on the religious imagination disappeared, and previously unorthodox ideas, including conversionist millenarianism, received a wider hearing than ever before. In the intoxicating atmosphere of those tumultuous times, many supporters of the parliamentary cause—politicians, preachers, scholars, and ordinary people alike—expected the conversion of the Jews and the coming of the millennium in the near future.[14] Some prophesied that these would occur in 1655; others said 1656, the date most popular among the Fifth Monarchists, a radical Puritan sect that believed the "fifth monarchy" of Jesus and the saints was at hand. Among those who shared these views, a few urged the immediate readmission of the Jews in order to hasten the coming of salvation. In January 1649, Johanna Cartwright and her son Ebenezer, Baptists who had fled to Amsterdam during the Marian persecutions, petitioned Thomas Fairfax and the Council of the Army to repeal the expulsion edict of 1290. Believing that redemption was at hand and that repeal of the ban would appease God's anger over the innocent blood being shed in England, they urged that the Jews be allowed to trade and dwell in England "under the Christian banner of charity and brotherly love" as they then did in the Netherlands. This was the first serious effort to recall the Jews to England.[15]

Reports about the growth of pro-Jewish sentiment in England reached Amsterdam, arousing the interest of Jews and Christians alike, including one of the communal rabbis of the Sephardim, Menasseh ben Israel (1604–57).[16] A Portuguese New Christian by birth, Menasseh was raised and educated in Amsterdam and, like many Jews of converso origin, was fluent in several European languages and familiar with intellectual and religious currents outside the Jewish community. He maintained an active correspondence with statesmen, divines, and scholars in several countries in northern Europe and was frequently consulted by them on matters of Jewish scholarship. He was also in contact with English religious sectarians who had taken refuge in Amsterdam; from them he learned of the religious and political changes convulsing their country. As the child of parents who had suffered at the hands of the Inquisition, Menasseh had two preoccupations that inclined him to respond with enthusiasm to the news from England. First, he was concerned with finding new lands of refuge for Jewish settlement and colonization. At one time, for example, he thought of dedicating his *Conciliador* (1632–51), a Spanish-language work reconciling apparent contradictions in the Hebrew Bible, to Queen Christina of Sweden, in order to make her more amenable to a proposal to settle Jews in her country.[17]

This concern was hardly unique to Menasseh ben Israel. From the time of the expulsion, New Christian and Jewish leaders labored to find lands of opportunity to which persecuted conversos could migrate. Indeed, one motive of the converso courtiers who financed Columbus's voyages of exploration was the desire to discover a new world in which former Jews and their descendants could start their lives afresh. In the 1650s, in particular, a concerted effort was made by Sephardim in Amsterdam and elsewhere to secure permission for new Jewish settlements in northern Italy, the Caribbean, and the Guyanas.[18] In this sense, Jewish efforts to gain readmission to England were part of a broader strategy of securing new places of refuge for persecuted New Christians.

Menasseh ben Israel's interest in Jewish resettlement in England had a further dimension. Menasseh was a messianist, and, like those English divines who linked the recall of the Jews to the Second Coming, he imagined that the return of Jews to England would accelerate the coming of the messianic age. While all Jews believed that one day God would send a descendant of the royal house of David to redeem them from exile and restore them to their ancient homeland, Menasseh lived in the expectation that these events would occur sooner rather than later, a belief shared by increasing numbers of Jews in the mid-seventeenth century, as the messianic excitement surrounding Shabbetai Zevi in the 1660s revealed (see below). Menasseh's messianism was stimulated by the arrival in Amsterdam in 1644 of a Portuguese New Christian, Antonio de Montezinos (ca. 1604–ca. 1647), who claimed to have met a group of Indians in a remote part of present-day Colombia who were descendants of the biblical tribe of Reuben, one of the so-called ten lost tribes. To Jews inclined to look for signs that the end of exile was at hand, this revelation was of great moment: the discovery of Jews in the New World meant that God was fulfilling the prophecy that the Jews would be scattered "from one end of the earth to the other" (Deut. 28: 64) before the end of days. Yet there remained one corner of the world from which Jews were still absent—England (called *ketseh ha-arets* [the end of the earth] in medieval Hebrew). Jews in a state of messianic expectation, like their Christian counterparts, could thus view the return to English soil as preparation for the advent of the messianic age.

Protestant millenarians in Holland and England, who had their own reason for being interested in the discovery of the lost tribes—they viewed the conversion of all the descendants of the ancient Israelites (rather than just the Jews of Europe) as a precondition for the Second Coming—heard rumors of Montezinos's encounter and turned to Menasseh ben Israel for his opinion. He responded by writing *The Hope of Israel* (1650), in which he discussed Montezinos's story, weighed various theories about the origins of the American Indians, and reaffirmed his faith in the traditional messianic promises made to the Jews. To the

English translation published in London in 1650, he appended a dedi-
cation to Parliament and the Council of State, in which he attributed
messianic significance to their activities. The whole world, he wrote, was
watching "that they may see whither all these things do tend, which the
great Governor of all things seems to bring upon the world by so great
changes . . . and so all those things, which God is pleased to have fore-
told by the Prophets, do and shall obtain their accomplishment."[19]

Publication of *The Hope of Israel* in England marked the start of a
campaign by Menasseh ben Israel to obtain government approval for
Jews to resettle there. When an English mission came to The Hague
early in 1651 to negotiate an alliance with the United Provinces, it visited
the Sephardi synagogue in Amsterdam, where a special blessing was said
in its honor and the honor of the English commonwealth. Menasseh
was present and probably discussed with the ambassadors his hopes for
obtaining permission for Jewish resettlement. Later in the year he sent
a petition for readmission (now lost) to the Council of State, where it
was discussed on 10 October. The response must have been more pos-
itive than negative, since in November a passport was issued for Menasseh to come to London to discuss the matter in person. However, the
outbreak of the first Dutch War (1652–54), following passage of the anti-
Dutch Navigation Act of 1651 (see below), delayed his coming to England for several years. But the question of Jewish readmission remained
before the public, thanks to mounting millenarian excitement. When
Oliver Cromwell opened the Barebones Parliament on 4 July 1653, he
announced, "This may be the door to usher in the things that God has
promised, which have been prophesied of, which he has set the hearts
of his people to wait for and expect. . . . You are at the edge of the
promises and prophecies." Among them he included the prophecy that
"God will bring the Jews home to their station from the isles of the sea,
and answer their expectations as from the depths of the sea," as once
He led Israel through the Red Sea.[20]

When Menasseh petitioned the Council of State, he did so on his
own account, not as an official representative of the Amsterdam community. Yet it is clear from correspondence that has survived that his
diplomacy enjoyed the unofficial blessing of major communal figures.[21]
While it is not known whether they shared his messianic hopes, they
did share his concern with finding new territories for Jewish settlement.
This had become an even more acute problem in the 1650s, when there
was an influx into Holland of New Christian refugees from Spain, where
the Inquisition operated with renewed ferocity after 1645, and of Jewish
refugees from Brazil, where Dutch rule collapsed between 1645 and 1654.

In addition, they had a particular interest in gaining a foothold in England. The Navigation Act of 1651, which sought to promote English overseas commerce at the expense of the Dutch, required merchandise imported into England to be carried either in English ships or in ships belonging to the country where the goods originated. This threatened to disrupt trading links between Amsterdam and Barbados (the pre-eminent Caribbean center for the production of sugar), where there was a largely Dutch Sephardi community. The establishment of an outpost in London would allow Sephardi mercantile houses headquartered in Amsterdam to circumvent the Navigation Act. However, because Anglo-Dutch relations were strained at this time, the *mahamad,* or governing council, of the Amsterdam community was unable to engage in open negotiations with Cromwell and Parliament or to endorse formally Menasseh's diplomacy.

The Barebones Parliament failed to usher in the millennium or recall the Jews, and from mid-December 1653 Oliver Cromwell ruled as Lord Protector. The following year, with the Dutch War at an end, the campaign for Jewish resettlement was renewed. In September, Menasseh's son, Samuel Soeiro (d. 1657), traveled to London. He was accompanied by Manuel Martinez Dormido (d. 1667), a merchant and former *parnas* (member of the mahamad) of the Amsterdam community who had lost his fortune when the Portuguese drove the Dutch from Brazil and who hoped to gain the assistance of the English government, now allied with Portugal, in recovering it. Dormido presented two petitions to Cromwell on 3 November 1654, one asking for diplomatic intervention to regain his fortune, the other asking for permission for Jews to settle and worship freely in England. Significantly, the second petition did not propose that Jews be allowed to return on the basis of a limited toleration, with a charter setting forth the conditions in which they would be allowed to live, as was the custom in Central Europe at the time. Rather, it petitioned that they be allowed to be "dwellers here with the same equalness and conveniences which your inland born subjects do enjoy."[22] This was without precedent. Before the French Revolution, in seeking admission to new lands or in renegotiating previous charters of settlement, Jews asked that they be tolerated and accorded certain clearly defined privileges—not that they be treated the same as other persons. The language of this petition suggests that Menasseh and whoever else had a hand in its composition were fully aware of the demands for religious and civil equality then being aired by radicals and sectarians and perhaps also knew that Cromwell himself was sympathetic to them.

For unknown reasons, the Council of State decided on 5 December

1654 not to act on either petition. On his own, however, Cromwell intervened on behalf of Dormido, writing to the king of Portugal on 26 February 1655 to request that he and his sons be compensated for the losses they had suffered. Why he did so is not clear. Two months later, on 27 April, he issued a pass to Abraham de Mercado and his son, members of London's converso colony, to emigrate to Barbados. The pass, which also gave permission to the father to practice medicine there, stated explicitly that Mercado was a "Hebrew." Again, Cromwell's motive remains unclear. In these instances of kindness toward individual Jews, as well as in his later actions on behalf of a general Jewish resettlement, he never expressed his own views. What can be said with some certainty is that he shared the millenarian sentiments of his contemporaries and that even after the failure of the Barebones Parliament dashed many of his hopes he was "still confident that he enjoyed a special relationship with God."[23] In addition to whatever religious hopes he entertained, Cromwell also had immediate and pragmatic reasons for befriending Jewish merchants. Several New Christians in London had been providing him with political intelligence from abroad, and the most prominent among them, Carvajal, was also a major army contractor.[24] It is also likely that Cromwell saw the commercial advantages of attracting Jewish capital and enterprise away from England's chief rival, Holland, although it would be wrong to exaggerate the benefits he expected from their readmission.[25] England, after all, was not an economic backwater, like those German states that employed Jewish agents (known as *Hofjuden;* literally, "court Jews") to provide vital economic and fiscal services.

Whatever motives were at work, there is no question that Cromwell favored readmission and that this news was conveyed to Menasseh in Amsterdam, probably by his son Samuel, who returned from London in May. Menasseh sailed for England in September to negotiate Jewish resettlement directly with the Lord Protector. In the months before his departure, he published a short commentary in Spanish (illustrated with four etchings by Rembrandt van Rijn) on Daniel's interpretation of Nebuchadnezzar's dream, forecasting the coming of the messianic days. This would seem to indicate that the messianism that contributed to his initial interest in England still stirred his imagination. He also issued a letter, in the form of a broadside written in Portuguese, to the Sephardi communities of Europe, announcing his mission and requesting their prayers on his behalf. In this document, he failed (perhaps intentionally) to mention his messianic expectations and stressed instead the need to find a "refuge and remedy" for "those of our people who are today so oppressed," especially "the many souls who, dissimulating their religion, dwell scattered in so many parts of Spain and France."[26]

Menasseh arrived in London armed with a pamphlet (known by its short title, *The Humble Addresses*), written in English before his departure, in which he set forth the case for Jewish readmission. In the introduction he repeated his belief that the dispersal of the Jews to the four corners of the earth was necessary before their final ingathering could occur, but in the body of the pamphlet he emphasized the commercial utility of the Jews and their political trustworthiness and refuted a number of common slanders—that they practiced usury, killed Christian children, and tried to convert Christians. On 31 October, Menasseh presented his *Humble Addresses* to the Council of State, and two weeks later, on 13 November, he returned to Whitehall and submitted a seven-point petition, specifying the terms for readmission, including the right to adjudicate cases within the community on the basis of Jewish law. A majority of the Council and Cromwell favored Jewish resettlement, with some restrictions, but, aware that the issue was contentious, decided to seek broader support by convening a gathering of lawyers, merchants, and divines, whose advice would nominally be solicited.

The Whitehall Conference, as the gathering has come to be known, met in five sessions from 4 to 18 December but did not provide Cromwell with the advice he desired. Although support was forthcoming from the millenarian faction, merchants and more orthodox clergymen expressed strong objections, as they had in various pamphlets published since the question of readmission surfaced. The merchants feared that Jews would dominate certain areas of trade, enriching themselves at the expense of native Englishmen. (Menasseh's point about Jewish commercial expertise was a double-edged sword.) The clergy emphasized traditional religious arguments: the public exercise of Judaism in a Christian state was blasphemous, the Jews would seduce Christians from their faith, Christian children might be murdered for ritual purposes. When Cromwell realized that the conference would not give him what he wanted, he dissolved it.

The Whitehall Conference aroused both great hopes and fears, launching, for example, wild rumors about Jewish offers to purchase St. Paul's Cathedral, various English towns, and the libraries of Oxford and Cambridge. Having encountered greater opposition than he initially expected, Cromwell avoided making any public statement about readmission or taking any official action in the months following the conference.

Indeed, neither he nor the monarchs who followed him ever voided the expulsion order of 1290 or issued a formal invitation to Jews to return. In this sense, Menasseh's mission was a failure. Yet Jewish resettlement went ahead, but in an unexpected and indirect way that in the end provoked less hostility.

It should be recalled that when Menasseh arrived in London, there were already Jews — or, to be more precise, New Christians — living there, perhaps twenty families in all. When he negotiated with the government, he did not do so as a representative of this converso group, with whom he apparently had little contact. During his stay, for example, he did not lodge with them, nor did he turn to them for aid when in financial distress in late 1656. (Instead, he petitioned Cromwell, whom he addressed as "the alone succourer of my life, in this land of strangers.")[27] The New Christian merchants of London, it appears, were content to continue living as they had been and did not share Menasseh's vision of turning England into a major refuge for persecuted Jews. Foreign affairs intervened, however, to force a change in their strategy.

In October 1655, England went to war with Spain in order to break its monopoly of South American trade. Since the New Christians were formally subjects of the Spanish crown, their goods were subject to seizure. In March 1656, Antonio Rodrigues Robles (ca. 1620–90), a wealthy merchant of Duke's Place, was denounced to the authorities, who ordered that all his property, including two ships lying in the Thames, be confiscated. This forced Robles and other converso merchants fearful of losing their property to abandon the pretense that they were Spanish Catholics and to claim publicly that they were instead Jewish refugees. On 24 March, six leading members of the colony, along with Menasseh ben Israel, submitted a petition to Cromwell requesting permission to gather privately for Jewish worship and to acquire a burial ground. At the same time Robles submitted his own petition requesting the return of his property on the grounds that he was a Portuguese "of the Hebrew nation." The Council of State responded favorably to Robles's request on 16 May but failed to act on the larger question. No formal order of readmission was ever issued. Nonetheless, Cromwell must have provided the group with some assurances that they would not be disturbed, for in the months that followed an avowedly Jewish community emerged. During the summer Menasseh wrote to his brother-in-law in Amsterdam asking that a Torah scroll be sent to London. In the fall a cousin of Carvajal, Moses Athias (d. 1665), assistant *hazzan* (cantor) and teacher in the talmud torah (religious school) in

Hamburg, was brought to London to work for Carvajal and to act as religious functionary for the community. In December, the community rented a house in Creechurch Lane for use as a synagogue and in February 1657 acquired a plot of land in Mile End for use as a cemetery. It is difficult to believe that the leaders of the group would have taken these steps without Cromwell's having promised that they could live in England as professing Jews.

That the resettlement occurred in the informal way it did had important consequences for the later development of Jewish status. Commercial and religious opposition to Jews was certainly as strong as millenarian sentiment in their favor. By removing the issue of Jewish readmission from the public agenda, Cromwell denied the opposition an immediate target. With no official measure or declaration to debate, anti-Jewish sentiment lost its focus. Agitation against readmission gradually subsided, and since no mass influx of Jewish refugees occurred, contrary to Menasseh's hopes, the Jewish presence in London remained a very minor topic of interest for the rest of the century. Moreover, by failing to issue a charter setting forth the terms of Jewish residence (as was the practice elsewhere), the government left their legal status undefined and thus ambiguous. No document specified limits to the scope of Jewish economic activity, social intercourse, or religious practice. This was an unintended boon with far-reaching consequences. At a later date, when Jews sought recognition of their right to participate as full citizens in state and society, there was no restrictive ancien régime code to be debated and repealed.

After the restoration of the Stuart monarchy in 1660, City merchants fearful of competition sought several times to restrict Jewish activity. Their efforts failed because Charles II and James II were willing to protect the new community.[28] When the lord mayor and corporation of the City of London petitioned Charles soon after his return to enforce the expulsion decree of 1290, he refused to do so. He acted similarly four years later when the Conventicle Act of 1664 came into force, prohibiting religious services not in conformity with the Church of England (legislation which he had opposed). Although the intent of the law was to repress Christian nonconformity, the Earl of Berkshire and Paul Rycaut, an associate of merchants who traded with the Levant and resented Jewish competition, attempted to use it to blackmail the Jewish community into paying protection money to avoid prosecution. Dormido, who had remained in London, and the other two members of the mahamad of the newly established community petitioned the king for protection. The privy council responded on 22 August 1664 that no orders had been given to disturb them and that they might continue to live and trade as before, so long as they did so peaceably, without scandal to the government and in due obedience to the laws.[29]

In March 1673, cancellation of Charles's Declaration of Indulgence, which had conferred the right of public worship on Roman Catholics and Dissenters, provided another opportunity to the Jews' commercial rivals. At the Guildhall quarter sessions during the winter of 1673–74, the leaders of the community were indicted for riotous assembly on the grounds that they had gathered together for the exercise of their religion. They again petitioned the king, who in February 1674 issued an order in council to the attorney general to halt all legal proceedings against them. In the fall of 1685, with Charles dead since February, another attempt was made to prosecute Jews using legislation designed to suppress Catholicism. Carlton and Thomas Beaumont, relatives and dependents of Sir Robert Clayton, alderman and former lord mayor, initiated legal action that led to the arrest of thirty-seven Jewish merchants at the Royal Exchange for recusancy—failure to attend the Church of England—under an act of Elizabeth that imposed a fine of £20 a month for nonattendance. Like his predecessor, James issued an order in council to the attorney general to suspend all proceedings.

The willingness of Charles II and James II to protect Jews derived from different motives. Charles had no conscientious objections to Jews settling in his kingdom and in 1656, while still in exile, had negotiated with the leaders of the Amsterdam community, offering to protect them after his return if they provided him with money, arms, or ammunition. Although no agreement was concluded, Charles and his advisors remained convinced of the Jews' usefulness, and a number of families followed him to London in 1660. Bribery also appears to have played a role in securing his protection: in December 1660, in response to the City's petition to the king, the leading figures in the community raised a fund of more than £2,000—clearly intended for bribes to the court— to counter the efforts of the City merchants.[30] In the case of James II, a different motive was at work: as defender of the Catholic cause, it was in his interest to protect all non-Anglican groups.

The accession of William of Orange to the throne in 1688 further strengthened the position of the new community. His Jewish subjects in Holland had long been able to trade freely and were prominent in several areas of international commerce. The firm of Machado and Pereira in Amsterdam had supplied his armies since 1672 and had also organized the commissariat for his English and Irish campaigns in 1688. In addition, Francisco Lopes Suasso (d. 1710) of The Hague had helped to finance his expedition to England with a loan of two million crowns. As king, William encouraged a number of wealthy Sephardim from Amsterdam to settle in London. He also continued to engage Machado and Pereira to supply his armies on the continent and in 1700 knighted their London agent, Solomon de Medina (ca. 1650–1730), for his services — the first professing Jew to be so honored.[31] With his long-standing links to major Jewish entrepreneurs, William was not inclined to overturn Jewish resettlement, although he was quite willing to exploit their presence for his own financial needs, as we will see.

In the half century after the readmission, a small but steady trickle of Sephardim made their way to London — professing Jews from Holland and Dutch and English colonies in the Caribbean, New Christians from the Canary Islands, the Iberian Peninsula, and France. At the outset of Menasseh ben Israel's mission to Cromwell, there were about twenty households of New Christian origin in London; at the end of the decade, about thirty-five. In 1684, according to a list prepared for the mahamad by Abraham Israel Zagache, there were 414 Sephardim; in 1695, the number was 499.[32] (The total number of Jews living in London was somewhat greater since Ashkenazim, Jews of Central and East European origin, were already migrating to England at this time, although not in great numbers.) Yet Menasseh's hope that England, like Holland, would become a major refuge for persecuted conversos was not realized. At the end of the century, the Sephardi communities of Amsterdam, Venice, Livorno, and Hamburg each outnumbered London's, despite four and a half decades of unrestricted settlement.[33]

The Sephardim who settled in London during this period included overseas merchants, commodity brokers, dealers in precious stones and jewelry, commercial clerks, and several physicians, as well as persons with little or no capital or training — peddlers, servants, vagabonds, and the like. The overseas merchants traded in a wide range of products: wine from the Canaries, sugar from Barbados and Jamaica, brazilwood from Portugal and the Azores, linen from northwest Europe, bullion from Spain, diamonds and other precious stones from India. They also exported English goods (textiles primarily) and re-exported colonial products.[34] Linked by ties of commerce, kinship, and a common past to Sephardi and New Christian merchants in ports elsewhere in Europe and in the New World, these London merchants constituted part of a transatlantic mercantile fraternity. Their agents abroad were other Sephardim or, in the case of Spain and Portugal, conversos who chose to remain Catholics. The goods in which they traded and the routes over which they operated were for the most part familiar to them before their migration to London.

The overseas merchants stood at the apex of the communal social structure, although as a group their role in London's international commerce was modest, being dominant only in the diamond trade with India. A handful of families, like the da Costas, the Henriqueses, and the Francias, amassed truly great fortunes, but most overseas merchants traded on a less impressive scale. For example, of the 800 cargoes imported by 26 Jewish merchant houses between Christmas 1675 and Christmas 1679, 700 were imported by only 7 firms. These 7 firms also exported over 400 of the 500 cargoes shipped by 19 Jewish houses during the same period. The modest character of most Jewish overseas trade (and Jewish economic activity in general) is also reflected in the distribution of contributions to communal expenses. In the period 1669–77, only 54 percent of heads of household did sufficient business to pay the *imposta,* a tax levied by the Sephardi community on the value of goods bought or sold by members. In 1669, of the 24 persons who paid the imposta, 5 paid two-thirds of the total; in 1677, of the 42 who paid the tax, 5 paid one-half of the total. Two decades later this imbalance in communal wealth remained: in 1695, only 36 of the 127 heads of household in the Sephardi community possessed non-landed property worth £600 or more.[35]

Brokers, jewelers, and retail merchants[36] were less numerous than the overseas merchants, although with the increase in government borrowing and the growth of a financial market from the 1690s, brokering government and other securities featured increasingly as a field for Sephardi enterprise. Alongside these persons of property there also developed a group of Sephardim sufficiently impoverished that they depended on communal charity to survive. In the nine years 1669–77, about one-third of the total income of the synagogue went to poor relief, the major portion of which was paid to persons resident in London (rather than itinerant Jews from abroad). Some were persons once financially secure who had suffered business reverses, but others were part of a permanent unskilled underclass—casual laborers, street traders, itinerant peddlers, beggars, vagabonds, and criminals—which was found throughout the Sephardi Diaspora in the seventeenth and eighteenth centuries.

The founders of the community attempted to replicate the religious customs, congregational structure, and communal practices of the Amsterdam community, of which it was an offshoot and, to some extent, a dependency. In 1663, a governing committee (mahamad) of three persons was constituted and bylaws (*ascamot*), based on those of the Amsterdam community (which, in turn, were based on those of Venice), were drafted.[37] The bylaws, which were adopted on the eve of Passover 1664, assumed that the new community enjoyed the same degree of legal autonomy and coercive authority as the Venetian community and vested in the mahamad almost absolute power over members. The first ascama forbade, under threat of the ban (*herem*), the formation of any other Sephardi congregation in London or even an assembly of ten persons for worship, except in cases of weddings or during periods of mourning. Another required members who had business disputes with each other to turn for arbitration in the first instance to the mahamad. And another forbade the hiring away of female servants already employed by other members, threatening transgressors with a £5 fine. The mahamad also forbade, again under threat of herem, the publication of books in any language, whether in England or abroad, without prior permission. This and the bans on engaging in religious arguments with non-Jews and on making proselytes were intended to safeguard the security of the community as a whole, for to risk offending Christians would be "to disturb the liberty which we enjoy and to make us disliked."

In 1664 the community also appointed the North African–born Jacob Sasportas (1610–98), then living in Amsterdam, as rabbi, or *haham*, as the religious head of the Sephardi community was known. Unlike Moses Athias, who had been brought from Hamburg to lead services in 1656, Sasportas was a respected rabbinic scholar. He arrived in London in early summer 1664 but left in a panic for Hamburg the following summer to escape the Great Plague. His flight abroad may not have been due entirely to his fear of contagion, however. During his short tenure, he clashed repeatedly with the lay leaders of the community over the question of religious discipline, provoking them with attacks on wealthy members who committed religious transgressions, such as refusing to have their sons circumcised or to undergo circumcision themselves. He insisted that he alone had authority in religious matters; they preferred to turn a blind eye to even major transgressions of Jewish law for the sake of communal harmony.[38] After his departure, the mahamad did not rush to fill the vacancy, waiting five years to appoint a successor. In 1670, Joshua da Silva of Amsterdam became haham, serving until his death in 1679. The post then remained vacant for two years, until the appointment of another Amsterdam rabbi, the Spanish-born translator and bookseller Jacob Abendana (d. 1685), in 1681. Abendana and his brother Isaac (d. 1699), who gave private Hebrew lessons at Oxford and Cambridge from the early 1660s, maintained close ties to Christian Hebraists in England and Holland, and with their support worked on translating the *mishnah* (the earliest compilation of rabbinic law) into Spanish and Latin.[39]

In 1689, five years after Abendana's death, Solomon Ayllon (ca. 1655–1728), a Salonican-born kabbalist and crypto-Sabbatean who was visiting Europe to collect funds for the Jews of Safed, a center of Jewish mysticism in the Land of Israel, was persuaded to remain in England and accept the post of haham. His tenure was as stormy as Sasportas's.[40] The Sephardim of London, unlike their kith and kin in Amsterdam, displayed little enthusiasm for the messianic movement surrounding Shabbetai Zevi (1626–76), either in its initial stage in 1665–66 or in its later manifestations. Indeed, news of the messianic claimant and his followers made a greater impact on Christians in London than on Jews.[41] Ayllon was unable to keep his beliefs and prior activities abroad a secret and on several occasions was denounced to the mahamad for heresy and loose living. The mahamad refused to take action against him, not because they shared his Sabbatean sympathies, but probably because they wished to maintain communal peace and had little taste for a theological witch-hunt. The agitation against him eventually proved too much, however, and in 1700 he resigned and accepted an offer to become rabbi of the Portuguese community in Amsterdam, where controversy over his Sabbatean past again enveloped him in 1713–14.[42]

Meanwhile, the building in Creechurch Lane that had been purchased for use as a synagogue in 1657—and then remodeled and enlarged in 1674—proved unable to accommodate the growing community. So in 1699 the congregation purchased a site in Bevis Marks, a short street in the easternmost ward of the City of London, and the following year began erecting a larger, more opulent structure, which was completed and dedicated in 1701. The synagogue, for the most part unaltered, is still in use as a place of worship, although towering office blocks surround it and few Jews, let alone Sephardim, live in the neighborhood.

The most pressing religious problem facing the Sephardi community in the half century after the readmission was making the transition from New Christian to professing Jew, a problem that confronted communities everywhere with large numbers of former conversos. Most of the Sephardim who settled in England in the seventeenth century had lived

as Catholics, not Jews, for much of their lives. At the time of the resettlement, persons of Jewish origin in Spain and Portugal had been cut
off from a living Judaism for more than a century and a half. They knew
only a truncated, clandestine Judaism, without the supporting institutional framework of synagogues, academies, and rabbinate. Educated
New Christians who wanted to hold on to their ancestral religion were
able to acquire indirect knowledge of Judaism through reading anti-
Jewish polemical literature and the works of Christian Hebraists or from
hearing sermons preached at autos-da-fé. In some instances they even
had direct access to a living Judaism through contact with professing
Jews who made their way into Spain and Portugal for short periods or
with Jews whom they met while abroad on business.[43] Yet even if not
completely sealed off from Jewish influences, the conversos knew and
observed a Judaism that had atrophied and fragmented under inquisitorial scrutiny and social pressure. With every new decade, it became
increasingly difficult to transmit a knowledge of Hebrew, liturgical practices, and ritual observances. New Christians migrating from Catholic
lands brought with them "a pastiche of fragments, inherited from parents, gleaned haphazardly from books, disorganized, with significant
gaps, sometimes distorted."[44] Some New Christians brought only an
awareness of Jewish origins, their decision to flee having been made for
them by the Inquisition, whose indiscriminate persecution of New
Christians often extended to families who had given up all Jewish practices and sought full absorption into Christian society.[45]

Once settled in London, out of reach now of the Inquisition, some
New Christians failed to embrace Judaism and continued to live as
Christians. Indeed, the very first conversos to arrive tended not to affiliate with the newly established Jewish community—only one-third of
those resident in London before 1659 were buried in the Sephardi cemetery in Mile End.[46] Moreover, among those interred there were conversos, such as Alvaro da Costa (1646–1716) and Fernando Mendes
(1647–1724), who, while living, had never declared themselves Jews and
had refused to be circumcised.[47] Later arrivals usually affiliated with the
congregation in Bevis Marks but frequently experienced difficulty in
accepting the full regimen of traditional belief and practice. It should be
recalled that Jacob Sasportas antagonized the lay leaders of the community in 1665 when he reproved wealthy congregants who were lax in
their observance of the *mitsvot* (divine commandments), including circumcision. On one Sabbath he expelled uncircumcised males from the
synagogue. In the stormy argument that ensued about the binding char-

acter of the mitsvot, one of the Francia brothers, who were themselves circumcised but had not circumcised their sons, stood up and announced, "Gentlemen, all this is suited either to very great fools or very wise men," whereupon he removed his *tallit* (prayer shawl), threw down his prayer book, and walked out.[48]

It is significant that, after Sasportas's departure for Hamburg, the mahamad urged Jorge and Domingo Francia (d. 1688) to rejoin the synagogue, without, however, requiring them to renounce their heterodox views. They did so, both eventually serving as parnasim.[49] This suggests that what bound the community together in its first half century or so was less an allegiance to Jewish practice than kinship, a shared past, and a common language and cultural outlook.[50] Because these bonds outweighed formal adherence to the Jewish religion, it was not uncommon to find within one family persons with different religious affiliations. In the wealthy Mendes da Costa family, for example, some were members of the synagogue in Bevis Marks, others of the Church of England or the Roman Catholic Church, including, among the latter, a physician who left a bequest to the synagogue's charity fund and was buried in its cemetery.[51] Moreover, whether Christian or Jewish in affiliation, former New Christians tended to choose marriage partners from families of New Christian background, thus reinforcing group cohesion.

In seventeenth-century Amsterdam, as well, former conversos experienced difficulty in making the transition from Christianity to Judaism. This group included famous heretics like Uriel da Costa (1585–1640), Juan de Prado (ca. 1615–ca. 1670) and Baruch de Espinoza (1632–77), whose breaks with Judaism and Jewry were dramatic, as well as a larger number of persons who lived quietly on the fringes of the Jewish community, taking no part in its communal life, but connected to it through common origins and family connections.[52] Yet it may have been more difficult to make the transition in London than elsewhere. Those settling in major Jewish centers, like Amsterdam, Venice, Livorno, and Constantinople, came to communities with resources and means for reeducating them in the fundamentals of Judaism and integrating them into normative Jewish life. In London, circumstances were less conducive to successful reintegration. The community was small, the learned and pious few in number. It lacked, moreover, corporate legal status, unlike most Jewish communities elsewhere at this time, so that its religious and lay leaders were at a disadvantage in influencing the behavior of new arrivals. To be sure, the bylaws of the congregation, which were based on those of Venice, where Jews lived in a ghetto, assumed that it enjoyed legal autonomy and thus could discipline those who would not conform, but the reality was different. The London community was among the first in Jewish history to be constituted on a voluntaristic basis, although its leaders would not have described it in such terms. (The Jews of Amsterdam were in a similar position.) Jewish residents could choose to affiliate with the community or remain on its margins, but even those who became members were at liberty to ignore the dictates of the communal leadership — although, of course, they could be denied synagogal honors and burial in the communal cemetery if they persisted in their disobedience.[53]

The historical experience of the Sephardim prior to the resettlement also influenced their social and cultural integration into English society. Before their expulsion, Iberian Jews were not compelled to live in physical ghettos, nor did they seek to segregate themselves from Christian influence in cultural ghettos of their own making. In addition, those who remained in the peninsula after 1492 lived as Christians within Christian societies. In matters of language, costume, deportment, and taste, they were not markedly dissimilar from their neighbors. They were "the first considerable group of European Jews to have had their most extensive and direct personal experiences completely outside the organic Jewish community and the spiritual universe of normative Jewish tradition." As nominal Catholics, they had "full access to the mainsprings of Western theological, philosophic, and scientific learning."[54] Many received a university education at a time when Jews elsewhere were generally barred from higher education. This meant that when conversos reached London and reasserted their Jewish identity, their acculturation to English habits of thought and behavior was relatively smooth, requiring no fundamental reassessment of the relationship between secular and Jewish culture. They began to relinquish Spanish and Portuguese in favor of English, to adopt current fashions in dress and personal adornment, to acquire a taste for English recreations and entertainments, and to seek entry to gentile social and cultural groups. Those who grew rich in international trade purchased homes in the countryside around London and took up country pursuits, as was the custom among merchants and financiers who had made their fortune in the City.[55]

While the anglicization of the Sephardim was advancing at a rapid pace in the first half century after readmission, Jewish civil and social status remained ambiguous. No charter was issued or legislation passed regularizing Jewish residence, thus leaving undefined the precise limits of their rights and duties. In this statutory vacuum, court decisions helped to define what the new residents could and could not do, although, by nature, the rulings were limited to specific matters. In 1667, for example, the Court of King's Bench ruled that Jews might give evidence in a court of law and be sworn on the Hebrew Bible, while in 1684 it ruled that they might sue for the recovery of debts.[56] In the fiscal sphere, Jews were not subject to special taxation — with the exception of one brief period, at the start of William's reign, when measures were taken to tap their wealth for the Irish and French campaigns. In late 1689, a bill imposing a special levy of £100,000 on the Jewish community was introduced into Parliament and given a first reading, but it died after the mahamad countered with a vigorous protest. In February 1690, William considered but then dropped a forced loan scheme. However, in fixing the poll tax for that year, Parliament assessed Jewish merchants at a higher rate than other foreign merchants, a provision that was eliminated in poll tax legislation in subsequent years.[57]

The major disabilities facing Jews were those barring their access to public life: they could not hold civil office, become freemen of the City of London, attend the ancient universities, or enter certain professions, since doing so required the taking of an oath "upon the true faith of a Christian" or, in the case of the universities, being a communicant of the Church of England and subscribing to its Thirty-Nine Articles. It is important to remember, however, that these oaths and requirements, which in some cases predated the readmission, were created to exclude not Jews but Christians whose loyalty to church and state was suspect.[58] Disabilities such as these, moreover, were not considered a social stigma or barrier to economic success. The community of the resettlement was a mercantile community of foreign origin with little interest in holding public office or diversifying its occupational base.

In the world of commerce, there were few serious obstacles to the deployment of Jewish capital and talent. Perhaps the most onerous was the cap on the number of Jewish commodity brokers on the Royal Exchange — 12 out of 124 — which the City of London imposed in 1697 in the course of a general reform of the Exchange. (This did not limit the number of Jewish stockbrokers, who carried on their business elsewhere, only the number of sworn commodity brokers.) Some Jewish merchants may also have been frustrated by exclusion from chartered trading companies like the Russia Company and the Levant Company. (The East India Company, on the other hand, admitted Solomon de Medina in 1691.) Foreign-born Jews were also disadvantaged in that they had to pay alien duties, as did other merchants born abroad, regardless of their religion. To remedy this, most Jewish merchants obtained patents of endenization from the crown, which allowed them to pay the same duties as native-born merchants. Endenization was, however, a less desirable way of gaining citizenship than naturalization, for there was some question whether endenized persons were allowed to own real estate or transmit it to their heirs. But Jews born abroad had no option, since applicants for naturalization were required to take the sacrament in the Church of England and to swear the oaths of supremacy and allegiance "upon the true faith of a Christian."[59] Jews born in Britain did not face these difficulties: they were citizens from birth and thus enjoyed the same property rights and paid the same customs duties as other native-born persons. Indeed, there is some evidence that Jewish merchants in the Netherlands intentionally sent their wives to give birth in London so that their children would be British citizens.[60]

There is no question that the Jews' position in England at the end of the seventeenth century was superior to that of Jews in other European states—in large part, as we have seen, because the state ignored their presence most of the time and left their legal status ill-defined. Yet it would be incorrect to infer from this that the Jews of England no longer encountered the old vulgar prejudices or were accepted as members of the English nation, differing only from their Christian neighbors by virtue of their religion. The Sephardim of England, like Jews everywhere in early modern Europe, continued to be seen as a distinct national group, with their own peculiar cultural habits, mental outlook, religious customs, historical memories, and future hopes for national redemption. Moreover, however willing they were to tolerate Jews, Englishmen continued to view these differences in a negative light. When Samuel Pepys visited the synagogue in Bevis Marks on Simhat Torah in 1663, he saw only "disorder, laughing, sporting, and no attention" and thought the worshippers "more like brutes than people [who] know the true God." He had not imagined, he wrote in his diary, that there was "any religion in the whole world so absurdly performed as this." John Greenhaigh, who visited the synagogue a year earlier, also drew on the vocabulary of barbarism to record his impressions: "Lord . . . what a strange, uncouth, foreign, and to me barbarian sight was there."[61] In both learned and popular discourse, Jews were still viewed as an obstinate people, clinging to old superstitions, refusing salvation, harboring hatred toward Christendom.[62]

It is difficult to know how the Jewish community itself assessed its position. Judging by the ascamot of 1664, the Sephardim viewed their status as uncertain and perhaps even precarious. As noted, several ascamot—the ban on religious disputations and proselytism and the censoring of books—were intended to prevent members of the community from offending Christian sensibilities. It would seem from this that the communal leadership felt insecure about Jewish status and perhaps imagined that unless they minimized the opportunities for conflict, the community might once again be expelled. These fears were not groundless. Commercial rivals in the City of London tried unsuccessfully on several occasions, the last being in 1685, to undo the resettlement. Aware that the greatest threat to its security came from other City merchants, the Sephardi community instituted in 1671 what soon became a regular practice—presenting each lord mayor on his succession to office with a "gift" in order to secure his friendship if the need arose. In most years the gift took the form of a purse containing fifty guineas, presented on a silver salver bearing the shield of the congregation. The Dutch and Huguenot merchant communities also made similar gifts to the lord mayor but, interestingly, they ceased doing so in 1749, convinced that their position was secure, while the Sephardim continued the practice for another forty years.[63]

During the next century, Sephardim continued to settle in London, although not in large numbers. They were joined now by thousands of Ashkenazim from Holland, Poland, and the German states, the earliest of whom arrived at the end of the seventeenth century and initially affiliated with the congregation in Bevis Marks. The new arrivals, whose culture and history differed in major ways from their predecessors, soon founded their own institutions and quickly outstripped the Sephardim in numbers, if not yet in wealth and influence. They swelled the size of the London community, making it by the end of the eighteenth century one of the largest urban Jewries in Europe. They also established small outposts in a dozen county towns and seaports, thus giving a provincial dimension to English Jewry. Although the Sephardim continued to distinguish themselves in trade and finance and thus occupied a prominent place in the public eye, their inability to sustain growth and stem drift and defection threatened their influence within the Jewish community as a whole, leaving open the possibility that they would become little more than a historical curiosity. This, however, is to get too far ahead of our story.

A LYONESS.

"A Lyoness." Polly de Symons, wife of the diamond broker Lyon de Symons
and sister of the communal magnates Abraham and Benjamin Goldsmid.
James Gillray's caricature of 1801. From a private collection.

CHAPTER 2

Bankers and Brokers, Peddlers and Pickpockets (1700–1800)

The Jewish community of the resettlement period was overwhelmingly Spanish and Portuguese in origin. In the first decades following readmission, some Ashkenazim migrated to London (there were almost no Jews elsewhere in Britain then), but they were too small in number to create communal institutions of their own. A few were wealthy merchants, but most were humble traders, itinerant peddlers, and longtime vagabonds who traveled the length of the Diaspora. By 1690, however, there were enough Ashkenazim to support their own synagogue, and from this time the Ashkenazi population grew at a rapid pace.

By 1720 at the latest, there were more Ashkenazim than Sephardim, who then numbered about 1,050. At mid-century, when there may have been seven to eight thousand Jews in the country, Ashkenazim constituted two-thirds to three-quarters of that population. In the early decades of the nineteenth century, when the Jewish population of Britain stood at twelve to fifteen thousand, the number of Sephardim remained about what it had been at the mid-eighteenth century—a little more than two thousand persons. (By contrast, Roman Catholics in England and Wales, who also stood outside the social mainstream, numbered 115,000 in 1720 and 700,000 in 1840.)[1] Some of the growth of the Ashkenazi population was due to natural increase, but most was due to an almost uninterrupted flow of poor immigrants from the Continent. In the first half of the eighteenth century, about six thousand Ashkenazim migrated to Britain; then between 1750 and 1815, another eight to ten thousand arrived, most of them before the Revolutionary and Napoleonic wars, when immigration was difficult.[2] It is this migration, rather than that of former conversos in the seventeenth century, that created the demographic foundation for English Jewry.

The great majority of the Ashkenazim who settled in Britain in the eighteenth century came from the German states, with smaller numbers from Holland and Poland. Those who were described as Dutch, moreover, were often German Jews who had migrated to Holland only a short time before. Thus, with some exceptions, the Ashkenazi migration was Central European in origin.[3] It was motivated largely, though not exclusively, by the deteriorating economic position of German Jewry. Before emancipation, all Central European states and cities placed obstacles in the way of Jewish trading activity and limited the number of Jews permitted to live in their territory. Some cities banned Jewish settlement altogether, while a small number confined those whom they did tolerate to involuntary ghettos. As the Jewish population expanded, as a result of both natural increase and immigration from Poland, the opportunities for gaining a settlement and earning a living remained constant or even diminished. As a consequence, many Jews were forced to uproot themselves and seek their livelihood elsewhere. Some took to the roads permanently, moving in bands from community to community, begging charity and at times turning to criminal activity. By the end of the eighteenth century, there were more than ten thousand *Betteljuden* (beggar Jews) in Germany (in comparison to a stable Jewish population of two hundred thousand).[4] Some of the Ashkenazi migration to England stemmed from this itinerant population. Other arrivals were young persons, usually with few resources, who wished to improve their lot and realized the difficulties in doing so in circumstances where Jewish economic activity was hedged around with restrictions. In addition, in a small number of cases, the desire to escape the confines of traditional Jewish life was also a motive, especially from mid-century on, when the old order in German Jewry began to crumble.

A small number of Sephardim also migrated to Britain during the eighteenth century, most of whom were impoverished, unlike their seventeenth-century predecessors. The most concentrated influx came between 1720 and 1735 as a consequence of renewed inquisitorial activity in Spain and Portugal. In some cases, the refugees were so destitute that they were unable to pay their fares, and, thus, the Sephardi synagogue arranged with British captains to pay their passage on arrival. After this, immigration from Spain and Portugal slowed to a trickle, the last New Christian arriving in 1798. In all, about three thousand Sephardim arrived directly from the peninsula in the eighteenth century.[5] In addition to these former conversos, small numbers of Sephardim also migrated from impoverished communities in Italy, North Africa, Gibraltar, Holland, and the Ottoman empire (including the grandfather of Benjamin Disraeli, who came from Cento, near Ferrara, in 1748).[6] Among this group were paupers from Amsterdam and Bordeaux whose passage to London was paid by their communities in exchange for a promise not to return — a common strategy at the time for dealing with pauperism. Amsterdam, for example, sent fifty-six paupers to London between 1759 and 1814.[7]

Most immigrants in this period, Sephardi and Ashkenazi alike, came with few material resources or artisanal skills and on arrival took to low-status itinerant trades to earn a living, hawking goods in the streets of London, buying and selling old clothes and other secondhand goods, peddling notions, gimcracks, and inexpensive jewelry in the provinces.[8] Their choice of occupation was not surprising: these trades required little capital or knowledge of English and were already mainstays of the Jewish economy on the Continent. With a few shillings' worth of goods, frequently obtained on credit from shopkeepers in the Jewish quarter, immigrants fresh off the boat were able to commence business. When a recently arrived old clothes man from Hanover was asked in a court of law in 1783 how he carried on business without knowing any English, he replied, through an interpreter, "There are so many of my country people who generally assist me." When then asked what he did when they were not around, he answered, "I generally make a motion" — that is, he made himself understood by gesturing.[9] Thus, despite the absence of legal obstacles to occupational diversification, the mass of Jews remained in traditional Jewish trades.

In London, Jews came to monopolize or were strongly identified with the trade in certain goods: oranges and lemons, spectacles, costume jewelry, sponges, dried rhubarb, lead pencils, inexpensive framed pictures, and, to a lesser extent, slippers, cakes and candies, glassware, sealing wax, belt buckles, and buttons. In the countryside, itinerant Jewish peddlers tended to specialize in the sale of inexpensive jewelry: shoe buckles, watches, watch chains, rings, snuff boxes, crystal buttons, shirt buckles. In fact, the trade in shoddy watches was so closely identified with Jewish peddlers that such watches were known as "Jew watches" in the late eighteenth and early nineteenth centuries. The most characteristic Jewish street trade, however, was the buying and selling of old clothes. Before the advent of mass-produced consumer goods, most British families regularly purchased secondhand merchandise, including the cast-off garments of the middle and upper ranks.[10] Jewish old clothes men and dealers catered to the needs of an expanding urban population that could not afford to purchase new clothing. Hundreds of them fanned out each day through the streets and squares of middle-class and aristocratic London to purchase articles now deemed unfashionable or too worn by their owners. In Rag Fair, an open-air market held daily in Rosemary Lane, near Tower Hill, Jewish dealers purchased the used goods collected earlier and offered them for sale to the hundreds of customers who jammed the area, making it at times nearly impassable.

The trades in which the mass of Jews concentrated were widely considered low-status and disreputable. This judgment derived in part from the goods offered for sale, which were frequently of poor quality or soiled and tattered, and in part from the manner in which business was conducted, for these trades were not only practiced in the streets but in a manner regarded as aggressive and rude. The poet and essayist Robert Southey complained about "Hebrew lads who infest you in the streets with oranges and red slippers, or tempt school boys to dip in a bag for gingerbread nuts," while a commercial traveler of the early nineteenth century regretted that he never could leave London by coach "without being besieged by a small army of Jew boys," who offered him "oranges, lemons, sponges, combs, pocket books, pencils, sealing wax, paper, many-bladed pen knives, razors, pocket mirrors, and shaving boxes — as if a man could not possibly quit the metropolis without requiring a stock of such commodities." Dealers in secondhand clothing were especially notorious for their volubility and aggressiveness. They shouted out the virtues of their goods and frequently grabbed hold of passersby and maneuvered them forcibly into their shops. An American visitor to London in 1802 recorded that he was accosted at least fifteen times while passing through Rag Fair.[11]

The disreputable character of these trades also derived from their association with criminal activity. Dealers in secondhand merchandise, Jewish and Christian, were notorious for purchasing stolen goods. Some Jewish dealers were, in fact, professional fences with close ties to criminal gangs and regular outlets for disposing of the goods they bought. Henry Fielding, who as a London magistrate was familiar with the criminal underworld, wrote in 1751 that there were several Jewish receivers who regularly shipped goods to Rotterdam, where they had warehouses and agents. In a survey of crime in the metropolis published in 1796, the police magistrate Patrick Colquhoun described a class of Jewish scrap-metal dealers who purchased stolen goods in the seaports and carted

"Sweet China Oranges." Luigi Schiavonetti's engraving of 1794, after a painting of Francis Wheatley, one of a series of pictures exhibited by Wheatley at the Royal Academy from 1792 to 1795. From a private collection.

them to London, where they disposed of them.[12] In general, dealers in secondhand goods were not concerned about their provenance. Street traders were also notorious for unscrupulous selling practices, such as misrepresenting their goods, and for passing counterfeit coins while making change. At the end of the century Jewish orange and lemon vendors appeared regularly at the Old Bailey for passing bad coins, while

The Times warned its readers in 1795 that "at this season the Jew fruitmen should be particularly guarded against."[13]

Criminal activity among the Jewish lower class was not the result of their occupational profile alone. Equally important was their poverty. In this, they were no different from other impoverished residents of the metropolis. Most Jews sentenced to death or transportation at the Old Bailey committed offenses characteristic of urban crime in general: shoplifting, burglary, stealing from carts and warehouses, picking pockets, assault and robbery. Some of these offenders lived off illicit dealings alone, and among them were members of organized gangs, the most notorious of which was the one responsible for the Chelsea murder case of 1771, in which nine Jews broke into a house in the King's Road and shot and killed a servant in the course of the robbery. Others, however, turned to crime only on occasion, usually when in dire straits. The extent of Jewish crime cannot be determined with any precision, so it is impossible to know whether lower-class Jews were disproportionately represented in London's criminal ranks. What is clear is that the extent of Jewish crime was sufficient to attract unfavorable attention. Public officials and social reformers commented frequently about the problem from the 1770s on; some even proposed that the community be made to bear collective financial responsibility for the misdeeds of individual members.[14]

While the majority of immigrants came from the lowest rungs of Central European Jewish society, their ranks also included skilled craftsmen, shopkeepers, religious functionaries, and small-scale merchants and brokers. Most common among the first group were pencil makers, glass cutters and engravers, watchmakers, jewelers, tailors, hatters, shoemakers, and pen and quill makers. While German guilds excluded Jews from membership and thus prevented the growth of an artisanal class within Central European Jewry, the skills represented here either fell outside the pale of guild supervision or were linked to the purchase and repair of secondhand goods, a Jewish specialty everywhere in pre-Revolutionary Europe. This group of artisans, along with shopkeepers and other merchants, became the backbone of Anglo-Jewish institutional life. They constituted the majority of regular synagogue worshippers and members of *hevrot* (societies) devoted to traditional learning and practice. They were also the founders of Jewish friendly societies, which, aside from providing the usual death and sickness benefits, offered a range of religious services. The Path of Rectitude Friendly Society, for example, provided a rabbi to teach mishnah during the period of mourning. These artisans and shopkeepers also formed Masonic lodges whose membership was largely Jewish, whose ritual was modified for Jewish usage, and in which the dietary laws were observed.[15]

Over the eighteenth and early nineteenth centuries, this stratum of Jewish society expanded, in part from immigration, but largely as a result of economic mobility. Imbued with a capitalist work ethic and armed with centuries of marketplace experience in buying and selling, Jews were well positioned to benefit from the rapid expansion of personal consumption in the eighteenth century. The latter part of the century witnessed "such a convulsion of getting and spending, such an eruption of new prosperity, and such an explosion of new production and marketing techniques, that a greater proportion of the population than in any previous society in human history was able to enjoy the pleasures of buying consumer goods."[16] Street vendors moved up to shopkeeping; old clothes men acquired fixed premises; shopkeepers were transformed into wholesalers, importers, and owners of emporiums; pawnbrokers and dealers in secondhand goods became jewelers and silversmiths; hawkers of oranges and lemons, grocers and wholesale fruit and vegetable merchants. One crude measure of the expansion of this segment of the community is the increase in Jewish names in directories of shopkeepers and merchants. In *The London Directory for the Year 1774*, there are only seven Cohens and Levys; in *The New Annual Directory for the Year 1800*, there are seventeen; in *The Post Office Annual Directory for 1815*, there are forty-one.

At the pinnacle of the Ashkenazi community was a small group of overseas merchants, gem dealers, loan contractors, and commodity and stockbrokers, who, like their impoverished coreligionists, migrated to England for economic reasons. The first Ashkenazi of substantial wealth to settle in London was Benjamin Levy (d. 1704), son of a prosperous Hamburg merchant, who arrived about 1670. Not untypically, he engaged in a variety of commercial and financial transactions. He speculated in the shares of chartered companies, discounted bills, was active in many branches of overseas commerce, dealt in precious stones and, after the reorganization of the Royal Exchange in 1697, was one of the twelve licensed Jewish brokers. (The only other Ashkenazi licensed broker at the time was Abraham Franks [d. 1748].) From the end of the century, family firms in Ashkenazi centers in northern Europe—Hamburg, Frankfurt, and Amsterdam, preeminently—sent their scions to trade and increase their fortune in what was becoming the most dynamic economic center in the world. In the early 1740s, Aron Goldsmit (1715–

1782), the younger of the two sons of the Amsterdam magnate Benedict Goldsmit (1686–1736/7), extended his family's mercantile and financial activities to London. His descendants, who spelled the name Goldsmid, prospered and occupied leadership positions in the community until the early twentieth century. (Most of them, however, eventually left Judaism.) In 1752, Yehiel Prager (d. 1788)—known more commonly by his English business name, Israel Levin Salomons—was sent by his widowed mother and two older brothers in Amsterdam to establish a branch in London. At his death, he was one of the wealthiest East India merchants in the Jewish community, leaving an estate of £48,000. At the end of the century, Mayer Amschel Rothschild (1743–1812) of Frankfurt sent his son Nathan (1777–1836) to England to purchase and ship textiles to the family warehouse in Frankfurt, thereby circumventing the need to use English agents.[17]

Although Ashkenazim outnumbered Sephardim before mid-century, the latter were more numerous at the uppermost level of the community, even at the end of the century. This is not surprising, of course, given the earlier arrival of the Sephardim and their previous involvement in far-flung trading enterprises. With a few exceptions, however, there was little difference in the character of the business activities of the two groups. Both Sephardi and Ashkenazi houses traded with the West Indies and North America and played a major role in the diamond and coral branch of the East India trade. (Sephardi merchants, for obvious reasons, were prominent in the trade with the Spanish and Portuguese colonies, while Ashkenazi merchants were not.) They acted as importers, exporters, and brokers of precious metals and negotiated and traded in bills of exchange. They supplied British troops overseas, raised funds for the government, loaned money to high-living aristocrats, and operated in the stock and commodity markets.

The prosperity of the Anglo-Jewish elite was linked to Britain's transformation into a major geopolitical and economic power in the eighteenth century. The growth of a broad-based domestic consumer market stimulated the demand for imports and thus intensified the need for the financial and brokerage services in which the Jewish elite specialized. London, now the largest city in Europe, with a population of over nine hundred thousand in 1800 (almost twice that of Paris), provided unprecedented opportunities for buying and selling. Enriched by the rise in grain prices and land rents after 1760, landowners flocked to the metropolis to enjoy its pleasures, consume its luxury goods, display their wealth, invest their surplus income, and see and be seen in society. The string of wars that Britain fought with France and its allies between 1689 and 1815 caused military spending to skyrocket, forcing the government to resort to short- and long-term borrowing schemes. To raise funds, it issued interest-bearing securities, which in turn led to the development of a sophisticated financial market in which lenders could sell to third parties their claims on the state. Jewish merchants and entrepreneurs profited from these developments. They helped to supply the state with the funds it needed to fight its wars and to provision its armies. Samson Gideon (1699–1762), who initially amassed a fortune speculating in lottery tickets, government securities, and shares of the joint stock companies, became the most important underwriter of government loans at mid-century and left a fortune of £580,000 at his death. In addition, Jews operated as both brokers and jobbers in the booming financial market that resulted from expanded government borrowing.[18]

When Jews first settled in England in the seventeenth century, they made their homes in the City of London and the streets immediately to the east. The growth of the community in the eighteenth century did not change this pattern of settlement. Most Jews, immigrants and native-born alike, continued to live in close proximity to each other in the east side of the City, where the principal synagogues were, and in Houndsditch and Goodman's Fields to the east. Even opulent merchants and financiers who could afford to purchase homes in the newly developed leafy squares of the West End continued to live in the area, many in the four streets of elegant houses surrounding Goodman's Fields—Prescott, Mansell, Leman, and Alie Streets.[19] In the second half of the century, small colonies appeared outside the area of major concentration. A number of skilled artisans and shopkeepers settled west of Temple Bar, that is, outside the City borders, in order to do business among the affluent population of Westminster and to circumvent the christological oaths that prevented Jews from becoming freemen of the City, a prerequisite to opening a retail shop. A cluster of small traders also grew up south of the Thames in the Borough.[20]

At the same time that London Jews began to disperse geographically within the metropolis, others began to settle in provincial market towns, resorts, and naval ports. There had been a few Sephardi families, mostly engaged in army contracting, living in Dublin and Cork in the late seventeenth and early eighteenth centuries, but these diminutive colonies were temporary, the result of English campaigns to subdue Ireland. Regular communal life in the provinces—measured by the acquisition of a cemetery, the commencement of public worship, or even the establishment of a formal congregation—began in the decades after 1740, although the settlement of individuals and families predated this. Some communities owed their origins to itinerant peddlers who settled down and became shopkeepers. In other instances, London traders and craftsmen were attracted by the growing demand for consumer goods and services and the decay of local regulatory controls on commerce.

At the end of the century, there were about twenty towns outside London with clusters of Jewish residents, although not all could be described as organized communities.[21] Some were old market towns, like Canterbury, Exeter, Gloucester, Norwich, and Oxford; others were resorts and spas, like Bath, Brighton, and Cheltenham; those with the largest concentrations were naval ports, like Chatham, Portsmouth, Plymouth, and Sheerness, all but the last having established congregations before mid-century. The Portsmouth community, the largest outside London, had fifty or so families by 1800—an indication of how small the early provincial communities were. Most, in fact, counted no more than a handful of families. It should also be noted that most communities were in the southern and eastern parts of the country. The Midlands and the North, which became home to the largest provincial centers in the industrial age, attracted few Jews in the eighteenth century. There was no permanent settlement in Manchester, for example, until the late 1780s and early 1790s.[22] This is not to say that Jews avoided these regions completely. In fact, there was almost no town of consequence in Britain in which Jews were completely absent, even if the Jewish presence was limited to one or two isolated traders or artisans.

The growth of Jewish communities in the coastal towns was a direct consequence of the expansion of the royal navy in the eighteenth century. The "blue water" strategy of successive governments—giving priority to naval rather than land forces to contain France and its allies—required not only maintaining growing numbers of ships and sailors but also sinking money into support services and infrastructures in the ports—dry docks, stores, roperies, building yards—all of which provided opportunities for petty commercial activity. Jewish watchmakers, jewelers, silversmiths, engravers, pawnbrokers, and purveyors of optical goods served both the civilian and naval populations in the ports. In addition, Jews were prominent as slopsellers, outfitting sailors with clothes and sailing gear, and as naval agents, providing sailors with goods on credit or loaning them money against receipt of wages or prize money. They also exchanged foreign money for crews returning from abroad and sold inexpensive watches, rings, and other trinkets to ship-bound sailors not permitted to go ashore for fear they might desert.[23]

In market and resort towns as well, Jews appeared as dealers in jewelry, silver, watches, and a range of secondhand goods. They were also found in a narrow range of artisanal trades—as spectacle makers, embroiderers, engravers, watchmakers, clock makers, goldsmiths, pencil makers, button makers, and, in Bristol and Birmingham, glass makers. Some shopkeepers also supplied goods on credit to itinerant Jewish traders who made their headquarters in the provinces rather than in London. One such shopkeeper in Falmouth, Henry Moses, also known as Zander Falmouth, accorded credit to hawkers on the condition that they return every Friday to Falmouth to be counted in his *minyan* (prayer quorum). On Sunday mornings they would settle their accounts and furnish themselves with whatever goods were needed for the coming week. In some cases he advanced them the money to purchase a peddler's license (which not all Jewish peddlers troubled to do), but here too he added a stipulation: that they had to have their full Jewish name inserted in the license.[24]

The growth of the Jewish population in the eighteenth century, its dispersion, and its predominantly Ashkenazi cast led to the formation of new synagogues and other voluntary associations rooted in traditional religious culture. The earliest immigrants from Central Europe joined the Spanish and Portuguese congregation in Bevis Marks, despite the unfamiliarity of its liturgy and rituals, but by 1690 there were enough Ashkenazim of means to establish a congregation of their own on a nearby site in Duke's Place, in the eastern quarter of the City. The chief mover in its foundation was Benjamin Levy, who was a native of Hamburg, like many of its other founding members. In its early years, a series of rabbis served the new congregation, none of whom remained in office long enough to have much impact. Then, in 1704, Moses Hart (1675–1756), who was a cousin and onetime business associate of Levy's, before branching out on his own, and who succeeded Levy as lay head of the Ashkenazim, brought his brother Aaron (1670–1756) from Breslau and installed him as rabbi, a post which he held, without great distinction, for half a century.[25]

In earlier accounts, it was common to refer to Hart as the first chief rabbi because he was the religious head of the congregation that eventually became known as the Great Synagogue.[26] To describe him as such, however, is an anachronistic misrepresentation of the character of his authority and the community he served. From their origins, London synagogues were voluntary bodies, completely independent of the state, their authority moral rather than statutory. There was no communal-wide body embracing all Jews in London. Similarly, before the Victorian period, there was no supracommunal institution uniting synagogues in London and the provinces, although many individuals and congregations outside the metropolis voluntarily accepted the religio-legal preeminence of the Great Synagogue's rabbi. The Portsmouth congregation, for example, submitted questions of *halakhah* (Jewish law) to Aaron Hart and relied on him to license their ritual slaughterers. But they did so because he was the most prominent representative in England of traditional religious authority, not because he occupied any formal chief rabbinical post. The formal institution of the chief rabbinate came into being only in 1842, when representatives of twenty-six congregations elected Nathan Marcus Adler (1803–90) to the post.

The true nature of Hart's position is best illustrated by reference to the development of additional Ashkenazi synagogues in London. In 1704, several gem dealers with ties to Hamburg, including Marcus (or Mordecai) Moses (d. 1735), son-in-law of the famous memoirist Glückel of Hameln (1645–1724), attempted to set up a *bet midrash* (prayer and study hall) in a private home in St. Mary Axe, a few hundred yards from Duke's Place. Since prayer was an integral part of bet midrash routine, Moses Hart viewed this development as a threat to the financial base of the existing Ashkenazi synagogue and, possibly, as a challenge to his brother's authority. In concert with the head of the Sephardi community, which was also eager to prevent breakaway groups, he persuaded (perhaps bribed) the Court of Aldermen of the City of London to intervene and prohibit its establishment. Relations between Marcus Moses and the brothers Hart worsened over the next two years. In 1706, Moses accused Aaron Hart of improperly writing a conditional bill of divorce for a debt-laden ne'er-do-well about to sail for the West Indies. A scandal erupted, ultimately involving scholars and merchants in Rotterdam, Hamburg, and Amsterdam. Charges and countercharges were made, rabbinical courts convened, pamphlets penned, reconciliations tried and abandoned. The upshot of the dispute was that Moses opened a synagogue in his home in 1707. The congregation that formed around it built a synagogue in Fenchurch Street in 1726, which it occupied until the late nineteenth century and which became known eventually as the Hambro Synagogue, after the city from which its earliest members came. At the time of its move, Moses Hart again asked the City authorities to close it, but this time they failed to take action.[27]

As the Jewish population of London expanded in the second half of the century, additional synagogues and minyanim emerged to meet the needs of an increasingly diverse and dispersed community. In 1761, a group of small merchants, some of whom were members of the Great Synagogue, purchased Bricklayers' Hall in Leadenhall Street for use as a house of worship. Their motive for establishing a congregation of their own was undoubtedly a desire to be independent of the existing congregations, in which synagogal honors and offices were, in effect, reserved for the rich. Enraged by the secession, which signified a loss of both authority and revenue, the leaders of the Great Synagogue, with the concurrence of the Hambro, ordered their rabbi to refuse to officiate at religious rites for members of the breakaway group. This had no impact on the new congregation, which became known eventually as the New Synagogue. About the same time artisans and shopkeepers living on the western border of the City established a minyan and sickness and burial society that later evolved into the Western Synagogue. In their case geographical distance from the established congregations was the chief motive, although, here too, the desire for religious independence from the great magnates may also have been a consideration.[28]

In addition, a number of small minyanim and hevrot were established by new arrivals from Germany and Poland who had a stronger commitment to traditional study and ritual observance than that was common in England. A hevrah called Mahzikei Ha-Torah (Upholders of the Law), which later evolved into the Rosemary Lane Synagogue, was established in 1748. About 1770, a Talmud study group and minyan, Hevra Shaarei Zion (Gates of Zion), formed around Moses ben Judah of Minsk, who lectured on the Talmud and delivered sermons, some of which were published in London in 1772 (*Sefer even shoham* [The book of onyx]). Toward the end of the century, a similar group formed around the Lithuanian-born Pinchas ben Samuel, whose *Midrash Pinchas*, a commentary on Talmudic legends, was published in London in 1795. Two Polish minyanim were established in Houndsditch, the center of the old clothes trade, in the early 1790s, one, Hevra Shas (The Six Orders of the Talmud), being devoted to the study of the Talmud. In the same decade there also came into being a minyan for *maariv bizmanah*, that is, for evening prayer at its proper time—a reference to the custom of anglicized Jews of reciting the evening service earlier than permitted because of the late hour at which the sun sets in England in the summer.[29]

Although there was tension between old and new synagogues initially, it was not long before they began to cooperate on matters of mutual concern, like poor relief and *shehitah* (ritual slaughter). In regard to the poor, for example, each synagogue assumed responsibility for relieving its own members and their families. There were, however, many Jews in need of assistance—recent immigrants especially—who had no claim on the charity funds of any synagogue and yet expected help. In order to distribute the financial burden of relieving such Jews, the major Ashkenazi synagogues, beginning in 1759 with an agreement between the Hambro and the Great, divided the expense of relieving the unaffiliated poor. Because this and other arrangements among the City synagogues were voluntary, there was much wrangling over terms and on occasion a complete breakdown of cooperation. This occurred, for example, in 1765 over the question of rabbinical authority. Hart Lyon (1721–1800) served as rabbi of the Great Synagogue from 1758 to 1764 and was recognized as the chief religious authority in the country by the Hambro Synagogue, which contributed to his salary, and by communities outside London as well. But when the Great Synagogue chose David Tevele Schiff (d. 1791) as his successor in 1765, the Hambro went its own way, appointing as its rabbi an unsuccessful candidate for the Duke's Place post—Israel Meshullam Solomon (1723–94), son of the well-known anti-Sabbatean controversialist Jacob Emden (1697–1776). Each man claimed to be the chief Ashkenazi rabbinical authority in England, and the dispute was resolved only in 1780 when Solomon left London to take a post in Russia.[30]

The most salient characteristic of English Jewish religious life in the eighteenth century was its laxity and ignorance. A minority of Jewish men, whether recently arrived or native-born, continued to practice Judaism in the traditional fashion, regularly attending synagogue, observing the full regimen of dietary, Sabbath, and festival laws, cultivating Talmudic learning. Those who did tended to be associated with small minyanim and hevrot in London, although strict traditionalists were found even in the major synagogues. From mid-century, however, it is clear that such persons were not representative of the mass of Jews. The general level of knowledge and practice in England was markedly lower in the second half of the century than elsewhere in Europe, with the possible exception of the Sephardi communities of southwestern France. (Equally low standards were to be found in communities in the West Indies and North America, which were, of course, closely linked to London.)

The weakening of traditional practice and knowledge was most pronounced among the very rich and the very poor. Among the former, laxity was widespread by the 1730s or 1740s. The laws of *kashrut*, for example, were observed casually or not at all. In 1733, Abigail Franks (1696–1756) of New York wrote to her son Naphtali (1715–1796), then living in London, to warn him never to eat a meal "unless it be bread and butter" at the home of her brother Asher Levy (1699–1742), "nor no where else where there is the least doubt of things not done after our strict Judaical method." Rabbi Hart Lyon complained in the late 1750s that as a result of Jews feasting with non-Jews on Christian holidays "the Christmas pudding which the Christians prepare in memory of the apostles is more favored than the *matsot*." When his son Solomon Hirschell (1761–1842) arrived from Germany in 1802 to assume the post of rabbi of the Great Synagogue, he announced that he would punish with excommunication "all such Jews who indulge their appetites with wild fowl."[31]

The wealthy were not punctilious about the observance of the Sabbath either. Brokers and jobbers opened their mail, walked through Change Alley to learn whether there had been a rise or fall in the market, discussed business matters with one another, and even gave instructions to buy and sell securities and bills of exchange. "Their day of rest," observed the physician Meyer Schomberg (1690–1761) in 1746, "is not a day of rest for them either in this world or the next, because they go to feed themselves at a nearby place, eating of the produce of the land that it is forbidden to eat and drinking the wine and liquor that make maids merry, in the company of gentile women." The anonymous author of *A Letter to the Parisian Sanhedrin* reported at the turn of the century that there were wealthy Jews who attended synagogue on Sabbaths and festivals but immediately afterwards rushed off to do business in the coffee houses and at the exchange. Synagogue attendance in general was not robust. By the end of the century, two of the three large Ashkenazi congregations in the City were experiencing difficulty in gathering a minyan for daily services, despite the increased number of Jews living in London.[32]

In their sexual habits the wealthy also broke with normative Jewish practice. Defying rabbinic ordinances regarding female modesty, married women appeared outside their homes with their own hair visible, attired in low-cut gowns, their flesh exposed to public view. Their husbands embraced the sexual code of aristocratic society, patronizing brothels, keeping mistresses, fathering children out of wedlock. Stage literature of the first half of the century contains numerous references to the philandering of opulent Sephardim. Henry Fielding's *Miss Lucy in Town,* first produced in 1742, is set in a high-class brothel patronized by wealthy Jews, for example. Communal leaders like Joseph Salvador (1716–86) and later the brothers Benjamin (1755–1808) and Abraham (1756–1810) Goldsmid were openly linked with fashionable courtesans. Samuel Vita Montefiore (1757–1802), an uncle of Sir Moses, fathered at least four children out of wedlock. Whether Jewish women of the same social stratum behaved similarly, flaunting traditional sexual morality, or whether a double standard operated, remains unknown; if they did breach traditional restraints, they were more discrete than their husbands and escaped public rebuke.[33]

In prosperous Jewish circles, the spread of religious laxity was linked to a broader process of adaptation to upper-class patterns of thought and behavior. Some deviations from traditional practice, such as conducting business on the Sabbath or eating gentile food, were explicit transgressions of Jewish law. Other new habits, while not violations of religious law, were nonetheless departures from previous patterns of cultural and social separatism and thus represented a break with tradition in the larger sense of the term. Economic success brought in its wake familiarity with upper-class living standards and social habits and kindled an interest in emulating them. Jews who had made their fortunes in the City began to adopt the habits, values, tastes, and outlook of the upper class. They copied their mode of dress, personal adornment, and home decoration, adopted their manners, pursued their recreations. They attended the theater and the opera, gossiped and played cards in coffee houses, collected paintings and had their portraits painted, hosted lavish parties and entertainments, patronized musicians and singers, took the waters at fashionable spas in the wake of too much rich living, acquired homes and even extensive estates in the countryside.[34]

The purchase of country homes and the subsequent pursuit of rural pleasures, such as hunting and racing, are potent symbols of this process of acculturation. In the first quarter of the century wealthy Sephardim with their primary residence in London started to purchase or rent homes in nearby villages or the surrounding countryside to which they could retreat on weekends or in summer. Members of the da Costa clan had purchased houses in Hampstead and Highgate, then villages on the northwest fringe of London, in the last quarter of the seventeenth century. As other Sephardim—and then, later, Ashkenazim—made their fortunes, they followed suit. The largest cluster of Jewish country homes was to the southwest of London, near the villages of Richmond, Isleworth, Teddington, Mortlake, and Twickenham. Some were princely edifices, intended to advertise their owners' good fortune. The Roe-hampton mansion of the merchant banker Benjamin Goldsmid featured a dining room sixty by forty feet, numerous drawing rooms, a ballroom, a library, a synagogue, and extensive gardens with an artificial lake and grotto. So common was ownership of a country home among wealthy Jews that when the Palestinian rabbi Haim Yosef David Azulai (1724–1806) visited London in spring 1755 to collect funds for the Hebron yeshivah, he found that most of his potential contributors were in the country.[35]

Jews who acquired country homes were following a well-trodden path. Parvenu merchants and financiers routinely purchased country estates in order to display their material splendor, advance their claims to gentility—the ownership of a landed estate being the foundation of genteel status—and establish the foundation for their descendants' entry into upper-class circles. Jewish ambitions were not as far ranging, at least not initially. Nonetheless, the acquisition of country homes worked to isolate their inhabitants from the Jewish community and its institutions, even if only intermittently, and simultaneously to bring them into closer contact with families from the traditional ruling class, who were their immediate neighbors. It was said of Benjamin and Jesse Goldsmid, in regard to their first country home at Stamford Hill, that they gained "the friendship of all the gentlefolks for many miles round the spot and reciprocal visits were as frequent as the return of day, each being emulous to become more and more agreeable to the strangers, till the most complete union was formed in all the neighbouring villages of Tottenham, Edmonton, and several miles round with the family."[36] Whether intended or not, this mode of living contributed to weakening the wealthiest families' links to Judaism and ultimately to hastening the departure of their descendants from the community altogether, the family of Benjamin Goldsmid being a prime example: following his death in 1808, his wife and children were baptized in the Church of England.

The rich were not alone in abandoning the regimen and self-segregation of traditional Jewish life. The Jewish poor, the largest section of the community by far, underwent an equally striking transformation, proving no more immune to the attractions of the larger society than the wealthy. Some adopted a casual attitude toward observance of religious rites and customs, performing them only intermittently or haphazardly; others failed to observe Judaism at all and lived essentially outside any religious framework, especially those who derived their livelihood from crime. None of the gang involved in the notorious Chelsea murder case of 1771 was a practicing Jew, for example. While being examined by Sir John Fielding after their arrest, one of the gang started abusing another. When Fielding told him to stop, as it would do him no good to revile his brother Jew, another member burst out: "He a Jew? He's no Jew; he is more Christian as Jews." The breakdown of traditional values was particularly acute in the realm of sexual discipline and family life. From the 1750s at the latest, cohabitation outside the bounds of marriage was not unusual, both between Jews and between Jews and non-Jews. Even synagogue-going Jews were to be found living in such relationships. Early Jewish friendly societies attempted to bolster the respectability of their artisanal and shopkeeping membership by excluding men who were cohabiting with gentile women. Jews were also to be found keeping brothels and working as prostitutes. Whether their clientele was largely Jewish or mixed is not known.[37]

The Jewish poor, like the Jewish notability, also absorbed non-Jewish habits and tastes, but in their case they embraced, not the standards of upper-class gentility, but rather the rough-and-tumble ways of their impoverished gentile neighbors, with whom they lived in close proximity, frequently sharing the same buildings and rooming houses. They abandoned the traditional Jewish garb of Central and Eastern Europe, eventually acquiring a reputation for flashy attire. They were often quarrelsome, undisciplined, riotous, violent, and hostile to authority. They routinely employed physical force to settle scores, defend themselves, and protest verbal slights. The most striking example of their acculturation was the passion they developed for prizefighting, both as spectators and participants. From the 1760s through the 1820s, several dozen Jews achieved fame in the boxing ring, including the greatest fighter of the period, Daniel Mendoza (1763–1836), whom early historians of the sport credited with introducing a more "scientific" form of boxing, one emphasizing finesse and agility over brute strength. When Jewish boxers fought, friends and coreligionists flocked to the ring, and matches became rallying points for ethnic assertiveness, as well as opportunities for heavy wagering. When Mendoza fought, for example, he was always billed as "Mendoza the Jew." On occasion, Jewish women also fought for prize money. In 1795, a boxing magazine reported a well-fought match in a field near the New Road in London between Mary Ann Fielding and "a noted Jewess of Wentworth Road," who was seconded by Mendoza. Fielding knocked the Jewess down over seventy times in a fight lasting one hour and twenty minutes.[38] It is difficult to imagine a more striking example of the transformation of traditional Jewish life.

The acculturation and secularization of the Jews in eighteenth-century England was more advanced than elsewhere in Europe. As we have seen, this was in large part due to a unique set of circumstances: the voluntary nature of communal bodies and their corresponding weakness; the relative openness of social life in a booming, undisciplined, poorly policed metropolis; the multiplication of opportunities for intensive social contact with Christians. There was another determinant as well. Historians routinely describe Central European Jewish communities at this time as socially isolated, culturally autarkic, and loyal to religious tradition. While this characterization is not altogether incorrect, I suspect that the seeds of change were more widely sown in these communities than has been acknowledged. If so, it follows then that those Jews who migrated to England in the Georgian period were not untouched by change before they crossed the Channel or the North Sea. Indeed, it is possible, although it cannot be documented, that those who emigrated from Central Europe were those whose attachment to tradition had already been loosened. Once settled in England, they found themselves in circumstances that encouraged behavior toward which they were already inclined.

The characteristic patterns of Anglo-Jewish life in the eighteenth century foreshadow those of Western Jewries in the following two centuries, when widespread acculturation, partial integration, and ample secularization were the norm. In this sense, the abandonment of tradition in Georgian England inaugurates the beginning of the modern era in Jewish history. There are, however, historians who reject this interpretation, arguing that these departures do not add up to the beginning of a new mode of Jewish life. They maintain that these changes were mere "variations" or "deviations" from tradition, not "elements of a new process that would lead ultimately to a new structure of society." They make this assertion because for them the test for significance is the consciousness or mental attitudes of historical actors. In their view, the decisive rupture between old and new came "only when deviation was justified on the basis of new concepts that contradicted the value system of tradition"—that is, only when Jews repudiated traditional patterns in a systematic, intellectually coherent, self-conscious manner, challenging rabbinic norms in the name of reason, science, liberalism, or some other enlightenment creed, as Moses Mendelssohn (1729–86) and his disciples did in Central Europe.[39]

This is an inappropriate standard for gauging the historical significance of changes in Jewish life. It privileges the ideological activity of philosophers, publicists, and patrons over the day-to-day behavior of inarticulate, intellectually undistinguished persons—the great mass of the Jewish people, in other words. It reflects a Germano-centric view of Jewish history that is unable to incorporate the experience of Jews in English-speaking countries into the larger framework of modern Jewish history. It implies that intellectuals set the pace of historical change and the masses follow, a dubious proposition in most historical contexts.

Yet, despite its inutility, this way of viewing the origins of Jewish modernity does serve to highlight a notable feature of the transformation of Jewish life in England: the absence of an intellectual movement promoting Jewish modernization. In Central and, later, Eastern Europe, groups of reform-minded intellectuals (*maskilim*) actively championed the acquisition of gentile dress, deportment, language, and manners; the intellectual reconciliation of Judaism and secular Western thought; the broadening of Jewish educational and cultural horizons; and the reformation of Jewish occupational structure. In England, these changes (with the exception of occupational diversification, which failed everywhere) occurred without such circles. English Jews who embraced new habits and attitudes rarely articulated their motives for doing so. They felt no need to appeal to a body of ideas to justify their break with tradition or to reinterpret Judaism in the light of enlightenment ideals. They adopted the habits of the surrounding population because they wanted to feel comfortable in their new home and to pursue pleasure and success unimpeded by traditional constraints. At the same time, there were no strong external forces working to preserve Jewish separatism or strengthen Jewish piety. The government did little to stop Jews from living and working as they pleased (what restrictions there were will be discussed further on) while the community, a network of voluntary associations rather than a corporate body, did little to control personal behavior. Because communal sanctions, as well as rabbinic authority, were weak, those who wished to break with tradition were not forced to confront its guardians and articulate a rationale for their dissent.

Although there was no movement for the modernization of Jewish life in England, there were publicists and intellectuals in the last third of the century whose work paralleled that of the maskilim in Central Europe. A few Hebrew scholars who were familiar with secular literature (an unusual accomplishment at the time in the Ashkenazi world) wrote in a modernized Hebrew style, frequently on themes of general interest.[40] Abraham Abrahams (d. 1792), also known as Abraham Tang, translated William Congreve's drama *Mourning Bride* into Hebrew in 1768, defended the radical John Wilkes and democratic principles in a small English-language pamphlet in 1770, published an English translation of *Pirkei avot* (Sayings of the fathers) in 1772, and wrote a Hebrew treatise on pagan mythology in 1773, in which he displayed a knowledge of Greek and Latin authors, as well as of modern European scholarship on religion. In the introduction to this work, which was never published, he maintained that a knowledge of classical mythology was of paramount importance to Jews since the rabbis of antiquity knew this material and sometimes borrowed Greek styles in creating *aggadot* (edificatory tales). Jews who were ignorant of Greek literature, Abrahams believed, could not comprehend the aggadot in rabbinic literature. The jeweler Jacob Hart (ca. 1745–1814), a more conservative thinker than Abrahams, defended Judaism against the attacks of pagan chroniclers and recent enemies of religious faith (Locke, Bayle, Spinoza, Hobbes, Hume, Voltaire, Bolingbroke, and Paine) in *Sefer milhamot adonai* (The wars of the lord) in 1794. His defense of tradition, while not remarkable in itself, showed him to be familiar with a broad range of ancient and modern authors. Among other sources, it drew on a High Church Tory polemic against the use of Newtonian natural philosophy to attack revealed religion.

Hart was steeped in traditional rabbinic culture and was no revolutionary. He viewed secular learning as a handmaiden to Torah, the bedrock of his outlook. A similar perspective was articulated by the anonymous author of a 1771 tract, *Sefer giddul banim* (The education of children), which was published in Judaeo-German in order to reach a broader audience. The author of this short pamphlet advocated modest reforms in the traditional system of educating male children. He urged that they be taught to understand, not just recite, the blessings and prayers, so that they would become familiar with the principles of Judaism, even suggesting that in order to accomplish this they first learn to pray in their native language, not in Hebrew. He argued that they should acquire a thorough, grammatically sound knowledge of the Hebrew Bible before going on to study Talmud and that, in addition, they should learn either French, because of its usefulness in commerce, or Latin, because of its importance for medicine. The author also cautioned parents about teaching their children fabulous aggadot incompatible with human reason.[41]

At the very end of the century there were critics of traditional Jewish life, writing largely in English, who adopted a more radical position.

The most articulate was the literary historian and anthologist Isaac D'Israeli (1766–1848), father of the future prime minister. In *The Curiosities of Literature* (1791–1834), his novel *Vaurien* (1797), an essay on Mendelssohn (1798), and then much later *The Genius of Judaism* (1833), he attacked the Judaism of his time in a manner similar to that of the radical, post-Mendelssohnian maskilim in Germany. He explicitly rejected the authority of rabbinic law, which he characterized as obsolete and arbitrary, dismissing the rabbis of antiquity as "dictators of the human intellect" and "a race of scheming schoolmen," who had imprisoned the Jewish people in "a mass of ritual ordinances, casuistical glosses and arbitrary decisions." He called for a radical reform of traditional Jewish education, whose exclusive focus on religious texts he blamed for the Jews' alleged intellectual inferiority, aesthetic degeneracy, and physical temerity. He urged Jews to reject every "anti-social principle" in their culture that marked them off so that they might fuse socially and politically with their fellow citizens.[42]

What set Jewish writers in England apart from their counterparts in Germany was the boldness with which they advanced their views. They polemicized about religious and political issues without fearing the wrath of state or communal officials. The shoemaker and later hatter David Levi (1742–1801) attacked the Christian interpretation of biblical prophecies in several volumes in English. He was as brash in his defense of Judaism as Moses Mendelssohn was circumspect in his, a contrast that highlights the level of security that Levi and other London Jews felt. Similarly, Abraham Abrahams's intervention in national politics— his public identification with the radical Wilkes and his denunciation of ministerial impudence—would have been unthinkable at this time in the German states.

The relative isolation of these writers, the fact that they did not constitute an intellectual coterie or social movement, mirrors the weakness of Jewish intellectual activity in general in England. In this regard, it is important to remember that London was on the cultural periphery of the Jewish world in the eighteenth century. It was a raw, rowdy, untamed place without well-established traditions of scholarship and piety. Communal affairs were in the hands of worldly merchants and brokers without much religious or secular learning. The mass of Jews were poor, unlettered, and largely immune to religious discipline. Given these circumstances, it is understandable that few scholarly figures, whether traditionalist or modernist, migrated to England and that those who did come did not remain permanently or succeed in creating learned circles or permanent institutions. The rabbis who served the Ashkenazi synagogues of London, for example, came from Germany and Poland and after some time in England returned there (or at least made the attempt) to take up more attractive positions. Hart Lyon, rabbi of the Great Synagogue from 1758 to 1764, complained repeatedly that there was no respect for learning and learned men in London and that he was unable to fulfill the mishnaic precept "raise up many disciples" (*Pirkei avot* 1:1) since he had no pupils, "not even a colleague [*haver*] with whom I could pursue my studies." The few advanced students of the Talmud were "scattered into different, distant parts of the town" and "live therefore a lonely life and cannot profit from one another." His successor, David Tevele Schiff, made virtually the same complaint: "I have no pupil and not even any one to whom I can speak on Talmudic subjects."[43]

The only major figure in European Jewish thought who resided in England in the eighteenth century was the Venetian-born David Nieto (1654–1728), rabbi of the Spanish and Portuguese community from 1701 to his death.[44] A graduate of the University of Padua in medicine, Nieto was familiar with the secular learning of his age, like many Sephardi rabbis in Western Europe, and maintained scholarly relations with a range of learned Christians in England and abroad—an impossibility, it should be added, for Ashkenazi rabbis in England at this time, since they lacked a secular education. As religious head of the London Sephardim, Nieto faced challenges that were more or less specific to Sephardi communities and were rooted in earlier developments. As indicated in chapter 1, it was not unusual for Sephardim with a converso background to experience difficulty in embracing normative rabbinic Judaism. The confused character of their religious identity and fragmented knowledge of Judaism made them susceptible to a number of heretical currents, including neo-Karaism (opposition to the oral law or to the literal understanding of rabbinic aggadot), Sabbatean messianism, and deism. In numerous sermons, tracts, and philosophical works aimed specifically at former conversos, most of them published in Spanish, Nieto defended rabbinic Judaism against its detractors. When crypto-Sabbatean supporters of his predecessor, Solomon Ayllon, attempted to blacken his reputation, by falsely accusing him in 1703 of expressing pantheistic views, he proved himself to be an able controversialist and political infighter. His major work, *Matteh Dan* (Rod of Dan; 1714), a defense of the oral law in dialogue form, has been reprinted numerous times and has become part of the intellectual arsenal of Orthodox Judaism.

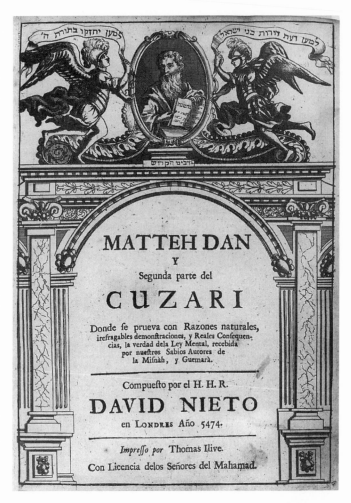

The title page of the Spanish edition of David Nieto's *Matteh Dan* (1714), a defense of the oral law and rabbinic tradition, addressed to ex-conversos. Courtesy of the Harlan Hatcher Graduate Library, University of Michigan.

The only other Jew in England who made a mark on Jewish culture of the period was Ephraim Luzzatto (1729–92), like Nieto a native of Italy and a graduate of the University of Padua in medicine.[45] Luzzatto settled in London in 1763 and was employed to provide medical treatment to the Sephardi poor. He brought with him the Italian Jewish tradition of writing secular Hebrew poetry and in 1766 published a collection of his poems, *Eleh benei ha-neurim* (These are the children of youth), that attracted the attention of maskilim on the continent and was later reprinted in Germany and Austria. He was also the author of a Hebrew cantata, *Geulah* (Redemption), celebrating the unrelieved spiritual happiness of the messianic age, which was performed in 1776 at the home of Abraham Mendes Furtado (1766–1821). Like Nieto and the handful of Ashkenazi scholars who wrote in Hebrew, whether in a modern or traditional vein, his work was addressed to a European-wide Jewish audience rather than specifically to local readers.

Although there is little information regarding Jewish schooling in the eighteenth century, it is clear that the Ashkenazi community lacked educational institutions that were common even in much smaller communities in Germany and Poland.[46] A communally supported elementary school for the Ashkenazi poor (talmud torah) was established in 1732, but it was no longer functioning during the rabbinate of Hart Lyon, who, lamenting the absence of communal schools, asked, "What will be the future of Judaism if this state of affairs continues?"[47] It was revived later in the century, but it educated few boys (no provision was made for girls) relative to the number of poor within the community. Those parents who were financially able either hired Hebrew tutors for their sons or sent them to private elementary schools (*hadarim*), where instruction was limited to reading Hebrew and translating the Pentateuch into Yiddish, the native language of the teachers (*melammedim*). (As early as the first decade of the century, one melammed complained of the difficulty of teaching Bible to boys who had been born in London because they lacked familiarity with Yiddish.)[48] One indicator of the low level of Hebrew knowledge in England was the appearance in 1770 of an English translation of the prayerbook. (In British North America, where standards of Jewish observance and learning were even lower, an English translation was published between 1761 and 1766.) At a more advanced level, there was an Ashkenazi bet midrash, about which little is known, but no yeshivah, although Hart Lyon attempted, unsuccessfully, to establish one. The Sephardim were better provided. The synagogue established schools for both elementary and advanced religious studies, including, in 1731, a school for the daughters of the congregational poor. They were also in advance of the Ashkenazim in introducing secular subjects into Jewish schooling, adding English and arithmetic to the talmud torah curriculum in 1736.

Despite the low level of observance and the advance of acculturation, it would be an error to conclude that Jews were being rapidly absorbed into the surrounding society and ceasing to be Jewish. Social integration and, in particular, full assimilation through intermarriage and/or conversion lagged far behind secularization and acculturation—as was the case wherever Jews left behind the cultural and social isolation of the traditional community.

The most extensive social interaction between Jews and non-Jews developed at the top and bottom of the social ladder. At the top, the business activities of stock brokers, government loan contractors, military commissaries, and dealers in precious stones brought them into contact with the wealthy and the powerful, while their acquisition of country homes created the basis for the growth of social ties between their families and local landed society. In this, the Sephardim, whose historical experience accustomed them to extensive contact with Gentiles and who had arrived in England earlier, took the lead. Horace Walpole's voluminous correspondence contains numerous references to wealthy Sephardim who entered into upper-class social life in the neighborhood around Strawberry Hill, his famous "Gothick" villa at Twickenham. In June 1780, for example, in a letter to the Countess of Upper Ossory, he praised "an exceedingly pretty fire-work" in honor of the king's birthday that he had seen at the Thames-side home of Raphael Franco, a diamond and coral merchant.[49] Few Ashkenazim were sufficiently wealthy and acculturated in the eighteenth century to move in these circles. The Harts, the Franks and, at the end of the century, the Goldsmids were among the small number who did so.

It is difficult to know if those families who established social links with landed society saw this as the first step in a process that would lead directly to full absorption into the non-Jewish world. But whether intended or not, it was not uncommon for wealthy families, once established in the countryside, to lose their attachment to Judaism—through intermarriage and conversion—within a generation or two.[50] In the case of Samson Gideon (1699–1762), the wealthiest Jew in the country at mid-century, there is no question that he consciously embarked on a course of radical assimilation in order to secure a place in upper-class society for his family. He married a Protestant, baptized his newborn children, purchased a fine mansion in Erith, Kent, with superb views over the Thames (as well as extensive estates in Lincolnshire and Buckinghamshire), married his daughter Elizabeth to the second Viscount Gage with a portion of £40,000, and obtained a baronetcy for his thirteen-year-old heir, then at Eton, after being refused the honor for himself, since he remained a Jew. In other cases, it is clear that the dissolution of Jewish ties was the outcome of a more gradual process of acculturation and integration extending over two or three generations. Moses Hart, his son-in-law Aaron Franks (1692–1777), and Aaron's brother Isaac (d. 1736) were pillars of the Great Synagogue but also cultivated ties with the non-Jewish world; by the end of the century most of their descendants were Anglicans and members of landed society.

The poorest strata of Jews also enjoyed extensive social relations with non-Jews. Street traders, old clothes men, itinerant peddlers, porters, servants, beggars, and criminals lived on close physical terms with their gentile neighbors. They lodged in the same narrow streets and crowded courts, frequently in the same buildings. Free of the rigid conventions that governed socializing in higher ranks, they mixed easily with non-Jews in the streets, public houses, theaters, and open spaces of the City and adjacent areas. Poor Jews whose ties to traditional religion were weak drank, ate, caroused, whored, and cohabited with non-Jews from the same milieu. One indicator of the intimate socializing that developed at the bottom of the social hierarchy was the increase in mixed gangs of pickpockets, housebreakers, and shoplifters from the 1770s on.[51] Here too sustained social intercourse led to intermarriage and complete alienation from Judaism.

The mass of Jews, however, continued to socialize and marry within their own community, irrespective of their attachment to Jewish ritual and worship. Moreover, they continued to think of themselves as Jews first and foremost, as members of a distinct people, and not as Englishmen, even if they were native-born citizens who had known no other homeland. In this respect, they were no different from their ancestors, who had lived in conditions of much greater isolation from the surrounding society. Jews in England began to think of themselves as English—as well as Jewish—only in the mid-nineteenth century, when the majority of the community was native- rather than foreign-born and the flow of immigration dramatically slower. Before then they did not concern themselves about how to combine or reconcile the claims of Jewish peoplehood and British citizenship. Their group identity and social cohesion remained more or less intact, except at the uppermost and bottommost reaches of the social ladder, where drift and defection were making inroads by the end of the eighteenth century.

The non-Jewish world also viewed the Jews in their midst as a separate people, regarding even native-born, highly acculturated Jews as different in kind, marked off by a distinctive, irreducible essence or otherness that remained despite their adaptation to English conditions. In fact, the belief in Jewish distinctiveness was so embedded in popular consciousness that converted Jews, including the children of Jews baptized at birth, were commonly referred to as Jews. Thus, the memoirist Sir Nathaniel Wraxall, in commenting on the generosity of Sir Sampson Gideon (1745–1824), the baptized son of a Sephardi father and a Protestant mother, wrote that he might have furnished the prototype of the virtuous Jew in an essay of Richard Cumberland, while, in a less flattering vein, the *Annual Register* of 1806 referred to Jamaican-born Sir Menasseh Masseh Lopes (1755–1831), landowner, Member of Parliament, and Anglican since 1802, as "a Jew baronet."[52]

The belief in the otherness of the Jews was an inheritance of centuries-old Christian theological contempt for Judaism. In sermons, tracts, and learned treatises, eighteenth-century churchmen, especially those in the High Church camp, repeated hoary, theologically derived accusations, denouncing Jews as blasphemers, deicides, infidels, children of the devil, allies of Antichrist, outcasts, and outlaws. In an editorial against the Jewish Naturalization Bill (see below) in 1753, for example, the *Westminster Journal* declared that the essence of Judaism was "an avowed contempt of Christ, an implacable hatred to Christians and an impious detestation to Christianity."[53] The medieval libel that Jews murdered Christian children in order to obtain their blood for religious purposes was voiced on occasion, as were other medieval fantasies, like the belief that Jews were distinguished by a peculiar smell.

Views such as these circulated everywhere in Europe at this time, in both Protestant and Catholic countries. The damnation of the Jews and their essential malevolence were stock beliefs in the mental universe of most men and women living in Christian societies in the age of enlightenment, as they had been for centuries. What is striking about England is that in the eighteenth century these beliefs lost much of their appeal and ceased to inspire either popular behavior or official policy toward Jews, at least most of the time. Their decline was undoubtedly linked to the evolution of an establishment Christianity in the eighteenth century that was moderate, worldly, and practical. Exhausted by the religious strife of the previous century and fearful of the social consequences of sectarian enthusiasm, the Anglican hierarchy sought to make the established church an inclusive, national body. They de-emphasized doctrinal divisiveness and crusading zealotry and minimized the transcendental and the mysterious, urging instead sobriety, moderation, moral duties, and good works. Latitudinarian churchmen viewed religious virtuosity and excessive piety with suspicion. "Enthusiasm is a very horrid thing," declared Joseph Butler, bishop of Durham.[54]

Liberal notions of religious toleration toward those outside the established church gradually took hold. While intended initially to respond to the growth of Christian diversity, they eventually had an impact as well on attitudes toward Jews. The Lockean argument that the state had no legitimate interest in examining the religious beliefs of its citizens as long as they adhered to the civil laws was explicitly applied to the Jewish population during the naturalization controversy of 1753. Reason and Nature, it was argued, dictated that persons not be barred from settling and trading in England on account of their religious beliefs. One tract asked, "What law in Nature can there be against any person's enjoying the common privileges of a society or nation into which they were joined by their own consent and loyal obedience to the rules of that polity?" Some Englishmen were so intoxicated with notions of toleration that they argued that Jews were no different than other human beings. The anonymous author of *A Looking-Glass for the Jews* (1753) emphasized the remarkable similarity between Jews and Christians: however different in terms of religion and nationality, they derived from one common stock.[55] To concede the common humanity of the Jews in mid-eighteenth-century Europe was a radical break from old ways of thinking.

At the same time that the concept of religious toleration was sinking roots, urbanization was removing many ordinary people from the influence of formal Christian doctrine altogether. In London and the mushrooming industrial centers of the Midlands and the North, much of the population never set foot in church and knew virtually nothing about Christian teaching—about Judaism or anything else. In Birmingham, it was said in 1788, "the great mass of the people give themselves very little concern about religious matters, seldom if ever going to church."[56] This does not mean, of course, that unchurched folk were immune to the influence of old prejudices. As we shall see, by the eighteenth century much anti-Jewish hostility existed independently of any theological framework, even if religious animosity was its initial inspiration.

Traditional Christian doctrine about Jews was also counterbalanced in the eighteenth century by a strong philosemitic current.[57] Millenarian views that inspired radical Puritans and others to seek Jewish readmission in the 1650s continued to influence attitudes toward Jews in the next century and beyond. Despite the drop in religious intensity, millenarian speculation never disappeared, nor did the associated conviction that the conversion of the Jews was linked to the Second Coming and that England had a special role to play in ushering it in. Pamphlets, tracts, sermons, and treatises on millenarian themes circulated widely, especially during the Revolutionary and Napoleonic wars, when evangelical Christians mistook social and political upheaval for the birth pangs of the millennium. Conversionist philosemitic views in particular reached a wide audience during the controversy over Jewish naturalization in 1753. One of the most frequently articulated pro-Jewish arguments in that debate was that naturalization would promote the Jews' integration into Christian social circles and result ultimately in their conversion. As one clergyman explained to his fashionable London congregation, extending the privileges of Englishmen to the Jews would incline them "to cultivate a friendship and familiarity with us; which, of course, must bring them, in due season, to a conformity of manners, and an imitation of our ways and customs." Jews would then come to entertain more favorable feelings toward non-Jews, and "these more favourable sentiments concerning us may be improved, e'er long, into a more favourable opinion of our religion," resulting in the end in conversion to Christianity.[58] Conversionist philosemites also reevaluated the traditional doctrine that God had eternally damned the Jews for killing Jesus. One anonymous writer even propounded the novel idea that the Jews of his age were no more responsible for the crucifixion than the descendants of the English alive in the reign of Charles I were for his death.[59]

It is difficult to assess the weight of conversionist philosemitism in creating a climate favorable to Jews in the eighteenth century. What can be said with certainty is that Britain possessed a religious tradition that was absent in most European states—Holland was the notable exception—a tradition that emphasized inclusion rather than exclusion. Yet it was, as we have seen, only one of several currents in religious life. Moreover, it is impossible to know how widely diffused this kind of philosemitism was. Perhaps it was expressed only during periods of heightened consciousness about Jews and was less important in the final analysis than the waning of Christian fervor and the inability of church or chapel to wield influence in areas of rapid population growth.

The most frequent and widespread expressions of anti-Jewish sentiment were couched in secular rather than religious language. In public and private discourse, Jews were branded as unscrupulous, untrustworthy, rapacious, lustful, and filthy. Their chief crime was not, as it had been, their rejection of Jesus, but rather their embodiment of unrestrained, morally unfettered, economic individualism. Critics alleged that they were consumed by an almost inhuman thirst for wealth that crowded out other emotions and that they employed any means, legal or otherwise, to gain their end. One described them as "a hard-dealing, hard-hearted people, taking all manner of advantage of the necessities of others," while another held them to be "the subtlest and most artful people in the world . . . so dexterous in bargaining that it is impossible for Christians to expect any advantage in their dealings with them."[60] Both elegant brokers and ragged street traders, native-born and foreign-born alike, were accused of unsocial or criminal commercial practices, and from the late 1760s there emerged the notion, stimulated by the growth of crime among the Jewish poor, that there was a great chain of Jewish criminality stretching from the meanest street tough to the wealthiest loan-contractor. As the police magistrate Patrick Colquhoun wrote at the end of the century, "From the orange boy and the retailer of seals, razors, glass, and other wares in the public streets to the shop-keeper, dealer in wearing apparel, or in silver and gold, the same principles of conduct too generally prevail."[61]

Jews reacted to gentile hostility and criticism in several ways. Unburdened by the demands of respectability, the poor tended to respond to verbal insults and physical assaults in kind. The Jewish poor in general, not just criminals and prizefighters, enjoyed a reputation for rowdiness, toughness, and violence. Graphic evidence of this can be seen in an anonymous engraving of a boisterous tavern scene featuring a bearded Jew delivering a blow to the mouth of a fellow who has grabbed his beard. When Thomas Dibdin's play *Family Quarrels* opened in 1802, Jews in the audience took offense at certain lines and reacted by disrupting the performance, making it impossible to hear a single sentence.[62]

Wealthier Jews, eager to enhance their social status, reacted in more complex ways. To some extent, their efforts to acquire the trappings of genteel rank—country estates, rich furnishings, Old Masters, liveried equipage, correct manners and bearing, etc.—can be viewed as an effort to escape the association of the Jew with commercial chicanery and street ruffianism. However, it would be wrong to attribute the rapid acculturation of successful Jewish merchants and their families solely to a desire to flee the common construction of Jewishness. Georgian society in general was deeply imitative. The *British Magazine* observed in 1763: "The present rage of imitating the manners of high-life hath spread itself so far among the gentle-folks of lower-life, that in a few years we shall probably have no common people at all."[63] Upstart manufacturers, bankers, and overseas merchants strained to emulate their betters, establish county families, and cultivate friends in high places. It was assumed that rich bourgeois families would use their wealth to secure a place in landed society. To what else were they to aspire? In this respect, well-to-do Jews who embraced an upper-class lifestyle were both reacting to a specifically Jewish problem and acting no differently from others in a similar economic position.

The efforts of Jewish merchants and brokers to enhance their status were threatened, however, by the disreputability of Jewish street traders and criminals and the readiness of Gentiles to lump together and condemn all Jews, rich and poor alike. Consequently, the communal elite took steps to control and reform the poor. In 1766, following the first great surge in Jewish criminal activity, the parnasim of the Great Synagogue began cooperating with the authorities to check Jewish crime. They supplied the Bow Street magistrate Sir John Fielding with information about Jewish fences and excommunicated several of them in order to disassociate the community from their activity. In 1770, during the same week that Fielding testified before a House of Commons committee about housebreakers taking their loot to Jewish receivers, the Great Synagogue advertised in the newspapers that it was offering a reward for the detection of persons buying stolen goods. The following year Ashkenazi leaders aided the government in apprehending the Chelsea murder gang and then afterward placed an announcement in the London newspapers distancing themselves from this "set of foreign miscreants who stain our religion by calling themselves Jews." They also excommunicated the members of the gang and urged the government to restrict the flow of poor Jews from northern Europe, which, in fact, it tried unsuccessfully to do.[64]

Beginning in the late 1780s, the Ashkenazi leadership began to view the problem of the Jewish poor as a social issue that required a more constructive response, one that would directly address the roots of Jewish misbehavior. In 1788, it initiated the first of many schemes to reform the manners and morals of the children of the poor and teach them useful skills. In that year the Ashkenazi Talmud Torah, a traditional charity school for Hebrew studies, was reorganized in a revolutionary direction. Hebrew instruction was de-emphasized; Talmud was made an elective; secular subjects (reading, writing, arithmetic) were added. When boys left the school at age thirteen, they were apprenticed to respectable Jewish artisans, mainly tailors, glass cutters, watch finishers, and pencil makers. But the reformed Talmud Torah did little to cure the problem of Jewish poverty and misbehavior—it enrolled only eighteen boys in 1793 and twenty-one in 1803—so from 1795 on communal notables began projecting, and raising money for, more ambitious schemes. None of these was implemented until the start of the next century, however.[65]

Although leaders feared that lower-class disreputability would strengthen popular hostility, thereby threatening their own advancement, there were, in fact, fewer obstacles to Jewish integration in England than elsewhere in old regime Europe. Jews who wanted to mix in landed society—and had acquired the necessary qualifications—were generally able to do so. Crude stereotypes alone were not sufficient to keep them out. The gentry and aristocracy did not constitute a closed caste and were accustomed to absorbing a flow of new wealth from below. The barriers between upper and middle ranks were penetrable and elastic, unlike elsewhere. Property, even Jewish property, counted and could not be ignored. Landed families were willing to mix with Jews, moreover, without expecting or demanding that they first convert to Christianity. Of course, many wealthy Jews, especially Sephardim, became members of the established church in the eighteenth century, but this usually came after their integration into landed society and was intended to complete a process of social absorption and cultural identification that was already far advanced. In this, they resembled Catholic gentry and Quaker businessmen who, finding it "a strain to be a gentleman without being an Anglican," also changed their religious affiliation.[66]

Jewish legal status as well was more favorable than public expressions of hostility might suggest. Jews born in England were citizens of the state, which was not true in other European countries before the French Revolution. The legal disabilities they faced were generally the same as those faced by others who were not members of the Church of England. This meant that they could not serve in Parliament, vote in parliamentary elections (in theory—in fact, they did vote), hold municipal office, be called to the bar, obtain a naval commission, or matriculate or take a degree at Oxford and Cambridge. In all of these instances, they were debarred not by statutes specifically excluding them but by the requirement of swearing a christological oath or taking the sacrament in the Church of England. There was also some legal confusion whether Jews could own real estate—a statute from 1271 barring them from doing so was unearthed in 1738—but this does not appear to have prevented rich Jews from acquiring property in the countryside.

The great mass of Jews, who could hardly aspire to sit in Parliament or hold a naval commission, suffered little from legal inequality. There were no restrictions on the trades they might follow, the goods in which they might trade, the areas in which they might live. Nor were they subject to special taxes, tolls, levies, or extortions. The statute book simply ignored their presence, itself a reflection of the attenuated role of central government in domestic matters (excluding taxation, of course). In general monarchs and ministers did not bother themselves much with raising cultural standards, improving social welfare, or regulating economic practice. For most Jews, the only important disability was exclusion from the freedom of the City (and thus from being able to operate a retail business within its boundaries) due to the impossibility of swearing the required oath. However, it was possible to evade this either by selling retail out of an ostensibly wholesale warehouse or by establishing a business just over the City's boundaries. The City also limited the number of Jewish commodity brokers on the Royal Exchange to twelve. This disability, of course, affected only the wealthiest members of the community.

Jews who were not born in England faced an additional disability. As aliens (rather than as Jews), they suffered from extensive commercial discrimination: they could not purchase land; they could not own, or share in the ownership of, a British vessel; they were barred from the colonial trade; and they were subject to various alien duties, some twice as high as those native merchants paid. Foreign traders who settled in England could obtain relief by becoming naturalized citizens, which required application to Parliament for a private naturalization act, an expensive procedure available only to the wealthy. Professing Jews, however, could not become naturalized citizens in this way since a statute of 1609 required applicants to receive the sacrament before their bill was introduced. But they could obtain a kind of second-class naturalization, known as endenization, by the purchase of royal letters-patent, also an expensive procedure. Denizens were permitted to engage in the colonial trade but were not exempt from paying alien duties and thus remained at a serious commercial disadvantage.

The ill-fated Jew Bill of 1753, whose passage provoked the most extensive public debate over Jewish status in eighteenth century Britain, was an attempt to change this by allowing foreign-born Jewish merchants to avoid the sacramental requirement.[67] The initiative came from the leaders of the Sephardi community, there being few foreign-born Ashkenazi merchants wealthy enough to benefit from legislation like this. Joseph Salvador, a prominent merchant in the diamond and coral trade and in trade with Spain and Portugal, and also a frequent adviser to the government on financial matters, approached the Duke of Newcastle in January 1753, requesting legislative relief from the sacramental test. Salvador himself had been born in England but was clearly acting on behalf of the Sephardi leadership. He may also have hoped that an improvement in naturalization procedure would strengthen, by inference, the position of Jews in regard to the ownership of freehold property. The government, which owed Salvador and his friends a favor for their assistance in financial matters, agreed to introduce the legislation. The bill, whose proper title was the Jewish Naturalization Bill, was a modest measure, limited in scope, and it passed through the early stages of the parliamentary process without serious opposition. At later stages it encountered greater hostility but nonetheless became law in late May.

This was not the end of the affair, however, but its start. Monopolistic merchants who opposed a more open economy and critics of the government (country squires and High Churchmen who disliked the political corruption and religious latitudinarianism of the Pelham ministry) mounted a noisy campaign to repeal the Jew Bill. Their initial motive was undoubtedly to promote their own factional and economic aims by exploiting popular feelings, by activating antipathies that were not far beneath the surface. In doing so, they turned discussion about a legislative act of limited scope into a full-scale debate about the place of Jews in English society, the first time this had happened since readmission. (In 1740, Parliament had passed—with no outcry—the Plantation Act, which included a provision allowing foreign-born Jews resident in the American colonies for seven years to become naturalized citizens without offending their religious beliefs.) Petitions were gathered, pamphlets written, meetings convened, sermons delivered. Their language was intemperate and their tone alarmist, even hysterical. As noted above, opponents of the act resurrected crude medieval libels and made extravagant claims about the consequences of the legislation. Britain would be swamped with unscrupulous brokers, jobbers, and moneylenders, who would use their ill-gotten gains to acquire the estates of ruined landowners. Moreover, because dominion followed property, Jews would control Parliament (which would be re-named the Sanhedrin), convert St. Paul's to a synagogue, circumcise their tenants, and perpetrate countless other anti-Christian crimes. At times hostility overflowed the boundaries of rhetorical excess, and Jewish peddlers were insulted and harassed.

Significantly, those who clamored for the act's repeal ignored its actual provisions, which were modest, benefiting a few dozen wealthy merchants, at most. The reason for this is that the clamor was first and foremost an exercise in "forging the nation," to use the subtitle of Linda Colley's seminal work.[68] The eighteenth century witnessed the making of a xenophobic, deeply Protestant, anti-Catholic culture uniting the inhabitants of Scotland, Wales, and England. More often than not, the "other" against which Britons defined themselves in this period was Catholic and French—not surprisingly, since Britain fought a chain of major wars against France between 1689 and 1815. However, given the ubiquity of centuries-old stereotypes about Jews, it is not surprising that these too were pressed into service at times in defining what was British. The "Jews" to whom the act's opponents referred were largely imaginary creatures, constructed to represent threats to British national traditions, Christianity, manhood, and landed property. Once the Pelhams, who were alarmed by the outcry and worried about the approach of a general election in 1754, withdrew their support and Parliament repealed the act (in November), the furor died down. Most Britons were not preoccupied with Jews, real or imaginary. The opposition to the Pelham administration was not interested in translating the anti-Jewish sentiments they exploited during the controversy into legislation curbing Jewish economic activity, land purchases, or social integration. They had other fish to fry. Still, the vein of bigotry they tapped in 1753 was genuine—the agitation would not have been effective otherwise—and available for use at other times. For example, during the Old Price Riots of 1809 (sixty-seven nights of populist rioting inside and outside the Covent Garden Theatre), protestors who were angered by the management's hiring of Jewish thugs to maintain order made use of anti-Jewish slogans that were unconnected to the conflict. Rioters carried placards bearing the slogan "Oppose Shylock and the whole tribe of Israel," while one pamphleteer, recalling King Edward's hanging of 280 Jews in one day, lamented that "things were better managed in former times than they are at present."[69]

Since Jewish disabilities were not intolerable and native-born merchants increasingly outnumbered those born abroad, communal leaders made no further effort to seek legislative relief. Jewish legal status remained unchanged until the next century, when a more acculturated leadership, with a different set of priorities and needs, mounted a campaign to remove all legal disabilities setting Jews apart from their fellow citizens. Until that time, Jews remained second-class citizens—like Protestant Dissenters and Roman Catholics. However, given the pervasive inequality that was the lot of Jews elsewhere in Europe before the French Revolution, their position was by comparison enviable, as the steady stream of immigrants from Central and Northern Europe seeking a better life in Britain testifies.

OLD CLOTHES

A Jewish old clothes man. Thomas Lord Busby, *Costume of the Lower Orders of the Metropolis* (London, 1822). From a private collection.

CHAPTER 3

Poverty to Prosperity (1800–1870)

At the start of the nineteenth century, most Jews in England were immigrants or the children of immigrants—impoverished, poorly educated, dependent on low-status street trades and other forms of petty
commerce, popularly identified with crime, violence, and chicanery,
widely viewed as disreputable and alien. Over the next three-quarters of
a century, the social character of the Jewish community was transformed
dramatically. Poverty ceased to be its defining characteristic. On the eve
of mass migration from Eastern Europe, the majority of Jews in Britain
were middle class. They were native English speakers, bourgeois in their
domestic habits and public enthusiasms, full citizens of the British state,
their public and personal identities increasingly shaped by the larger
culture in which they lived—even if their gentile neighbors viewed them
as less than fully English. On the basis of this ascent from poverty to
respectability, Jewish legal status, communal organization, and religious
life also were transformed, and Jewish identity reshaped.

The low economic status of English Jewry at the start of the century
resulted from decades of unrestricted immigration from Holland, the
German states, and, to a lesser extent, Poland. The Revolutionary and
Napoleonic Wars virtually halted the flow, but it resumed after 1815 and
continued unabated until the 1830s, when the United States became the
chief destination for Ashkenazim fleeing poverty and persecution in
Central and Eastern Europe. By 1830, there were about twenty thousand
Jews living in London and perhaps another ten thousand in the provinces. In the next two decades, immigration slowed, and there was also
some out-migration to the United States. This caused the community

to grow at a more modest pace. At mid-century, London Jewry numbered between twenty and twenty-five thousand, provincial Jewry between ten and twelve thousand.[1]

The population balance between London and the provinces remained
unchanged in the nineteenth century, but outside the metropolis old
communities stagnated or declined, and new ones flourished. The end
of the Revolutionary and Napoleonic Wars hit the economies of naval
towns with substantial Jewish communities—Plymouth, Portsmouth,
Sheerness, Falmouth, Chatham. These communities either grew little in
the Victorian period or went into decline, their members leaving to seek
their living in London or the Midlands, where commercial opportunities
were expanding because of the industrial revolution.[2] Birmingham,
Manchester, and Liverpool (more important as a commercial port than
a manufacturing center) became magnets for Jewish settlement, rapidly
outstripping the towns of the South and East. In 1851, there were about
1,500 Jews in Liverpool, 1,100 in Manchester, and 780 in Birmingham.[3]
Smaller communities grew up in other burgeoning industrial towns
(Sheffield, Nottingham, Glasgow, Leeds, Coventry), in Hull, because it
was a port of disembarkation for transmigrants to the United States,
and, after 1850, in seaside resorts and inland spas (Brighton, Bath, Rams-
gate). In all, there were thirty-six towns in 1851 with organized congregations and at least another dozen or so with a handful of Jewish families
each.[4]

German Jews continued to settle in Britain after the 1830s,[5] but the
complexion of the migratory flow changed. Unlike the mass of immigrants in the Georgian and Regency periods, those who arrived in the
Victorian age tended to be drawn from the "respectable" ranks of
German Jewry—in part, a reflection of the social and economic transformation of German Jewry that was under way.[6] Many of the men
were merchants and clerks with previous experience in large-scale trading ventures. They were attracted to England because of its unrivaled
mercantile and industrial pre-eminence, especially in textiles. With the
backing of established merchant houses in Germany, they opened offices
and warehouses in Bradford, Leeds, Manchester, and Nottingham to
purchase goods for export to family and business associates on the Continent. In addition, London's position as the largest center of conspicuous consumption in the world attracted wholesale and retail merchants,
purveyors of jewelry, cigars, antiques, toys, picture frames, leather
goods, and other luxury items. Jewish banking clans in Germany also
sent representatives to take advantage of new opportunities in govern-

ment loans, international trade, and railroad, mining, and industrial securities. From Frankfurt alone came sons of the Stern, Worms, Erlanger,
Speyer, Schuster, and Goldschmidt families. A handful of refugees from
the abortive revolutions of 1848, including Karl Marx (1818–83), also
found their way to London, but, whether baptized or not, they tended
to eschew Jewish circles and institutions.

In addition to middle-class immigration from Germany, there was
also a small but steady trickle of impoverished Jews from Eastern Europe—contrary to the popular myth that the pogroms of 1881 inaugurated immigration from Poland and Russia. Two Polish synagogues
were established in London in the 1790s and had evolved from minyanim organized even earlier. Well before 1881 Jews born in Russia and
Poland were a significant minority within the Jewish population. In 1851,
25 percent of the Jews in Birmingham engaged in trade were natives of
Poland or Russia; in 1861, immigrants from the tsarist empire were 19
percent of the Manchester community. (If Polish Jews from Posen and
Galicia, who were citizens of Prussia and Austria respectively, are included in the total, then the proportions would be even higher.) Significantly, by mid-century Polish and Russian Jews were considered a
major burden on communal funds. An editorial in the *Jewish Chronicle*
in 1846 urging readers to contribute generously to Jewish charities attributed the pressure on communal resources to newly arrived immigrants from Poland and Russia, while an editorial in 1854 asking for
special donations to an East End soup kitchen explained that current
funds were unable to handle the great influx of Polish Jews.[7]

The tide of immigration before and after the Revolutionary and Napoleonic wars and then the reduced but steady flow after the 1830s meant
that poverty continued to characterize much of the community well into
the Victorian period. At mid-century 25 to 30 percent of London Jews
were in receipt of occasional or regular poor relief; in addition, another
35 to 40 percent of men were dependent on street trading, market trading, and artisanal work. Thus, at a minimum, half of the Jews in London
were impoverished or barely making a living. Even among the Sephardim, poverty was widespread. In 1829, twelve hundred of the twenty-
five hundred Sephardim in Britain were receiving regular or occasional
relief from communal funds. The pattern was much the same in the
provincial cities. In Birmingham, for example, the majority of Jewish
males in 1851 were struggling glaziers, slipper makers, tailors, and hawkers.[8] In all, the percentage of Jews living in poverty or on its margins at
mid-century was not much different from that in the general population.

As was the case in the previous century, Jewish poverty went hand in hand with crime, squalid surroundings, low-status trades, and coarse behavior. In the 1810s and 1820s, there was a marked increase in the incidence of Jewish criminal activity in London, if the skyrocketing rate of Jewish convictions at the Old Bailey is any guide. When the notorious Ikey Solomons (ca. 1785–1850), a leading receiver of stolen goods in London in the 1820s, stood trial at the Old Bailey in 1830, his misdeeds were reported at length in the daily press and in several sensational pamphlets.[9] In the following decades, the number of Jewish street criminals fell as immigration slowed and acute poverty waned, but Jews remained active in socially marginal occupations—as dealers in battered odds and ends, worn-out clothing, rags and rubbish; as keepers of brothels, wine rooms, saloons, gambling dens, billiard rooms, and sponging houses; as fences, crimps, sheriff's officers, prizefighters, and prostitutes.[10]

Even when conducted honestly, these occupations inspired revulsion. When the French socialist and feminist Flora Tristan visited London in 1830, she noted in her journal that the "great heaps of old worn-out clothes" she encountered in Petticoat Lane (the open-air old clothes market in the East End) gave off "such a strong odour that it turned our stomachs; we came away from the filthy place with a feeling of nausea."[11] Charles Dickens despised "the red-headed and red-whiskered Jews [in Holywell Street] who forcibly haul you into their squalid houses, and thrust you into a suit of clothes whether you will or not," while Thomas Carlyle associated the old clothes dealers of Monmouth Street—"the brood of money-changers who nestle in that Church and importune the worshipper with merely secular proposals"—with crude materialism. The Rev. John Mills, author of a sympathetic account of British Jewry in 1853, distressingly concluded: "The old clothes trade has always been characterized as singularly opprobrious, and its merchants as notoriously unjust, and consequently has been the universal bugbear to stigmatize the Jewish people."[12]

For religious and pragmatic reasons, the leaders of Anglo-Jewry believed that relief of the Jewish poor was a communal responsibility. From their establishment, synagogues in London and the provinces dispensed charity to both distressed members and, to use the language of the period, the "casual" and "strange" poor (immigrants and others with a less firm "claim" on the congregation). Extra-synagogal charities were organized to meet a variety of special needs. They distributed food, fuel, and clothing during the winter and at festivals; relieved orphans, widows, invalids, the aged, and the blind; provided marriage portions, medical care, clothing for newborns, and burial for the indigent dead.[13] In addition, at a time when rich and poor still lived in close proximity, wealthy individuals dispensed charity on a face-to-face basis to those who called at their offices or homes or importuned them in the street. Chief Rabbi Solomon Hirschell, for example, provided regular assistance to a number of once comfortable Jews, now fallen on hard times and too embarrassed to apply for aid, with funds provided him by wealthy congregants.[14]

Alongside traditional motives for extending aid to the Jewish poor, there was an additional concern shaping philanthropic activity in the late-Georgian and Victorian periods. The intimate connection between poverty and disreputability alarmed acculturated middle-class Jews because it threatened their social achievements and, from the 1830s, their efforts to improve Jewish civil status. In their view, given the common tendency to view all Jews — rich and poor, cultured and coarse — as part of one undifferentiated mass, the misbehavior of the poor fueled anti-Jewish sentiment in general and thus threatened their own successful integration. In response, beginning in the late eighteenth century, communal leaders established a network of philanthropic institutions designed not only to provide assistance to the poor but also to reform their manners and morals and provide them with the means to join the ranks of the respectable. From this time until World War II, both religious idealism and social and economic self-interest characterized philanthropic activity toward the poor.

The earliest effort of this kind, discussed in the previous chapter, was the reorganization of the Ashkenazi Talmud Torah in 1788. In addition to providing a rudimentary Hebrew education, the Talmud Torah aimed to keep its graduates from swelling the ranks of Jewish street traders by apprenticing them to artisans within six months of their thirteenth birthday. The school enrolled few students, however, and thus contributed little to reducing poverty and crime. In 1795, Benjamin and Abraham Goldsmid launched a campaign to raise funds for a major poor relief scheme, whose details have not survived, and by 1797 had collected £20,000. At this point, the scheme's backers quarreled, the Goldsmids became disgusted and withdrew their attention; the principal was left to draw interest for the next ten years, when it was devoted to another project (see below).[15]

Meanwhile, Joshua Van Oven (1766–1838), a surgeon active in communal affairs, introduced a bold proposal to control poverty and crime — the creation of a communally financed agency, with quasi-governmental powers, for the relief and reformation of the Jewish poor. The impetus for his proposal was the publication in 1800 of a new, enlarged edition of the police magistrate Patrick Colquhoun's *Treatise on the Police of the Metropolis,* which described Jewish criminal activity in detail and suggested that there was a uniform code of corrupt commercial ethics to which all Jews adhered. Van Oven gained the support of Abraham Goldsmid and other communal magnates, and a proposal was sent to Parliament to create a Jewish poor relief board with the authority to erect a workhouse, hospital, old-age home, and trade school and to expel idle and troublesome foreign-born Jews. One-half of the parish poor rates paid by Jews was to be diverted to finance the board's work. The leaders of the major Ashkenazi synagogues supported the measure, but the Sephardim refused because they did not want to be associated, for status reasons, with the Ashkenazim, whom they regarded as socially inferior, and because they believed they would be forced to pay a disproportionate share of the expense. Ashkenazim outside the Goldsmid circle also criticized the Van Oven scheme, primarily because it gave the rich enormous power over the poor—which, in truth, was its supporters' objective. To control poverty and crime, the elite wished to resurrect, with parliamentary support, the police powers of the quasi-autonomous, pre-modern *kehillah* (corporate community). In the end, whether because of opposition or other reasons, the scheme's backers abandoned it at a meeting in April 1802.

Future efforts to improve the poor were more modest in scope and utilized voluntary associations rather than state power to achieve their ends. In 1807, a group of wealthy Ashkenazim established the Jews' Hospital in the Mile End Road with funds raised by the Goldsmid brothers a decade earlier. The hospital consisted of two separate departments: an old-age home, whose purpose was exclusively charitable, and a trade school, whose goal was to keep children from the temptations of the streets and at the same time train them to be productive citizens. Hebrew instruction was limited to two hours a day. The remainder of the time was devoted to teaching secular subjects and practical skills—shoemaking, chair making, and cabinetmaking, in the case of the boys; knitting, washing, ironing, cooking, needlework, and housecleaning, in the case of the girls. On leaving the hospital at age twelve or thirteen, the boys were apprenticed to artisans and the girls put into domestic service, generally in Jewish homes. The school emphasized the reformation of manners and morals as much as it did the acquisition of useful skills. The children lived on the hospital grounds and were subject to a prisonlike regimen and constant supervision. In the eyes of the school's benefactors and management, they were a rowdy, immoral, uncivilized lot, whose old habits needed to be eradicated in order to render them fit members of society.

While the enrollment of the trade school department of the Jews' Hospital was larger than that of the Talmud Torah, its overall impact on the extent of Jewish poverty in London was limited. From its inception to 1844, it apprenticed 135 boys and placed 88 girls in domestic service—an average of less than half a dozen children per year. Moreover, because enrollment was limited to the children of the "respectable poor" (persons who had lived in London for ten years and had a claim on one of the three City synagogues), those most in need of help and most likely to damage the community's reputation—the poorest, the least anglicized, the most recently arrived—were automatically excluded from receiving assistance.

The most extensive scheme to educate and reform the poor was put into effect with the opening of the Jews' Free School (JFS) in 1817. Based on the Lancastrian monitorial system of the British and Foreign Society schools (a labor-saving method of teaching by rote that utilized older students, coached by the master, to teach less advanced students), it was able to provide large numbers of the poor with a rudimentary secular and religious education. Jewish parents, as eager as the school's founders to see their children abandon street trading, rushed to enroll them. Within a few weeks of the JFS's opening, there were 184 students. In June 1822, a new school building was dedicated in Bell Lane, Spitalfields, to meet increased demand, and by August of the following year there were over 550 students enrolled. In 1870, before mass migration from Eastern Europe commenced, there were 1,600 boys and 1,000 girls. For the school's managers and supporters, its overriding task was the civilization of the poor, especially the immigrant poor. Echoing the language of middle-class reformers in general, Moses Angel (1819–98), JFS headmaster from 1840 to 1891, told a London School Board committee in 1871 that the school's pupils were dehumanized, "ignorant even of the elements of sound" (that is, unable to speak English properly), and that their parents were "the refuse population of the worst parts of Europe," living "a quasi-dishonourable life"—by which he meant that they were street traders and thus liars and cheats.[16]

Educational schemes to promote social change multiplied after the opening of the Jews' Free School. In the late 1810s, middle-class Jews living to the west of the City established a small free school for boys—

there were only twenty students in 1825—that evolved eventually into the Westminster Jews' Free School. Like the Jews' Hospital, funds were allotted to apprentice boys to trades when they left the school. A girls school was added in 1846 and by the end of the decade there were about one hundred students in all.[17] In the major provincial communities— Liverpool, Birmingham, and Manchester—free schools were established in the early 1840s. (Unusually, the Birmingham school enrolled the children of all ranks.) As in London, a major objective was the moral reformation of the poor. As one of the early backers of the Manchester school urged in seeking to mobilize support, "the character of our nation in the estimation of others was to be best maintained by the early and judicious education of our humbler classes."[18]

In addition to their concern about "the character of our nation in the estimation of others," the promoters of these schools were also worried about missionary inroads among the Jewish poor.[19] The conversion of the Jews was much talked about in the eighteenth century, but no organization or institution was created to undertake the actual task of bringing them into the fold. The spread of evangelicalism in the late eighteenth and early nineteenth centuries, with its emphasis on practical activity to make England a more Christian nation, engendered sympathy and support for organized initiatives to convert Jews. The London Missionary Society, which was established in 1795 to convert the inhabitants of Africa and the Indies, set up a special committee in 1806 or early 1807 to work among the Jews of the metropolis. Members of this committee became dissatisfied with the meager financial resources allotted them, broke from the parent body in 1808, and established what eventually became the world's largest organization devoted exclusively to evangelizing Jews, the London Society for Promoting Christianity among the Jews.

From the start, missionary groups concentrated their efforts on the most vulnerable section of the Jewish population—the lower class. In particular, they took advantage of the inadequacy of communal provision for the education of the poor to establish free schools in or near Jewish neighborhoods. The first such school opened in 1807 with a dozen children in attendance. It and other missionary endeavors among the poor failed to produce many converts; they were—in fact, if hardly in intent—somewhat counterproductive. The prospect of losing children to the missionaries alarmed communal leaders and, in tandem with their interest in making the poor respectable, helped to loosen their philanthropic purse strings. This fear was a factor in the opening of the

Jews' Hospital in 1807, the Jews' Free School in 1817, and the Jews' Infant Schools in 1841. Outside London, where there were no conversionist schools at this time, concern in general about the vulnerability of the Jewish poor to Christian propaganda featured in discussions leading to the establishment of communal schools that combined secular and religious instruction.[20]

Efforts were also made to reach the adult poor, whose lack of religious devotion and social discipline continued to trouble communal leaders. The short-lived Jews' and General Literary and Scientific Institute (1845–59), known popularly as Sussex Hall, was created, in imitation of the mechanics institutes of the period, to raise the cultural level of Jewish shopkeepers, street traders, and artisans living in the City and the East End. It offered classes in Hebrew, French, and German, lectures on Jewish and general subjects, art exhibitions, displays of scientific instruments and curiosities, concerts, and a circulating library. But, unable to compete with more lively places of amusement or to attract sufficient financial support from the wealthy, it closed in 1859. The Jewish Association for the Diffusion of Religious Knowledge, which was founded the following year, pursued similar goals through religious channels. In addition to a Sabbath school in the East End, which enrolled over four hundred students in 1864, it sponsored Sabbath afternoon lectures and a Friday evening scripture class. The latter was established to provide young men in the Jewish quarter with a healthy alternative to dance halls, gambling dens, public houses, and the like. Between 1860 and 1879 the Association also published 120 tracts, two to eight pages in length, to instruct the Jewish lower class in the principles of their religion and middle-class values. The tracts retold biblical stories and moral fables from midrashic literature and explained the meaning of Jewish holidays and practices. The poor were told, for example, that "the eating of forbidden food generates disease." The tracts also urged their readers to consider "the immense advantage of a frequent and plentiful use of water" and warned them to avoid unnecessary expenditures. Mothers, in particular, were alerted to the danger of allowing their daughters to visit places of amusement. "A smart bonnet, a flounced dress, light kid gloves, will soon empty their purses, and for one night's display of foolish finery, they must forego decent and wholesome cleanliness, perhaps for weeks."[21]

As charity schemes multiplied, concerns emerged about their mode of operation and their impact on recipients. First, the City synagogues, which divided responsibility for assisting new arrivals among themselves according to a series of "treaties," felt overwhelmed by what seemed to be a ceaseless tide of needy foreigners. Second, a reappraisal of the principles of charity-giving was underway in English society, and this led supporters and managers of Jewish charities to look critically at their own philanthropy. Before the Victorian period, assistance to the Jewish poor was provided without regard to the circumstances (material, moral, or otherwise) that led to their impoverishment. In general, no moral stigma was attached to poverty or the receipt of charitable aid. Indeed, the giver, rather than the recipient, was the focus of interest, since assisting the poor was a mitsvah, and benefits in this world and the next accrued to those who performed it. As Israel Zangwill (1864–1926) emphasized in his comic tale *The King of Schnorrers* (1894), the rich were to be grateful to the poor for allowing them to be charitable. The incessant moralizing of the Victorian age—in particular, the belief that the poor were responsible for their poverty and that unsystematic giving further demoralized them, destroying their will to improve, rendering them permanent paupers—influenced the outlook of communal leaders. They became concerned that the existing jumble of independent charities promoted duplication, waste, and inefficiency—there were seven clothing charities alone in London—and, by their failure to investigate the merit of applicants, encouraged mendicancy and idleness. In this regard, it should be noted that most poor relief societies were voting charities, in which the size of donors' subscriptions determined the number of votes they were allowed in choosing who was to be aided. Thus, the whims of donors took precedence over the moral fitness of recipients in the selection process.

One solution to the problem of poverty would have been to allow the Jewish poor to obtain relief in the same manner that the Christian poor did. After passage of the 1834 Poor Law Amendment Act, this often meant incarceration in the grim, ratepayer-supported workhouses whose uninviting character was intended to deter able-bodied persons from seeking assistance. Poor Jews were entitled to be admitted to these hated institutions, but very few were. Communal leaders preferred to take care of their own rather than throw them on to the state. Their reasons for doing this were mixed. They did not want the Jewish poor incarcerated in a Christian institution whose routine and discipline made the observance of Jewish law virtually impossible. In addition, the forced separation of husbands, wives, and children that was standard practice in all workhouses was offensive to Jewish tradition and sentiment. Even more they feared that allowing the Jewish poor to increase the cost of maintaining the workhouse system would spark resentment, despite the fact that, as ratepayers, they already contributed to its support. They preferred, instead, to treat poverty internally, thus hoping to enhance the reputation of the community in Christian eyes.

In 1859, growing discontent with the state of Jewish charity—and the suffering caused by the severe winter of 1858–59—prompted leaders of the three Ashkenazi City synagogues (the Great, the Hambro, and the New) to establish a centralized relief agency, the Jewish Board of Guardians. Charged initially only with administering aid to the foreign poor, the Board, prodded by its moving spirit, the banker and stock broker Lionel Louis Cohen (1832–87), slowly expanded the scope of its work, rationalizing, consolidating, abolishing indiscriminate almsgiving.[22] By the time of the mass migration from Eastern Europe, it dominated Jewish charity work in London, a position it has occupied until the present, although no longer under its Victorian name. (Its growth and methods will be discussed in chapter 4, in the context of East European immigration.) Provincial communities with multiple charities and synagogues followed London's lead in centralizing and consolidating relief work. Manchester created its own board in 1867, Birmingham in 1870, Liverpool in 1876, and Leeds in 1878.[23]

In the end it is difficult to assess the contribution of these philanthropic undertakings to the increasingly middle-class character of the community. The conclusion of an earlier historian that the apprenticeship schemes of Jewish charities were "largely responsible for raising the condition of the Jewish poor in the first half of the nineteenth century" is naive and without factual basis.[24] Too few were apprenticed to effect such a transformation, and, in addition, many of those who received artisanal training did not follow the trades they had been taught but turned to petty commerce, believing it offered a surer livelihood. Still, it would be wrong to discount the impact of communal schools and charities completely. For some individuals, communal aid provided the foundation for later mobility. The millionaire West End moneylender Samuel Lewis (1838–1901), for example, was the son of a failed peddler, who abandoned his family, leaving them to survive on aid from the Birmingham Hebrew Philanthropic Society. Lewis received a free education at the Birmingham Hebrew National School, and, when he left school at age thirteen and set out as a country peddler, the Philanthropic Society funded his initial stock of cheap jewelry and steel pen nibs.[25]

In addition to charitable aid from the wealthy, there were other sources of support available to Jews seeking to escape poverty. Street traders and itinerant peddlers routinely obtained goods on credit from Jewish shopkeepers and wholesale merchants, most of whom had started in similar circumstances. This allowed penniless immigrants to begin trading on their own soon after their arrival. In addition, artisans and traders in London, like their Christian counterparts, formed friendly societies to tide them over difficult times. These mutual aid associations, the earliest of which were founded in the 1790s, provided benefits during illness, at death, and in the week of confined mourning (when work is forbidden), thus acting as a financial cushion for families who otherwise might have tumbled into poverty. To bolster their members' claim to respectable status, most societies were selective about whom they admitted. The United Israelites and the Guardians of Faith barred men who cohabited with non-Jewish women or were not married according to Jewish law, while the latter also excluded men who kept their shops open on Saturday mornings and personally attended to business then.[26]

Mutual assistance, communal schools and charities, experience in buying and selling, growth of the domestic consumer market, as well as assimilation of its roughest elements into the English lower class—all contributed to the gradual transformation of Anglo-Jewry in the first two-thirds of the nineteenth century. Evidence of this process before its completion can be seen in the decline of street trading as a common Jewish occupation in London by mid-century. In the 1790s, when street trading was the most common Jewish occupation in the metropolis, Patrick Colquhoun estimated there were two thousand Jewish old clothes men; a half-century later Henry Mayhew thought there were only five to six hundred. In the street trade in oranges, Mayhew recorded, the Irish had almost completely replaced the Jews. The marriage registers of the Sephardi synagogue tell a similar story. In the 1840s, over 20 percent of the grooms were hawkers and general dealers; in the 1860s this proportion dropped to 11 percent and in the 1870s to 9 percent.[27]

In the provinces, Jews remained prominent in peddling much later than in London. In small towns and villages, with few or no shops and a limited range of goods, itinerant traders found customers well into the second half of the century, if not beyond, in more remote areas of the country. In Birmingham, in the late 1860s, almost all the fathers of children enrolled in the communal free school were hawkers. Jews who peddled in the countryside, especially if married, tended to make their headquarters in cities with established communities, to which they would return to rest on the Sabbath and replenish their stock, after having made their rounds in the surrounding countryside. Jewish itinerant traders also tended to specialize in certain lines, especially inexpensive jewelry and watches. While some ended their days in obscurity, others were able to amass sufficient capital to become shopkeepers and lead a settled existence. The story of Joseph Harris, a native of Poland who landed at Hull in 1851, at age sixteen, is not unusual. With £2 from an uncle in Hull and 12 shillings left from money his father had given him, he went into business as a peddler of inexpensive jewelry and hardware. At first, knowing no English, he indicated the price of goods with his fingers, and, until he was able to save £4 for a peddler's license, confined himself to working in small villages where he was unlikely to be arrested. He eventually established a regular schedule, visiting the same towns in the North once a month, and confined his trade to watches, which he had made to his own specifications with his name on them. When he settled down and married in his twenties, he was worth about £90 (the equivalent of more than £3,000 in the 1990s).[28]

At the same time that Jewish street trading declined, the number of Jews in skilled manual work increased, both in London and the provinces. This was due in part to the shift in the source of Jewish immigration from Central to Eastern Europe, where Jews had long been prominent as artisans, and in part to the apprenticeship schemes of Jewish charities, which were designed to transform the children of street traders into skilled workers. In the early Victorian period, Jewish boys were being apprenticed to tailors, shoe and boot makers, cigar makers, pencil makers, pen and quill makers, cabinetmakers, glass cutters, watchmakers, picture framers, turners and carvers, manufacturing jewelers, and broom and brush makers, among others.[29] Some of these trades — those associated with clothing, footwear, and furniture, primarily — were entering a long period of deterioration, or "de-skilling," becoming notorious as sweated industries, characterized by poor wages, seasonal work, subcontracting, shoddy products, and insanitary working conditions. Workers in these trades generally faced a bleak future. Nonetheless, some prospered, by producing goods for the top end of the market or by becoming "sweaters" themselves, turning out cheap, mass market goods. In addition, some skilled workers accustomed to selling their products directly to the public moved entirely into retail and became independent, substantial businessmen. For example, frame makers evolved into picture and antique dealers, watchmakers into jewelers and pawnbrokers, makers of pencils, pens, and quills into stationers.[30]

The most common avenue for mobility, however, was retail trade.

The expanding native-born middle ranks of English Jewry were filled with the children and grandchildren of peddlers, old clothes men, and market traders who had become respectable, if modest, businessmen. A striking illustration of this can be seen in the aforementioned orange trade. As noted, by mid-century, Jews were no longer the dominant group hawking oranges in the streets of London, having been replaced by the Irish. However, they remained prominent at the wholesale end of the trade: the fruit market in Duke's Place, where street traders purchased oranges and nuts, was entirely Jewish. A similar development occurred in the secondhand clothing trade. Jews increasingly moved out of the lower end of the trade and into its slightly more salubrious branches, becoming pawnbrokers, slopsellers, auctioneers, salesmen with fixed premises, or stallholders in the covered wholesale exchange erected in Houndsditch in 1843. The latter was a bustling international mart, regularly attracting wholesale dealers from France, Belgium, Holland, and Ireland, as well as every city in Britain. A few entrepreneurs then made the leap from slopselling (or slopselling and pawnbroking) into manufacturing inexpensive garments. (Tailoring and shoemaking also served as launching pads for entry into the field.) The two biggest firms in England in the 1830s and 1840s were those of the Moses and Hyam families, both of which grew out of slopselling.[31] Despite the Enlightenment hope that, in the absence of legal barriers, agriculture and the crafts would save the Jews from poverty and make them productive citizens, it was commerce that became the vehicle for the economic transformation of Anglo-Jewry, as it was in all western countries.

Already by mid-century there was a substantial Jewish middle class in London and the provinces. Vivian Lipman's careful estimate of the social structure of London Jewry in 1850 puts the size of the financial haute bourgeoisie and the upper ranks of the middle class at 5 percent of the total and the remainder of the middle class at 30 percent. Thirty years later, at the start of the mass migration from Eastern Europe, a majority of Jews in London had entered the middle class. According to the estimates of the early social scientist Joseph Jacobs (1854–1916), first published in the *Jewish Chronicle* in 1883, 14.6 percent of the Jewish population of London belonged to the financial haute bourgeoisie and upper-middle class (annual family income of £1,000 or more) and 42.2 percent to the rest of the middle class (annual family income in the £200–£1,000 range). This was at a time when less than 3 percent of families in England and Wales earned £700 or more and less than 9 percent earned between £160 and £700. In Manchester, soon to become the largest provincial community, the proportion of middle class Jews in 1871 was smaller—between one-third and one-fourth of the total.[32] In fact, the extent of economic mobility since the start of the century was greater than these estimates indicate, since the total population included thousands of recent arrivals whose low status statistically diluted the achievements of the native-born, as well as the foreign-born who had been in the country for several decades.

At the pinnacle of the communal hierarchy in London were two hundred households whose wealth derived from finance-related activity in the City—merchant banking, commodity and stock brokerage, foreign loans, and currency and bullion transactions. Some of these families—Rothschilds, Cohens, Mocattas, Goldsmids—had been wealthy since the late eighteenth century or earlier. Others—Franklins, Montagus, Samuels, Spielmanns—acquired their wealth in the mid-nineteenth century. The foundation of the Montagu fortune, for example, was the successful silversmith and watchmaking business of Louis Samuel (1794–1859) in Liverpool. Still others—Sassoons, Bischoffsheims, Sterns, Worms—arrived in England in the mid-nineteenth century to open branches of financial houses that were already well established elsewhere. Whatever the origins of their fortunes, it was London's unrivaled position as the financial services capital of the world and the extraordinary opportunities it offered that undergirded their prosperity. These families tended to marry among themselves, especially those in the first two groups, which had the effect of concentrating their wealth and their influence within the community. They dominated the management of communal organizations (synagogues, charities, schools) and the conduct of Jewish politics throughout the nineteenth century and well into the twentieth, although not with one mind or without challenge from below, as we shall see.[33] In the large provincial communities, on the other hand, the dominant families were less wealthy and derived their fortunes from commerce and manufacturing rather than finance, a reflection of the economic profile of provincial cities. In Manchester, for example, the leading figures were cotton merchants, clothing manufacturers, jewelers, and dealers in "fancy" and optical goods.[34]

Beneath the financial upper crust, a new stratum of the middle-class emerged in the Victorian period, composed of professionals (physicians, solicitors, barristers, architects, dentists, and ministers) and other educated white collar workers (journalists, accountants, managers, and teachers). The formation of this group reflected the trend toward professionalization and specialization of activity characteristic of Victorian

society in general and the increasing acculturation and embourgeoisement of the Jewish community in particular, for without a solid economic base, entry into the professions was impossible. In the case of
barristers, the requirement of swearing a christological oath blocked the
entry of Jews until 1833, when Lincoln's Inn allowed Francis Henry
Goldsmid (1808–78) to take a modified oath.[35] But in general restrictive
oaths and practices were not a major impediment to occupational diversification. Even after barriers disappeared, British Jews—unlike Jews
in Central Europe—did not flock to the professions, at least in the Victorian period. Jacobs estimated that less than 4.5 percent of London's
Jews belonged to the professional stratum in the 1880s.[36] While there
were a number of reasons for this, the most important was that the
stigma attached to finance and commerce, traditional areas of Jewish
activity, was mild by comparison with other countries. In the absence
of this pressure, there was no widespread flight from "Jewish" occupations.

The expansion of the middle class was accompanied by the dispersion
of its more prosperous members to new suburban districts. Previously,
the wealthy, the middle ranks, and the poor, Jew and Gentile alike, lived
in the same neighborhoods (although not in the same streets and
squares). The nineteenth century saw "the systematic sorting-out of
London [and other cities as well] into single-purpose, homogeneous,
specialized neighborhoods" with strict social segregation.[37] Until about
1825, almost all London Jews lived in the City and the streets immediately to the east, with small colonies in the Strand, Covent Garden, and
Pall Mall. The one exception were wealthy Sephardim, who began to
disperse around 1800—to Kennington, Islington, Bloomsbury, Mayfair,
Kensington, and Belgravia—a reflection undoubtedly of their increasing
detachment from synagogue life. The Ashkenazi upper crust remained
in the traditional area of Jewish settlement until the 1820s, when they
began leaving for the West End. In 1825, Nathan Rothschild (1777–1836)
moved to Piccadilly, Moses Montefiore (1784–1885) to Green Street and
then Park Lane, and Isaac Lyon Goldsmid (1778–1859) to Regent's Park.
In the 1830s and 1840s, well-to-do families moved northward to Finsbury Square and Finsbury Circus and westward to Bloomsbury and
Marylebone. Then, in the 1860s and 1870s, fashionable families pushed
further west to Bayswater and areas north of Hyde Park and Kensington
Gardens. More ordinary middle class families tended to disperse northward, to Islington, beginning in the 1840s, then to Canonbury and
Highbury in the 1860s, and then northwestward, in the 1870s, to St.
John's Wood, Maida Vale, and West Hampstead. Less affluent middle-

class Jews moved to Dalston and Hackney, starting in the 1870s. At the same time, as the City declined as a residential area, Jews pushed eastward into Whitechapel, expanding the area of Jewish settlement in the East End. However, most London Jews, probably about two-thirds, continued to live in the old districts, whether in the 1850s or the 1880s—although by the latter decade this was due to mass immigration from Eastern Europe rather than the presence of native-born Jews.[38]

Jews left the City and the East End for the same reasons that other Londoners did—to escape congestion, noise, and filth and to find housing that reflected their status in the social hierarchy. They did not scatter at random throughout the suburbs but clustered in new colonies along a few lines of dispersion. This suggests that the drive for full or complete assimilation into English society was not a primary factor in the process of suburbanization. Still, the new districts were far less "Jewish" than the old—Jews were a smaller percentage of the population and Jewish institutions less visible—and in the long term this contributed to a weakening of Jewish ethnic and religious ties. Residential segregation also contributed, more immediately, to the shift in Jewish attitudes toward poor relief discussed above. It was much easier for well-to-do Jews to embrace the harsh ethos of the new philanthropy once they no longer lived alongside the poor and encountered their distress face-to-face.

The embourgeoisement of most native British Jews in the nineteenth century transformed more than the material conditions of their lives. Entry into the middle class influenced how they educated their children, comported themselves in public, worshipped in their synagogues, and thought about themselves and their relationship to state and society. Material success and acculturation to middle-class English habits and values engendered, in turn, further efforts to reduce, but not obliterate, differences that set Jews apart. In particular, it sparked efforts to harmonize the practice of Judaism with middle-class standards of decorum and piety. It also generated a revolution in Jewish self-consciousness. While previously Jews had thought of themselves primarily as Jews, members of a distinct people with a history and destiny of their own, now they came to identify more intimately with the country in which they were living, seeing themselves as both Jews and Englishmen. Once this shift in self-definition occurred, they then found the remaining legal disabilities setting them apart (however inconsequential in practice) an intolerable burden and began to campaign for their removal. It is to this complex of interrelated changes, which economic mobility made possible, that we now turn.

To begin, greater affluence allowed families to support their children

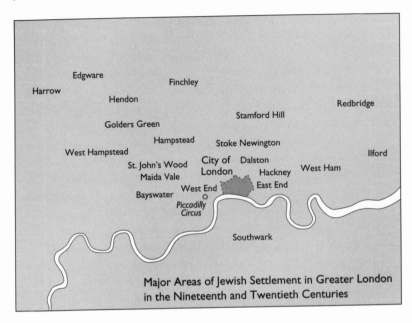

Major Areas of Jewish Settlement in Greater London in the Nineteenth and Twentieth Centuries

into their adolescent years, instead of putting them to work at age twelve or thirteen, and this, along with the assimilation of English cultural norms, created a demand for secular education at the secondary level. Since education in England was organized on a denominational basis— there was no system of state education until after 1870—fee-paying boarding schools developed to cater to wealthy families who chose not to send their sons to local, non-Jewish day schools or to educate them at home, as had been customary in the eighteenth century. The earliest was that of the Posen-born maskil Hyman Hurwitz (1775/6–1844), established at Highgate in 1799. It was acquired by Leopold Neumegen (1787–1875), also a native of Posen, in 1821 and moved to Kew in 1842, where it continued until 1875. On Neumegen's death, the *Jewish Chronicle* remarked that "there is scarcely a family of any position amongst us whose members have not received a portion of their education at the school he conducted for many years so successfully." Other Jewish boarding schools included those of H. N. Solomon (1796–1881) at Edmonton; Louis Loewe (1808–88), orientalist and aide to Moses Montefiore, at Brighton and later Broadstairs; Raphael Isaac Cohen at Dover; and H. Berkowitz at Gravesend. These schools educated only male children, of course. Wealthy families, to the extent that they troubled themselves with their daughters' education, had them taught at home or sent them to private local schools, such as that of the Belisario sisters at Hackney or the Segré sisters at Cheetham Hill, Manchester.[39]

The few communal schools for middle-class children that were established at this time were not successful. In 1855, Chief Rabbi Nathan Marcus Adler opened a "public day school for the sons of our middle class" in Finsbury Square, then an attractive residential area. The school, which offered both religious and secular instruction and was linked to Jews' College, the seminary for training Anglo-Jewish ministers, was never able to attract broad support and closed in 1879. Indeed, a number of leading figures opposed its establishment at the start because they believed, in the words of the *Jewish Chronicle*, that "a separate Jewish school would positively prove injurious to the interests of the community by fostering a spirit of exclusiveness . . . and by perpetuating certain disagreeable peculiarities." (They did not object, however, to separate schools for the Jewish poor.) When the solicitor Herbert Bentwich (1856–1932) tried to establish a fee-paying Jewish day school for middle-class children in North London in 1880–81, he found few parents in the district who took any interest in the project.[40]

Most ordinary middle-class families in London and elsewhere preferred to send their sons to local non-Jewish schools whose charters did not restrict admission to Christians. University College School in Gower Street, which was linked to the nonsectarian University College, to whose establishment in 1828 Jews contributed, imposed no religious tests and welcomed Jewish students from its inception. In the 1830s, its first decade, over forty Jewish boys were enrolled. The City of London School, St. Paul's School in West Kensington, Manchester Grammar School, and King Edward VI School in Birmingham—as well as a host of less selective schools—also accepted Jewish boys, although in the case of St. Paul's they were not exempt from attending chapel until 1882. However, few boys from well-to-do observant Jewish families attended public schools before the 1870s, either because they were not welcome or because their parents were unwilling to place them in institutions in which chapel attendance and New Testament instruction were required and the observance of the dietary laws, the Sabbath, and the festivals almost impossible. On the other hand, status-conscious families who were already on the road to radical assimilation were sending their sons to Eton and Harrow as early as the 1860s.[41]

Before the end of the century, few students with a secondary education went on to university. In part, this was because of the historical link between Oxford and Cambridge and the Church of England. Jews were permitted, in theory, to matriculate at Cambridge but were not able to take a degree until 1856, when passage of the Cambridge University Reform Act abolished the religious test for graduation (subscription to the Thirty-Nine Articles of the Church of England). But the colleges, which controlled admissions, were not eager to accept Jews — some refused outright to do so — and placed obstacles in their way, such as requiring attendance at chapel. Mayer de Rothschild (1818–74) entered Magdalene College in October 1837 but later that academic year transferred to Trinity College, where the authorities were more understanding about his absence from chapel. His cousin Arthur Cohen (1830–1914), later a prominent barrister and communal leader, was refused admission at both Trinity and Christ's and was accepted at Magdalene only through the intercession of his uncle Moses Montefiore and Mayer de Rothschild with the Prince Consort, who was chancellor of the university. Few Jewish applicants could hope for this kind of assistance. Cohen completed his work in 1853 but did not take his degree until 1858. At Oxford, on the other hand, Jews were unable to either matriculate or take a degree until passage of the Oxford University Reform Act of 1854. Even then the colleges balked at accepting Jews. When the authorities of Worcester College discovered that Sackville Davis (1829–1913), who was admitted in 1859 on the assumption that he was a member of the Church of England, was an unbaptized Jew, they tried to get rid of him, and only the threat of legal action, backed by prominent London Jews, caused them to back down.[42] There was one further obstacle to Jewish attendance at the ancient universities: the atmosphere was suffused with Christianity. Gothic architecture, chapels, clerical faculty, Latin benedictions at dinner, and countless other Christian symbols combined to create a setting in which many Jews would have felt uncomfortable. It was as if they sensed the power of these quintessentially English spaces to shape the identities of those who inhabited or passed through them.[43]

However, even if there had been no obstacles at the ancient universities, there is still reason to believe that Jewish undergraduates would have remained few in number in the nineteenth century. English universities were not centers of intellectual ferment or launching pads for occupational mobility. Unlike their continental counterparts, they did not provide training or certification for professional careers to which Jews were attracted. For the first three-quarters of the century, Oxford and Cambridge were "educators, first and foremost, of the clergy of the

Establishment." Over 70 percent of graduates in the first half of the century became Anglican clergymen and over 50 percent in the third quarter.[44] In addition, an English university degree did not confer the status that a German or Austrian degree did. There Jews embraced higher education as a means of shedding the taint of commerce and demonstrating their commitment to *Bildung* and *Kultur*. This, it was believed, would help them obtain civil and social equality. For ambitious English Jews, on the other hand, the road to social acceptance ran through the City of London, not Oxford and Cambridge. Manners and money counted more than cultural virtuosity. If university education had been of vital social or economic importance, communal notables would have made the removal of religious tests a matter of high priority, or parents would have sent their sons to universities abroad or in Scotland, where religious tests were not required of students. (The nonsectarian University College, London, and the provincial civic universities, which were not established until the second half of the century, were socially and intellectually inferior to Oxford and Cambridge and did not attract substantial numbers of Jews until the twentieth century.)

The spread of secondary education reinforced the Englishness of English Jews, even those educated in all-Jewish schools. It exposed them to early- and mid-Victorian middle-class values and encouraged them to think of themselves as English, as well as Jewish, as rooted in the life of the country rather than tossed onto its shores by circumstance. At the same time, Jewish business and professional men became participants in the burgeoning associational life of middle-class society, as members of literary and philosophical societies, dining clubs, musical societies, Masonic lodges, subscription libraries, chambers of commerce, and choral groups, and as sponsors of mechanics institutes, art galleries, schools of design and technology, and other schemes to spread entrepreneurial ideals and civilize the cities. These institutions, which one historian has described as the "arteries" of society, expressed the primacy of the public voluntary sphere in the shaping of British civil society. They undertook tasks that in other countries were performed by the state or established corporations.[45] Independent of church and chapel, as well as of aristocratic society, they provided a quasi-neutral setting in which Jews were not at a disadvantage because of their religion. In new industrial centers outside London, where landed upper-class influence was weak, they constituted the major avenue for the integration of successful Jewish businessmen into local society.[46]

In London, on the other hand, the wealthiest families continued to imitate patterns of upper-class social life, seeking confirmation of their status through the acquisition of country estates and the pursuit of rural pleasures. Nathan Rothschild's sons—Lionel (1808–79), Anthony (1810–76), and Mayer—became landed magnates, acquiring thousands of acres in the Vale of Aylesbury in Buckinghamshire, and then played the role to the hilt. They built grand houses on their estates (or renovated more modest existing structures), filling them with exquisite examples of antique furniture, porcelain, and other precious objects, and took up gardening, farming, steeplechasing, and foxhunting and stag hunting with gusto. They entertained the political elite of the nation on a grand, opulent scale, both in London and the country, and, aside from their numerous relations, rarely included other Jews in their dinners, hunting weekends, and musical evenings. Thanks to their extensive landholdings, they also became great political magnates: they were the largest single electoral influence in the borough of Aylesbury by 1850, having replaced the Duke of Buckingham.[47]

More ordinary middle-class Jews in London, those beneath the haute bourgeoisie of finance on the social ladder, were less aggressive in pursuing integration into gentile circles. Because there were tens of thousands of Jews in London, there was ample scope for families of more modest means than the Rothschilds to exercise their need for sociability and recognition within the boundaries of their own community—at fundraising dinners and committee meetings of charities and schools and, at home, in an endless round of teas, dinners, card parties, musicales, and the like. The same was true for the lower middle class. Entertainment and sociability could be found without having to look outward. Jewish-owned taverns, coffee houses, billiard rooms, and gambling clubs in the eastern precincts of the City and the East End offered opportunities for conviviality and recreation within a mostly Jewish milieu. The Saturday night balls at Howard's Assembly Halls in Aldgate, for example, catered to an almost all-Jewish clientele. While a three-person Jewish band played, a journalist noted in 1838, top-hatted nobs, puffing "elegantly" on their cigars, waltzed with their pretty partners.[48]

After 1830, Jews who mixed in gentile society became increasingly sensitive to the remaining legal disabilities that set them apart from other citizens. Because they were acculturated second- and third-generation residents of Britain, the equals in every other sense of the non-Jews whom they met, they viewed the simple existence of legal disabilities as an indictment of their character, even if these disabilities were of little consequence in day-to-day affairs. Barriers to public office and elite institutions implied that Jews as a group were inferior, not altogether English, and untrustworthy. As Isaac Lyon Goldsmid, one of the leaders of the emancipation effort, told Sir Robert Peel in 1845, the Jews "desired to be placed on an equality in point of civil privileges with other persons dissenting from the established church not so much on account of the hardship of being excluded from particular stations of trust or honor, as on account of the far greater hardship of having a degrading stigma fastened upon us by the laws of our country."[49] As noted, earlier generations had been satisfied with England's relative toleration, which explains why the campaign for Jewish emancipation in Britain was inaugurated decades later than in France and the German states. Not until substantial numbers of Jews had achieved middle-class status and redefined the nature of Jewish identity was there real interest in removing the few remaining barriers to full civil equality and the right to participate in public affairs.

Emancipation came to the Jews of Britain in piecemeal fashion between 1830 and 1871, rather than in a single comprehensive legislative act.[50] Moreover, some Jewish disabilities were discarded by local bodies and corporations without recourse to parliamentary action. In 1830, for example, Jews gained the right to become freemen of the City of London — and thus the right to operate retail businesses within the City's boundaries — when the Court of Common Council ruled that they need not take the Christian form of oath. This decision came after a struggle waged by the Nonconformist glass manufacturer Apsley Pellat and other evangelical millenarians, members of the Philo-Judaean Society. This group, though firm believers in the ultimate conversion of the Jews, was critical of the aggressive and unscrupulous methods of the London Society for Promoting Christianity among the Jews. They also were eager to remove legal obstacles to Jewish integration, believing that this would bring them into closer contact with Christian civilization and thus prepare the ground for their conversion.[51] In 1833, as we saw earlier, Jews became eligible to practice as barristers when the benchers of Lincoln's Inn permitted Francis Henry Goldsmid to take the required oath in a form acceptable to his conscience.

The central battleground for the emancipation campaign, however, was Westminster. Again, evangelical Christians, not Jews, took the earliest initiative. In June 1827, a petition of several members of the Philo-Judaean Society urging the repeal of the "oppressive" laws under which Jews labored was read in the House of Commons, but nothing more was heard of it. A second Philo-Judaean petition suffered the same fate, as did that of Moses Levy of Great Alie Street, which was read in June 1828. What brought magnates like Nathan Mayer Rothschild and Isaac Lyon Goldsmid into the struggle and marked the start of a concerted Jewish effort was repeal of the Test and Corporation Acts in 1828 and passage of the Catholic Emancipation Act in 1829. This legislation, which allowed Nonconformists and Roman Catholics respectively to hold national and local offices, marked the start of a decades-long parliamentary campaign to reform the political life of the country—to root out "Old Corruption" (rotten boroughs, placemen, fundholders, monopolies, aristocratic privilege), hobble the established church and the landed interest, and empower the urban, often Nonconformist, middle-class population. Landmarks in this campaign were the First Reform Act of 1832, which disenfranchised most rotten boroughs, redistributed their seats among underrepresented urban areas, and increased the electorate in England and Wales; the Municipal Corporations Act of 1835, which made possible the incorporation of new industrial cities and expanded urban self-government; and repeal of the protectionist Corn Laws in 1846, which had benefited landowners at the expense of the cities.

Against this background of political reform, the first Jewish emancipation bill was introduced in 1830. It was defeated in the House of Commons on its second reading, but another attempt was made in 1833, on the heels of the Reform Act of 1832, and this time the reformed Commons passed the bill. In what became a pattern, it was defeated in the House of Lords. Various measures to remove Jewish disabilities, as well as measures merely to alter the oath required of persons elected to Parliament, met the same end—passage in the Commons, defeat in the Lords—in 1834, 1836, 1841, 1848, 1849, 1851, 1853, 1856, and 1857. (In 1854, the Commons rejected Lord John Russell's Parliamentary Oaths Bill, but this was because it abolished the special oath for Roman Catholics mandated in the Catholic Emancipation Act, in addition to omitting the words "on the true faith of a Christian".)

Gentile support came from four political groups, each with its own reason for backing emancipation: Whigs, who were ideologically committed to religious freedom and civil rights; progressive Tories (Canningites and, after 1846, Peelites), who had broken with the mainstream of their party and supported religious liberty and other Whig measures; evangelical Tories, who were eager to promote Jewish integration as a prelude to their conversion; and Radicals and Nonconformists, who wanted to weaken the influence of the Church of England and saw

Jewish emancipation as another blow to its privileged position. After the Reform Act of 1832, these groups tended to dominate the lower house of Parliament.

Opposition to Jewish rights came primarily from Tory High Churchmen and ultra-conservative evangelicals. On religious grounds, they were unsympathetic to Jews and Judaism, in addition to which they were resentful that political necessity had led to granting Catholics and Nonconformists their rights and angry that state intervention in church matters in general was on the rise. After Catholic emancipation, they were loath to consider any further dilution in the Anglican character of the state. This explains their stubborn resistance over three decades to all proposals to allow Jews to become members of the national legislature.

Other measures to remove Jewish disabilities, on the other hand, evoked no comparable response. In 1835, Parliament quickly approved the Sheriff's Declaration Act in order to allow David Salomons (1797–1873), a banker who had just been elected one of the two sheriffs of the City of London, to assume office without having to take the Christian form of oath. That same year Parliament also approved legislation revoking the power of returning officers at elections to demand voters take the oath of abjuration in its Christian form before voting. This formally enfranchised Jews who were otherwise qualified to vote, although in practice Jews had exercised the franchise since the end of the previous century, it being the practice of election officers in some boroughs to dispense with the oath. In 1845, Parliament passed the Jewish Municipal Relief Act, which allowed Jews to assume all municipal offices without having to take the required oath "on the true faith of a Christian." Here, too, legislation followed what had already become practice, at least outside London: Jews were elected to municipal office at Southampton in 1838, Birmingham in 1839, and Portsmouth in 1841. In 1846, the Religious Opinions Relief Act extended the protection given to Nonconformist chapels, schools, and charities to Jewish institutions. It also established undisputed entitlement to own land. And, in 1854 and 1856, as we have seen, passage of the Oxford University Reform Act and the Cambridge University Reform Act respectively opened the way for Jews to take degrees at the ancient universities, although barriers to holding fellowships and participating in university governance were not removed until passage of the Universities Tests Act in 1871.[52]

The willingness of a majority in the reformed Commons to seat Jews and, even more, the willingness of majorities in both Commons and

Lords to admit Jews to other areas of public life suggest that opposition to Jewish integration in general was neither wide nor deep. If it had been, it is unlikely that Parliament would have approved the relief acts discussed above. What opposition there was, to be sure, was genuine, but it gained importance only because the question of Jewish access to Parliament was part and parcel of a larger debate about church-state relations and the boundaries of the political nation that raged for most of the nineteenth century. Opposition to the Jew Bill of 1753 had been far more intense and popular. Even the Earl of Shaftesbury, an evangelical opponent of emancipation, conceded that it was not an issue that generated much excitement: "The popular voice, to take it in the full extent of the term, is neither upon one side or the other. There is, upon the whole, a general apathy upon the question. Where any feeling is entertained in its regard, that feeling is deep and serious; but that feeling has not, however, pervaded the whole mass of the community."[53]

Confident of England's assimilative capacity, most respectable Victorians did not view Jewish integration as a threat to the health of state and society, even if they continued to describe Jews in ways that were, by later standards, blatantly antisemitic. Much of what Britons wrote and said about Jews in the nineteenth century was careless and conventional, the result of unthinking, unreflective habit. To take a well-known example: Charles Dickens created Fagin, the very model of the demonic Jew and, with the exception of Shylock, the most influential Jewish character in English literature, during the first decade of the campaign to remove Jewish disabilities. Yet he was, as far as we know, no opponent of emancipation. Indeed, in the 1850s and 1860s, when Dickens became aware of the implications of his portrayal of Jews (in *Oliver Twist* and his journalism), he moderated his treatment and eventually created Riah, the impossibly good Jew of *Our Mutual Friend* (1864–65), to offset the repulsive villainy of Fagin.[54]

Within the Jewish community as well, excitement about the emancipation campaign was absent—largely because the mass of Jews stood to gain little from the removal of the few remaining disabilities. How many peddlers and shopkeepers, after all, considered running for Parliament or sending their sons to Oxford or Cambridge? The London correspondent of a New York Jewish newspaper reported in 1850 that Anglo-Jewry as a body was "quite indifferent" about emancipation and that only a few ambitious individuals cared whether Jews would be allowed into Parliament. A "Hebrew gentleman" told the social researcher Henry Mayhew that "so little did the Jews themselves care for 'Jewish emancipation,' that he questioned if one man in ten, actuated solely by his own feelings, would trouble himself to walk the length of the street in which he lived to secure Baron Rothschild's admission into the House of Commons."[55]

Even within middle-class ranks, support for political emancipation was not universal. Well-to-do persons of moderate ambition were more or less content with what they had. The turnpike farmer Lewis Levy (1786–1856) told the Commons that he desired neither to have the franchise nor to be admitted to Parliament and that all his Jewish friends were equally indifferent. All he asked was a law declaring the ability of Jews to hold landed property.[56] Some religious traditionalists feared that participation in public life would weaken Jewish faith and practice. Moses Montefiore, for example, while not a vocal opponent, was no enthusiast either. Conservative in disposition, an observant Jew who did not go into society much, he was concerned that emancipation would lead Jewish officeholders to neglect their religious duties and refused to support an aggressive public campaign.[57] Chief Rabbis Solomon Hirschell and Nathan Adler shared his outlook. They were unable to oppose the wishes of men like Goldsmid, Salomons, and Rothschild and thus did not refuse their formal backing, but they were not in the front ranks of emancipation supporters. A few traditionalists even opposed emancipation in the earliest years of the campaign. The colonial entrepreneur Moses Levy not only felt that emancipation would endanger Judaism — he cited as proof the low state of observance in France and Holland — but also argued that Jews constituted a separate nation and were incapable of becoming Englishmen. In a similar vein, the Hungarian-born rabbi Joseph Crool (1760–1829), then a private tutor in Hebrew at Cambridge, opposed emancipation on the basis of the traditional doctrine that the Jews were in exile and must await divine redemption in their own land.[58]

Thus, almost until the end, the emancipation campaign was not a broad-based communal effort but rather the work of a handful of ambitious, well-connected City men, whose close government contacts allowed them to put the question of Jewish disabilities on the national agenda. Initially, Isaac Lyon Goldsmid attempted to build broader support by mobilizing the Board of Deputies of British Jews, a hitherto somnolent body.[59] The origins of the Board can be traced to a committee of Sephardim, formed in 1760 at the accession of George III, to negotiate Jewish status with the new monarch and his ministers. Ashkenazi leaders objected to being unrepresented in the delegation that subsequently called on the lord chancellor, the Duke of Devonshire, and it was eventually agreed that representatives, or deputies, from all major London synagogues would meet in the future whenever it became necessary to represent Jewish interests to the government. This group, from which the Board of Deputies evolved, met infrequently until the beginning of the emancipation era—five or six years between meetings were not uncommon—and its role in communal life was negligible.

The Board, in which Montefiore's was the dominant voice, at first supported the efforts of Rothschild and Goldsmid, although it tempered its support with caution and left most of the actual work to the activists, especially Goldsmid, who pursued the cause relentlessly. (Rothschild died in 1836.) However, as Goldsmid and his son Francis continued their forceful lobbying and pamphleteering, Montefiore became concerned that the Board's role was being usurped. In 1836, after failing to restrain the Goldsmids and their new ally, young David Salomons, the Board notified the chancellor of the exchequer that it was the only official channel of communication for the secular and political interests of the Jews. (The Board continued to make this claim throughout the nineteenth and twentieth centuries, although there was no legal basis for it.)

In the next stage of the campaign, the activists embarked on a new, more confrontational strategy, one that led to a temporary break with the Board but in the end produced success. As we have seen, in 1835, Salomons was elected one of the two sheriffs of the City of London, moving Parliament to pass the Sheriff's Declaration Act so he could take office. At the end of the year, he was elected an alderman for the ward of Aldergate but was prevented from taking office because he could not take the oath in its Christian form. He then took legal action against the Court of Aldermen, which he lost on appeal almost four years later. In 1839, when the Board of Deputies refused to help with the expenses of a further appeal to the House of Lords, Salomons resigned from the Board. Meanwhile, he was adopted as Liberal candidate for Parliament for New Shoreham in 1837 and for Maidstone in 1841 but lost both times. In 1844, he stood for alderman of Portsoken Ward and won but was not allowed to take office. He took his grievance to Sir Robert Peel, the prime minister, and Lord Lyndhurst, the lord chancellor, and the latter agreed to sponsor a municipal emancipation bill, which passed in 1845. This time the Board of Deputies backed Salomons's initiative, even establishing a public subscription to finance the campaign. However, theirs was not the only Jewish deputation to see the prime minister. The Goldsmids, who had by now quarreled with Montefiore and the Board

in regard to Reform Judaism, told Peel that British Jews would be satisfied with nothing less than complete emancipation.

The strategy that Salomons worked out between 1835 and 1845 became, in the end, the Jewish road to Parliament. In 1847, five Jews were
adopted as Liberal candidates for Parliament—two sons of Nathan
Rothschild, Lionel at the City of London and Mayer at Hythe; Salomons at Greenwich; and the Goldsmids, father and son, at Beverley and
Great Yarmouth respectively. Lionel alone won that year—and four
more times before he was finally allowed to take his seat—but the more
combative Salomons won Greenwich at a by-election in 1851 and after
taking the oath (but without the offensive words) spoke and voted before being excluded. Rothschild's and Salomons's strategy shifted the
debate from an abstract issue—the place of Jews in a Christian legislature—to a specific, practical matter: Could Parliament exclude the legally elected representatives of British voters, especially when the house
to which they were elected saw no impediment to their admission? At
the same time, the election of Jews to municipal office and the bestowal
of a knighthood on Montefiore in 1837 and Salomons in 1855 and bar-
onetcies on Goldsmid in 1841, Montefiore in 1846, and Anthony de
Rothschild (1810–76) in 1847—made the exclusion of Jews from Parliament appear ever more anachronistic. In 1858, the Conservative leadership, exhausted and aware that its intransigence at this point was harm-
ing the party, relented. A face-saving compromise was reached: each
house would determine its own form of oath. By 1860, four of the five
Jews who had been candidates in 1847 had won election to the Commons.

In the last stages of the emancipation debate, Jewish interest in gaining admission to Parliament broadened. The Board of Deputies took a
more active stance, orchestrating a cascade of petitions following Rothschild's fourth election victory in 1857, while Jews outside the inner circle
of notables also began to identify with and support the efforts of their
wealthy co-religionists. In the City of London, there were several hundred Jewish electors, concentrated in its eastern wards, whose votes
Rothschild and other Liberals actively solicited. "However little the Jewish community as a whole might have cared for the matter," the historian
of the English Jewish vote has noted, "Liberal politicians appeared as
suppliants before it, forcing it to sit up and take notice."[60] In 1847, at
the initiative of Joseph Mitchell (d. 1854), proprietor of the *Jewish Chronicle,* the Jewish Association for the Removal of Civil and Religious Disabilities was formed to agitate on a popular basis for emancipation. (Its

usual venue was the Fishmonger's Arms, St. James Place, Aldgate.) It drafted petitions to Parliament, held a mass demonstration at Sussex Hall, and attracted 120 members at its prime. However, it folded the following year in the face of indifference from the leading emancipationists.[61] Nonetheless, popular interest continued to grow, a trend to which the first Jewish newspapers, the *Voice of Jacob* and the *Jewish Chronicle*, both established in 1841, made a critical contribution. (The two papers merged in 1842 and then split in 1844. The *Voice of Jacob* ceased publication in 1848.) The Jewish press provided the only popular communal forum for the discussion of emancipation, religious reform, poor relief, and Jewish suffering abroad. It broadened the outlook of its readers and helped to define their Jewish interests and consciousness.[62]

In the provinces, the emancipation campaign attracted more popular support than in London, for there, in the absence of powerful figures like Rothschild, Goldsmid, and Salomons, men of lesser rank were able to take part in communal affairs. Among those who wrote pamphlets, organized petitions, or orchestrated pro-emancipation motions in municipal councils were a Norwich optical goods merchant and a Truro jeweler. Popular interest in emancipation was stimulated as well by the internal strife that engulfed provincial congregations in the 1840s and 1850s over issues of synagogue governance. British congregations at the time had two classes of members: free, or privileged, members and seatholders. (There were also persons who attended services regularly but were unable to afford any class of membership.) The former monopolized synagogue affairs: they alone elected officers or were eligible to be elected, imposed fines, assessed financial contributions, chose who received synagogue honors, and determined who was admitted to free membership. Discontented English-born seatholders, businessmen who supported the great reform movements of the day, challenged the system, denouncing it as contrary to the liberal spirit of the age.[63] It was only natural that such men took a keen interest in the fate of emancipation.

In the context of European Jewish history, the emancipation debate in Britain was unique: Christian champions of the admission of Jews to the political nation did not set conditions for their emancipation. In most European states, emancipation was conditional. In return for equal rights, Jews were expected to abandon their social cohesion, national consciousness, ritual separatism (short of conversion, of course), and skewed occupational profile. Napoleon's leading questions to the so-called Parisian Sanhedrin of 1806 and 1807, with their emphasis on the gap between Jewish beliefs and practices and those of civil society, embodied the conditional or contractual approach to emancipation. For, in effect, Napoleon told the assembled notables that unless they responded appropriately to his questions, that is, repudiated Jewish separatism (for example, the ban on intermarriage), emancipation would be withheld. In the Russian empire, where emancipation was no more than a vague hope in the nineteenth century, those who favored the integration of Jews into Russian society insisted that they first prove their worthiness by abandoning traditional beliefs and habits that both kept them apart from and posed a threat to Russian society.

In the English debate, those who favored emancipation did not make their support conditional. In their view, Jews had demonstrated their worthiness for admission to the political nation. They were sober, diligent, hard-working, loyal citizens, already active participants in important spheres of life, save one—the political. Whether they continued to pray for their return to Jerusalem and the restoration of the Davidic monarchy and Temple cult or to socialize and marry exclusively among themselves was of little interest. Opponents of emancipation, to be sure, harped on the otherness of the Jews, but from their perspective no amount of assimilation—with the exception of baptism, in which case Jews ceased to be Jews—would be efficacious. For them, it was not Jewish separatism or particularism but the Jewish religion itself that disqualified Jews from a legislative role in a Christian state. Reforming Judaism, giving its doctrines a more universal cast and its practices a more Protestant tone, would not have made its adherents more acceptable as legislators. The debate, then, tended to focus less on the habits of the Jews than on the nature of the state and the place of the established church and its adherents within it. As such, it was a debate conducted largely among Christians, as one student of emancipation remarked, rather than between Christians and Jews.[64]

This is not to claim, of course, that in the emancipation era, or later, that Jews never experienced pressure to conform to English norms or that they never felt insecure or even on trial, their behavior subject to close scrutiny. Few Jews in England or elsewhere who pursued integration were able to escape such pressures. But the source of these assimilatory pressures was not an implicit contract between communal leaders and their liberal friends, struck during the three-decade long debate on emancipation, by which Jews pledged to rid themselves of disagreeable traits and separatist habits in return for admission to Parliament. In the debate itself, advocates of Jewish emancipation did not demand that

Jews regenerate themselves, abandon commerce, modernize their religion, or transform themselves into "English citizens of the Mosaic persuasion." The liberal essayist and MP Thomas Babington Macaulay admitted that there was some truth to the anti-emancipation charge that Jews were a separate people, but then argued that as long as the government treated them as it did its other citizens they would feel loyal to it—and that satisfied him and most other friends of the Jews as well.[65]

The unconditional nature of Jewish emancipation in Britain had profound consequences for the development of Anglo-Judaism in the Victorian period. At the beginning of the century, Judaism in England—its forms, customs, and doctrines—differed little from the Judaism of Central Europe, except in regard to levels of observance and piety, which were markedly lower. A Jewish merchant from Frankfurt or Prague who attended a Sabbath service in London in the eighteenth century would have felt at home. (However, he would have been surprised by the number of empty seats and the behavior of his fellow worshipers after leaving the synagogue.) In the nineteenth century, the communal elite introduced reforms into London's traditional synagogues in order to make them conform more closely to middle-class notions of decorum and gentility. The earliest step to make Jewish worship more dignified occurred, actually, in the mid-eighteenth century, when the Great Synagogue ordered its hazzan to wear canonicals (the long black gown with two white ribbons hanging at the front of the neck worn by Protestant divines), but this was an isolated incident.[66] In the 1820s, some of the London congregations introduced (or considering introducing) minor reforms such as limiting the number of mi-she-berakhs, requiring hazzanim to chant the liturgy in a straightforward rather than florid style, and prohibiting children from interrupting the reading of the scroll of Esther with noisemakers on Purim. In the late 1820s, the Spanish and Portuguese Synagogue considered, but rejected, a package of more radical reforms: introducing instrumental music into the synagogue, abolishing the repetition of the amidah, reducing the number of recitations of the kaddish, allowing women to join in the chanting of the service, allowing sermons in English (rather than Portuguese).

Some of these reforms were designed to make attendance at synagogue more attractive to congregants who could read but not understand Hebrew and were impatient with the length of the traditional service. But most of them, particularly those initiated by the Ashkenazi congregations, were cosmetic in character, undertaken within the parameters of traditional practice and designed to enhance the dignity of the service. They addressed the externals of Jewish worship rather than its doctrinal content. The men who backed their introduction were aware that Jewish worship was widely perceived as indecorous and irreverent and wanted a form of service that conformed to their social rank, their comfortable mode of living, and their self-image as well-mannered men of property. Modernizing ideological considerations, such as those that drove the earliest reformers in Germany, were absent or muted. There were no attempts to tamper with liturgical references to the messianic age or the chosenness of the Jewish people.

After 1840, the desire for change sharpened, resulting in the end in the establishment of independent Reform congregations in London and Manchester.[67] The catalyst in the case of London was an internecine Sephardi dispute. Members of the Sephardi congregation, by virtue of their longer residence in the country and their converso past, were more acculturated on the whole than members of the Ashkenazi congregations. Throughout the 1820s and 1830s, discontent mounted at Bevis Marks about the indecorous state of public worship, as well as the high-handed, unbending nature of congregational governance. (The latter precipitated Isaac D'Israeli's withdrawal from the congregation in 1817.) When the elders agreed in 1830, for example, to permit sermons in English, they stipulated that the text had to be submitted to them beforehand to ensure that it did not contain "any thing inimical to our religious doctrines or any matter hostile to the established institutions of the country."[68] One major bone of contention was the refusal of the elders to permit the establishment of a branch synagogue in the upscale West End, where the wealthiest families now lived. Moses Montefiore willingly walked the four-and-one-half miles from Park Lane to Bevis Marks (since Jewish law prohibits riding on the Sabbath and festivals), but others stayed home, demanding revision of ascama one, the congregational bylaw from 1664 that prohibited members from gathering for public worship within six miles of Bevis Marks.[69]

In 1840, after more than two decades of wrangling, a number of wealthy families withdrew from the congregation and, with a handful of equally prosperous Ashkenazi families, the Goldsmids at their head, founded the West London Synagogue of British Jews, the first non-Orthodox congregation in the country. Their secession, they declared, was motivated by their unhappiness about undignified services and poor attendance, which they attributed to five causes: one, "the distance of the existing synagogues from the places of our residence"; two, "the length and imperfections of the order of service"; three, "the inconvenient hours at which it is appointed"; four, "the unimpressive manner in which it is performed"; and, five, "the absence of religious instruction [sermons] in our synagogues."[70] Their overall object, in the words of the Sephardi founders, was "to arrest and prevent secession from Judaism—an overwhelming evil, which has at various times so widely spread among many of the most respected families of our communities."[71]

While the stated motives of the founders appear sufficient to explain their actions, it has been suggested that they attached political hopes as well to the establishment of a Reform congregation.[72] According to this interpretation, those who championed the reform of Judaism in England, like their counterparts in Germany, believed that by modernizing their ritual they would prove themselves worthy to be emancipated. Isaac Lyon Goldsmid, one of the most outspoken emancipationists, clearly believed that the establishment of a Reform synagogue would promote the removal of civil disabilities. In 1831, when the Board of Deputies refused to ask the government for full emancipation, as Goldsmid urged, he threatened that he "would establish a new Synagogue with the assistance of the young men; he would alter the present form of prayer to that in use in the Synagogue at Hamburg," which was established in 1817. And, in 1845, after having led his own delegation to see Sir Robert Peel, he explained that his object had been to place before the prime minister "certain facts connected with the advancement of British Jews in the several branches of letters and science, in the different learned professions, as well as in the improvement of the worship of the synagogue, during the last few years."[73]

Aside from Isaac Lyon Goldsmid, who, in fact, did not join the congregation until 1843, there is no evidence that the founders (his relatives aside) held such views. Most of the reforms introduced in the new congregation were moderate measures that responded to social rather than political needs: *shaharit* began at a later hour, *aliyyot* and *mi-she-berakhs* were abolished, the *mussaf amidah* was shortened, and English sermons were introduced. Even though Isaac and his son Francis insisted that there was no national dimension to contemporary Jewish life, nothing of a nationalist or particularist nature was eliminated from the liturgy, although this was the practice in Reform congregations in Germany and later the United States. The London reformers retained Hebrew as the language of prayer and left unaltered prayers about the chosenness of the Jews, the coming of the messiah, the return to Zion, and the restoration of the Temple cult. The one major break with tradition was the abolition of the second day of the festivals.[74] The Goldsmids' concern about excessive holy days preventing Jewish participation in public life perhaps contributed to this departure from established practice. But more decisive was the hostility of the synagogue's first religious leader, David W. Marks (1811–1909), to practices that were introduced by the rabbis in antiquity and lacked biblical sanction. His bibliocentric, neo-karaitic approach to Judaism, which shaped liturgical and ritual practice in the new congregation, was unique and owed nothing to the Hamburg Temple, in particular, or the German Reform movement, in general.

Traditionalists reacted harshly to the establishment of the West London Synagogue, despite the moderate character of the reforms introduced there. Urged on by Moses Montefiore, a bitter, intransigent opponent of Reform, Chief Rabbi Hirschell drew up an indictment of the reformers in late summer 1841, charging them with rejecting the authority of the oral law and banning them from participation in the religious life of the community. (Although labeled a "caution," the document was in effect a herem.) The members of the Sephardi *bet din* (law court) also appended their signatures to the document, there being no haham at the time. It was published and ordered to be read in all British synagogues on 22 January 1842, five days before the formal consecration of the new congregation's house of worship (a former dissenting chapel) in Burton Street, off the Euston Road. The most serious consequence of the "caution" was the refusal of the Board of Deputies, which Montefiore headed, to allow the Reform congregation to be represented on the Board and to authorize its secretary to register marriages. (The Marriage Registration Act of 1836 conferred on the Board of Deputies sole authority to certify to the Registrar-General the names of marriage secretaries of congregations of "persons professing the Jewish religion".) In Montefiore's view, members of the Reform congregation were not professing Jews. This meant that couples from the West London Synagogue were forced to marry in a public registry office before celebrating their marriage in a religious ceremony. The Reform congregation obtained the legal right to certify its own marriages only with passage of the Dissenters' Chapels Bill in 1857. Members of the congregation became eligible to sit on the Board (as deputies for other congregations) in 1874, but the synagogue itself did not gain representation until 1886.

The founders of the West London Synagogue were not zealots for religious innovation. Following the initial reforms, they made few additional changes in the worship service. In the second half of the century, an organ, a mixed choir, and some English prayers were introduced and the petition for the restoration of sacrificial offerings was removed. Separate seating for men and women, on the other hand, was maintained until 1918. Membership increased modestly—there were about 150 families at mid-century—and remained overwhelmingly middle to upper-middle class in composition. The staid respectability of the congregation inspired Israel Zangwill to quip that the congregation was "a body which had stood still for fifty years admiring its past self."[75]

Nor were the founders religious crusaders, eager to build a movement to reform the practice of Judaism throughout Britain. A second Reform congregation was established in Manchester in 1856 and a third in Bradford in 1873, but neither owed its origins to initiatives emanating from London. In Manchester, discontent with the highhanded rule of central communal authorities in London (the Chief Rabbi and the Board of Deputies) as well as middle-class social concerns about heightening the solemnity of worship led to the establishment of a separatist Reform congregation. A majority of the founding members were German-born and one of the leading agitators for change, the language teacher Tobias Theodores (1808–86), understood the intellectual foundations of German Reform, but most did not look to Germany for guidance in doctrinal and ritual matters. The new congregation adopted the prayer book and ritual of the West London Synagogue but retained the second day of festivals. In Bradford, on the other hand, the influence of German Reform was substantial. The founders of the synagogue, the first in the city, were well-to-do, assimilationist-minded German textile merchants. Their outlook was shaped more by conditions in Germany, where they had been born and raised, than in Britain and, accordingly, they imported their first religious leader, Rabbi Joseph Strauss (1844–1922), from Germany.

The failure of Reform to make headway in Victorian England—in contrast to its progress in Germany and the United States—requires explanation. To start, its lack of success was *not* due to widespread adherence to traditional standards of observance. Most English Jews at this time were not Orthodox in the usual sense of the term (strict observance of kashrut, Sabbath rest, festival rituals, etc.), despite belonging to congregations whose ritual and religious leadership were Orthodox.[76] Although absent from their workplaces on the Sabbath—the old clothes market in Houndsditch was shut, as were the large Moses and Hyam clothing stores—most men were not to be found in synagogue. They preferred, rather, to devote their Saturdays to visiting theaters, music halls, concerts, exhibitions, race courses, and public houses. Those who attended synagogue included not a few who hired Gentiles to mind the store in their absence. Nor were most Jews strict in their observance of the dietary laws. Many families purchased kosher meat that was unsalted and unporged. For most, observance of kashrut outside the home was limited to avoiding meat, pork, and shellfish. There were, of course, strict traditionalists, recent immigrants to a large extent, who were as Orthodox in their private habits as in their public worship, but they were a minority without great influence in communal life.[77]

Why, then, were so few British Jews attracted to Reform Judaism, given such widespread indifference to traditional practice? The chief reason is that there was no compelling need to alter the public face of Judaism, that is, its theology and worship service. As we have seen, the political pressures that caused Jews in Germany to denationalize Judaism in the hope of gaining full emancipation were absent. There was no public clamor that Jews renounce particularist rituals and doctrines in order to be integrated into society. There was also, at the same time, a disincentive to tamper with ancient public observances. Religious tradition was closely identified in England with the dominant political and ecclesiastical establishment. The commercial and financial magnates who governed Anglo-Jewry were aware of the prestige accorded ancient institutions and customs in elite culture and were receptive to a form of Judaism that emphasized venerable traditions, hallowed ceremonial forms, and hierarchical religious leadership. Though disinclined themselves to accept the full discipline of that form of Judaism,[78] they nonetheless expected their synagogues and communal functionaries to do so. Eager to strengthen their social position, they saw in Orthodox Judaism a parallel to the venerable, tradition-minded Church of England. On the other hand, the schismatic character of Reform invoked comparison with low-status, sectarian Nonconformity.

Solomon Hirschell's successor, the Hanoverian Nathan Adler, who served as chief rabbi from 1845 until his death in 1890, exploited this identification to combat Reform Judaism and to enhance the status and power of his office as well.[79] His predecessors had exercised limited authority and cannot be said to have influenced the course of Anglo-Jewish history. But from the start Adler set out to invigorate the chief rabbinate in the belief that a strong, centralized rabbinical establishment, with supreme authority over the public religious and educational life of the community, was required to preserve traditional Judaism. Within two years of his arrival, he issued his *Laws and Regulations for All the Ashkenazi Synagogues in the United Kingdom,* in which he claimed absolute power to determine liturgical forms, license and discipline religious functionaries, supervise schools, and even approve the establishment of new congregations throughout Great Britain. With the backing of the Montefiore-dominated Board of Deputies and the acquiescence of most provincial and metropolitan congregations, Adler accomplished much of what he set out to do. He created an authoritarian episcopal system that swept away congregational autonomy and rabbinical independence. (His authority, in fact, extended beyond Britain's shores to encompass congregations throughout the Empire.) In concentrating power in the hands of one person, Adlerism, as its critics called it, was unique in modern Jewish history. The authority of the *grands rabbins* of France and *Oberrabbiner* and *Landesrabbiner* of Germany was weak by comparison. In this sense, Adler's system was as radical a departure from Jewish tradition as the changes introduced at the West London Synagogue of British Jews.

Adler's restructuring of religious authority did not go unchallenged. Several provincial synagogues balked at surrendering their independence. Liverpool, which had refused to read Hirschell's ban on the reformers in 1842 (from distaste for religious intolerance rather than sympathy for religious reform), objected to the promulgation of his *Laws and Regulations* because no congregations had been consulted. Manchester, which had also refused to read the ban, waged a running war with Adler in the 1850s over the question of local autonomy.[80] In 1850, Manchester obtained Adler's permission to appoint as its minister the Hungarian-born, German-educated political refugee Solomon Schiller-Szinessy (1820–90). Adler agreed—on the condition that Schiller-Szinessy, an ordained rabbi, Ph.D. of the University of Jena, and dynamic preacher, refrain from making rabbinical decisions and introducing liturgical changes without his (Adler's) consent. To Schiller-Szinessy, whose qualifications were the same as Adler's, this stipulation was a slap in the face. With the support of influential congregants, whose local pride bristled at claims of metropolitan supremacy, he began to exercise rabbinical functions independently and gave himself the formal title "Local Rabbi," which led, of course, to repeated skirmishes with Adler.

Manchester also clashed with the chief rabbi over the anti-Reform *herem* of 1841. The original ban had prohibited marriages with members of the breakaway synagogue. In 1849, under pressure from communal magnates who were bound to the reformers by family and business ties, Adler lifted the ban on individual members, although he still refused to recognize their synagogue as a Jewish congregation, the effect of which was continued exclusion from the Board of Deputies. In 1853, four members of the Reform congregation were elected to the Board as deputies for four small provincial congregations but were not allowed to take their seats. (For reasons of convenience, provincial communities often chose London residents as their representatives.) This angered Manchester Jews, whose two delegates had supported the Reform deputies, and, along with earlier disputes, helped to crystallize Reform sentiment. In fact, local pride and resentment of Adler's monopolization of religious authority may have contributed as much to the emergence of a Reform synagogue there as concerns about decorum and sermons.

After the disputes of the 1850s, Nathan Adler never again faced a serious challenge to his authority. However, in 1870, when the promoters of the United Synagogue scheme, a federation of London's largest Orthodox Ashkenazi congregations, were drafting a charter for the new institution for submission to the Charity Commissioners and attempted to insert a clause giving the chief rabbi sole control over all religious matters, the Home Secretary, who was responsible for presenting the Charity Commissioners' report on the proposed union to Parliament, objected, and the clause was deleted. The government was then in the process of disestablishing the Anglican Church of Ireland, and it would not have been consistent or wise to arm the ecclesiastical representative of the Anglo-Jewish elite with the power of the state.[81] The chief rabbinate thus remained without broad statutory support, its state-authorized power limited to licensing marriage secretaries.

Adler was successful in large part because he enjoyed the backing of the communal notables (with the exception, obviously, of those who were members of the Reform congregation). They shared his distaste for radical innovation and schism, as we have seen, while he preached an accommodationist Orthodoxy compatible with their everyday needs. Like other modern Orthodox rabbis in nineteenth-century Europe, Adler embraced cultural assimilation, secular education, and participation in public life. He sought to maintain an Orthodox posture while living in the modern world. As he announced in his installation sermon in 1845, his was the difficult task of finding "the golden mean," of mediating between those who desired "rapid innovation" and those who trusted in "steadfast adherence to whatever time has sanctified, even though it be contrary to the law."[82]

Adler's brand of traditional Judaism well suited the needs of acculturated British Jews. Though uninterested in theological reforms to uni-

versalize Judaism, they were eager to have dignified, musically harmonious services. Many also wanted shorter services at more convenient
hours. They voiced their desire to improve the tone of public worship
before the Reform secession occurred and continued to do so throughout the century. Immediately after the formation of the West London
Synagogue of British Jews, for example, the Western Synagogue, which
had refused to read Hirschell's herem from the pulpit, fearing it would
spread intolerance, introduced several reforms to heighten the dignity
of public worship. It adopted a new system of congregational finance
in order to eliminate the selling of liturgical honors during the service
and required its newly hired minister, H. A. Henry (1806–79), to deliver
regular English-language Sabbath sermons.[83] When Adler took office,
he sanctioned changes like these because they did not conflict with Jewish law. During his chief rabbinate, he banned toddlers from attending
services; forbade congregants to chatter, gossip, or leave their places;
ended the sale of liturgical honors and limited the announcement of
monetary offerings; and encouraged the introduction of all-male choirs.
The most radical innovation he sanctioned was the division of the Sabbath and festival morning service to accommodate West End Jews who
did not want to attend services that customarily began at 8:00 or 8:30
in the morning. Yielding to pressure from communal oligarchs, he ruled
that the early service (*shaharit*) might be held from 8:30 until 9:30 and
then a second service (*kriyyat ha-torah* and *mussaf*) might follow, after a
break, from 11:00 until 1:00. In another marked departure from tradition, he also sanctioned the introduction of a confirmation ceremony
for both boys and girls at the Bayswater Synagogue in 1864.[84] This willingness to accommodate nonideological, cosmetic changes within a formally Orthodox framework also worked to dampen interest in a separatist Reform movement.

During Adler's tenure, and with his encouragement, a new kind of
religious leader—a pastoral, preaching Jewish clergyman—emerged,
giving a unique cast to Anglo-Judaism.[85] Before the Victorian period,
the few ordained rabbis in England performed the same functions as
rabbis elsewhere in Europe. They answered questions of religious law,
adjudicated cases brought to communal courts, supervised minor religious functionaries, and taught Talmud and codes. Services were conducted by hazzanim, or readers, as they were known in England. In
small communities, these officiants functioned as ritual slaughterers, cir-
cumcisers, Hebrew teachers, and congregational secretaries as well. Neither rabbis nor readers preached regularly, although the former custom-

arily gave a legal discourse on the Sabbaths before Yom Kippur and Passover.

In the 1840s and 1850s, as more Jews attained bourgeois status, absorbed English tastes, and identified their fate with England, the idea arose that the community needed readers who would preach regularly in English, visit the sick and the poor, and, more generally, reflect the cultural level of the community. The *Jewish Chronicle* editorialized in 1861 that "the qualifications of a minister should extend beyond the beauty of his voice" and that his preeminent duty should be "to expound the principles of Judaism from the pulpit in choice and earnest language." At a time when most officiants were natives of Germany or Poland and lacked both secular education and rabbinical ordination, some advocates of the new model demanded that British birth also be a requirement, the assumption being that "the locality of the office demands, for the self-respect of Judaism, a slight knowledge of society." (That their chief rabbi was a native of Germany seems not to have bothered those who demanded British-born ministers). Strict traditionalists, on the other hand, were unsympathetic to these demands: one of them remarked that he could not find any "John Bullism" in Judaism.[86]

This new model of spiritual leadership took hold in the Victorian period, as it did in other Western countries. But, unlike elsewhere, Anglo-Jewish ministers were not ordained rabbis but rather well-mannered, sweet-voiced clergymen who preached and led services but were not trained to carry out traditional rabbinic functions, like answering halachic questions and teaching Talmud and codes. The emergence of the modern Anglo-Jewish religious leader in this form was the direct consequence of Nathan Adler's determination to monopolize Ashkenazi rabbinic authority in Britain. Jews' College, the seminary he opened in 1855 to train modern clergymen, did not give its students advanced training in traditional legal texts and so did not prepare them for rabbinic ordination. Thus, when Adler's own son Hermann wished to study for the rabbinate, he traveled to Prague to attend the yeshivah of the renowned Solomon Rapoport.

Although Adler refused to accord rabbinical status to other religious leaders in the community, there were, in fact, several men with traditional training and ordination, like him products of Central and East European yeshivot, including his nemesis Solomon Schiller-Szinessy. The Hambro Synagogue, the most traditional of the City congregations, employed successively two readers who were both ordained rabbis and talmudic scholars: Herman Hoelzel, a native of Hungary who had studied at the Hatam Sofer's yeshivah in Pressburg, served from 1845 to 1852; and Samuel Gollancz (1820–1900), a native of Prussian Poland who had studied at several yeshivot in the Posen area, including Akiba Eger's, served from 1855 to 1900. The members of Adler's bet din were also ordained rabbis, although Adler refused to allow them to be called to the reading of the Torah by their rabbinic titles.

By centralizing religious authority and preventing the emergence of an independent, native-born rabbinate, Adler and his lay supporters helped to guarantee the institutional hegemony of Orthodox Judaism in Britain. Their success stands in marked contrast to the failure of traditionalists to stop the spread of Reform in Germany, Hungary, and the United States during this same period. However, this achievement was not without its downside. The stifling of religious innovation robbed communal life of the intellectual ferment that accompanied the debate about Reform in more open, pluralistic communities and that stimulated the creation of scholarship and religious thought across the denominational spectrum. At the same time the failure to produce a corps of well-educated rabbis, equally at home in traditional sources and modern scholarship, deprived the community of potentially significant intellectual resources and, together with almost universal indifference to higher education and scholarly activity, reinforced its status as a cultural backwater. It is no accident that Victorian Jewry failed to produce notable religious thinkers, Talmud scholars, or practitioners of Wissenschaft des Judentums. As the historian Isaak Markus Jost (1793–1860) noted after visiting England in 1841, "No English rabbi has a place in the Jewish learned annals. Everybody was too busy to study, and no honour lured and confirmed those thirsting for knowledge." And, when the learned Morris Raphall (1798–1868), minister of the Birmingham Hebrew Congregation, left England to take a position in New York in 1849, the lack of serious patronage of scholarship was held responsible. The *Jewish Chronicle* indicted communal leaders for being "not yet alive to the value of the mind."[87] Similar complaints continued to be voiced throughout the nineteenth and twentieth centuries.

What there was of Jewish scholarship in Victorian England was largely imported from Central Europe. The bibliographer Joseph Zedner (1804–71), Hebrew librarian at the British Museum from 1845 to 1869, was a native of Glogau who returned to Germany on his retirement. Emanuel Deutsch (1829–73), a prominent contributor to learned journals on Judaism, Islam, and the ancient Near East, the major inspiration for the Jewish themes in George Eliot's remarkably sympathetic novel *Daniel Deronda* (1876), and an assistant librarian at the British Museum from 1855 to 1872, was raised and educated in a strictly Orthodox milieu in Silesia and came to London in 1855 by way of Berlin. Adolph Neubauer (1831–1907), hired by the University of Oxford to catalogue the Hebrew manuscripts in the Bodleian Library in 1868 and then to teach rabbinic Hebrew from 1884 to 1900, was a native of Hungary who had studied at the University of Prague and Solomon Rapoport's yeshivah and at the University of Munich. Michael Friedländer (1833–1910), principal of Jews' College from 1865 to 1907, translator of Maimonides and Abraham ibn Ezra, author of popular works on Judaism, and expert on the Jewish calendar, was a native of Posen and a graduate of the University of Halle.[88] Adler, of course, was also foreign-born and-educated, as were both his successor (and son) Hermann and Herman's successor Joseph Hertz (1872–1946). Indeed, the first chief rabbi to be both born and educated in England—Israel Brodie (1895–1979)—took office only in 1948.

Parallel to the emergence of the chief rabbinate, the Board of Deputies became the representative of the Jewish community in its relations with the state.[89] Before the emancipation campaign, the Board was of little importance. Then, in 1835, probably due to the influence of Montefiore, who served as its president, with a few breaks, from 1835 to 1874, it adopted a constitution and instituted regular meetings. Its membership increased as more congregations were established and chose to send representatives. When Montefiore became president in 1835, only Bevis Marks and the three large Ashkenazi synagogues in the City were represented. In 1860, there were deputies from six London and nine provincial congregations; in 1879, the numbers were fourteen and thirteen respectively.[90]

Although its members came exclusively from the non-Reform segment of the Jewish haute bourgeoisie, the Board thought of itself as the representative of the political interests of the entire community, a view that the government shared. In 1836, as noted above, it was awarded statutory authority to certify marriage secretaries, a power it used subsequently to punish congregations that rejected the chief rabbi's authority. After its reorganization in 1835, the Board became the most important channel for making Jewish interests known when laws affecting Jews (primarily in respect to Sunday trading, marriage, divorce, education, and burial) were under consideration in Parliament. It also intervened with government officials to protest administrative arrangements, at both the local and national levels, that discriminated against

Jews. It succeeded, for example, in having the Home Office rescind an order compelling Jews in prisons to work on the Sabbath and festivals. It also was successful in convincing various examining bodies to make alternative arrangements for Jewish students when competitive examinations fell on a Sabbath or festival.

At the urging of Moses Montefiore, the Board also became active in the defense of persecuted Jews in non-Western countries.[91] There was a precedent for this—Moses Hart and Aaron Franks had appealed to King George II in 1745 to protest Maria Theresa's expulsion of the Jews from Prague—but in the Victorian period the circumstances were different. The Board's intensive diplomacy on behalf of oppressed Jewries rested on the enhanced legal and social standing of English Jews in the mid-nineteenth century, the access of leading members to government ministers, the expansion of British imperial power, a liberal moralistic foreign policy, and the fortunate confluence of British foreign policy interests and Jewish concerns. The Board did not initiate this new role on its own, but acted in response to requests for assistance from beleaguered communities in Eastern Europe, the Middle East, and North Africa, which tended to have inflated notions of the extent of Anglo-Jewish, especially Rothschild, wealth and influence.

The Board first became involved in overseas diplomacy at the time of the Damascus blood libel of 1840. With the backing of the government, Montefiore and Adolphe Crémieux (1796–1880), a lawyer and politician, and vice-president of the Consistoire Centrale in Paris, journeyed to Alexandria to intervene with the Egyptian ruler Mehemet Ali, whose territory included Syria, to release the Jews who had been imprisoned in Damascus for allegedly murdering a Capuchin priest and his servant in order to obtain their blood for baking matsot. Their mission was successful: Mehemet Ali freed the prisoners and issued a firman declaring the Jewish people innocent of ritual murder, as did the sultan in Constantinople. Whatever talent Montefiore and Crémieux brought to their task, their success depended ultimately on the readiness of the British government to exert its influence on behalf of Jews in the region. It did so in the Damascus case, and again later in the century, because it saw an advantage in supporting a group in the Ottoman Empire through which it could extend its influence. In the Damascus case, there was the additional opportunity of frustrating the designs of its rival France, which protected Catholic interests in the Middle East and in this case defended its consul in Damascus, who had played a key role in the genesis of the libel.

Montefiore, with the backing of the Board of Deputies, undertook other dramatic missions to defend persecuted Jews. He went to Russia in 1846 and 1872 to intercede with the tsar; to Rome in 1859 to reclaim seven-year-old Edgardo Mortara from the papal authorities, who had taken him forcibly from his parents, claiming that he had been secretly baptized by his nurse; to Romania in 1867 to intercede with Prince Carol; and to Morocco in 1863–64 to free two Jews falsely accused of murder and to prevent the outbreak of a general persecution. Few of these missions were successful; none effected a permanent improvement in Jewish status. Nonetheless, Montefiore acquired a larger-than-life reputation throughout the Jewish world. Requests for his assistance poured in from communities in distress, beseeching him once more to set off on a mission of deliverance. Perhaps what he symbolized—Western Jewish confidence, wealth, and access to power mobilized in the defense of persecuted Jews—was more important than what he in fact accomplished.

Although their diplomacy met with little success, the very willingness of communal notables to mobilize government support on behalf of foreign Jews is noteworthy. It indicates that they retained a sense of kinship with Jews elsewhere, even unwesternized Jews. This, in turn, suggests that acculturation and integration failed to erode completely the old, pre-emancipation understanding of Jewish peoplehood. For those who held the reins of communal power, at least, Jewishness remained more than a religious identity. It continued to include sentiments, much like familial bonds, that transcended the borders of contemporary nation-states. Acculturation and integration in England, while destructive of tradition, clearly did not entail full assimilation. Despite their intensive pursuit of Englishness, communal leaders were not transformed into the proverbial Englishmen of the Mosaic persuasion. Their Jewishness and Englishness coexisted, often in harmony but on occasion otherwise, as parts of their public and private identities.

In Victorian Britain, at least before the end of the century, the pressures that caused Jews elsewhere to abandon traditional notions of peoplehood, collective fate, and mutual responsibility were muted. British Jews were free to express their ties to Jews abroad without fear of endangering their own struggle for civil equality and social acceptance. In this sense, the diplomatic activities of Montefiore and the Board of Deputies, like the failure of Reform Judaism, testify to the confidence of communal leaders about their own status. It is important to stress this, for the contrary has been argued: that English Jews in the age of emancipation were insecure, fearful that their social and legal gains would be taken from them if they failed to lead exemplary lives, act according to English norms, and remain unobtrusive.[92] While such fears can be found to some extent everywhere during the last two centuries, they were not pervasive in England at this time, certainly not among those who shaped the institutional life of the community. Only toward the end of the century, with classical liberalism under attack and nationalism and anti-semitism on the rise, did such fears gain ground and begin to shape communal policy—especially in regard to the newcomers from Eastern Europe.

Chief Rabbi Hermann Adler in full ecclesiastical costume. Leslie Ward's *Vanity Fair* caricature of 1904. From a private collection.

CHAPTER 4

Native Jews and Foreign Jews (1870–1914)

Between 1881 and 1914, 120,000 to 150,000 East European Jews settled permanently in Great Britain, effecting a radical transformation in the character of Anglo-Jewry. Their poverty, occupations, and foreignness drew unwanted attention to them and native-born Jews alike, fueling the fires of xenophobia and antisemitism. By virtue of their numbers, they swamped the established community and gave Anglo-Jewry, once again, a foreign-born, lower-class cast, which disappeared only in the mid-twentieth century. Furthermore, their behavior rubbed against the comfortable grain of native Jewish patterns, creating intracommunal friction. Their old world religious practices offended those accustomed to the polite but somnolent atmosphere of anglicized synagogues. They balked at recognizing the authority of the chief rabbi, his reverend ministers, and the Board of Deputies, while, in politics, a vocal minority embraced radical causes—socialism, anarchism, Zionism—that were believed to threaten native Jewish interests. But, at the same time, they guaranteed the demographic survival of British Jewry into at least the twenty-first century. For without this infusion of new blood, the small, increasingly secularized, native-born community, left to itself, would have dwindled into insignificance, as drift, defection, and indifference took their toll.

It is impossible to know the exact number of East European immigrants who settled in Britain. This is in part because the government began to collect figures on the arrival of aliens only in 1890 and then failed to identify Jews as such. But even if such figures were available, they would not indicate the number of Jews who became permanent residents, since many who landed at British ports did not intend to remain in the country and soon left for the United States. In fact, due to intense competition on Atlantic emigrant routes, it was cheaper at times to sail from Northern Europe to Hull and Grimsby and then from Liverpool to America than to make the trip directly. Some arrivals continued their journey after a few days, but others remained for weeks, months, even years. And some never left at all, whether from inertia, a lack of funds, personal ties, or unexpected good fortune. Thus, the number of foreign-born Jews in Great Britain at any point during the period of mass migration was substantially greater than the number who in the end became permanent members of the community. This had the effect of raising immigrant visibility and thus contributed to the widespread perception that unregulated immigration was a social evil.[1]

Contrary to popular myth, East European immigration did not begin with the pogroms that swept through Bessarabia and Ukraine in 1881. Polish Jews first arrived in London in the eighteenth century, part of a long-term westward migration from Central and Eastern Europe that has yet to run its course. Their numbers increased noticeably in the 1840s. By mid-century, as noted earlier, Polish and Russian Jews were considered a major burden on communal funds in London, Liverpool, and Manchester. In 1850, they constituted about one-tenth of the Jewish population in Manchester; at the end of the decade, more than one-fifth; by 1875, between one-half and two-thirds. When Joseph Jacobs calculated the size of British Jewry in 1883, he estimated that twelve thousand Russian and Polish Jews had settled in Britain in the previous fifteen years. In the next two decades, the pace of immigration jumped. It hit new peaks in the years 1903 to 1906 and then fell when the restrictionist Aliens Act took effect that year, only to increase again just before World War I. During this period, the number of immigrants each year ranged from three to eight thousand persons.[2]

The most fundamental cause of emigration from Eastern Europe was the failure of the Jewish economy to grow as rapidly as the Jewish population. Between 1800 and 1900, the Jewish population of the Russian empire shot from one million to five million persons, exclusive of the one million who emigrated before the end of the century. (The Jews of Galicia, who enjoyed Habsburg tolerance but contributed to the migration current nonetheless, increased from 250,000 to 811,000.)[3] During this same period, tsarist policy toward Jews oscillated between schemes to coerce their russification (through military service or education in state schools, for example) and measures to accomplish the reverse, that is, to isolate them from contact with sections of Russian society considered too weak to resist their alleged depredations—the peasantry, in particular.[4] Measures with the latter goal in mind constricted Jewish economic activity and caused increasing immiseration over the course of the century. As the number of Jews exploded, the government repeatedly imposed limits on their ability to support themselves. With the exception of certain privileged persons, Jews were forbidden to live outside the Pale of Settlement, Russia's westernmost provinces, and thus were denied access to those cities and regions where industrialization was creating new opportunities. At the same time, the government undertook steps to remove Jews from border regions and the countryside and concentrate them in the Pale's overcrowded cities. There artisans and petty traders faced mounting competition from each other and, in the case of the former, from factory production as well. General conscription of Jewish males, imposed in 1873, as well as countless arbitrary acts of cruelty, made material immiseration seem even more unbearable.

In this context the pogroms of 1881 and the repressive legislation that followed were more catalyst than cause. Spreading fear and despair throughout Poland and Russia, they convinced the young that they had scant hope for a better future under tsarist rule. They accelerated a decades-old movement, causing migration to assume a momentum and life of its own. Personal exposure or immediate proximity to mob violence was not necessary to set people in motion. The first waves of immigrants to Britain came disproportionately from northern districts in the Pale, which were hardly touched by the pogroms of 1881. In Habsburg Galicia, which remained relatively free of pogroms throughout this period, a higher proportion of Jews migrated than in Russia. Here economic backwardness propelled migration—to Britain, the United States, and the Habsburg capital, Vienna.[5]

Like earlier Jewish immigrants to Britain, most—about 60 to 70 percent—settled in London, primarily in the East End. Long a point of arrival for newcomers, the East End offered opportunities for employment, was home to synagogues and other institutions necessary to lead a traditional Jewish life, and, above all, was the chief residence of fellow Yiddish-speaking Jews who had arrived earlier in the century. East European Jews were also attracted to Manchester, with its growing clothing industry, and in much smaller numbers to established provincial communities such as Liverpool, Birmingham, and Glasgow, where they found opportunities in tailoring, market trading, and peddling. The one new center to emerge at this time was Leeds, whose community numbered a mere 144 persons at the time of the 1851 census but then began to expand in the 1860s with the arrival of Russian and Polish Jews seeking employment in its burgeoning men's clothing industry. Its population then shot from almost one thousand in 1871 to about twenty thousand on the eve of World War I.[6] Small but once flourishing communities in southern seaports and pre-industrial market towns failed to attract immigrants, and most disappeared, while new communities were founded or existing ones reinforced in manufacturing and mining towns in the North, the Midlands, and Wales. By the end of the century, for example, there were small Jewish trading communities in most industrial towns in the valleys of South Wales. In addition, communities in port towns on the indirect "land" route to the United States—Grimsby, Hull, and Newcastle on the eastern coast and Liverpool on the western coast—grew as transmigrants failed to resume their journey.[7]

As a result of East European immigration, the Jewish population of Britain was close to 300,000 on the eve of World War I. Communities were to be found in dozens of locales in England, Scotland, and Wales—as well as in Belfast, Cork, Limerick, and Dublin. Still, 80 percent of Britain's Jews chose to live in just three places: London (180,000), Manchester (30,000), and Leeds (20,000). The communities in Liverpool (8,000), Glasgow (7,500) and Birmingham (6,000) accounted for another 7 or 8 percent. Given this degree of geographical concentration, the history of British Jewry from the end of the nineteenth century to the present is in essence the history of these six communities. What happened elsewhere, however piquant or arresting in human terms, reveals little about the main currents of Anglo-Jewish history.

The newcomers found employment in two broad areas of economic life—retail trade (shopkeeping, pawnbroking, street and market trading) and small workshop manufacture. In a break with previous immigrant custom, only a minority (certainly less than one-third) earned their living on a regular basis as small traders. To be sure, it was still not difficult to take up peddling: Jewish warehouses gave credit on lenient terms; communal charities and kith and kin offered loans to purchase stock; little knowledge of English was required. But in London the rewards were less certain than before due to the increase in retail shops. Nonetheless, when immigrants in depressed industries were out of work, which was often, they took to peddling and market trading temporarily. In this sense, the line between workers and traders was not hard and fast: immigrants moved back and forth as the economic climate changed. However, in provincial communities in the Midlands, the

Sunday market in Petticoat Lane, London. *The Graphic,* 16
November 1889. Courtesy of the Harlan Hatcher Graduate
Library, University of Michigan.

North, Scotland, and Wales, immigrant traders were more common.
For example, in 1891, 35.2 percent of employed Jews living in the Gorbals, Glasgow's immigrant quarter and poorest working class area,
worked as hawkers, peddlers, and travelers, while another 13.4 percent
earned their living as dealers and shopkeepers.[8] In other words, almost
half made their living in petty commerce. Immigrants in provincial
towns found opportunities in adjacent rural districts, in mining villages

and mill towns, to which they journeyed from their homes on a daily or weekly basis. (Polish-born Michael Marks [1863–1907], cofounder of the Marks and Spencer empire, launched his career in retailing as an itinerant peddler visiting the villages around Leeds.) Some became weekly payment travelers (known as Scotch drapers or tallymen), taking orders door-to-door for handkerchiefs, bedding, household textiles, children's clothing, shawls, and even boots. They delivered the ordered goods on their rounds the following week and then called weekly until the goods were paid for.[9]

Most immigrants, however, entered the British economy as workers in sweated industries (see below), not as peddlers and costers. In London, Manchester, and Leeds, the characteristic immigrant worker was employed in a small, insalubrious workshop producing inexpensive clothing, footwear, or furniture. Almost two-thirds of male workers in London in 1901 were found in these three trades, with tailoring representing almost half the total. In Leeds, where the growth of the Jewish community was linked to the men's clothing industry, 72 percent of employed adults in 1891 were in the tailoring trade. The link between the industry and the Leeds community was so close that even as late as the 1920s 62 percent of men who married in local synagogues were tailors or in some way connected to the trade. By contrast, in Glasgow, as in other small provincial communities, workshop manufacture was less dominant. In the Gorbals in 1891, 33 percent of employed persons were in tailoring and 13 percent in other areas of manufacturing, mainly cigarettes and picture frames.[10]

Immigration from Eastern Europe, in addition to transforming the occupational structure of British Jewry, also marked the reappearance of Jewish women in the working population. In the Georgian period, women routinely worked in shops, market stalls, and streets, either on their own or alongside their husbands. The straitened circumstances in which most families lived required women to be active in economic life. However, as Jewish families achieved middle-class status and came to share Victorian values about female roles, women withdrew from the marketplace and confined their activities to the domestic sphere, with an occasional foray into public life for philanthropic work. With no economic task to perform, they took on new roles—as managers of households bursting with children, servants, and possessions; as overseers of social calendars crowded with dances, teas, dinners, at-homes, concerts, each with its own elaborate protocol of correct behavior and dress; and even as informal religious guides to their children, a role traditionally performed by fathers.

Yet Jewish women never disappeared completely from the market-place, since need always forced some native-born women either to make their own living or supplement what their husbands earned. But because East European immigrants arrived almost penniless, like Central European Jews a century earlier, large numbers of women again entered the labor force, not as street traders this time, but as workers in the same sweated industries as men (with the exception of cabinetmaking).[11] In the ready-made garment trade, women worked as basters, fellers, buttonhole makers, and, less frequently, as cutters, pressers, and tailors, the latter being largely the domain of male workers. In the cap-making workshops of Stepney, the center of the London trade, there were as many female as male workers in 1911. In cigar and cigarette making, where the introduction of machines had reduced the need for skilled male hands, women came to outnumber men.[12] Women immigrants were also active in traditional areas of commerce. They kept food shops, sold clothing and household items in markets and from their homes, worked as credit drapers, newsagents, tobacconists, and shop assistants. For all of these women, work was a necessity, either because the chief breadwinner in the family earned too little or because, as widows or abandoned wives, they had to support themselves and possibly young children as well. Accordingly, immigrant women tended not to leave the workforce after they married, in contrast to the pattern that developed in the next generation. What changed after marriage was the venue of work, with subcontracted home-work, such as buttonhole making or cap making, replacing outside employment. Although it paid less well, home-work allowed women to take care of household chores and mind their children while continuing to contribute to family earnings. Many also earned extra income by taking in boarders.

The distinctive occupational profile of the immigrants is explained by their previous work experience in Eastern Europe and by the opportunities for employment they found in their new home. In the Pale of Settlement, one-half the workforce at the end of the century was employed in handicraft and industrial manufacturing (largely of clothing and footwear) and somewhat less than one-third in trade.[13] The occupations of those who traveled to Britain roughly reflected this distribution. In a sample of about nine thousand immigrants who received aid at the Jews' Temporary Shelter in the East End between 1895 and 1908, 29 percent said they had been garment workers, 11 percent boot- and shoemakers, 8 percent carpenters, and 23 percent traders.[14] On arrival, then, most immigrants found work similar to that which they or their relatives had performed in the old country.

The immigrants were able to do this because those who had preceded them had established an economic beachhead in these areas. It is sometimes assumed that the Jewish connection with small-scale manufacturing began with mass migration in the 1880s, but in fact it started much earlier. There were Jewish workshops in London and Manchester producing clothing, footwear, hats and caps, furniture, cigars, and waterproof garments (in the case of Manchester) from the 1840s.[15] Communal philanthropy before 1880 tended to reinforce this connection. The Jews' Hospital apprenticed most of its male inmates to masters in these trades, while in 1861 the Board of Guardians introduced a hire-purchase scheme that allowed tailors and dressmakers to acquire sewing machines from the Board by making small weekly payments. (It was discontinued in the late 1870s when the manufacturers introduced a scheme of their own.) The Board also enabled workers in other trades—glaziers, carpenters, cabinetmakers, shoemakers, printers, and bookbinders—to purchase tools and equipment on a similar basis.[16]

When the number of East European Jews reaching Britain accelerated in the 1880s, immigrant districts—the East End in London, Strangeways and Red Bank in Manchester, the Leylands in Leeds, the Gorbals in Glasgow—were already dotted with small workshops, presided over by Russian- or Polish-born masters who had themselves been poor a decade or two earlier. Given this and, of course, the character of the Jewish economy in Poland and Russia, it should astonish no one that the bulk of the newcomers went to work in the sweated workshop sector of manufacturing. While it was not unknown for immigrants to seek and be refused employment in Gentile-owned enterprises,[17] the impact of discrimination on occupational choice in the immigrant generation was, overall, minimal. Most newcomers never looked for work outside the Jewish sector, preferring to labor among their own kind, in trades they already knew well, for masters who, however harsh, at least spoke their language and were sometimes willing to accommodate their religious requirements.

To the misfortune of the immigrants, the trades they entered were in decline and characterized by low wages, long hours, irregular or seasonal employment, and poor working conditions. Earlier in the century the production of numerous consumer goods had shifted from a skilled artisanal basis, in which one individual crafted an item from start to finish, to a workshop and outwork basis, in which entrepreneurs provided raw materials to laborers paid by the piece, each of whom performed only part of the manufacturing process, often in his or her own home. Extensive division of labor and subcontracting, along with the introduction of the sewing machine in the clothing trades in the 1860s, permitted masters to exploit both skilled and unskilled workers and either to forestall or to compete with factory production. Goods produced in this fashion were "cheap and nasty," intended for the low end of the market, the working and lower-middle classes, whose income and appetite for ready-made, mass-produced footwear and clothing were on the rise. This mode of production, known as "sweating," a reference to the unventilated, fetid rooms in which workers toiled, was well established in the tailoring and shoemaking trades by the 1840s, as was the term itself, decades before it became associated with East European Jews.[18]

The arrival of tens of thousands of immigrant workers fueled the growth of the sweating system. Because work was subcontracted and a minimum of capital required to set up as an "independent" master, hundreds of small workshops sprang up in immigrant districts. In London, there were over one thousand by the late 1880s, most with a handful of workers. A survey prepared for the pioneer urban investigator Charles Booth in 1888 found 571 workshops making men's coats in less than one square mile in and around Whitechapel. Of these, over 70 percent employed fewer than ten workers, while less than 3 percent employed more than twenty-five workers.[19] In the clothing industry, immigrant workshops manufactured garments for merchants and wholesale clothiers, both Jewish and gentile, who supplied them with cloth, often already cut. In Leeds, which was unique in this respect, large factories subcontracted work to immigrant workrooms when demand was high, which had the advantage of allowing the factories to operate with less fixed capital than would otherwise be required.[20] The dependence of small masters on wholesale clothiers and large merchants meant that work was seasonal and irregular, and security of employment nonexistent. Masters hired and fired as orders rose and fell. Because new workers continued to arrive, flooding the labor market, there was little incentive to retain a permanent staff, especially since many tasks required little skill and were easily learned. This stream of new arrivals also guaranteed that wages remained low, a problem aggravated in trades like slipper making in which the workshops were fighting a rearguard action against increasingly mechanized factory production.

Working conditions in immigrant trades were notorious, attracting the attention of social reformers, journalists, politicians, and public health officials. Workshops were housed in garrets, cellars, backrooms in private homes, stables, disused sheds, crumbling warehouses. Most were overcrowded, dimly lit, poorly ventilated, littered with refuse, and permeated with foul odors. Toilet facilities were scandalous. It was not unusual for inspectors to find floors smeared with feces, toilets leaking water onto workroom floors, and unenclosed urinals. In Leeds, for example, in 660 inspections at 182 Jewish establishments in 1891, the local medical officer's staff found 301 cases of defective ventilation, 226 cases of dirty workrooms, and 180 cases of dirty toilets. In addition, they found that 59 workshops lacked any form of drainage and 55 were without indoor toilets.[21] The health of workers who toiled fourteen- to eighteen-hour days in conditions like these suffered irreparable damage. Tailors, for example, contracted respiratory diseases from working in damp, steamy, overheated workrooms and inhaling toxic fiber particles. Their eyesight, like that of others who performed close work in dim light, was damaged as well. Women workers, according to one physician, were commonly afflicted with "malformation of the vertebrae, pains in the back, swelling of the veins and of the articulations, tumors at the femur and legs, malformation of the pelvis, disorder in the menses, eczema, miscarriages."[22] How widespread were work-related health problems? In Leeds, one out of five Jewish military recruits in World War I was rejected—three times the rate for non-Jews—the chief reasons being lung disease and myopia. In London, tuberculosis dominated the agenda of the Board of Guardian's Sanitary Committee from the late 1890s until World War I.[23] Although government regulation of workshop labor was introduced in 1867, enforcement provisions were inadequate. Further legislation in 1871, 1878, 1891, 1895, and 1901 eliminated loopholes and strengthened inspection, so that in the decade and a half before the war some progress in tackling unsanitary conditions was made. But, in general, even with adequate legislation, local authorities were ill-equipped to police the ocean of small workshops in which immigrants labored.[24]

The low wages, insecure employment, and unspeakable working conditions that characterized the sweated trades sparked the formation of a vocal workers movement in the immigrant community.[25] The first industrial dispute in which Jewish workers took collective action actually predated the period of mass migration by two decades. In the winter of 1857–58, London Jewish cigar workers, most of Dutch origin, struck their Jewish employers, accusing them of halving wages when trade was depressed and then recruiting foreign workers willing to work for less.[26] But it was the expansion of the sweated labor system from the 1870s that created widespread worker discontent and thus the basis for collective protest. The initial impetus came from radical ideologues who had received their political education in the tsarist empire. In 1872, Louis Smith (d. 1931), a veteran of the Polish revolt of 1863 and the Paris uprising of 1871, arrived in London and soon founded a union of Lithuanian tailors in Whitechapel, the first in modern Jewish history. It enrolled 72 members but collapsed after a few weeks, following which Smith left for the United States.

The next attempt came four years later and was, like the first, rooted in the revolutionary politics of the Russian empire. In August 1875, Aron Liberman (1849–80), a radical maskil and revolutionary socialist, advocate of both the reform of Jewish society and the overthrow of the tsarist regime, arrived in London, having escaped a government raid in Vilna. Liberman became a writer and typesetter for Peter Lavrov's London-based *Vpered!*, the leading Russian revolutionary journal of the period, but also turned his attention to the immigrant workers of the East End. Unlike many East European radicals, he embraced rather than rejected Jewish national solidarity, believing that Jewish workers should constitute an autonomous unit within the international socialist movement.[27] To mobilize the immigrant masses, he established in May 1876 the Union of Hebrew Socialists in London (Agudat ha-sotsiyalistim ha-ivrim be-London), whose task would be to forge a trade union of Jewish clothing workers. The Union met twenty-six times before its demise in December and at its peak counted thirty-eight members. Its campaign to mobilize workers on behalf of socialism, launched at a well-attended public meeting on 26 August, was a total failure. Liberman's intemperate attacks on religious leaders as part of the exploiting class created a storm, alienating many potential members. In addition, few workers were interested in socialism as a solution to their distress. The new tailors union that was formed rejected Liberman and his Jewish socialism. Although three hundred members were recruited by mid-September, the union was moribund within a few months, its treasurer absconding to America with its funds. In 1883, Isaac Stone, one of the ten original members of the Union of Hebrew Socialists, made another effort to organize a tailors union, but it too rapidly collapsed.

In Leeds, meanwhile, workers succeeded in creating trade unions without help from refugee intellectuals. In 1876, they created the Leeds Jewish Working Tailors' Society, inspired to a large extent by the Leeds branch of the Amalgamated Society of Tailors. In the Leylands, as opposed to the East End, Jewish workers were less isolated from other workers and more aware of the quickening pace of unionization during the 1880s and 1890s. At the same time, local trade unionists viewed the unionization of sweated labor as a matter of self-preservation: raising wages and improving conditions among foreign workers would eliminate unfair competition and benefit unionized English workers. Although Jews in the Leeds tailoring industry formed their own labor organization, there was, nonetheless, a marked degree of interaction with local trade unionists and socialists. In 1884, the Jewish tailors union, along with the newly founded pressers and machinists unions, affiliated with the Leeds Trades Council. The next year, when the tailors struck, for the first time and with some success, winning a reduction in hours, a gentile boot maker and socialist, James Sweeney, served as secretary of their union. When the tailors next struck in 1888—this time without success—Sweeney and two other gentile members of the Socialist League directed their strike. The Jewish unions collapsed after this defeat, but with the formation of the Leeds branch of the Gasworkers' and General Labourers' Union in 1889, tailors, machiners, and pressers formed a Jewish branch of the general union. At its peak, it enrolled almost 50 percent of the immigrant tailoring force. This arrangement lasted only until late 1891 or early 1892, but when immigrant workers reorganized in 1893, their new union developed close ties with the English union representing workers in the wholesale clothing factories, and in 1915 the two joined four other unions to create the National Union of Tailors and Garment Workers.

In Manchester as well, Jewish trade unionism developed within the context of the larger labor movement. The earliest steps in the immigrant sector were taken when a deputation of cigarette makers who wished to form a union approached the Manchester and Salford Trades Council for advice in February 1889. They established a local branch, with a Jewish secretary and a largely Jewish membership, of a national union, the Cigarette Workers and Tobacco Cutters Union. That same year Jewish male workers in the waterproof garment industry established a general union whose membership was largely but not exclusively Jewish. (Female workers were, with few exceptions, Christians.) Jewish cabinet makers joined the East Manchester branch of the general union that represented workers in the cheaper end of the trade, while Jewish boot- and shoemakers affiliated with the local branch of the National Union of Boot and Shoe Operatives, accounting for one-half of its members in 1890. In fact, the only explicitly Jewish union to be established in Manchester was in tailoring, which employed more Jews than any other trade. Unionized English tailors and the Trades Council encouraged and aided its establishment in 1890 and gave active support and guidance when it conducted its initial strike that year.

In London, on the other hand, where there was less interaction between English and Jewish trade unionists, there was, concomitantly, more input from radical émigré intellectuals. The latter gained a voice in the immigrant community in 1884 when Morris Winchevsky (1856–1930) and E. W. Rabbinowitz (1853–1932) established the first radical Yiddish newspaper anywhere, *Der Poylisher Yidl* (The little Polish Jew). Sixteen weekly issues appeared, and then Winchevsky, who objected to Rabbinowitz's policy of accepting advertising from bourgeois politicians and religious organizations, left to establish his own nonpartisan socialist organ, *Der Arbeter Fraynd* (The worker's friend), which first appeared in July 1885. With articles on the sweated trades and capitalist exploitation, Winchevsky aimed to arouse the social consciousness of the immigrants and mold them into a radical mass movement. To this, he added elements of national solidarity and populism, urging Jews, like other oppressed peoples, to unite to help one another and defending the immigrants' honor and language (Yiddish) against the slanders of acculturated native Jews.

That same year a group of radicals close to Winchevsky acquired premises in Berner Street in the East End for a workers educational club. The Berner Street Club, as it was known, soon became a base for union and radical activity throughout the immigrant community. In 1886, the club took control of *Der Arbeter Fraynd,* providing it with a home and its own printing press. The club offered a range of activities—lectures on politics, economics, and literature; plays, concerts, and dances; English-language classes for new arrivals—and, although many came for social, not political, reasons, it still served to heighten political consciousness in the East End. Radical societies and trade unions met there; William Morris and other members of his Socialist League (the only English socialists sympathetic to Jewish workers)[28] addressed immigrant audiences there; strikes, rallies and marches were planned there. In the second half of the 1880s, "London was even considered the hub of the emergent [worldwide] Jewish labor movement, and its socialist journal, *Arbeter fraynd,* enjoyed a following in New York."[29]

At first, the Berner Street Club and *Der Arbeter Fraynd* served both social democrats and anarchists, who managed to overcome their ideological differences in order to work together. Within a few years, however, cooperation became difficult and then impossible. By 1888, the anarchists, who had formed their own group, the Knights of Labour, emerged as the larger, more active element. In 1891, in the wake of a series of London tailors strikes in 1889–90 that failed, they gained control of both the club and the newspaper. In the next few years, most of the leading social democrats in London, including Winchevsky, the newspaper's then editor Philip Kranz (1858–1922), and assistant editor Benjamin Feigenbaum (1860–1932), left for the United States, where they believed the ground was more fertile for building a mass Jewish workers movement. (There were ten times as many Jewish workers in the United States, as well as precedents for political mobilization on the basis of a foreign language.) The more sectarian anarchists thus came to dominate radical East End politics until World War I. Forced to vacate their Berner Street premises in November 1892, they remained homeless, wandering from one meeting place to another, until 1906, when they opened a new club in a former Methodist church in Jubilee Street, which, as before, attracted a diverse group of politically minded immigrants — social democrats, anarchists, Bundists, Zionists — as well as immigrants more interested in the club's dances, lectures, plays, concerts, chess matches, bar, and library. In 1898, the German Gentile Rudolf Rocker became associated with East End anarchism and soon emerged as its dominant figure. A superb orator in Yiddish, Rocker devoted his life to the immigrant workers cause until he was deported, as an enemy alien, at the start of World War I.[30]

The scope of radical influence in the East End is difficult to gauge. In terms of numbers, both anarchists and social democrats failed to create mass movements of like-minded believers and remained little more than sect-like coteries. Their failure was due, in part, to their aggressive atheism, which manifested itself in incessant attacks on Jewish religious customs and leaders. Although most immigrants were not scrupulous in their observance of traditional ritual, they were not militant atheists either, ready to throw overboard their inheritance. Speeches and articles lampooning Yom Kippur and Passover, which were observed almost universally in immigrant districts, repelled rather than attracted potential followers, as did the anarchists' notorious Yom Kippur balls. Nonetheless, it is clear that as agitators and publicists they contributed to the political education and empowerment of sweated workers and in this fashion encouraged the growth of trade unionism. In addition, in periods of intense labor activity, they offered counsel and support to those engaged in collective action, occasionally moving into positions of leadership.

Although indifferent or hostile to ideological radicalism, East End workers were not averse to engaging in collective action of a pragmatic kind to improve their lot. In the mid-1880s, more than a dozen unions formed under worker leadership in the tailoring, shoemaking, cigarette, cabinetmaking, and stick-making trades. Small and unstable, many were gone before the end of the decade. But, then, as militant strikes of unskilled English workers—match girls in 1888 and dockers and gas workers in 1889—rocked London, Jewish trade unionism acquired a new lease on life. Inspired by the "new unionism," which advocated the organization of all unskilled workers and the use of aggressive tactics, new unions formed and old ones revived. In September 1889, as many as ten thousand garment workers went out on strike for a twelve-hour day and a ban on taking work home at the end of the day. They obtained a reduction in hours but soon employers were undermining the negotiated agreement, and unsettled conditions returned. The following year boot- and shoemakers and stick makers also conducted mass strikes. In the clothing trades, the subdivisional system of labor made unified action difficult. Between 1880 and 1910, separate unions represented, at one time or another, ladies' tailors, gents' tailors, machiners, pressers, plain machiners, underpressers, waistcoat makers, military tailors, and trouser makers. In 1896, there were thirteen Jewish trade unions in London; by 1902, thirty-two, of which twenty-six had been founded in the previous six years. A mass strike of three tailoring unions in 1906 gained little, and workers quit in droves. A semblance of stability came only when small unions amalgamated and when, in the wake of a successful mass strike of East and West End workers in 1912, unions representing half of London's organized Jewish tailors became branches of the national Tailors' and Garment Workers' Trade Union.

English labor leaders at the time often maintained that Jews were reluctant and unsuccessful trade unionists because of their assertive individualism and chaotic indiscipline. This essentialist assessment, which, in truth, reveals more about English constructions of the Jew than it does about Jewish workers, missed the mark completely. Immigrant Jews failed to build stable, powerful unions because of the structure of the sweated trades, especially in London, rather than because of allegedly innate character traits. The multiplication of small workshops, the division of the manufacturing process into unskilled or semiskilled tasks, the abundance of cheap labor, the lack of social distance between masters and workers, the seasonality of work, and the tyranny of fashion—all combined to hobble trade union activity in sweated trades. In London, in particular, where small-scale production of consumer goods and luxury items was the dominant form of manufacturing, trade unionism in general made little progress, certainly in comparison to the Midlands and the North. London was, in Eric Hobsbawm's words, "a trade union desert." From this perspective, the immigrant record was similar to that of other London workers. Indeed, in tailoring, it was better: in 1914, of the 8,300 male and female tailors in London who were unionized (out of a total of 65,000), 5,600, or 65 percent, were Jewish and 2,700, or 35 percent, were English — at a time when Jews were 30 percent of the total number of tailors.[31]

The industrial strife and radical politics of the immigrant quarter have suggested to some historians that this period witnessed the emergence of a Jewish working class. In their view, repeated clashes between workers and masters, along with ideological guidance from socialist and anarchist activists, led sweated workers to view themselves as a discrete social formation, with class interests that set them apart from other Jews, among them being a collectivist, communitarian vision of the future. According to this perspective, full-blown class warfare raged in the immigrant community, with modern class relationships eventually replacing older ties of ethnic and religious solidarity.[32] This perspective replicates for Anglo-Jewry the once-popular view of early-twentieth-century British society, which, it was believed, witnessed the consolidation of two polarized classes and the domination of the political process by class conflict. Marxist and Marxisant historians found evidence for their view in the explosive growth of trade union membership, unprecedented industrial unrest (with waves of strikes in the late 1880s and the early 1910s), and the formation of the Labour Party in the first decade of the new century.

The view that a Jewish working class came into being in this period is a minority view, but the language of class is so pervasive that historians of all political shades routinely use the term "working class" in regard to the immigrant community. To the extent that this characterization is meant to convey the occupational structure, poverty, working conditions, and labor struggles of the East European community, it is apt. It is also useful as a heuristic device to underline the transformation in the occupational makeup of the lowest strata within the Jewish community — from street traders to sweated workers. However, to claim more than this is problematic. Jews were not oppressed proletarians in the Marxist sense, working in large industrial enterprises, waiting to have their class consciousness awakened. In the small workshops where they toiled, they and their employers shared a common culture and background. Workshop masters were not acculturated, well-to-do native-born Jews with their own distinctive values but themselves uprooted aliens, earlier arrivals usually, who had managed, by saving and/or borrowing, to set themselves up as petty capitalists.[33] Joseph Finn (1865–1945), general secretary of the United Ladies' Tailors Union from 1893 to 1895, noted that 90 percent of the masters in the mantle trade in the first decade of the twentieth century were former members of his union.[34] That Jewish masters exploited Jewish workers is without question, but it must be remembered that they in turn were subject to merciless exploitation at the hands of the largely English wholesale houses and retail merchants for whom they worked on a contract basis. Under intense pressure to produce more goods at lower prices—there was always another competitor bidding to do the same work for less—their failure rate was high. Workers rose into and fell from master status with regularity. Viewing them as two distinct social formations, each with its own value system and cultural outlook, separated by a great divide, is a distortion. Just as the gap between capital and labor in British society was not deep and irreconcilable, so too the difference between masters and workers in immigrant society was not hard and fast.

Most workers, moreover, aspired to be independent, to leave the ranks of those who labored for someone else, even if few succeeded. In this regard, it should be remembered that those Jews who left Eastern Europe were not fatalistic. They uprooted themselves because they believed they could take fate in their own hands and change their life chances. Driven, ambitious, more optimistic than pessimistic, they viewed economic betterment as something within their reach. After all, they had before them evidence of the possibilities of mobility: the masters who employed them were former workers like themselves. The opportunity structure of garment manufacturing also fueled their aspirations. Ambitious men could set up as producers with relative ease: it required only a few pounds, lent in some cases by the Jewish Board of Guardians.[35] Using their own homes as shops, putting family members to work while toiling themselves alongside their hired hands, sweated workers transformed themselves into small manufacturers. (Whether they remained so is a different matter.)

If Jewish workers harbored bourgeois aspirations, then how can this be reconciled with their support for trade unionism? In fact, there is no contradiction. Like their British counterparts, most Jewish workers who joined unions did so for immediate, short-term, pragmatic ends—to raise wages and improve working conditions—rather than for radical, ideology-fueled, political goals. Such behavior, utilizing collectivist means to achieve individualist ends, is not inconsistent with aspirations for mobility. This is not to say that socialism made no converts among the immigrants or that those who had been converted earlier in Eastern Europe lacked influence. Their message repeatedly stirred workers to organize in defense of their own economic interests but, in the end, failed to convince the majority that the capitalist system needed to be overthrown. The pioneer sociologist and demographer Jacob Lestschinsky (1866–1976), himself a socialist, estimated that in 1907 there were only two hundred Jewish socialists in London.[36] However, since the Jewish radicals of the East End were vocal, high-profile activists whose interests at times meshed with those of nonideological workers, their views and perceptions, including their insistence on the class character of immigrant society, have been accorded undue weight—both by historians and by leaders of the native community at the time.[37]

To label immigrants as working class also risks missing one other dimension of their economic behavior. As I noted above, although only a minority of the newcomers regularly earned their living in petty commerce, a much greater number took to market or street trading at one time or another in their lives. When out of work or underemployed or when trade took a permanent downturn, as in boot making after 1900, sweated workers became hawkers, market traders, tallymen, peddlers, costermongers—petty capitalists, if you will. While the number who gained practical business experience in this fashion cannot be known, the evidence from oral histories suggests that it was not uncommon.[38] This is important because it seems likely that retail trade, rather than small-scale manufacturing, provided the most common way out of poverty for immigrants and their descendants.[39] Unfortunately, because social mobility has not been a major theme in British historiography, in contrast to the United States, there are no quantitative studies of changes in immigrant economic status that would indicate its contours and frequency.

In the absence of such work, an alternative indicator of economic improvement before World War I is geographical dispersion, movement out of areas of first settlement, with their crowded streets, substandard housing, and lack of amenities. In London, before 1900, better-off immigrants were found living to the east of the old Jewish quarter, in Stepney Green, Bow, and Poplar; to the north, in Victoria Park, Hackney, and, to a lesser extent, Dalston; and even to the west of the City, in Soho and Notting Hill. Enough East European tailors, dealers, stall-holders, and small shopkeepers lived in Notting Hill by 1900, for example, to establish a congregation. By the 1890s, 30 percent of the members of the East London Synagogue in Rectory Square, Stepney Green, which adhered to the anglicized ritual of the mainstream United Synagogue, were foreign-born.[40] In the provinces, a similar development occurred; new immigrant residential concentrations appeared in Hightown and Higher Broughton in Manchester and Camp Road and Chapeltown in Leeds.[41]

When outsiders visited the East End (or its provincial counterparts), they tended to see its filth, congestion, and bewilderingly foreign character, and often little else. The inhabitants of immigrant districts seemed to be dark, alien, ill-mannered creatures. Their speech, gestures, dress, comportment, shop signs, and wall posters (in Yiddish) revealed their foreign origins. Even the smells encountered there were un-English: "a blended and suffocating odour, as of fried onions and burnt bones, dirty clothing and stale fish, decaying vegetables and over-ripe fruit," as the socialist journalist Robert Blatchford observed.[42] The reality was more complex. What outsiders could not see was the rich organizational life of the immigrants, the extensive network of institutions they created to meet their religious, cultural, social, and political needs. In London and the largest provincial communities, they created a sophisticated, almost self-sufficient subculture of their own. The Jewish East End became for more than a few newcomers to London, especially those who failed to learn English, a social and cultural ghetto they rarely left.

With few exceptions, immigrants chose to worship in synagogues of their own rather than those of the established community, even when the latter were nearby. The solemn atmosphere, English-language sermons, begowned clerics, choral music, and stately architecture of English synagogues were unfamiliar, intimidating, and smacked of Christian influence—in addition to which, their membership fees were beyond the reach of all but the most successful newcomers.[43] Instead, immigrants worshipped in small, self-administered congregations, known as hevrot (societies, literally), housed initially in homes, workshops, and other makeshift premises. In these unassuming surroundings, they were able to worship in the informal, enthusiastic manner to which they were accustomed, to enjoy liturgical honors frequently and at little cost, and, in general, to feel at ease with their compatriots and their God. Some hevrot were established by persons from the same East European locale, such as the Krakow and Berdichev hevrot in Manchester, the Marianpol hevrah in Leeds, and the Kalisch, Kovno and Lodz hevrot in London. Still others were characterized by a specific orientation within traditional Judaism, such as Hasidism, or devotion to a particular religious obligation, such as visiting the sick, reciting Psalms, or studying the Talmud. In addition to serving as houses of worship, most hevrot also functioned as friendly societies, providing sickness, death, and mourning benefits. The largest were able to employ rabbis of their own, fellow immigrants, to teach Talmud, render legal decisions, and deliver homilies at life-cycle events, while the smallest were forced to rely on their own members to conduct services and do whatever teaching they could. In time many hevrot grew into small and medium-sized synagogues and acquired premises of their own.

The male children of the new arrivals, with the exception of those enrolled in communal schools, received after-school religious instruction in the hundreds of hadarim (private, one-room schools) that sprang up in immigrant districts. In 1891, for example, there were already more than two hundred hadarim in the East End, enrolling about two thousand boys, ages five to fourteen, who paid weekly fees of 6d. to 1s. 6d. Run by poorly paid, much maligned melammedim, the hadarim provided an elementary, unsystematic knowledge of liturgical and biblical Hebrew. In some cases, hevrot maintained their own hadarim or banded together to do so, in which case the level of instruction improved somewhat. Eventually, immigrants in the largest cities established their own communal religious schools, known as talmud torahs, to provide supervised, graded instruction in improved physical surroundings on an after-school and Sunday basis. In 1904, the talmud torahs in the East End enrolled between 2,500 and 3,000 students; another 3,000, it was estimated, were being educated in hadarim. In 1910, the Manchester Talmud Torah enrolled 600–700 children. The best Hebrew instruction was found in the innovative schools established by Zionists, in which Hebrew was taught as a modern language, according to the *ivrit be-ivrit* (literally, Hebrew in Hebrew) method. The most famous was the Redman's Road Talmud Torah of J. K. Goldbloom (1872–1961), which in 1914 had over 600 children at its main site in East Stepney and another 350 at an annex in Bethnal Green. Similar ivrit be-ivrit schools were opened in Leeds, Glasgow, and Liverpool, while the Manchester Talmud Torah also adopted the method for a number of years.[44] Early in the century, small circles of pious immigrants established yeshivot—the first in English Jewish history—in London (1903), Manchester (1911), Leeds (1912), and Liverpool (1914).[45]

Although immigrant religious and educational institutions were Orthodox in character, it cannot be inferred that most immigrants remained (or ever were) steadfast in their observance of Jewish law. Granted, they showed little interest in the demure, latitudinarian Anglo-Judaism of the native community or its Reform offshoot, but for many this had less to do with religious principles than with cultural and status differences. Immigrant institutions reflected the only form of Judaism known in Eastern Europe. However, in terms of personal observance, the religious behavior of immigrants exhibited greater diversity, ranging from obsessive devotion to outspoken hostility. Some had loosened the yoke of religious law before emigration—even Russia and Poland were not cut off from the winds of change—but most arrived with at least a nominal attachment to Jewish practice. In the communities from which they came, however, Jewish observance had been embedded in the fabric of daily routine; it was what one social scientist has dubbed "milieu piety."[46] But in Britain, the social and cultural framework was different. Immigrants encountered a broader range of acceptable forms of behavior and suffered no formal or informal sanctions if they departed from communal norms. Added to this were economic pressures to work on the Sabbath.[47]

This meant that the institutional profile of the immigrant community was Orthodox, but, on close inspection, the behavior of all or even most of its individual members was not. Alongside those who remained loyal to old ways, there were others who, while not rejecting the authority of traditional Judaism, adopted a selective attitude toward its customs and laws. The Rumanian-born writer Maurice Samuel (1895–1972), who grew up in Manchester before World War I, wrote many years later that the religious life of his family, which was not atypical, would have seemed "grotesquely eclectic or haphazard" to a truly Orthodox Jew. They ate only kosher foods but did not keep separate sets of dishes and utensils for meat and milk; they attended synagogue on the major festivals but not on most Sabbaths. They fasted on Yom Kippur and the Ninth of Av, recited Psalms on solemn, critical occasions, like births and serious illness, and strictly observed traditional mourning rites. His father, he recalled, "having lapsed into average piety from a higher standard in Rumania," no longer recited weekday morning prayers, wrapped in tallit and *tefillin,* but on the Sabbath, though failing to attend synagogue, he abstained from work and smoking. Most immigrants eventually became more casual or lax in their observance than this. On the first day of Passover in 1903, for example, according to a newspaper census of religious worship in London, only about a quarter of the adult immigrant population attended services. In Sheffield, most men in the immigrant congregation worked on Saturdays—the majority were market traders—and came to synagogue only on Rosh Ha-Shanah and Yom Kippur or to say kaddish for their parents.[48]

For immigrants who no longer found fulfillment in religion, fraternal orders and Jewish nationalist societies (the latter will be discussed in chapter 5) provided institutional frameworks for companionship and sociability. While many hevrot functioned as friendly societies, mutual aid societies also flourished, some patterned on the English model, with elaborate rites, ornate costumes, and secret passwords. The first, Achei Brith (Brothers of the covenant), was established in 1888. In London in 1901, there were 13 Jewish orders (Achei Brith, Achei Emeth [Brothers of truth], the Grand Order of Israel, and the Hebrew Order of Druids were the largest) with 71 affiliated lodges and a further 117 independent lodges, whose membership totaled almost 23,000 persons. In addition, there were Jewish lodges of English orders, mainly the Ancient Order of Foresters (750 members in 1911), and independent friendly societies (that is, not linked to hevrot), some of which were organized on a trade basis, others on place of origin. As protection against economic distress, the lodges and friendly societies were more popular and effective than trade unions. The lodges, in particular, performed important social functions as well. Their rituals and costumes fed their members' sense of self-esteem, while their complex hierarchy of grandiloquently titled offices and ranks provided opportunities to gain recognition.[49]

In addition, successful immigrants established charities to offer aid to needy fellow newcomers. While the native community supported an extensive relief network, to be discussed below, whose resources were greater than those of the immigrants, its agencies imposed conditions that excluded many would-be recipients and conducted business in a manner that both humiliated and intimidated clients. Immigrant-initiated charities operated on more traditional Jewish lines, attempting to preserve the dignity of those whom they aided. Typical of such charities was the Russian Jews' Benevolent Society in Manchester, founded in 1905 by successful shopkeepers belonging to the Bardichever Synagogue. The society provided interest-free loans and, beginning in 1910, distributed meat before the Passover festival. Unlike the city's Jewish Board of Guardians, it dealt with applicants in their own language, questioned them in their own homes, rather than requiring their presence at a quasi-public hearing, and exerted no pressure to change their cultural and religious habits.[50]

In London, Yiddish-language newspapers of various political and re-ligious outlooks, including three dailies by the 1890s, served the immi-grant community. Touring companies offered melodramas, lightweight musical comedies, operettas, and Yiddish translations of stage classics. At first, they performed in rented halls and clubs, later in purpose-built theaters, the most famous of which was the Pavilion Theatre in the Whitechapel Road, which presented Yiddish-language productions from 1906 to 1935.[51] Immigrants with sufficient command of English, as well as their English-educated children, of course, also attended En-glish music halls, then at their zenith, and the newest mass entertain-ment, the cinema. For the young seeking to meet the opposite sex, there were dances at local halls, visits to coffee houses, and, in London, prom-enades along the wide pavements of the Whitechapel Road. For men, young and old, there were gambling dens, billiard halls, boxing clubs, and race tracks. In general, only those born or raised in England or those living in small provincial towns regularly ventured outside their own communal turf in search of entertainment or pleasure.[52]

The most sustained interaction between the immigrants and English culture occurred in local, state-supported schools. Although Jewish char-ity schools (to be discussed below in the context of native anglicization schemes) continued to educate substantial numbers of poor children, most received their basic education at board schools, that is, state-financed, nondenominational primary schools run by municipal boards of education established under authority of the Education Act of 1870. In the East End, there were sixteen board schools by 1905 that were overwhelmingly Jewish in composition. In these "Jewish" board schools, the calendar was adjusted to accommodate the Jewish Sabbath and festivals, and Judaism classes were offered after regular school hours.[53] Along with "Christian" board schools and Christian voluntary schools, which some Jewish students attended, they introduced the sons and daughters of the immigrants, ages five to thirteen, to English cul-ture: its language, literature, customs, values, traditions, myths, recrea-tions. As vehicles for anglicization, they reached greater numbers of immigrant children than the schools and clubs sponsored by the native elite. In fact, while some parents refused to send their children to com-munal schools because of their explicit commitment to anglicization and low standards of Hebrew instruction, they willingly sent them to non-denominational board schools.[54] What they failed to realize, however, was that state education worked just as effectively to reshape their chil-dren as did the elite's communal schemes. In a myriad of subtle and not so subtle ways, children learned to regard whatever was English as preferable to the old world habits of their parents. One scholarship boy at the Davenant Foundation School in the Whitechapel Road recalled, "The unspoken but quite clear message of that school was: 'Now, if you accept what we have to offer, we might, after seven years of concentrated endeavour, turn you out as a passable imitation of an educated member of the English middle class.'" The teachers maintained "a deafening silence" about their students' culture, showing "not a jot of awareness" of their "sensibilities, embarrassments and particular kinds of ignorance." This produced a growing feeling "that you came from a substandard culture although you probably couldn't express it," another former student remembered.[55] The decline of Yiddish and religious observance, so noticeable in the interwar period, was rooted to a great extent in this school-based exposure to English culture.

The un-English character of the aliens, as well as their numbers, unsettled communal leaders, causing them to seek ways to accelerate their anglicization. This effort, more than any other item, dominated the agenda of the established community in the decades before World War I. Before we can examine the anglicization campaign, however, we must first understand what alarmed communal leaders about the newcomers. But to do this, it is necessary to expand the context of the discussion and examine changes occurring in the political climate in England and the relationship between these changes and views about the place of Jews in English society. To anticipate what follows, it can be said that England discovered it had a "Jewish Question" in the last decades of the nineteenth century.

Before the late 1870s, Jews did not loom large in the political or cultural imagination of the English. There was no widespread obsession with Jews at any level of society as there was in German-speaking lands, no leap to define what was English by reference to what was Jewish. In politics and culture, the "other" was more likely to be a Catholic, an Irishman, a Frenchman, or one of England's colonized peoples than a Jew.[56] It can even be said that in the debate over Jewish legal disabilities the Jews themselves—their religious beliefs, social habits, occupational profile—were a side issue. For it is now agreed that parliamentary emancipation "concerned Jews only incidentally" and was, at bottom, part of an ongoing debate about the place of the Church of England in national life, a debate into which the issue of Jewish disabilities was inserted.[57] Nonetheless, in that debate notions of the national collectivity were articulated with the potential to marginalize or exclude Jews. Thomas Babington Macaulay, for example, argued that emancipation would cure the Jews of their "exclusive spirit." Realizing that they owed their good fortune to the state that treated them as equals, they would become patriotic Englishmen. What he omitted to say was what would occur if they failed to transcend their former clannishness and become good citizens. On close examination, there was, then, some ambiguity about the character of emancipation, about the terms on which Jews were to be included in the political nation, although at the time it had no impact.

During the same decades that Jewish disabilities were being debated in Parliament, Jews and Judaism were topics of discussion in other public forums as well. Conversion-minded evangelical Christians pilloried Judaism in sermons, lectures, pamphlets, newspaper articles, and books, harping especially on its "degeneration" into "rabbinism." Alexander McCaul's *The Old Paths* (1837), which claimed that Christianity was the continuation of true Hebraic religion and that contemporary Judaism was a corrupt, scheming invention of the ancient rabbis, sold ten thousand copies in its first year and appeared in a second edition in 1846.[58] While works like *The Old Paths* caused few, if any, Jews to change their religion, they were effective in reinforcing hoary stereotypes about Jewish "legalism" and "talmudism." Beginning in the 1850s, liberal religious thinkers also contributed to the defamation of Judaism. Belief in the historical, evolutionary character of revelation led them to view Judaism as a primitive or arrested stage in the development of true religion. In presenting their own vision of Christianity, they denigrated Judaism as a narrow racial religion of prohibitions and punishments, the possession of one people, without universal import. The new critical biblical scholarship from Germany, with its evolutionary bias, reinforced this kind of supersessionist understanding of Israelite religion and further strengthened the view that contemporary Judaism was fossilized and unspiritual. Although expressed in Victorian theological garb, these characterizations of Judaism were not, in fact, new.

At a more popular level, in novels, newspapers, and the theater, malicious or crude images of Jews were common fare.[59] Charles Dickens, William Makepeace Thackeray, and Anthony Trollope, as well as dozens of less talented scribblers, unhesitatingly incorporated grasping, lisping Jews into their fiction and journalism. Whether they balanced them with saint-like Jews, like Dickens, or with equally corrupt and squalid Christians, like Thackeray, is beside the point. They manipulated stereotypical Jewish characteristics for artistic ends because they knew intuitively that these would strike a chord with their audience. This is the reason that Jewish readers were so delighted with the publication of George Eliot's

Daniel Deronda in 1876. Her celebration of Jewish family life and idealized Jewish characters—the visionary Mordechai, the devout Mirah, the high-minded Daniel—were genuinely novel. Eliot was also the first major writer to portray Jews living happily in an intact family situation, rather than as isolated individuals, like Fagin in *Oliver Twist,* or members of broken families, like Shylock in *The Merchant of Venice.* The *Jewish Chronicle* was rapturous, believing that Eliot's Jews would counter the "bad" Jews that novelists regularly fed the public.[60] This also explains why Jewish writers before Eliot, like Grace Aguilar (1816–47) and the Moss sisters, Celia (1819–73) and Marion (1821–1907), populated their work with impossibly noble Jews.[61]

Recourse to negative representations was routine and unthinking—one example will have to suffice. In September 1852, the Great Synagogue in Duke's Place, London, reopened after having been closed for renovations. The event was marked with a celebratory weekday afternoon service, to which *The Times* sent a reporter. His sneering account of the occasion drew on a common stock of crude popular images that marked Jews as alien and inferior. To reach the synagogue, he wrote, he was forced to pass through "narrow courts and squalid streets reeking with mouldy odours" and "strange alleys impregnated with the scents of fried fish and mouldy wardrobes." The male worshippers, whose respectable dress surprised him, were remarkable for their "much begemmed fingers and shirt fronts, radiant with every variety of precious stone." What convinced the reporter that he was in the midst of "a distinct race" was their faces, which "were not European or, at all events, were not English." The service itself was "not consonant with our notions of reverence and religious propriety." The reader chanted the prayers in a "nasal snuffling tone"; some congregants burst into "wild ejaculations, which tapered off into growling murmurs"; others muttered to themselves; still others were "half-singing, half-talking, the whole forming a chaos of uncouth sound."[62]

Paradoxically, these images do not correlate with the actual legal and social status of Jews. Just as Charles Dickens was no implacable enemy of the Jews, despite his diabolic Fagin, so it is doubtful that *The Times* correspondent wished to deny Jews a voice in local and national politics or bar them from sitting on juries, owning landed estates, or entering the learned professions. Clearly, there was a gap between how Jews were represented and how they fared in social and political life. The former reflected inherited beliefs, the accumulation of centuries of Christian contempt, while the latter testified to more immediate realities. Few

Englishmen felt compelled to pursue the logic of their inherited views, perhaps because their faith in them was half-hearted and inconsistent with other, competing views, or perhaps because other "others"—Catholics, the Irish, and the non-white peoples of the British Empire—absorbed their energy and interest even more. Whatever the reason, English statesmen, clerics, and men of letters, as well as those for whom they wrote, were not obsessed with Jews, viewing them as a source of national degeneration or casting them as the antithesis of authentic Englishness. (There were, of course, exceptions, like the journalist and radical William Cobbett, who, in his idealization of preindustrial England, associated Jews with rampant capitalism and corruption.)

In the late 1870s, this started to change. Public attention became focused on Jews more frequently and intensely than before, and, while Britain was not gripped by the kind of *Judenhetze* that seized Germany, Austria, and France, there was, nonetheless, a "Jewish Question" by the turn of the century. Liberal and Radical criticism of Disraeli's policy toward Turkey in the period 1875–78 and, in particular, his apparent indifference toward the massacre of Bulgarian Christians, marked the start of this new, more insistent concern with Jews. Critics explained Disraeli's policy by reference to his racial origins: Jews and Turks, both oriental peoples, were allied against the Ottoman Christians. Some went further: they indicted English Jews as a body for supporting Disraeli's "anti-Christian" policy and claimed that British interests were being subverted to serve those of Jewish bondholders. Both accusations implied that Jews were unpatriotic, their attachment to British interests tenuous.[63]

The Boer War (1899–1902) triggered similar accusations of Jewish manipulation of British foreign policy. Liberal and socialist critics of imperial expansion claimed that Jewish financiers in London and Jewish mine owners in Johannesburg had pushed Britain into war in order to safeguard and extend their interests in South Africa. Again, the charge was that Jews were cosmopolitan and unpatriotic, committed above all to their own far-flung material interests. What was novel in this was the conspiratorial note, the contention that there was an international Jewish capitalist network capable of bending journalists and statesmen alike to its own ends. This view, moreover, was not confined to a lunatic fringe but was common in respectable Liberal and Labour circles.[64]

The same theme, that alien Jewish financiers conspired to corrupt British politics, was later struck in the Marconi scandal of 1912 and the Indian silver affair of 1913. In the former case, the postmaster general,

Benjamin Disraeli. Carlo Pellegrini's *Vanity Fair* caricature of 1869. From a private collection.

Herbert Samuel (1870–1963), was accused of awarding a telegraph contract on unusually favorable terms to the (English) Marconi Company,
whose managing director, Godfrey Isaacs (1867–1925), was a brother of
the attorney general, Sir Rufus Isaacs (1860–1935). Samuel and Isaacs,
as well as other Liberal politicians, were also accused of using official
information to speculate in Marconi shares. In the Indian silver affair,
Herbert Samuel's elder brother, Sir Stuart Samuel (1856–1926), MP for
Whitechapel, and his first cousin Edwin Montagu (1879–1924), parlia-

mentary undersecretary for India, were accused of obtaining a secret contract for the family bullion brokerage firm, Samuel Montagu & Co., to purchase £5 million of silver for the Indian government.[65] In neither case was there legal wrongdoing, but the mere appearance of illicit activity was sufficient to unleash a stream of crude antisemitism that, again, was not limited to the political fringe. The most virulent attacks in the Marconi affair were launched by Hilaire Belloc and the brothers Cecil and G. K. Chesterton, whose hostility to Jews was linked to their opposition to liberalism, their backward-looking Catholicism, and their nostalgia for a medieval Catholic Europe that they imagined was ordered, harmonious, and homogeneous.

The Jew baiting at the time of the Boer War and the Marconi scandal was linked to a broader protest, mounted in the main by the Radical wing of the Liberal Party, against the growing visibility of successful businessmen in national life and their challenge to what were seen as traditional English values. Critics of the new plutocrats took aim at a wide range of targets: the growing love of luxury and display, the self-indulgence of the very rich, the raffishness of the Prince of Wales' set and later Edward VII's court, the sale of honors to "cosmopolitan" financiers and businessmen, the promotion of shaky ventures, and the scramble for instant wealth.

Frequently, but not invariably, the attack on plutocracy took on an anti-Jewish cast. While the baiting of rich Jews was not novel, the social phenomenon that inspired this bout of rich-Jew antisemitism was the startling increase in the number of very wealthy Jews and their admission into high society in the half-century before World War I. This period was the golden age of the City of London, the apogee of its influence in world trade and finance. Jewish families in banking, brokerage, and international trade amassed enormous fortunes, thanks in great part to the City's ascendancy. Some, like the Rothschilds and Goldsmids, traced their roots in England to the eighteenth century; others, like Ernest Cassel (1852–1921), Maurice de Hirsch (1831–96) and the Sassoons, were newcomers, attracted to London because it was the hub of international finance and trade. They were joined by a handful of "Randlords," like Alfred Beit (1853–1906) and Barney Barnato (1852–97), "obscure" men who had acquired their fortunes in the diamond fields and gold mines of South Africa. The number of Jewish millionaires in Britain during this period, relative to other top wealth holders, was unprecedented. Jews constituted 12 percent of non-landed millionaires who died in the 1890s, 14 percent in the 1900s, and 23 percent in the 1910s. (In contrast, in the decades from 1920 to 1970, the number was never more than 9 percent.)[66]

Material success kindled their social ambition. By the 1880s, rich Jews had made their way into the drawing rooms and dining rooms of smart society, their entrance made possible by aristocratic willingness to absorb new wealth whatever its origins, industrial, financial, or mercantile, American or Jewish.[67] The most visible sign of Jewish integration into high society was the inclusion of wealthy Jews—Rothschilds, Sassoons, Cassel, Hirsch, and the newspaper proprietor Edward Levy-Lawson (1833–1916)—in the intimate circle of the Prince of Wales.[68] This, and other dazzling social triumphs, underwritten in every case by lavish entertainment and opulent display, bred resentment and envy. Old aristocratic families rooted in country life, those who held aloof from London's "smart set," were shocked by the admission of Jews into high society.

The Duchess of Buccleuch, a bitter opponent of "the vulgarism and ostentations of the smart set and notable for her insuperable objections to the publicity of illustrated papers and society gossip," only once stooped "to entertain a Jew, whom she did not know, as a specially marked compliment to the Prince of Wales."[69] Antisemites of the Belloc-Chesterton school viewed this incursion as a sign of national degeneration.

But, above all, it was immigration from Eastern Europe that focused attention on Jews. The number of newcomers in itself was not the problem—the Jewish population never exceeded one percent of the total population of Britain—but, rather, their concentration in three or four urban centers, the East End of London preeminently, which was already the focus of much middle-class concern. From the 1860s, educated opinion increasingly believed that the presence of a nonindustrial, casual laboring class in the heart of the capital—described variously as immoral, vicious, besotted, atheistic, and feckless—threatened Victorian civilization.[70] A growing literature, both serious and sensational, highlighted the social problems of "Outcast London" in general and the East End in particular, starting at least a decade before Jewish settlement in the area evoked concern. The poverty, overcrowding, and sweated labor associated with the new arrivals fed the debate about the condition of the masses, heightening existing anxieties about moral and physical degeneration and national competitiveness. One historian of opposition to immigration has even concluded that "had economic deprivation and social concern not given the East End prominence, the immigrants would have gone unnoticed."[71] At the same time, the fact that the immigrants were Jewish added another dimension to the debate. Essentialist notions of Jewish behavior, rooted in centuries-old ill-will but expressed often in up-to-date racial language, were evoked to explain the baleful consequences of Jewish immigration.[72]

Discussion of the aliens was linked to social realities, but it was also clouded by intolerance and fear. Residents of the East End and middle-class visitors alike viewed immigration as a foreign invasion, turning once-English districts into "little Jerusalems" and "little Palestines." Native workers felt overrun and displaced as immigrants flooded in and occupied street after street. With Jews accounting for almost one-half the population of Whitechapel and St. George's in the East, a witness told the Royal Commission on Alien Immigration in 1903, "the feeling is that there is nothing but the English going out and the Jews coming in." A local borough councilor complained that as he walked through Mile End or Cable Street he saw that "the good old names of tradesmen have gone, and in their places are foreign names of those who have ousted Englishmen out into the cold." In Whitechapel, a Christian social worker noted, "the English visitor feels himself one of a subject race in the presence of dominant and overwhelming invaders."[73] The districts into which Jews moved already lacked sufficient housing, as a result of slum clearances and demolitions for railways, warehouses, and streets that started in the 1860s. Willing to suffer overcrowding and pay higher rents (offset in part by taking in lodgers), the newcomers exacerbated the housing shortage. The increased demand allowed landlords to raise rents and demand so-called key money, which in turn made East End housing a speculative investment for successful immigrants. The result was that native, non-Jewish tenants were forced to seek lodging elsewhere.[74]

The immigrants were also held responsible for introducing the sweating system, with its low wages and terrible working conditions. Considered more pliant and adroit than native workers, assumed to be content with a lower standard of comfort, the immigrants were blamed for undercutting and replacing local artisans. For critics of unfettered capitalism like J. A. Hobson and Beatrice Potter, immigrant virtues—thrift, industriousness, sobriety, drive—were vices. They saw hard-working immigrants as fierce individualists, devoid of social morality, bent on underselling their competitors. Although unbiased observers noted that sweating was well established before the mass migration from Eastern Europe, Jews became linked with it in the popular imagination. And, while most Jewish workers did not compete with English workers (except in branches of men's tailoring), the sweeping accusation that aliens caused low wages and swelled the casual labor force took hold, becoming an idée fixe.

In addition to the issues of housing and employment, the basic strangeness of the immigrants—their language, diet, gestures, religion, work and social habits, even poverty—provoked indignation and unease. Unaccustomed to mass immigration (aside from the long-established flow from Ireland), Englishmen regarded the establishment of foreign "ghettos" in their midst with alarm. They regarded the aliens as filthy, clannish, indecent, impious, and, in the view of some, subversive. They were affronted because the aliens worked on Sundays, slept outside on hot summer nights, ate herring and black bread, and read Yiddish newspapers. Their fundamental grievance, of course, was that the immigrants were not English, a truth recognized at the time by Canon A. S. Barnett, warden of the Whitechapel settlement Toynbee Hall, who noted that "the prejudiced Englishman is apt to call 'dirty' whatever is foreign."[75]

Sensational crimes in East London became focal points for the articulation of anti-alien sentiment. The trial and conviction of the immigrant stick maker Israel Lipski (1865–87) for the murder of Miriam Angel in 1887—he had poured nitric acid down her throat—sparked street fights between Jews and non-Jews in the East End. At his execution, a crowd waiting outside Newgate Prison broke into prolonged cheering when the signal came that he had been hanged. According to the *Evening Standard*, the murder underlined how Polish Jews, "a social cancer," blighted the districts they occupied, lowering the standard of living and morality alike. The unsolved Jack the Ripper murders the following year—six East End prostitutes were killed and disemboweled from August to November 1888—provoked hysteria and near riots. Rumors spread like wildfire: no Englishman could have committed such horrible crimes; the women were victims of ritual murder; the murderer was a *shohet* (ritual slaughterer), knowledgeable in anatomy, steeped in talmudic fanaticism, with his own arsenal of knives. When one of the victims was found near the Jewish anarchist club in Berner Street, the *Church Times* claimed the murderer was a Russian Jewish anarchist. (Suspicion also fell on the Duke of Clarence, a son of Queen Victoria; a barrister who resembled the Duke of Clarence; a Russian secret agent; a local midwife; and a "mad" doctor, none of them Jews.) In the Jack the Ripper murders, social tensions and deep irrational fears linking Jews with blood, murder, and revenge mixed easily. The criminal acts of a band of non-Jewish Latvian anarchists and social democrats — their attempted robbery of a Tottenham rubber factory in 1909 ("the Tottenham Outrage") and burglary of a Houndsditch jeweler in 1910, as well as the shoot-out in which two of them died in 1911 ("the siege of Sidney Street") — suggested that the East End harbored wild revolutionaries and prompted calls for strict immigration controls. And the rise of London as a way station in the burgeoning Jewish traffic in prostitution between Eastern Europe and Argentina drew further unwanted attention to the immigrants, adding the charge of sexual corruption to the list of ills they brought with them.[76]

In the mid-1880s, massive unemployment, which owed little to the Jewish influx, and fears of worker violence sparked the first calls to restrict immigration.[77] In response to the outcry, the House of Lords appointed a Select Committee on the Sweating System in 1888 and, that same year, the House of Commons established a Select Committee on Alien Immigration. Neither recommended legislative action. As a rule, Liberals opposed aliens legislation because of their faith in free trade, whether in goods or persons. Conservatives tended to be more protectionist in their views, but the leadership was not yet ready to abandon free trade and free asylum. In the 1890s, pressure mounted outside Westminster to slow or halt the flow. The Association for Preventing the Immigration of Destitute Aliens, which was run by the antisemitic publicist Arnold White and the Tory democrat and Fair Trader the Earl of Dunraven, met for the first time in 1891. The Trades Union Congress passed resolutions against free immigration in 1892, 1894, and 1895, arguing that alien Jews undercut British labor. And in the election of 1892, most Conservative candidates in the East End demanded restrictions on immigration. But the Liberals, in office from 1892 to 1895, remained firm in their commitment to free trade and unrestricted immigration.

When the Conservatives returned to power in 1895, the government was unenthusiastic about introducing aliens legislation. The prime minister, Lord Salisbury, did not share the views of those in his party who wished to attract working-class voters with measures to remedy unemployment and regulate labor. Intraparty pressure came from backbenchers, many representing East London constituencies, who, whatever their personal views, recognized the electoral appeal of an anti-alien mix of populist protectionism and patriotic nationalism, the latter shading at times into blatant antisemitism. Sir Howard Vincent, MP for Sheffield and head of the anti-alien camp in Parliament in the second half of the

1890s, introduced immigration bills, unsuccessfully, in 1897 and 1898, as did Lord Hardwicke in the Lords in 1898.

After 1900, the Conservative leadership was less able to withstand backbench demands to regulate immigration. The British Brothers League, an anti-alien pressure group founded in 1901 by William Evans-Gordon, MP for Stepney and successor to Vincent as leader of the anti-alien campaign, claimed a membership of twelve thousand, concentrated mostly in the East End. It staged enthusiastic public meetings, including one at the People's Palace in January 1902 that attracted more than four thousand persons, and gathered forty-five thousand signatures on an anti-alien petition. Popular agitation in the East End, reinforced by rich-Jew antisemitism, lent weight to demands in parliament for legislation to protect the nation from the invasion. Bowing to pressure, the government, now led by Arthur James Balfour, announced the appointment of a Royal Commission on Alien Immigration in March 1902. Its report, issued in August 1903, concluded that there was no case for a total ban on immigration but recommended that several classes of undesirable immigrants be excluded, that immigrants be banned from settling in overcrowded districts, and that undesirable aliens already in the country be repatriated. Balfour introduced a bill incorporating these recommendations in 1904, but the Liberal opposition prevented it from passing. The following year a less exclusionary bill passed and became law in August, the Liberals this time offering mere token opposition. The Aliens Act empowered immigration inspectors to exclude immigrants without means, unless they were seeking admission solely to avoid religious or political persecution. Although the Liberals swept back into power in a landslide victory in the election of 1906, they made no effort to repeal the law, which was a popular measure, but their enforcement of its provisions was half-hearted.[78]

Given the zeal of the restrictionists, the act that passed was narrow in scope, admitting even pauper aliens if they were victims of persecution. Thus the law discouraged, but failed to halt, the East European influx. The annual number of immigrants from the Russian empire dropped at first, but then, beginning in 1912, rose slowly to five thousand persons in 1914, which was, in fact, the annual average for the entire period 1881–1905. The decrease, however, resulted less from Jews being refused entry on arrival—a little more than four thousand were turned away between 1906 and 1910—than from smaller numbers seeking admission in the first place, for as word of the act spread in Eastern Europe, Britain became a less desirable goal for migrants than the United

States.[79] What can never be known, of course, is how much greater the flow would have been if there had been no controls whatsoever. That the Jewish community, then and now, would have been larger seems certain.

Although narrow in scope and loosely enforced, the act was a watershed in one important sense. In the two centuries before its passage, successive British legislatures ignored the presence of Jews in the country, except in those instances when Jews themselves demanded laws to relieve their disabilities. No government introduced legislation to regulate Jewish occupations, religious life, social habits, communal organization, residence, dress, or immigration, all of which were objects of legislation elsewhere in Europe in the eighteenth and nineteenth centuries. Broadly speaking, there were two reasons for this. First, unlike their counterparts in Central and Eastern Europe, Britain's governors did not view Jewish behavior as a threat to the social or moral fabric of the nation. They lacked that obsessive concern with Jews that surfaced periodically in German, Russian, Austrian, Hungarian, Polish, and even French political life. Second, for a complex of reasons, the British state was less inclined than other states to take legislative action in order to maximize public happiness and productivity. There was no tradition of a strong, bureaucratically swollen, centralizing state, endowed, in Matthew Arnold's words, "with stringent powers for the general advantage, and controlling individual wills in the name of an interest wider than that of individuals."[80] For most of the Victorian period, there was a broad consensus that state power was to be minimized and individual freedom and responsibility enhanced. Unnecessary state intervention was condemned as immoral, as destructive of personal character. But toward the end of the century, the confidence and prosperity that sustained liberal dogmas started to crumble. Britain's worldwide industrial dominance, especially in metals and heavy, chemical, and industrial engineering, was under attack from German and American competition; the rate of industrial profits was falling; the social consequences of unregulated capitalist development were becoming more blatant. Optimism was giving way to caution, unease, even outright pessimism. Fears about national decline—economic, cultural, racial—surfaced and took hold. England felt vulnerable and less confident than earlier in the century. The "old" liberalism was not working. From 1880, emerging political groupings demanded a more responsible, activist, tutelary state. Under the banner of communitarian social morality, they called for state intervention to restrain marketplace competition, restore the material and spiritual health of the nation, and, in an era of heightened imperial rivalries, strengthen its military and economic fitness. The Aliens Act of 1905 was part of the legislative response to this call. It signaled the decline of the once regnant "old" liberalism and heralded "a transformation of the regulatory ambitions of the British state and a reorientation of the idea of the nation."[81]

Despite heightened hostility to Jews in this period, antisemitism was neither as virulent or explosive as in other European states nor as successful in derailing Jewish integration. With one exception, violence before World War I was limited to random, localized outbreaks of short duration in working-class districts where Jewish immigrants were concentrated. Crowds leaving the mass meeting staged by the British Brothers League at the People's Palace in January 1902, for example, turned rowdy and attacked Jews and Jewish property, while in 1898, 1901, and 1903 there were attacks, sparked by the housing crisis, on Jews in Mile End, Shadwell, and Bethnal Green respectively. In Manchester, Leeds, and London, adolescent gangs harassed immigrants, crossing into Jewish districts on weekends when drunk, and street fighting erupted between them and Jewish gangs, but violence like this, to which antisemitism gave an edge but was not central, was common at the time. As a rule, immigrants rarely ventured into rough streets and districts known to be hostile to Jews, even when nearby. In this way, residential segregation tended to minimize friction. Still, even if violence was rare, both native and foreign Jews were nervous, fearing the worst. Pogroms in Russia and anti-Dreyfus riots in France, as well as minor eruptions at home, convinced them that mob violence was possible. In his Rosh Ha-Shanah sermon at the Great Synagogue in London in 1899, Hermann Adler told his listeners that events in Paris were "a handwriting on the wall," a warning "to be more cautious and circumspect than ever before." It even has been suggested that Simeon Singer (1848–1906), minister of the fashionable New West End Synagogue, counseled the unfortunate Israel Lipski to confess to Miriam Angel's murder in order to forestall violence.[82] The one major outbreak before World War I, the exception mentioned above, occurred in South Wales in August 1911, when working-class mobs looted and destroyed Jewish shops in Tredegar and ten surrounding towns, inflicting damage estimated at £12,000 to £16,000. A full explanation for the South Wales riots is still not possible. What is clear is that a mix of causes contributed to the violence, including xenophobia, Nonconformist antisemitism, Jewish rack-renting, and labor unrest.[83]

While violence was unusual, verbal abuse was both common and unremarkable. It was found throughout English society; neither the well-born and the middle ranks nor the poor and the disreputable thought twice about discussing Jews in terms that the latter considered offensive. Poor Jews met with taunts and catcalls in streets and markets; well-to-do Jews with barbs and slights in drawing rooms and clubs. The Bloomsbury set, for example, which took pride in its contempt for convention, was entirely conventional in its contempt for Jews, despite Virginia Woolf's marriage to one. When John Maynard Keynes wrote to her sister Vanessa in 1917 and 1918, he referred often to "Virginia and the Jew" and expressed his pleasure at visiting Vanessa and finding Virginia but "no Jew." Virginia herself expressed similar attitudes. In 1905, sailing with her brother Adrian to Portugal, she wrote to a friend that there were "a great many Portuguese Jews on board, and other repulsive objects, but we keep clear of them." When Leonard (1880–1969) proposed to her in 1912, she cited his Jewishness as an obstacle to accepting him. "You seem so foreign," she wrote him—which was odd, given his thoroughly upper-middle-class upbringing, his education at St. Paul's and Trinity College, Cambridge, and his total neglect of Jewish rites and lack of interest in his background. When Virginia told friends of her intention to marry Leonard, his Jewishness loomed large in the way she thought about him. She was going to marry "a penniless Jew," she announced more than once. Later, in 1930, she recalled her initial reaction to Leonard and his family: "How I hated marrying a Jew—how I hated their nasal voices, and their oriental jewellery, and their noses and their wattles—what a snob I was." But she never fully overcame her earlier feelings. In 1926, following a tea in honor of Gertrude Stein at the Sitwells, she wrote to Vanessa that the house "swarmed" with Jews. In her view Stein was conceited and her ideas dangerous, but "Leonard, being a Jew himself, got on very well with her." Quentin Bell recalled a visit by the Woolfs in the interwar years, at which, in response to a question being asked, Virginia blurted out, "Let the Jew answer." (Leonard replied, "I won't answer until you ask me properly.") In the published and unpublished versions of "the Jew in the bath" scene in *The Years* (1937), she associated the Jew Abrahamson with contamination. The Jew having a bath in the room opposite the narrator's leaves a line of grease around the tub, the thought of which disgusts her, imperiling her solitude and privacy.[84]

Significantly, sentiments like these were rarely translated into social and political action (the anti-alien agitation was one notable exception).

After all, Virginia did accept Leonard's proposal of marriage, whatever her reservations about Jews. This is not to say that there were *no* obstacles to the social integration of upper-middle-class Jews. There is evidence, for example, that from the end of the century Jewish men experienced difficulty in becoming members of certain clubs.[85] But outright bans were rare. The rigid exclusion of Jews from elite society that was the rule in Germany and the United States at this time was not duplicated in Britain. Neither high society nor the educated middle class closed its doors to Jews, even while viewing them as not quite English or even worse.

In political life, wealthy Jews faced few obstacles to finding a seat in Parliament.[86] Six unconverted Jews sat in the House of Commons in 1869, sixteen in 1906. After the Promissory Oaths Act (1871) made possible the appointment of Jews to ministerial office, neither Liberal nor Conservative leaders were reluctant to promote Jewish MPs. Sir George Jessel (1824–83) became solicitor general in 1871; Henry de Worms (1840–1903) undersecretary of state for the colonies in 1888. Three Jews — Herbert Samuel, Rufus Isaacs, and Edwin Montagu — held office under H. H. Asquith before World War I, a record not equaled until the prime ministership of Margaret Thatcher in the 1980s. Jews also qualified for honors, whether by virtue of their accomplishments or their contributions to party coffers. In 1885, on the recommendation of William Gladstone, Queen Victoria raised Nathaniel de Rothschild (1840–1915) to the peerage, although she had balked at so honoring his father sixteen years earlier. In 1895, Henry de Worms became Lord Pirbright and Sydney James Stern (1845–1912) Lord Wandsworth; in 1907, Samuel Montagu became Lord Swaythling. Jewish knights and baronets were even more plentiful. The first was Moses Montefiore, who was knighted in 1837 following his election as sheriff of London and then made a baronet in 1846 in recognition of his work on behalf of persecuted Jews abroad. By the end of the century, there were more than a dozen Jewish knights and baronets; in the decade and a half before the war, their ranks were swelled by an additional dozen.[87]

It is also significant that the Tories did not officially embrace antisemitism or make it central to their party's message, as did right-wing parties elsewhere in Europe. Of course, they exploited anti-alien sentiment and passed restrictionist legislation, but this was not the same as urging the revocation of emancipation and the exclusion of Jews from the national mainstream, the goal of their continental counterparts. Conservative MPs fighting for restrictionism, like James Lowther and

William Evans-Gordon, not wishing to be branded bigots, denied that anti-alien agitation was "aimed at the Jewish race."[88] Rather, they insisted, it was aimed at aliens, which in a formal sense was true, since neither Jews nor other national groups were mentioned by name in the Aliens Act. In fact, though, this was disingenuous: East European Jews were the only aliens entering Britain in large numbers at this time. What is significant is that restrictionists in Parliament felt compelled to deny their antisemitism. In other national legislatures, it was a badge of honor. Moreover, while antisemitism was central to the anti-alien agitation, especially outside Westminster, support in Parliament for the Aliens Act was not necessarily a vote against Jews. There were Conservative Jewish MPs, including the communal stalwart Benjamin L. Cohen (1844–1909), who supported the act but were not motivated by antisemitism, however strong their dislike of poor, foreign Jews.

If antisemitism in all its varieties was less acute in late-Victorian Britain than in other countries, this does not mean that it was insignificant in its consequences for Jewish behavior. Heightened, most often hostile, interest in Jews had a profound impact on both the private and public conduct of native Jews from the 1880s on. Being associated with alien, un-English customs, with superstition, dirt, clannishness, and crime, with cosmopolitan loyalties, unsettled prosperous Jews whose roots in the country went back several generations. They assumed that political emancipation had resolved Jewish status. They prided themselves on their acculturation and integration, their material and social accomplishments. Now they were less sure of where they stood. Their Englishness appeared open to question, their reception in some circles less warm or assured than before. While their reactions to this new set of circumstances varied, in intensity and kind, in general they strove to reassure their fellow citizens of their basic Englishness while working, at an institutional level, to address those conditions believed to be fostering ill will.

At one level the intensification of antisemitism encouraged native Jews to mute their distinctiveness even further. Their observance of Jewish rituals and customs continued to weaken. Their occupational profile, while still skewed toward commerce, broadened, although slowly. By the early 1880s, Anglo-Jewry included about two hundred professionals (barristers, solicitors, doctors, dentists, architects) as well as a handful of artists, university teachers, writers, scientists, army officers, and civil servants.[89] Well-to-do families began sending their sons to public schools in the 1870s; by the 1890s, there were about a dozen Jewish

Israel Zangwill in his early thirties. Walter Sicket's
Vanity Fair caricature of 1897. From a private
collection.

students at Cambridge, a few less at Oxford.[90] In politics, propertied
Jews in the late 1870s and the 1880s abandoned their monolithic support
for the Liberal party, to which they owed their emancipation, and began
giving their votes and money to Conservatives as well.[91] (This would
have been unthinkable in most European countries, where conservative
parties were invariably antisemitic, in terms of both personnel and programs.) In countless, less obvious, ways too, English Jews were coming
to resemble their socio-economic counterparts in the host population.

This trend would have continued even if there had been no rise in anti-semitism, but what this rise did was to hasten the process and, in some cases, move it in a more radical direction.

This acceleration can be seen in the introduction of religious reforms in the 1880s and 1890s in middle-class, mainstream Orthodox congregations. While respectful of tradition, most English-born Jews were not Orthodox in terms of personal practice. Nonetheless, they were content to remain within an Orthodox congregational framework, in large part because there was no compelling reason to do otherwise. However, in the last decades of the century, as a Jewish Question took shape, congregations in London and the provinces repeatedly petitioned the chief rabbi for permission to introduce changes in the worship service. Some of the changes requested, like eliminating repetition of the amidah, reading the Torah on a triennial rather than an annual cycle, and starting the Sabbath morning service later, were unrelated to the rise of antisemitism and indicated, rather, the advance of secularization and the resulting unwillingness to devote long hours to religious observance. But others were clearly intended to present Judaism in a more acceptable light. These included requests for confirmation services for girls, organ music on Sabbaths and festivals, and public recitation of the ten commandments, whose introduction was intended to demonstrate that Judaism and Christianity shared the same ethical ideals. Those who desired reforms were especially eager to remove liturgical poems (*piyyutim*) that detailed past persecutions and called on God to avenge the deaths of Jewish martyrs. There was also at this time increased concern with matters of decorum, in part, a reflection of growing affluence but also, in part, a response to the ever more common representation of Jews as crude and ill-mannered.[92]

The requested reforms left untouched the central sections of the liturgy, as well as the theological core of rabbinic Judaism, so the Adlers, whose permission was required for liturgical alterations in synagogues under their ecclesiastical authority, were able to sanction those that, in their view, did not violate halakhah. In 1880, for example, Nathan Adler approved the omission of most piyyutim. In 1892, Hermann Adler, who had succeeded his father as chief rabbi the year before, sanctioned a broader range of changes: the omission of the repetition of the amidah, the reading of the decalogue by ministers, the commencement of the Sabbath morning service at the late hour of 9:45, and the introduction of a largely English-language children's service on Yom Kippur and a confirmation-like service for students who completed synagogue reli-

gion classes. Congregations were not required to introduce these reforms, and as a rule those in less fashionable districts balked at doing
so. At the East London Synagogue, where there was little lay enthusiasm
for alterations in the service, traditional members left to form the Stepney Orthodox Synagogue when its reform-minded minister, Joseph
Stern (1865–1934), introduced a mixed choir in 1896.[93]

The Adler-sanctioned reforms of the 1880s and 1890s made native
Orthodoxy more genteel, thus widening the gap between it and immigrant Orthodoxy. But they were still too limited to satisfy some critics,
who in addition to being worried by increasing antisemitism were also
alarmed by spreading religious indifference, which they blamed on the
backward character of Anglo-Jewish Orthodoxy. They demanded a re-
vitalized, even more English Judaism, its ritual and theology adjusted
to the findings of modern scholarship.[94] They could not look to the
West London Synagogue of British Jews as a model, for it had changed
little since its opening in 1842 and had become almost as tradition-bound
as the United Synagogue. It was, moreover, even less successful in stem-
ming indifference: in the religious census conducted by the *British
Weekly* in 1886, the West London Synagogue attracted the smallest number of worshippers (measured as a percentage of seat holders) among
London synagogues. At a series of meetings that began in fall 1901 and
continued into winter 1902, a group dissatisfied with the state of English
Judaism, led by Lily Montagu (1873–1963), daughter of the banker Samuel Montagu, and the Oxford-educated biblical scholar Claude Goldsmid Montefiore (1858–1938), established the Jewish Religious Union.
Its object was to deepen "the religious spirit" among those unsympathetic to services as then conducted or unable to attend because they had
to work on Saturday mornings. Starting in October 1892, the Union
sponsored Saturday afternoon services in rented halls in the West End.
Most of the liturgy was in English; men and women sat together; a
mixed choir sang, with instrumental accompaniment; liturgical references to the restoration of the sacrificial cult, the return to Zion, and
resurrection of the dead were deleted. Since the Union was nondenominational in its aim and its services were viewed as a supplement to,
rather than a substitute for, the traditional Sabbath morning service, it
initially attracted the support of leading figures in mainstream Orthodoxy, including the ministers Simeon Singer, A. A. Green (1860–1933)
of the Hampstead Synagogue, and Joseph Stern of the East London
Synagogue, and the United Synagogue officers Albert Jessel (1864–1917)
and Felix Davis (1863–1916). However, these withdrew eventually, as

Montefiore and Montagu moved the Union in a more radical direction and criticism from Hermann Adler and other Orthodox leaders mounted.

In the years that followed, the Jewish Religious Union evolved into a separate denomination, known as Liberal Judaism, similar in its ritual and theology to the radical form of Reform Judaism then common in the United States. A synagogue was opened in 1911 in Hill Street, Marylebone, and the following year Israel Mattuck (1883–1954), a graduate of the Hebrew Union College in Cincinnati, was hired as its first rabbi. During the interwar years, the Liberal movement became more attractive than Reform Judaism to Jews seeking a modernized faith. Three new congregations were organized between 1921 and 1928 — in North and South London and in Liverpool. In the late 1920s, the three synagogues in London counted somewhat less than two thousand members, drawn almost exclusively from the prosperous, native-born section of the community.

Unlike Reform, Liberal Judaism broke root and branch with traditional Judaism, even its polite English form. Its major thinker, the well-born Claude Montefiore, was a theological radical, much influenced by German Reform Judaism, advanced biblical criticism, and the liberal Christianity of Benjamin Jowett, master of Balliol College, Oxford, where Montefiore was an undergraduate. Montefiore rigorously universalized Judaism, transforming it into a kind of Jewish Unitarianism. He rejected the divine character of the biblical text and the ritual laws that were derived from it, situating final religious authority instead in the conscience of the individual. Inspired by the Prophets more than the Pentateuch, he considered Jesus a Jew in the prophetic tradition and urged Jews to accept those of his teachings that were compatible with their own religion. Although Montefiore believed that Jews were divinely chosen to carry the universal message of ethical monotheism to humankind, which was standard Reform doctrine, he rejected the notion that Jews shared a distinct messianic future or fate. They were not a nation, not even a people, but rather a "religious brotherhood." Because Montefiore himself lacked the drive or talent to launch a movement, the task fell to Lily Montagu, who, aided by her wealth and social connections, became the first woman in Jewish history to lead a religious movement. Organizer, publicist, preacher (from 1918), and leader of services (from 1920), she functioned at times like a modern Reform rabbi.[95] That Liberal Judaism allowed her to do so was indicative of its unprecedented break with tradition.

Neither Montagu nor Montefiore—nor, for that matter, the several thousand Jews who embraced Liberal Judaism—were in conscious flight from their Jewishness. (Jews who were on the road to radical assimilation did not, as a rule, bother with even Unitarian-like Judaism.) But there is no question that their reforms bore the impress of the much discussed Jewish Question. Whether intentional or not, they responded to some of the most common complaints about Jews—their unassimilability, tribal attachments, clannishness, materialism, spiritual backwardness. The Judaism of Montagu and Montefiore suited the outlook of well-to-do Jews who, while wishing to remain identified as Jews, were also sensitive to non-Jewish opinion, perhaps even dependent on it for their own social and psychological well-being. For such Jews, narrowing the gap between Judaism and Protestantism was one strategy for asserting their Englishness, their sense of identity with other Englishmen. Montefiore himself wrote proudly in 1908 that he was "an Englishman of the Jewish persuasion."[96] If there had been no Jewish Question in England at this time, it is doubtful that a movement like this would have arisen.

On the communal periphery, the increase in antisemitism evoked expressions of Jewish self-hatred, a phenomenon encountered infrequently in Britain before this period. In the late 1880s and early 1890s, the writers Julia Frankau (1859–1916), Amy Levy (1861–89), and Leonard Merrick (1864–1939) published novels incorporating crude, antisemitic representations of Jews and Judaism, their object being to demonstrate their distance from other Jews. The first and most notorious, Frankau's *Dr. Phillips* (1887), painted a repellent portrait of middle-class Maida Vale Jewry, the social milieu in which Frankau herself was raised.[97] Her fictional Jews were uneducated, narrow-minded, clannish, vulgar, materialistic, and tasteless. Amy Levy was so depressed and self-hating, which in her case was linked to both her Jewishness and her sexuality, that she killed herself soon after her novel *Reuben Sachs* (1888) appeared. Even Israel Zangwill, who identified with and labored for Jewish causes throughout his life, voiced criticism of and alienation from Jewish life in ways that mirrored antisemitic constructions of Jews and Judaism.[98] Jews who worked and socialized largely with non-Jews were especially prone to expressions of self-hatred. Leonard Woolf felt so embarrassed by his background that he declined to invite his family to his wedding and, in his roman à clef *The Wise Virgins* (1913), a thinly disguised account of his courtship of Virginia, pilloried his mother as an overweight, large-nosed, full-lipped, oriental-looking, stiflingly conventional "Jewess." The Liberal politician Edwin Montagu dismissed his mother's entreaty that he consider marrying a Jew with the rejoinder that not only did he not like Jewish women but that it was wrong "to look for a wife in one set of people." When a character in Saki's novel *The Unbearable Bessington* (1913) declared that no one in England was really an antisemite, her companion replied, "I know a great many Jews who are."⁹⁹

At the communal level, British Jews did not create new agencies to combat antisemitism, as did their counterparts in Germany, Austria, and the United States. They relied, rather, on the Board of Deputies, which continued to pursue the kind of low-profile, behind-the-scenes politics that characterized its work during earlier decades. It functioned, with some success, as a lobby in Parliament to protect the religious rights of Jews serving in the armed forces and other public positions, but its response to more serious threats was weak and provoked calls for greater activism. In particular, its failure to offer an adequate response to a clerical-led, two-year boycott of Jewish shops in Limerick (1904–6), which decimated the community, drew strong criticism and fed discontent over communal governance, which erupted later, during World War I, into a public fight. At the same time, communal leaders urged Jews to curb behavior that attracted unfavorable attention and thus, in their view, contributed to antisemitism. In 1893, for example, the *Jewish Chronicle* chastised those who wore diamonds on "inappropriate occasions" and in "abnormal profusion" and dressed and talked in a "loud" manner. Preachers and editors also targeted unscrupulous Jewish moneylenders for inflaming antisemitism. As an act of "self-defense," the communal worker Oswald John Simon (1855–1932) proposed in 1898, at a time when the House of Commons was conducting a well publicized investigation of moneylending, that synagogues bar moneylenders from membership and reject their financial contributions.¹⁰⁰

The increase in antisemitism also shaped relations between native Jews and foreign Jews. Although sympathetic to the sufferings of Jews under tsarist rule, English Jews believed that unchecked immigration of East European Jews threatened their own status and well-being. It exacerbated existing social problems, such as housing and employment, in the East End, introducing a Jewish dimension to the condition-of-England debate. At the same time it raised the specter of Jewish separatism, suggesting that Jews were a distinct national group, incapable of assimilation. Native leaders reasoned that their community's previous immunity to continental-style antisemitism was due in great part to its willingness to become English. The new immigrant "ghettos" were both an embarrassment and a threat, with the potential, it was believed, to undo the social and political gains made by anglicized Jews. As the *Jewish Chronicle* editorialized, "As long as there is a section of Jews in England who proclaim themselves aliens by their mode of life, by their very looks, by every word they utter, so long will the entire community be an object of distrust to Englishmen."[101] To forestall the growth of rabid antisemitism, leaders of the old community labored to slow the alien influx, promote immigrant anglicization, and reduce tensions between the newcomers and their neighbors.[102]

Communal leaders acted from the start to discourage East European immigrants from settling in Britain, preferring that they remain in the Pale or, once having left, that they move on to the United States or the colonies. In London, the Jewish Board of Guardians, the central communal agency for poor relief, refused to assist immigrants who had been in Britain less than six months, in the belief that unrestricted access to communal funds promoted emigration among persons unable to support themselves. In 1884 and subsequent years, the Board inserted notices in the East European Jewish press warning would-be immigrants of the bitter hardships they would face in Britain. In 1888, Chief Rabbi Nathan Adler requested his rabbinical colleagues in Eastern Europe to preach against migration to London, where newcomers, he warned, would face poverty, overwork, irreligion, and the snares of missionaries. When an immigrant baker, Simon Cohen (known also as Simha Becker), opened a humble, none-too-sanitary shelter for the homeless and unemployed, including immigrants fresh off the boat, the Board succeeded in 1885 in having it closed, fearing that it would "tend to invite helpless foreigners to this country." This move drew protests from communal leaders more sympathetic to the immigrants. With the financial backing of Samuel Montagu, his brother-in-law and business partner Ellis Abraham Franklin (1822–1909), and the Polish-born stockbroker Hermann Landau (1844–1921), a Poor Jews Temporary Shelter was established to help transmigrants and new immigrants. But the most unequivocal indicator of the Board's resolution to slow the growth of a foreign colony was its repatriation policy. Between 1880 and 1914, it sent back about fifty thousand destitute persons who were believed to have little prospect of making a living in England and who agreed to return voluntarily.[103]

Although communal leaders worked to discourage immigration, most were disinclined to support anti-alien legislation. They preferred to regulate the flow of foreign Jews themselves—by discouraging it in the first place, by repatriating those who became a financial burden, by promoting transmigration to countries better suited in their view to receive immigrants, like the United States, Canada, South Africa, and Argentina. They also believed that immigration would decline if the Russian authorities ceased to persecute Jews and to that end publicized and protested conditions there, urging British officials to pressure the imperial government. However, when restrictionists and antisemites blamed immigrants for the social evils of the East End and Britain's national decline, they rallied to their defense, hailing their virtues—their industriousness, sobriety, thrift, thirst for education, and so forth. For although native leaders themselves were critical of the immigrants for their foreign ways and preferred that they go elsewhere, they also understood that the fates of the two communities were linked, that hostility to poor, unacculturated, foreign-born Jews could, and frequently did, become an attack on all Jews. This sense of interconnectedness, fortified by feelings of ethnic solidarity, however ambivalent and attenuated, also caused most native leaders to oppose government regulation of immigration (except in regard to criminals, the disabled, and the mentally ill). They feared that state intervention, even if it produced a desirable result (which, in fact, their own policies worked to achieve), would set an unfortunate precedent: one act to curb Jews could beget another, and this time native, not immigrant, Jews could be the target. The *Jewish Chronicle* warned: "The letters which spell exclusion are not very different from those which compose expulsion. What an admission against ourselves it would be to say, 'let us have no more Jews.'"[104]

Within the ranks of prominent Jews, however, a minority, most of whom were Conservatives, vocally supported legislation to restrict immigration. Chief among them was Benjamin Cohen, Conservative MP for Islington and president of the Board of Guardians from 1887 to 1900. An avowed restrictionist as early as 1894, he voted with his party in favor of the Aliens Bill in 1905, as did two other Conservative Jewish MPs—Harry S. Samuel (1853–1934) and Harry H. Marks (1855–1916), editor of the *Financial News* and son of the Reform minister David W. Marks. Both sat for East End constituencies (Limehouse and St. George's in the East, respectively) in which anti-alien sentiment was strong. Samuel defended his position in a letter to the *Jewish Chronicle* in 1902 with the argument that antisemitism would erupt if Jews were the only group to oppose restriction. He urged them to avoid the limelight, shun public debate, and accede to the restrictionist views of the majority.[105] Support for restriction also came from some earlier immigrants from Holland, Poland, and Russia, skilled artisans and shopkeepers mainly, who felt that the new immigrants threatened their social and economic status.

Although communal leaders split over the wisdom of government intervention, they agreed about the need to hasten the anglicization of the newcomers to avoid an antisemitic backlash. (They differed, as we shall see, about what anglicization meant and how it was to be effected.) To achieve this end, they harnessed a remarkable network of charities, some well established and others newly created, to the task of making the immigrants less foreign.[106] To be sure, most of these charities served altruistic ends as well, caring for new mothers, orphans, the incurably ill, the aged, and the tubercular. But built into these and other immigrant aid schemes was an explicit anglicizing dimension. Humanitarian and religious sentiments, rooted in centuries-old habits of communal self-help, became entangled with immediate, self-serving concerns about eliminating problems that attracted unwanted attention. The Sick Room Helps Society, for example, which was founded in 1895 to aid East End immigrant women with housework, cooking, shopping, and childcare during illness and confinement, also instructed them on matters of personal and domestic hygiene.[107] The Jewish Board of Guardians, the central agency for the relief of the Jewish poor in London since its establishment in 1859, worked both to instill middle-class values and discipline in its clients and to encourage their acculturation. It sent volunteers into their homes to offer advice on childrearing and hygiene and to tell them how to organize their lives. Welfare schemes like this were also intended to combat the influence of Christian missions, which offered an array of social services to win the hearts and minds of immigrant Jews in need of emotional and material support.[108]

Children and adolescents, in particular, were objects of anglicization schemes, since they were considered more malleable than their parents, who clung stubbornly, it was believed, to old-world habits and attitudes. Jewish charity schools, most of which predated the East European influx, expanded to accommodate children whose parents wanted them to receive both a Jewish and a secular English education. At the turn of the century, London's Jewish schools, which received state financial aid by this date, enrolled about 8,200 pupils.[109] Although nominally Orthodox and under the supervision of the chief rabbi, these schools placed more emphasis on transforming their students into little Englishmen and-women than into observant, learned Jews. The schools worked especially hard to eradicate the use of Yiddish, which was regarded as a major stumbling block to anglicization. Louis B. Abrahams (1840–1914), headmaster of the Jews' Free School in London, the largest elementary school in turn-of-the-century England, urged parents and their children to discard Yiddish, "that miserable jargon which is not a language at all." If they succeeded in wiping away "all evidences of foreign birth and foreign proclivities" and their children identified with "everything that is English in thought and deed," then, he reasoned, antisemitism would disappear.[110]

Communal leaders also labored to influence the rising generation through English-style youth movements and clubs. In 1895, Colonel Albert Edward Goldsmid (1846–1904), an eccentric career officer in the British army who had been raised as a Christian but returned to Judaism as a young man, created the Jewish Lads' Brigade on the model of the Church Lads' Brigade, whose origins were rooted in English fears about racial degeneration. Like its Anglican model and, later, Baden-Powell's Boy Scouts, the Jewish Lads' Brigade aimed to instill habits of orderliness, cleanliness, and honor in working-class adolescents who had left school and to transform them into healthy, manly, patriotic, and obedient citizens. At the same time, it had additional, specifically Jewish goals: to iron out the "ghetto bend" in immigrant lads; to refute charges that Jews were undersized, underdeveloped, weak, and sickly; to promote and give evidence of Jewish loyalty to Britain. The brigades' martial music, uniforms, drills, and parades, along with its athletic contests and annual encampments at Deal, added excitement and color to the lives of immigrant youth; by 1909, the movement counted between four and five thousand members in London and the provinces.[111] Its success encouraged the establishment of other boys and girls clubs in immigrant neighborhoods. The first was the Brady Street Lads' Club in Whitechapel, established with the financial support of Lady Rothschild in 1896. Others followed, both in London and the provinces. All featured athletic and recreational activities, including summer camps by the sea or in the countryside. Their aim was to offer alternatives to the temptations found in music halls, public houses, gambling dens, and the streets and to help immigrant youth rise in the world, while exposing them to English, especially public school, games and values. Inspired by the settlement house movement and in particular Toynbee Hall, the East End settlement established by Rev. Arthur Barnett in 1883, the sons and daughters of communal notables, many of them with public school and Oxbridge backgrounds, helped to establish and manage these clubs. Most notable was Basil Henriques (1890–1961), who founded the Oxford and St. George's Club in the East End in 1914 after an apprenticeship at Toynbee Hall, using it as a vehicle for promoting both public school values and his own spiritualized interpretation of Liberal Judaism.[112]

Immigrants who came into contact with assimilationist charities and agencies reacted with ambivalence to their overtures. On the one hand, they welcomed interest-free loans, recreational programs, medical care, evening classes, model tenement blocks, financial assistance, and other benefits. But, at the same time, they resented—adults more than children—the arrogant anglicizing framework in which these were provided. Philanthropists, teachers, club leaders, home visitors, and sanitary inspectors were often overbearing and paternalistic, making the objects of their charity feel inferior and despised. Maurice Samuel recalled that while the *Budagaren* (Board of Guardians) were "good, benevolent people" who "helped us economically" they also "made us feel that they regarded our mores as inessentials—and worse: as outlandish impedimenta that were unnecessary to Judaism and a deterrent to good English citizenship."[113] Immigrants like Samuel and his parents were not opposed to becoming English but preferred doing so at their own pace and in their own way. They did not embrace in toto the assimilationist, middle-class values of establishment philanthropists but took what seemed valuable to them while rejecting the rest. As an adult worker at the Jewish Boys Club recorded in the club log book in 1901 after "a very successful day at cricket": while the boys' behavior on the field was very good, they were still reluctant "to accept the umpire's decision as final." Their anglicization, in other words, was incomplete.[114]

The bitterest clashes between immigrants and natives occurred when religious issues were at stake. To the chief rabbi and his supporters, the immigrants' worship was irreverent; their places of worship, insalubrious; their spiritual leaders, unenlightened and out of touch with the demands of modern life. To yeshivah-trained immigrant rabbis and their followers, on the other hand, the sedate Judaism of the Adlers and the United Synagogue was inauthentic, having made too many concessions to gentile taste. The top-hatted, dog-collared reverend graduates of Jews' College who ministered to middle-class anglicized congregations were, in their view, deficient in rabbinic learning and casual in their performance of religious duties, despite their claim to represent Orthodox Judaism. One non-Jewish student of the East End remarked in 1900 that the immigrants regarded all English Jews as "reformers," including Hermann Adler, whom they saw as "the Chief Reformer."[115]

Native Jews were alarmed by the multiplication of independent hevrot, for they believed that they preserved immigrant separateness and blocked the anglicizing influence of native Jewish institutions. Some called for their destruction. More sober leaders worked instead to gain influence over them, hoping thus to minimize what they viewed as their worst features. From the 1870s, for example, several notables supported foreign-born *maggidim* (preachers) like Zvi Hirsch Dainow (1833–77) and Hayyim Zundel Maccoby (1856–1916), whose sermons attracted large audiences and who were themselves amenable to promoting moderate acculturation. They hoped, as well, that these popular preachers would combat the growth of East End socialism. The most ambitious attempt to anglicize immigrant religion originated with Samuel Montagu. Himself Orthodox in practice and belief, Montagu aimed to preserve the intensity of immigrant religion—in part, to offset laxity and indifference among native families—while guiding it in the direction of moderate acculturation. His project, the Federation of Synagogues, which he bankrolled from its establishment in 1887, united the larger hevrot in London, as well as several small synagogues that predated the East European influx. The Federation made loans to member congregations to improve their buildings, encouraged the amalgamation of small hevrot, insisted on the use of English in conducting its business, and gained a modest voice for immigrant Jewry in communal councils like the Board of Guardians and the Board of Deputies. By 1903, the Federation included thirty-nine small congregations, with 4,391 male seat holders, representing about 24,000 persons in all.[116] Although it was intended to complement rather than rival the United Synagogue—few immigrants could afford United Synagogue fees, in any case—tensions between the two bodies developed, rooted, in part, in personal and ideological differences between the Federation's chief sponsor, Montagu, and the head of the United Synagogue, the first Lord Rothschild, and, in part, in the deep cultural divide that separated immigrant and native Judaism.[117]

Several outspoken magnates opposed the creation of the Federation from the start, believing it would encourage immigrant separatism. The president of the Board of Guardians at the time, Benjamin Cohen (another brother-in-law of Montagu), declared in 1888: "It is not so much the federation as the extinction of many of these synagogues which is to be desired."[118] Cohen, Rothschild, and others remained unwilling to leave the religious anglicization of the immigrants to Montagu and the Federation. They also feared that the mass of East End Jews, who affiliated neither with the United Synagogue nor with the Federation, was escaping the civilizing influence of communal social control. Between 1888 and 1898, they proposed to the United Synagogue council a series of ambitious programs, known collectively as the East End Scheme, to address these concerns. At the heart of the scheme was the proposal, made by Lord Rothschild in January 1889, to erect a single great center of Jewish public service in the East End, with a 1,200-seat synagogue as its dominant feature. The scheme came to include, at one time or another, the erection of a large hall for meetings and overflow services, the transfer of the *bet midrash* and bet din to the center, the registration of official interpreters for the courts, the establishment of arbitration panels (to keep Jewish litigants out of the public courts and the public eye), the sponsorship of a provident society and savings bank, and the employment of a full-time minister, whose duties were to include elevating the social conditions of area residents "by inculcating lessons of morality, health, and cleanliness." In the end the United Synagogue dropped the scheme. Fiscal conservatives objected to its expense, while the Montagu camp argued that the "colossal synagogue" would not attract immigrant worshippers, who preferred the intimacy of small, informal conventicles in which they enjoyed frequent liturgical honors at little cost.[119]

The most persistent source of religious conflict was immigrant reluctance to recognize the preeminence of the chief rabbinate. The institution itself was unknown in Eastern Europe, where rabbinical authority was decentralized and derived from scholastic virtuosity rather than official appointment. The English character of the chief rabbinate and the congregations under its control, as well as its willingness to tolerate deviations from East European standards of Orthodoxy, led immigrant leaders to ignore or challenge its hegemonic claims. East European rabbis solemnized marriages and granted divorces on their own authority, which, while in accord with Jewish law, ran counter to civil law, which authorized the chief rabbinate to regulate such matters. Their activities affronted communal authorities and created potential legal problems for those whom they married or divorced. Children born of unregistered unions were illegitimate, for example. To combat *shtille huppah,* as the practice was known, the United Synagogue introduced "cheap marriages" at two small East End synagogues in 1877, on the assumption that couples who married outside ecclesiastical control were unable to afford the normal United Synagogue marriage fee. This, however, did not stop shtille huppah, which continued to bedevil the chief rabbinate and the Board of Deputies until after World War I.[120]

Immigrant rabbis also challenged the chief rabbinate's regulation of the slaughter and sale of kosher meat, claiming that its standards were lax, that it was more concerned with the convenience of Jewish housewives than the requirements of Jewish law. In 1891, when Hermann Adler failed to respond to requests for more stringent supervision of butchers licensed by the London Board of Shechita, a group of East End traditionalists, with the support of some Central European–born followers of Samson Raphael Hirsch (1808–88), founded a separatist community, Mahzikei Ha-Dat (Those Who Hold Fast to Religion), that eventually acquired its own *rav*, shehitah, butcher shops, talmud torah, and synagogue (in Brick Lane, Spitalfields). Mahzikei Ha-Dat threatened not only Adler's rabbinic claims but also the Board of Shehita's financial viability, since its butchers competed with the Board's. Adler and his bet din declared the meat slaughtered under Mahzikei Ha-Dat authority to be *tref* (not kosher) and tried to bully—and then cajole—the separatists back into the fold, but their efforts failed, as, indeed, did all subsequent efforts to control the emergence of independent, separatist Orthodox institutions.[121] Meanwhile, as the number of immigrant rabbinical authorities in Britain multiplied, Adler, who was not a respected halachic authority, faced additional challenges to his regulation of shehitah and kashrut. Three disputes with butchers who challenged his authority—in Liverpool in 1904, Manchester in 1907, and London in 1911—were so bitter that they ended in the civil courts. During discussions before the selection of Adler's successor in 1912, a group of foreign-born provincial rabbis insisted that the new chief rabbi should recognize their halachic autonomy, especially in regard to shehitah.[122]

Although an article of faith in assimilationist circles, the belief that immigrants would cling to their old world ways unless encouraged or coerced to give them up was, on balance, groundless. Immigrant acculturation in Leeds, where there were few native Jews and hence no broad anglicization campaign, differed little in the end from that in other cities. On the whole, the new arrivals were not interested in recreating the Jewish market towns and urban quarters of Eastern Europe in Whitechapel, the Strangeways, or the Leylands. Most viewed their migration and settlement as the start of a new life rather than a temporary exile from a beloved Russian or Polish homeland. They were not hostile to the idea of becoming English and took pride in their children's rapid progress in that direction. They and their children admired England—its imperial grandeur, its material wealth, its toleration (relative, of course, to what they had experienced in Poland, Russia, and Rumania)—and could be as effusively patriotic as their assimilationist counterparts. But they were, at the same time, sensitive to and resentful of the cultural arrogance and social condescension with which native Jews regarded their old habits and views, which, after all, were normative in the communities from which they had migrated. They welcomed opportunities to become English, but according to their lights, without being coerced to sacrifice their self-respect, religious passion, or native tongue.

The adaptation of the immigrants and their children to their new surroundings was also governed by a sense of Jewishness that was different from that of families long settled in the country. Before their migration, East European Jews had lived as members of a distinct national and religious unit with its own cultural and social traditions. They had not identified themselves as Russians, Poles, Ukrainians, Rumanians, Lithuanians, or even as hyphenated variants of them, but rather as Jews *period*. The kind of bifurcated identity that worked to harmonize both Jewishness and Englishness (or Germanness or Frenchness) was rare in Eastern Europe, where liberal nation states, with which Jews in the West identified, did not exist. Thus, immigrants from these regions viewed their Jewishness in a broader, more inclusive manner than native Jews. Their identity included a strong element of national-ethnic distinctiveness, almost an inchoate nationalism. In time, this led to clashes with the old, more assimilation-minded leadership over matters of communal governance and politics. The new creed of political Zionism, in particular, became a source of bitter conflict. However, since the battles over Zionism and communal control, which were linked, did not emerge full blown until after the close of the immigrant period, discussion of their origins will be postponed to the next chapter, which traces the fortunes of British Jewry from World War I to World War II.

Lucien Wolf. A. P. F. Ritchie's *Vanity Fair* caricature of 1911. From a private collection.

CHAPTER 5

The Great War to the Holocaust
(1914–1945)

The outbreak of World War I ushered in four decades of unparalleled horror in European history. Although British Jews escaped the death and destruction that swept over continental Jewish communities, they were not spared their repercussions and consequences. The collapse of the Russian, German, Austrian, and Turkish empires in the wake of World War I and the rise and fall of Nazism in the 1930s and 1940s forced communal leaders and organizations to confront a host of novel problems. While earlier crises abroad, such as the Damascus blood libel of 1840 and the Russian pogroms of 1881, had also sparked concern, the upheavals of the twentieth century were unprecedented in scope, complexity, and urgency. The challenges they posed taxed and then outstripped Anglo-Jewish resources and forced a rethinking of Anglo-Jewish understandings of emancipation and Jewishness. These upheavals also set in motion a train of unanticipated changes that rearranged the domestic landscape of British Jewry. Anglo-Jewish identities acquired a nationalist dimension. The old notable families disappeared from the communal scene, leaving governance in the hands of new men of East European background. With the exit of the old guard, the tolerant, latitudinarian Orthodoxy that had emerged in the Victorian period yielded to a more strident, sectarian traditionalism.

When Britain went to war in 1914, acculturated, middle-class Jews responded to the call to arms with enthusiasm. In sermons, editorials, and public statements, rabbis and notables beat the drum, identifying the British national cause with Jewish ideals. Their patriotism was genuine, unambiguous, and deeply felt, but it was also true that the war

183

offered them a welcome opportunity to disprove the charges of disloyalty, cowardice, and unmanliness that were the stock-in-trade of antisemites. In August 1914, with hostilities looming, the *Jewish Chronicle*,
which had urged neutrality as late as July, declared: "England has been
all she could be to Jews, Jews will be all they can be to England." Before
the introduction of conscription in 1916, most young men (perhaps 90
percent) from native families volunteered. Almost to a man, past and
present military-age members of the Jewish houses at the public schools
of Clifton and Cheltenham took a commission. This outpouring of patriotism, moreover, was not confined to the privileged strata: close to
ten thousand men were on active service before conscription came into
force.[1]

Behind the patriotism of middle-class Jews, however, lurked concern
and unease: wartime Germanophobia and renewed xenophobia nourished old hostilities, which, it was feared, would end in antisemitic violence.[2] Much of the native community traced its roots to German
lands, bore German names, and continued to maintain familial and business links with Germany long after emigration. Because of these links
and because of their hatred of the tsarist regime and its antisemitic policies, leading Jews, including the first Lord Rothschild and the journalist
Lucien Wolf (1857–1930), had been vocal opponents of entente with
Russia and war with Germany, refusing to succumb to jingoistic
German-bashing. Once war was declared, of course, their pro-German
or neutralist sentiments evaporated, but the damage was done. Jew-
baiting journalists like Leo Maxse and W. T. Steed charged that Jews
supported German interests, while even less hostile writers conflated
Jews and Germans on occasion. Unnaturalized Jews born in enemy
countries, including Polish Jews from Austrian-controlled Galicia, were
interned, along with other enemy aliens. Fearful of being accused of
disloyalty, the Board of Deputies refused to assist them or plead their
case, although urged to do so by the B'nai B'rith and the friendly societies, which represented a broader spectrum of communal opinion. Numerous families of German origin legally changed their names to escape
identification with the enemy: Ansbachers became Ansleys; Auerbachs,
Arbours; Hallensteins, Halsteds; Meyers, Merricks; Rothensteins,
Rutherstons; Schlosses, Castles; Waldsteins, Walstons; and so on. When
a German submarine sank the *Lusitania* in May 1915, Hun-bashing
reached a new pitch. East Londoners rioted for three days, smashing
and robbing German- and Austrian-owned shops, often making no distinction between enemy aliens and other foreigners. In response to the

anti-German hysteria that followed the sinking, prominent German-born Jews, like the laryngologist Sir Felix Semon (1849–1921) and the financier Sir Ernest Cassel, joined other German-born citizens in writing "loyalty letters" to *The Times* to affirm their allegiance to Britain.

As the war dragged on, the issue of Jewish military service—were Jews "slackers," evading their country's call?—became explosive. While well-established, anglicized families sent their sons to war with enthusiasm, immigrant families did not. In the Jewish East End and its provincial counterparts, few were eager to sacrifice themselves or their children in a war in which, in their view, Jews had no stake, a war, moreover, in support of the hated tsarist regime many of them had fled. During the period of voluntary enlistment, few immigrants joined up. The introduction of conscription (for unmarried men in January 1916 and for all men in April 1916) swept up the British-born sons of immigrants but not men of military age (18 to 41) who were born in the Russian Empire. As friendly aliens, they were exempt from conscription. The twenty-five to thirty thousand men who fell into this category were the only group of able-bodied men escaping military service. Their presence attracted scathing comments, which, old-line communal leaders believed, further fed the fires of antisemitism. In summer 1916, with few friendly aliens having volunteered, Home Secretary Herbert Samuel, himself a member of the communal oligarchy, announced that aliens who did not serve would be deported to Russia. To encourage their enlistment, a special recruiting office was opened at the headquarters of the Rothschild bank in the City of London, less than a mile from Whitechapel, but the results of this and other efforts, like recruiting posters in Yiddish, were disappointing. Samuel's announcement, moreover, sparked political resistance in the East End. Challenging the claim of the old anglicized elite to speak for the community as a whole, Jewish socialist groups, trade union branches, and friendly societies banded together to form the Foreign Jews Protection Committee. With substantial immigrant support and backing from a handful of well-known gadflies, like Israel Zangwill and the Sephardi haham Moses Gaster (1856–1939), it organized petitions, deputations, and mass meetings to protest repatriation. The government put off action from month to month but, after the Russian Revolution, pushed through legislation that eventually sent a few thousand Jews back to Russia. These moves, however, did little to dampen the popular belief that Jews were shirkers, stealing the jobs of brave British soldiers and growing rich to boot. In June 1917, a crowd of several thousand wrecked houses and looted shops in the Jewish quarter in Leeds, while onlookers stood by and made no effort to intervene; in September, two to three thousand Jews and Gentiles, wielding wood logs, iron bars, and flat irons, fought a pitched battle in Bethnal Green.[3]

There can be little doubt that Jewish status suffered during the war years, chiefly because of the controversy over alien conscription.[4] But at the same time, by dealing a fatal blow to the Turkish empire in the Middle East, the war itself advanced the fortunes of Jewish nationalism, linking them (for better or worse) to British foreign policy while propelling the Zionist movement from the periphery to the center of communal politics. Before the war, the Zionist movement in Britain was weak and uninfluential, despite long-standing Anglo-Jewish and Anglo-Christian interest in the Land of Israel. Christian interest was rooted in evangelical, millenarian dreams of Jewish restoration (and conversion) as a precursor to or accompaniment of the Second Coming. Victorians supported conversionist work in the Holy Land and applauded the establishment of a joint British-Prussian bishopric in Jerusalem in 1841. Toward the end of the century some Christians even envisioned the Land of Israel as a refuge for persecuted European Jews.[5] This evangelical, conversionist interest in the Land of Israel complemented and drew strength from widening diplomatic entanglement in the Eastern Question (the future of Turkey and its European and Middle Eastern possessions). Control of Egypt in particular became critical to British imperialists because it was the road to India. The opening of the Suez Canal in 1869, Disraeli's purchase of the single largest block of shares in the Suez Canal Company in 1875, and outright occupation of Egypt in 1882 sparked interest in expanding the British cordon sanitaire around the Suez Canal zone. Throughout the century, batteries of travelers, artists, orientalists, archeologists, missionaries, novelists, and pilgrims visited and wrote about Palestine's holy sites and ancient inhabitants, reinforcing the notion that the fortunes of Britain and Israel were linked.

To what extent Christian restorationism and British imperialism encouraged Victorian Jewish concern with the Holy Land is a matter of conjecture; at a minimum, they lent it an aura of legitimacy. In any case, well before the rise of modern Jewish nationalism, British Jews took an active interest in the Land of Israel and its small, impoverished Jewish communities, far more interest, certainly, than other Western Jewries. Between 1827 and 1874, Moses Montefiore made seven well-publicized trips to the Holy Land, in large part to promote the productivization of the Old Yishuv (the pre-Zionist, traditional Jewish community), which lived precariously on charitable funds collected in the Diaspora.

Montefiore's efforts to reform the Old Yishuv and place it on a firm economic base were not successful, but his trips generated intense public interest, nonetheless.[6] Moreover, while he was the best known Victorian Jew to concern himself with the Land of Israel (his fame was due, in part, to his talent for self-promotion), he was not alone.[7] The Bohemian-born journalist Abraham Benisch (1814–78), who edited the *Jewish Chronicle* from 1854 to 1869 and again from 1875 to 1878, ceaselessly promoted the economic productivization of the Old Yishuv and the establishment of agricultural colonies. In 1852, with the help of both Jews and Christians, he formed the short-lived Association for Promoting Jewish Settlements in Palestine. When the pioneer religious nationalist Yehuda Alkalai (1798–1878) visited London for six months in 1852, the *Jewish Chronicle* reported his activities; in the 1860s, it publicized the work of Moses Hess (1812–75) and Zvi Hirsch Kalischer (1795–1874) and, in 1880–81, the settlement schemes of Laurence Oliphant, a Christian mystic and former MP, who tried to obtain the sultan's permission to found a Jewish colony east of the Jordan River.

Montefiore and Benisch were not so-called proto-Zionists. Their interest in the Land of Israel was philanthropic and sentimental, nourished by traditional religion rather than political ideology. Two fundamental assumptions of political Zionism were absent in their thinking—one, that emancipation was a failure, and, two, that the creation of a sovereign state was the sole solution to its failure. Nonetheless, long-standing interest in the welfare of the Old Yishuv, especially the wish to make it economically productive, inclined some communal leaders to look favorably on the spread of Hibbat Tsiyyon, the Love of Zion movement that developed in Eastern Europe in the wake of the pogroms of 1881 and was the immediate precursor to the full-blown political Zionism of Theodor Herzl (1869–1904). Beginning in 1883, East European immigrants in London, Leeds, and Manchester founded Hibbat Tsiyyon societies to support the movement's fledgling agricultural settlements in the Land of Israel.[8] Members placed hundreds of collection boxes in immigrant homes, but, on the whole, the societies failed to generate much interest in the idea of national rebirth and collapsed after a few years. Most immigrants, after all, were struggling to make ends meet and had neither the time nor the energy for utopian dreams about rebuilding Zion. The London group, Hevrat Yishuv Erets Yisrael (Society for the Settlement of the Land of Israel), however, recorded one major gain: in 1885, it recruited the banker and communal magnate Samuel Montagu, then campaigning for the Whitechapel seat in Parliament, and he agreed to become the society's treasurer. Whether he joined because he was a strong critic of the *halukah,* the welfare system on which the Old Yishuv depended, and wanted to promote economic self-reliance, or because he was a shrewd electioneer and believed membership would attract votes, his recruitment marked the start of West End participation in the movement.

In the late 1880s, the movement revived, attracting about two thousand members at its height, among them a bevy of West End notables, including Montagu; Lord Rothschild; the Conservative MP Benjamin L. Cohen, the engineer Elim d'Avigdor (1841–95); Moses Gaster; Hermann Adler, then rabbi of the Bayswater Synagogue; Simeon Singer; and, most importantly, Col. Albert Edward Goldsmid, who later introduced himself to Herzl with the declaration "I am Daniel Deronda." Goldsmid stamped the movement's growing structure with a British military impress, dubbing local chapters "tents"; their leaders, "commanders"; the central office, "headquarters"; and its head, "the chief," a post he held from 1893. On the whole, its West End members were less ideological, less consumed by dreams of reviving the Jewish nation, than its more numerous immigrant members. The former supported the movement for mixed reasons: it offered an alternative to socialism; it directed immigration to the Land of Israel (rather than to Britain, where it created social problems); it encouraged Jews to settle on and work the land, thereby proving that Jews too were capable of healthy, productive labor; and it reinforced long-standing religious and philanthropic links to the Land. They also supported Hibbat Tsiyyon because it celebrated Jewish national pride without calling into question the status of Jews in Britain. When Herzlian Zionism, which urged the immediate creation of a Jewish state, overtook the movement, West End nationalist enthusiasm ebbed.

Theodor Herzl himself made few converts in Britain. He arrived in London for the first time in November 1895, three months before the publication of *Der Judenstaat,* to outline his ideas to the Maccabeans, a dining club of writers, artists, and professional men, and to meet privately with lay and religious leaders. His reception on this and a subsequent visit in July 1897 was polite—even enthusiastic, when he spoke to several thousand East Enders on a Sunday evening at the Jewish Working Men's Club—but unproductive. Few British Jews, whatever their background, were interested or willing to commit themselves. Sales of the English translation of *Der Judenstaat,* which appeared in 1896, were poor. Even the fourth Zionist Congress, which was held in London in 1900, failed to generate enthusiasm. In the understated judgment of the English Zionist Federation's own historian, "[its] effect on Anglo-Jewry did not come up to expectations and the Congress proved a merely transient incident in the vast Metropolis."[9] Most Jews were either too concerned with their own immediate problems to take an interest or believed that Herzl's political ideas were utopian and dangerous, fodder for antisemitic allegations about Jewish tribalism and separatism. Most also assumed that Zionism would remain on the periphery of communal life and eventually die of neglect.[10]

Still, small circles of enthusiasts emerged. The greatest number were immigrant veterans of Hibbat Tsiyyon societies, which, shorn of their West End leaders, merged into the Herzlite English Zionist Federation between 1899 and 1902, when Goldsmid wound up the affairs of the headquarters tent. Less numerous but more influential were middle-class, largely native-born Jews from professional and business backgrounds, residents of North and Northwest London rather than the East End, whose birth and wealth were too humble to qualify them for membership in the communal elite. This group included Herbert Bentwich, a solicitor; Leopold Greenberg (1862–1931), a journalist and publisher; Joseph Cowen (1868–1932), a clothing manufacturer; Jacob de Haas (1872–1937), a journalist; and Israel Zangwill. (The latter left the Herzlite mainstream in 1905, after it rejected the British government's offer of land in East Africa, to establish the Jewish Territorial Organization [ITO]). Resentful of their exclusion from policy-making positions in Anglo-Jewry, these "new" men found in Zionism a vehicle for opposing the oligarchic rule of the established elite.[11] In addition to these activists, the leadership of the movement also included the well-connected but ineffectual Sir Francis Montefiore (1860–1935), Sir Moses's great-nephew, and the contentious Rumanian-born Moses Gaster, a supporter of all manner of dissident causes.

In the prewar period, English Zionism was numerically and organizationally weak. Riven by personal squabbles and unable to compete with trade unionism, socialism, or traditional religion, it failed to win a substantial following in immigrant neighborhoods. In 1902, seven thousand persons were nominal members of groups affiliated to the English Zionist Federation; by 1917, before the government issued the Balfour Declaration, the number had dropped to four thousand. Nor was English Zionism successful in advancing its avowed policy of infiltrating and conquering established communal institutions. Indeed, in the ongoing struggle of professionals and businessmen to achieve greater influence in communal affairs, Zionist leaders played a subordinate rather than commanding role. Zionism did not go unnoticed, of course, drawing the fire of articulate thinkers like the radical theologian Claude Goldsmid Montefiore and the Cambridge rabbinics scholar Israel Abrahams (1858–1924). Like Zionism's integrationist opponents on the Continent, they argued that Jews constituted a religious community not a political nation, that the history of the Diaspora was not a record of unending travail, and that Zionism cast doubts on the Englishness and patriotism of the community. But the movement was too weak to sow panic or fear among its opponents or cause them to create a distinct organization to counter its influence.[12]

Soon after Britain went to war, leading figures in both the English Zionist Federation and the World Zionist Organization concluded that there was a good chance that at the end of the conflict the Turkish empire would be dismembered and that Palestine would fall within the British sphere of influence. With this in mind, they began to cultivate the support of government ministers, high-ranking civil servants, and influential politicians. (This was not the first time that Zionist leaders had pursued a British strategy. Herzl's diplomacy at the turn of the century had focused on London and met with some success when, in April 1903, Foreign Secretary Joseph Chamberlain offered a tract in East Africa for Jewish settlement. Chamberlain's motives, however, were pragmatic rather than sentimental; he wanted to increase the number of politically harmless, economically productive white settlers in East Africa to strengthen Britain's imperial hold there.) The key figure in the Zionist campaign was the Russian-born organic chemist Chaim Weizmann (1874–1952), who had arrived in England in 1904 to take a research post at Owens College, Manchester.[13] Well known within the Zionist movement prior to his arrival, Weizmann threw himself into its work in Britain. When the war broke out, he was among the two or three most influential Zionists in the country and in February 1917 assumed formal leadership of the English Zionist Federation. However, his standing and ability to negotiate on behalf of the movement derived less from the office than from his position in the World Zionist Organization's inner circle, his charm and eloquence, and his understanding of and admiration for the English establishment.

In wooing British officialdom, Weizmann and other Zionist spokesmen played several cards at once. They appealed to imperial concerns, arguing that a British-sponsored Jewish homeland would protect the northern flank of Egypt and, thus, the Suez Canal, the lifeline to India.

When, in 1915, the Foreign Office became worried about the pro-Germanism of Jews in the then-neutral United States, Weizmann and others exploited the crude fantasies of ministers and officials about Jewish power, urging them to declare their interest in Palestine in order to sway American Jews to the Allied cause. (American Jews were believed to wield great influence in Washington.) Later, following the Russian Revolution, when British statesmen became fearful that the new government would sign a separate peace treaty with Germany, they argued similarly that a British commitment to a Jewish homeland would win the hearts of Russia's Jews, who were thought to be powerful in the radical circles that favored withdrawal from the war. Lastly, they appealed to evangelical, ethical, and humanitarian sentiments. In the end, no one argument carried the day. Each contributed to some extent to the decision of the War Cabinet in November 1917 to commit Britain to "the establishment in Palestine of a national home for the Jewish people," to quote the words of the cabinet document (actually, a letter to the second Lord Rothschild [1868–1937]) later known as the Balfour Declaration because Foreign Secretary Arthur James Balfour signed it.[14] At the same time, the Russian-born right-wing Zionist Vladimir Jabotinsky (1880–1940), a great believer in the value of military training and discipline, led a campaign for the creation of a Jewish legion to fight alongside British troops in the liberation of the Holy Land. The War Office eventually consented and in July 1917 created a Jewish battalion of the Royal Fusiliers (known popularly as the Judaeans), which took part in the last phase of the Palestine campaign.[15]

Zionist diplomacy in the war years did not go unchallenged. Most (but not all) communal notables feared that the creation of a British-sponsored Jewish homeland would impede social integration and throw into doubt the legal status of Britain's Jews. As long as Zionism in Britain had been a low-key, ineffectual affair, they were content to more or less ignore it. However, the diplomatic strides that Zionism made during the war stimulated moves to counter its growing influence in Whitehall. Using similar methods of persuasion (memoranda, letters to the press, pamphlets, meetings with ministers and civil servants), the integrationist camp strove to influence the same public figures whom the Zionists were courting. The most prominent opponents of Zionism came from well-to-do families that had been settled in Britain for several generations and were accustomed to setting the community's agenda and representing its interests to the state. They viewed the Zionists as upstarts and usurpers and their program as a threat to their own status.

Edwin Montagu, secretary of state for India and son of the first Lord Swaythling, emerged as the fiercest opponent of the Balfour Declaration within the cabinet. Although a radical assimilationist who took no interest in Jewish matters, Montagu articulated his opposition to Zionism in "Jewish" terms. In a confidential memorandum to the prime minister in March 1915, he wrote that there was "no Jewish race now as a homogeneous whole" and that "the whole claim of the Jews to equality of treatment with those who profess other religions in the countries in which they find themselves is based on the fact that they are citizens of the countries in which they have been born and lived for generations."[16] But not all of the notables shared his outlook. Indeed, in contrast to other West European Jewish communities, there were an uncommonly large number who sympathized with and took a leading role in the Zionist movement, an indication, perhaps, that there was less pressure on English Jews to deny the ethnic dimension of their collective identity. Among them were Edwin Montagu's first cousin Herbert Samuel; the geneticist Redcliffe Nathan Salaman (1874–1955); Lord Rothschild and his brother Charles (1877–1923); the French-born James de Rothschild (1878–1957), who had moved to Britain in 1913 and whose father, Edmund (1845–1934), was the most important benefactor of the earliest agricultural settlements in the Land of Israel; and Sir Francis Montefiore, who was a first cousin of the anti-Zionist Claude Goldsmid Montefiore.

The institutional stronghold of the anti-Zionist camp was the Board of Deputies, which historically had articulated Jewish interests to government ministers and officials. Its membership consisted of representatives of congregations in London, the provinces, and the colonies. However, of the 143 deputies in 1917, 110 were residents of London, mostly members of upper-middle-class West End congregations. The majority of these London-based members had been elected by congregations outside the capital to represent them on the board.[17] Even more firm in its opposition was the overtly unrepresentative Anglo-Jewish Association, founded in 1871 to promote the welfare of unemancipated Jews in the Middle East, North Africa, and Eastern Europe and headed in the war years by Claude Goldsmid Montefiore. In 1878, the two bodies had established a Conjoint Foreign Committee to lobby the government on matters concerning persecuted Jews abroad. The Conjoint, as it became known, appointed the journalist Lucien Wolf its executive secretary at the start of the war, and he waged a skilled if unsuccessful campaign to counter the advances Weizmann and his associates were making. The conflict between the two camps came to a head in May 1917. Aware that it was being outmaneuvered in influencing the government at the highest level, the Conjoint published a manifesto in *The Times* on 24 May attacking Zionism for claiming that Jews everywhere constituted "one homeless nationality" and for "stamping the Jews as strangers in their native lands," thus "undermining their hard won position as citizens and nationals of those lands." Publication of the statement elicited outrage. The chief rabbi, Joseph Hertz, who had succeeded Hermann Adler in 1913, denounced it as unrepresentative, while the Board of Deputies voted by 56 to 51 on 17 June to condemn the statement and its publication and to withdraw from the Conjoint, thus effectively dissolving it. In the wake of the vote, the president of the board, David Lindo Alexander (1842–1922), a signatory to *The Times* letter, resigned.

Often viewed as an endorsement of Zionism, the vote at the Board of Deputies was, in truth, much more the start of a revolution in communal governance than a signal that Zionism had captured the hearts and minds of Anglo-Jewry. Although Herzl had urged his supporters to oust those who controlled communal bodies (a strategy known as "the conquest of the community"), the victory at the Board of Deputies was due even more to shifts in the social character of British Jewry than to the spread of Zionism. In the eighteenth and nineteenth centuries, there existed no alternative to the rule of the great banking and brokerage families (Rothschilds, Montefiores, Cohens, Mocattas, etc.). The middle ranks of the community were sparse. Professional men, merchants, and manufacturers deferred to the rule of the established oligarchy, at least in London. (In provincial cities like Manchester, which lacked a finance-based Jewish haute bourgeoisie, deference was weaker, and from the mid-Victorian period local, self-made leaders had challenged the authority of the London elite and its religious head, Chief Rabbi Nathan Adler.)[18] By the end of the century, however, the professional and mercantile upper-middle class was larger. Resentful of their exclusion from communal power and, at the same time, inspired by middle-class gains in the national political arena, business and professional men began to challenge the monopoly of the old families. Some were East Europeans who had made their way into the middle class within one generation, while others came from Central European families that had migrated to Britain earlier in the century. Confident, energetic self-made men, they believed that British Jews had gone too far in subordinating their collective distinctiveness to the pursuit of social equality. They wanted a more representative, assertive communal leadership, one less concerned with keeping a low public profile, which would confront antisemitism vigorously and openly, demand government protection of Jewish interests, and mobilize "the Jewish vote" in parliamentary and local elections.[19]

In the decade before World War I, these circles established forums and organizations to promote their views, while, at the same time, working to gain a foothold in core communal bodies, especially the Board of Deputies. In 1910, over the opposition of well-entrenched leaders like Claude Goldsmid Montefiore, these "new" men established a lodge of B'nai B'rith, an international fraternal organization. Led by the solicitor Herbert Bentwich, an ardent Zionist, B'nai B'rith championed Jewish interests that the Board of Deputies defended with little enthusiasm or firmness. The lodge provided legal aid to aliens who were refused admission by immigration officers at ports of entry, and Bentwich himself intervened at the Home Office on behalf of difficult cases. It lobbied MPs to safeguard Jewish interests in regard to the Slaughter of Animals Bill, the National Insurance Bill, and the Sunday Closing of Shops Bill, and protested the Russian government's reluctance to issue travel documents to British Jews. Viewing these initiatives as irresponsible, unwarranted interference, the Board of Deputies refused to cooperate with B'nai B'rith on most matters.[20] In large provincial cities, local leaders who felt that the Board of Deputies was too distant and passive created representative councils, largely as organs of communal defense.

Meanwhile, at the Board of Deputies, representatives of provincial synagogues and disaffected Londoners began agitating for reforms that would make it more democratic and responsive. Here the leading dissident was the statistician Simon Rosenbaum (1877–1950), a founding member of B'nai B'rith and its president in 1915, who moved to censure the board's president in 1911. In 1906, the *Jewish Chronicle* was purchased by Leopold Greenberg, owner of a successful advertising agency and one of the founders of the English Zionist Federation, and under him it became an advocate of dissident concerns of all kinds, not just Jewish nationalism.[21] It demanded the reform of the Board of Deputies, urged Jews to exploit their vote to gain political leverage, and criticized the halfhearted opposition of communal notables to the operation of the Aliens Act. On the cultural front, Joseph Hochman (1883–1943), minister of the New West End Synagogue, and Norman Bentwich (1883–1971), a barrister and Herbert's eldest son, launched a serious journal, *The Jewish Review*, in 1909 to take the place of *The Jewish Quarterly Review*, which transferred to the United States in 1908. It reflected the

Zionism of its founders but embraced other concerns as well. For example, it repudiated Montefiore's interfaith dialogue with Christian thinkers, urging Jews to give priority instead to their own Jewish education.

The vote at the Board of Deputies on 17 June 1917 was the outcome of years of accumulated resentment and dissatisfaction. It marked neither the end of the notables' rule nor the triumph of Zionism. The old families did not disappear from communal management until after World War II, while Zionists remained a minority within the community until the 1940s. Indeed, in the wake of their setbacks, the anti-Zionists rallied and counterattacked. One week after the government issued the Balfour Declaration Lionel de Rothschild (1882–1942), the educationalist Sir Philip Magnus (1842–1933), and the second Lord Swaythling (1869–1927) formed the League of British Jews to oppose the idea that Jews constituted a political nation. Lucien Wolf and Claude Goldsmid Montefiore provided the League with ideas, while Sir Philip's son Laurie (1872–1933), a journalist and man of letters, edited its newspaper, the *Jewish Guardian,* which appeared from 1919 to 1931. At the Board of Deputies, the election of new officers following Alexander's resignation revealed how limited were the goals of the majority of those who voted to condemn the Conjoint letter. Sir Stuart Samuel, a brother of Herbert Samuel and a non-Zionist, was elected president and Sir Philip Magnus was elected to one of the two vice presidencies. The other was filled by Lord Rothschild, who was a Zionist but whose election was due more to being a Rothschild than a Zionist. Cooperation with the Anglo-Jewish Association resumed, and the Conjoint was reconstituted as the Joint Foreign Committee, with Lucien Wolf as its executive secretary.

What the vote marked was the *start* of a transformation in communal governance that lasted several decades, concluding only in the 1950s. The shift was a drawn-out, bitter struggle punctuated by public skirmishes and conflicts. In the interwar period and during World War II, newcomers and outsiders repeatedly challenged the old elite and its policies on various fronts, including the battle against domestic antisemitism, the rescue of Jews from Nazism, the mandate for Palestine, and the protection of Jewish observance. The level of conflict between the contending parties was unprecedented in Anglo-Jewish history—in large part because the stakes were higher than they had ever been before. To some, with antisemitism threatening at home and abroad, the very existence of the Jews hung in the balance. To understand the communal strife of these decades, however, it is first necessary to look at the changes that were taking place in the lives of the East European immigrants and their children, since these changes underwrote their challenge to the rule of the notables.

In the first half of the twentieth century, the immigrants and, even more, their children began to move up the economic ladder. On the whole, their progress was less dramatic than that of their counterparts in the United States, with its more dynamic economy, but, by British standards, it was remarkable. It began in a modest way before World War I. Workers in immigrant trades became masters; market men became shopkeepers; their English-born children became clerks, typists, shop assistants, and travelers. During this period, Michael Marks made the transition from peddler to market trader in the markets of northern towns, and then, in Manchester, to shopkeeper and eventually founder and partner in Marks & Spencer, a nationwide chain of retail stores. Those who remained in sweated trades also experienced a modest improvement in their standard of living. Following the stagnation of real wages in the 1880s and 1890s, there was a small upturn in the standard of living of ordinary workers. One sign of this improvement was the movement of successful immigrants to more attractive residential areas before World War I—in the case of London, largely to districts contiguous to the East End (Hackney, Dalston, Stoke Newington, Clapton, Stamford Hill, and West Ham). It is remarkable that 22 percent of immigrant grooms who married in City and East End synagogues in the period 1910–14 were living in areas of secondary settlement.[22] During World War I, the pace of economic mobility quickened. Military contracts benefited the immigrant trades, accelerating the exodus from the old neighborhoods. The fictional Lakarins in Charles Landstone's novel *Blue Tiger Yard* (1927), manufacturers of "khaki tunics, army boots, service caps, [and] swagger canes," rise "on the crest of the khaki boom" and move to Highbury New Park in 1917.[23]

In the interwar period, the number of Jews who rose into the lower-middle and middle class increased substantially. To be sure, in areas of first settlement, the old trades (clothing, footwear, furniture) remained central to the Jewish economy, employing the great majority of male and female workers. Even in adjacent, less congested areas, like Hackney in London, Cheetham in Manchester, and Chapeltown in Leeds, these trades continued to employ thousands of Jews. However, the young avoided them when possible, for while wages and hours were better in the interwar period than before, conditions in the workshops were still squalid: cramped, dark, damp, poorly ventilated. Young men and women increasingly turned to white-collar work, finding employment as travelers, shop assistants, and secretaries, and, especially in the 1930s, to taxi-driving, hairdressing, entertainment, accountancy, and estate agency. Thus, while 70 percent of male and female teenagers joining Jewish friendly societies in East London in 1913 worked in the clothing and furniture industries, in 1930 the number was down to 50 percent. Equally significant: 30 percent of boys and 40 percent of girls were now office workers, shop assistants, and commercial travelers.[24]

As more and more Jews entered the lower-middle and middle class, the old immigrant neighborhoods lost their central place in Anglo-Jewish life. While before World War I the East End held at least two-thirds of London's Jews, by the 1930s it contained barely one-third. With immigration from Poland and Russia at an end, there were no newcomers to replace those who moved away, so the East End and its counterparts increasingly housed disproportionate numbers of the old, the poor, and the working class. Concurrently, the number of families with school-age children in areas of first settlement shrank. Thus, by the early 1930s, seven of the eleven elementary schools in Jewish streets in the East End were no longer used as schools, while enrollment at the Jews' Free School was half of what it had been at the turn of the century. Those who were able to leave the East End moved to districts in North London, as before the war, as well as to leafier, more up-market suburbs in Northwest London—Hampstead, Golders Green, Finchley, and Hendon. Already by 1930, the northwest suburbs housed about 10 percent of London's Jews. (In the interwar period, the United Synagogue admitted sixteen synagogues from these districts.) In the new neighborhoods in London, Manchester, and Leeds, lower-middle- and middle-class families outnumbered working-class families. In the boroughs of Stoke Newington and Hackney, for example, there were almost twice as many middle-class as working-class Jews in the late-1920s (middle class status then being defined as an annual household income of at least £250).[25] Symbolic of the improved fortunes of East European families was the growing popularity of annual holidays at the seaside or in the country. In 1930, for example, over one hundred kosher hotels advertised regularly in the Jewish press, ranging from luxury resorts in Bournemouth to simple boarding houses in Blackpool. Even the Isle of Man in the Irish Sea boasted two kosher boarding houses.[26]

Before World War II, the contribution of formal education to the rise of East European Jews was modest. State-sponsored primary education was universal, but secondary education was for an elite, those who excelled at test-taking *and* whose parents were able to dispense with their potential earnings while they continued their schooling. Most children left school at age fourteen. In Manchester, for example, only 24 percent of all Jewish children received a grammar school education as late as 1950. Still, Jews were well represented at secondary schools in or near Jewish districts; for example, 50 percent of the students at Clapton County School were Jewish, 40 percent at Hackney Downs Secondary School (The Grocers), 60 percent at the Central Foundation School.[27] But this was unusual. Most Jews did not receive a secondary education in the interwar period. Given this, it should be no surprise that the number of East European Jews who attended university—and then entered the liberal professions and other high-status occupations—was small. Outside London, there were fewer than one thousand full-time Jewish university students in the late 1930s, and of these about one-quarter were from abroad, that is, from the United States, other English-speaking countries, the Yishuv, and Germany. About two-thirds of Jewish students were reading medicine. (Law was much less popular, in part because few solicitors were willing to take Jews as articled clerks.) With the exception of Jewish students at Oxford and Cambridge, who came disproportionately from well-established families, few read arts or science subjects. Yet however small their absolute numbers, Jewish students were still "overrepresented" at the universities, even in the 1930s. Less than 1 percent of the population as a whole, Jews constituted 2 percent of the students at Oxford and Cambridge, almost 4 percent at Manchester, and over 7 percent at Leeds.[28]

As Jews moved into the middle class, abandoning the districts and trades of their parents or their own youth, they encountered new levels of ill-will and unpleasantness. In part, this was a matter of timing. Their embourgeoisement coincided with a period of industrial depression, long-term unemployment, labor unrest, and bad housing conditions, when the national mood was dark and anxious. Moreover, it took place at a time when news-making events abroad—the Bolshevik revolution, riots and armed revolt in Palestine, the rise of the Nazis—heightened the "Jew consciousness" of ordinary Britons. But it was not just a matter of bad timing. Residential and economic mobility brought Jews into contact with Gentiles more frequently than before. Earlier in the century social relations between immigrants and English men and women were limited, since the former tended to work and socialize among themselves. Now, for the first time, large numbers of Jews were moving into middle-class social space (clubs, schools, shops, restaurants, resorts, cinemas, theaters), disturbing their once homogeneous ethnic character. Jewish women shopping in Golders Green struck gentile observers as exotics, "decked as for some barbaric royal levee," courting attention "with their bold, brilliant eyes": "Bracelets swing from their wrists, chains of big, coloured beads loop their necks, earrings dangle from their ears, diamonds glitter on their pink-enamelled fingers."[29] The reaction to this "invasion" was similar to that which occurred in the United States in the interwar period: occupational and social discrimination, defamation, whispering and sniggering. This is not to claim that the "rise" of the Jews "caused" antisemitism. After all, antisemitism hardly needs flesh-and-blood Jews to flourish. Rather, it is to explain the direction and forms that it took in this period.

Anti-Jewish discrimination in the interwar period was not systematic, poisoning all Jewish contact with the larger society, but it was common enough that few Jews avoided it altogether.[30] Masonic lodges and golf, tennis, and motor clubs introduced membership bans. Restaurants and hotels advertised that they did not cater to Jews. Garages refused to rent cars to them because insurance companies would not issue short-terms policies to Jews and other "high-risk" groups. Admission to public schools and the most desirable colleges became more difficult. St. Paul's, for example, which had welcomed Jewish boys in the late-Victorian and Edwardian years, imposed an undeclared quota, as did University College, London. Those who were admitted to these and similar institutions often found themselves the objects of hostile comments, snide remarks, and, more rarely, physical attacks. Between 1918 and 1928, the London County Council refused to award university scholarships to children who were not British citizens or who had not been born, or had fathers who were not born, in Britain or the Dominions. Occupational discrimination became a problem for men and women seeking employment outside traditional Jewish trades. Newspaper advertisements for secretaries, clerks, and shop assistants specified that Jews would not be hired. Jewish teachers in particular experienced trouble in finding positions. Some changed their names, hoping thereby to get an interview at least. One East End–born teacher recalled a school inspector, who thought well of her as a teacher, strongly advising her to change her name because "it might be a great hindrance to you." In medicine, Jews routinely faced obstacles in obtaining hospital positions and promotions. The atmosphere at the London Hospital, in the heart of the Jewish East End, was markedly hostile to Jewish medical students. One instructor went so far as to allot the back seats in his lecture room to Jews.[31]

Two other resurgent forms of antisemitism heightened the impact of these discriminatory practices. One was the denigration of Jews in low and high culture; the other was ideological, right-wing antisemitism, the variety associated with fantasies and fears about Jewish plots to dominate the world.[32] In the 1920s and 1930s both popular and serious writers—T. S. Eliot, Graham Greene, Wyndham Lewis, H. G. Wells, John Buchan, Rudyard Kipling, Dorothy Sayers, Agatha Christie, Dornford Yates—populated their work with mythic, offensive Jews. One observer remarked in 1935 that "it is unusual to find a reference to a Jewish character in English fiction which is not in the Shylock tradition" and that "it is the rarest thing to find a Hebraic character presented in a normal light." Journalists, travel writers, and social commentators as well represented Jews in unflattering terms, describing them as clannish, oversexed, materialistic, averse to physical labor, alien, and corrupt. One account of East London, in describing the spread of Jews into streets beyond those in which they had been concentrated earlier, spoke of "their predatory noses and features which the word 'alien' describes with such peculiar felicity." Echoing a common anti-immigrant trope from the prewar years, it remarked: "One seems to be in a hostile tribal encampment, and it makes one afraid, not of them personally, but of the obvious tenacity, the leech-like grip, of a people who, one feels in one's English bones, flourish best on the decay of their hosts, like malignant bacilli in the blood." A card game of the 1930s, "Sexton Blake," based on a popular radio program of the same name, included cards picturing "Solly Silver, fence" and "Jake Smith, fence's agent," both drawn as swarthy, hook-nosed Jews.[33]

The common thread running through these ways of thinking about Jews was the notion of Jewish "difference." While the notion was hardly novel, its impact in the interwar period on how Jews thought and felt about themselves was more intense than before. The immigrant generation had lived more or less within its own social and cultural universe. Its social aspirations were limited. What Gentiles thought about Jews was irrelevant to what they thought about themselves. In any case, much of gentile opinion was simply inaccessible to them. This was far less true, however, for the next generation, young, English-educated men and women who came of age and entered the workplace from the 1920s to the 1940s. These upwardly mobile second-generation Jews were unable to escape gentile constructions of "the Jew"—and the more eager they were to succeed outside Jewish circles, the more baleful the impact of these ideas was on their own sense of self-worth and their attitudes to their Jewishness. Living and working outside immigrant neighborhoods, they repeatedly encountered corrosive reminders of gentile constructions of their difference.

Betty Miller (1910–65) brilliantly captured the emotional power of this "civilized" intolerance in her novel *Farewell Leicester Square* (written in 1935 but published only in 1941). The protagonist, Alec Berman, a successful film director who would like to think of himself as an Englishman, is married to a non-Jewish woman who cannot understand why he, as a Jew, lives in a perpetual state of unease and insecurity. Despite his good fortune, he is haunted by a sense that everything he has is built upon sand and can disappear in the blink of an eye. He tells his gentile wife that she cannot understand the emotional state—"a very special type of low-grade fear that's always there, behind every situation"—that even trivial incidents can induce in him, one of the "lucky" ones. "You don't know the sixth sense that tells you the man behind the counter, the boy who sells you a newspaper at the corner, has sized you up; the fact that such a momentary relationship is qualified." Endowed by Miller with self-understanding, Alec grasps how living in what he calls a "spiritual" concentration camp has left him with a "constant sense of inferiority." As he tells his wife, "You've never had the experience of hearing your own race casually vilified; and allowing the remark to pass . . . smiling even. . . . Degraded, again and again, not by the insult, but by your own reaction to it." For Jews like the fictional Berman, Jewishness was a stigma, which, in the words of the Gorbals-born, Oxford-educated memoirist Ralph Glasser, "burdened every step of our lives." Glasser and his friends never considered forsaking their Jewishness formally through baptism (they were socialists with no need for religion), but they hoped "at least to bury it beneath some protective colouring, so that we might go our private ways like everybody else."[34]

In sum, interwar intolerance was, in general, neither brutish nor shrill. Indeed, there was probably less social, occupational, and educational discrimination than in the United States. Few Britons were obsessed with Jews, viewing them as evil incarnate and the cause of national decline, just as few Britons were attracted to extremist political movements. Even for those who caricatured or excluded them, Jews were usually a side issue, not an obsession. Those who embraced what Saul Friedländer calls "redemptive" antisemitism, a worldview that attributes the degeneration of the nation to Jewish penetration and links its redemption to the destruction of the Jewish peril,[35] were very few indeed. While antisemitism (in all its forms) was more common and touched more Jews in this period than before, it was not so overwhelming that it caused thousands of Jews to seek relief in conversion or other forms of radical assimilation, as happened in Central Europe.

Still, brutish, shrill, ideological antisemitism was not altogether absent. In the years between the Bolshevik Revolution and the start of World War II, right-wing, conspiratorial antisemitism gained a hearing, if not broad popular support. In the aftermath of the upheaval that followed World War I, otherwise reasonable persons were prepared to consider the possibility that "the Jews" were a subversive force conspiring to dominate the world. In 1920, both *The Morning Post* and *The Times* published and discussed the notorious tsarist forgery *The Protocols of the Elders of Zion*. Gentile friends and acquaintances of Jews asked them in all seriousness whether there was indeed a shadowy Jewish force behind the dramatic collapse of the Russian, German, and Austrian empires.[36] A handful of reactionary antisemites—Arnold Leese, Henry Hamilton Beamish, Archibald Maule Ramsay, Nesta Webster—began to agitate against Jewish influence at this time and continued to stir up hostility to Jews throughout the interwar period. But few attended their meetings, and even fewer joined their organizations, which remained on the fringe of conservative politics. Once the Bolshevik scare and xenophobia of the immediate post–World War I years receded, few Britons were attracted to obsessional, "hidden hand" antisemitism. This version of the "Jewish Question" lacked broad popular appeal and propaganda value, even when manipulated by a gifted agitator like Sir Oswald Mosley.

In the mid-1930s, Mosley tried to introduce the "Jewish Question" into British political life.[37] When he founded the British Union of Fascists (BUF) in October 1932, he made no mention of Jews at all, but within six months his followers were assaulting Jews and distributing anti-Jewish handbills. Then, in a speech at the Albert Hall on the evening of 28 October 1934, Mosley launched a full-scale attack on Jews and their influence, inspired, it seems, by Hitler's recent successes and convinced, mistakenly, that Jew-baiting would attract votes. His accusations, on this and other occasions, were not original. He charged that Jews were a foreign, antisocial menace, exploiting British society and exerting disproportionate, deleterious influence. When denounced for turning to gutter politics, he claimed that he did so in self-defense, that the BUF was only responding in kind to Jewish attacks on the BUF. Both as an ideological movement and an electoral party, the BUF was an abysmal failure. At its peak, in the mid-1930s, it had around sixteen thousand members; at its suppression in May 1940, it had eight to ten thousand members. It never won a seat in Parliament or on a local council, even in East London, where its support was greatest and where it concentrated its efforts.

These failures have led some historians to minimize the importance of the BUF in Anglo-Jewish history and to conclude that at most it was a minor irritant.[38] While it is true that the impact of the BUF on British politics was small, this is a different issue from the question of how its activities influenced British Jews. The BUF's anti-Jewish campaign was not limited to conventional political tactics, such as distributing handbills or staging rallies. Like the fascist parties of Germany and Italy, which it consciously emulated, it used terror and violence to promote its ends. Uniformed members of the BUF (Blackshirts) marched through East London districts, singing Nazi songs and chanting anti-Jewish slogans. They daubed hate messages on walls and windows and staged outdoor street-corner rallies. They smashed windows in Jewish houses and shops, assaulted Jews out walking alone at night, often sending them to hospital, overturned the stalls of Jewish market traders, picketed Jewish shops, shouting antisemitic slogans and intimidating potential customers, and, on at least one occasion, threw flaming torches into Jewish shops. They desecrated synagogues with slogans and even with the severed heads of pigs. In October 1936, one week after an antifascist front of a hundred thousand Jews and Gentiles blocked a BUF procession through the East End ("the Battle of Cable Street"), the BUF retaliated with a small-scale pogrom in Mile End Road. A gang of 150 young Mosleyites smashed the windows of and looted twenty-nine Jewish shops in the Mile End Road and sixteen Jewish shops in Green Road. They set an automobile on fire and threw a man and a girl through a plate-glass window while the crowd shouted "Down with the Yids." In Manchester, they invaded Cheetham, the Jewish quarter, in uniform, making insulting remarks and attacking Jewish youth, often four or five times a week. In Oxford, they ragged Jewish students and pasted antisemitic labels on their doors.[39] Violence — and the threat of violence — sowed fear, panic, and terror throughout the community, not just among those who were its immediate targets. Moreover, because it occurred at the same time that Jews were reading about Nazi violence in Germany and viewing newsreel footage of Nazi rallies, book burnings, and marches, it had a more powerful impact than it might have had otherwise.[40] It was little comfort to Jews to know, assuming they could have known at the time, that the BUF was "doomed" to fail.

Concern about domestic antisemitism and, after 1933, events in Germany informed the conduct of communal politics until after World War II. Zionists and anti-Zionists, Reform and Orthodox, Communists, Labourites, Liberals, and Conservatives, rich and poor alike, were swept up in debates about how Jews should react and, more generally, how they should conduct themselves. Even Jewish notables, who were descendants of families settled in Britain for a century or more and who enjoyed close ties to the English Establishment, were unable to escape antisemitism's reach, despite the fact that they were rarely its immediate victims. Although their wealth and influence shielded them from physical harm, antisemitism still exacted a heavy toll. In their case, however, the toll was emotional, rather than physical or material, a blow to their self-esteem and self-image. Because they wanted to think of themselves as English to the core, simple knowledge that there were Englishmen who repudiated their claims, insisting instead that they were different in kind, was sufficient to be unsettling. It made them anxious about the future and caused them to wonder how secure their position was. Their anxiety, along with the fears of Jews who experienced discrimination, intimidation, and violence at firsthand, made communal politics in the interwar period and during World War II fractious and ferocious, perhaps more so than at any earlier time.

The divisions in communal life in the 1920s and 1930s were less clear-cut and the issues more complex than before World War I. With East European immigration at a near standstill and residential dispersion under way, the aliens issue lost its urgency. Time, exposure to English schools and mass culture, and increasing prosperity were at work, making the immigrants and their children less foreign in their speech, dress, habits, and tastes, although outsiders often failed to recognize the extent of this transformation and continued to think of the old Jewish districts as exotic enclaves. *The Times,* for example, in a series on "Alien London" in 1924, characterized the East End as "a strange and alien city" and "an Eastern stronghold," much like "a Jewish lane" in Odessa or in a Galician "ghetto," alive with "all the expressive gestures of the bazaars of the Near East" and home to "the backward" and "the less adaptable" element among the East European Jewish population."[41] Because of this perception, the communal establishment was unable to leave the East End and similar districts to their own devices. Reinforcing their concern was the growing social homogeneity of these districts, which, with the exodus of successful Jews to better neighborhoods, became more lower class in makeup than before. The traditional immigrant trades (small scale manufacture of garments, footwear, and furniture), which were plagued by high unemployment in the late 1920s and early 1930s and hard hit by the Great Depression, continued to provide the main source of jobs for those who had not moved to the inner and outer suburbs. For them, career choices and expectations of what the future would bring were limited. As the East End novelist Willy Goldman (b. 1910) remarked (with some hyperbole), the garment trade was "the unescapable destiny of an East End Jew." It was "all fixed at the cradle." The one detail about a son's future that remained to be decided was whether he should enter "ladies" work or "gents."[42] While it would be incorrect to say that a cloud of hopelessness had settled over the East End, there is little question that life there was drab and harsh. Hard-pressed market traders and out-of-work sweatshop workers, battered by class warfare and generational conflict, populate the 1930s East End "proletarian" novels of Goldman and Simon Blumenfeld (b. 1907). *The New Survey of London Life and Labour* concluded that the Jewish working class community of East London was "on the whole a poor community, its proportion of poverty being slightly greater than that of the surrounding non-Jewish population (13.7 per cent as compared with 12.1 per cent)."[43]

The poverty of the old immigrant districts, along with the estrangement of the second generation from the ways of their parents, created a fertile breeding ground for behavior, both social and political, that attracted unwanted attention and distressed communal leaders. The children of the immigrants were drawn to the popular culture of the non-Jewish population more than the Old World culture of their parents. Most showed little interest in religious worship or observance and blatantly disregarded the Sabbath. The Judaism of the immigrant synagogue, with its foreign-born, Yiddish-speaking functionaries, could not compete with the amusements of urban life. When the young went to synagogue, it was often to please their parents and avoid an open break. They preferred to spend their leisure time at the billiard hall, the cinema, the theater, the dance hall, the football stadium, the racetrack, and the boxing arena. Promenading in public, dressed to the hilt in up-to-the-minute fashion, was more popular than worshipping or studying, judging by the crowds that filled the main thoroughfares of immigrant districts on Friday nights and Saturdays.[44] Even more than before the war, British-born working-class Jews were enthusiasts for prizefighting, renewing a connection between Jews and the ring that had flourished in the late-Georgian period. They distinguished themselves as trainers, promoters, managers, and boxers, supplanting the Irish as the dominant ethnic group in the ring. A few were found in less savory niches in the world of working-class culture, as bookmakers, receivers of stolen goods, keepers of illicit gaming clubs (*spielers*), pimps, and enforcers. They were especially conspicuous in the racetrack gangs that thrived in the 1920s and 1930s, selling protection to bookmakers and helping them collect gambling debts, which were not enforceable at law.[45] The Tory Earl of Crawford thought that Jewish "control" of popular sports was far advanced: "prizefighting, dogracing, ordinary horse betting, and the disgraceful pools—in all these directions the Jew betting man is supreme." It is no coincidence that the head of the racetrack gang in Graham Greene's *Brighton Rock* (1938), the corrupt, vicious Colleoni, is a Jew. Indeed, the inspiration for the racetrack violence in the novel, in which razor-wielding Jews attack the Catholic antihero Pinkie, was a similar, widely reported incident at Lewes races in June 1936, although, significantly, at Lewes, the roles were reversed: the victims were a Jewish bookmaker and his Jewish clerk, while the attackers were rival gentile gangsters.[46]

The "irreligion" of second-generation working-class Jews and their fondness for low-life amusements alarmed lay and religious leaders. They believed that the association of Jews with illicit or vulgar activities offered grist to the antisemitic mill, providing Jew-baiters with evidence of Jewish deviance and depravity. They feared as well that the revolt of the young against parental control and religious discipline boded ill for the future of the community. In becoming English, it seemed, the second generation had thrown out the baby with the bath water. Communal leaders voiced concern about the radical turn that anglicization had taken and searched for means to "re-judaise" the East End young and stem their drift to hedonism and materialism. Rabbi Meir Jung (1858–1921), chief minister of the Federation of Synagogues, for example, created a network of Sinai Associations, the first in Whitechapel, which combined social and literary activities with Jewish study. But the chief instrument for middle-class influence was the youth club.[47] First established in the prewar period to promote immigrant anglicization, the clubs thrived in the 1920s and 1930s, attracting thousands of members. They fielded athletic teams; offered drama, music, and art classes; hosted concerts, lectures, debates, and dances; sponsored weekend rambles and summer camps; and operated savings banks and employment bureaus to help their members "get on." Some, like the Jewish Lads' Brigade, stressed public school and military values: obedience, manliness, self-discipline, physical fitness, patriotism. Others, like Lily Montagu's West Central Jewish Club in Soho and Basil Henriques's Oxford and St.

George's Jewish Lads' Club in the East End, incorporated religious worship and talks. All emphasized character-building, the molding of their members according to the values and traditions of respectable, native, middle-class Anglo-Jewry. In an era before the professionalization of social work, men and women from upper-middle-class backgrounds, like Montagu and Henriques, not only raised funds for the clubs but led their activities and managed their affairs on a day-to-day basis, often living in the district or even on club premises.

The same conditions that detached working-class youth from the religious culture of their parents also drew them to radical, collectivist politics. Before the war, few Jews in these districts took an active interest in politics of any kind. Most were unnaturalized aliens, with an unsure grasp of English, preoccupied, overwhelmed even, with keeping themselves and their families fed and housed. Their British-born, British-educated children, on the other hand, were alive to currents and crises beyond their immediate surroundings. Less willing to tolerate the world as it was, many of them embraced radical politics, especially in the 1930s and 1940s. At the center of left-wing activism in the old immigrant districts was the Workers' Circle (Arbeiter Ring), which functioned as both a friendly society and a cultural, social, and political club. Established by Russian-born Bundists in Stepney in 1909, membership was not limited to those who supported the Bundist program (a mix of Marxism and Jewish cultural nationalism) but included all who identified with the left—trade unionists, Labourites, Communists, anarchists, and Labor Zionists. In the interwar period, there were twenty branches, in both London and the provinces, two of which at least were Communist-controlled. Total membership of the Workers' Circle, which stood at thirteen hundred in 1922, peaked at about three thousand in 1939 and then declined after the war, as the Jewish working class shrank. Circle House in Alie Street, the London headquarters of the movement, opened in 1924 and hosted lectures, concerts, dances, debates, and classes. Workers gathered to read newspapers, play cards or chess, drink tea, and argue. There, in its modest canteen and its provincial counterparts, they found "consolation, a spiritual refuge from the struggle with the day-to-day world, a place to recharge their dreams," as Ralph Glasser recalled.[48]

In the mid-1930s, the Communist Party of Great Britain (CPGB) became a force in Jewish working class districts.[49] Before this, it had been a negligible presence, attracting only a hard core of ideologically committed veteran activists with links to pre-1918 East European politics. Membership in its Stepney branch, most of whose members were Jewish, leaped from 115 in 1934 to 500 in 1939. (The branch's Young Communist League counted an additional 250 members.) It attracted young men and women who wanted to build a better world but were disillusioned with the increasingly moderate Labour Party, a partner in the coalition National Government from 1931 to 1940, and its Irish-controlled Stepney branch, which was unsympathetic to Jewish concerns. It was also attractive because it was more than a political organization. It offered a meaningful, all-enveloping way of life. "To be a Communist," the East End–born Marxist historian Raphael Samuel (1934–96) recalled, "was to have a complete social identity, one which transcended the limits of class, gender and nationality." Jewish Communists lived "in a little private world of their own," within "intense neighbourhood networks and little workplace conventicles."[50] They gathered at the same cafes and attended the same lectures; they listened to readings and debates together and went on holiday and weekend rambles with each other. For some, Communism functioned like a religion, offering answers to ultimate questions, replacing a faith lost or never possessed, providing strength and solace.

Although few Jews became members of the CPGB, its influence in working-class Jewish districts from the mid-1930s to the mid-1940s was far ranging. It mobilized local residents to fight the British Union of Fascists, led rent strikes, organized anti-Nazi demonstrations, agitated to improve conditions in air raid shelters during World War II, and otherwise championed the immediate interests of Jewish workers and traders. One reason it succeeded in winning broad support, including, at times, the support of Jewish businessmen, was that it cooperated with non-Communist groups (trade unions, friendly societies, the Workers' Circle) in popular front–style organizations. The Stepney Tenants' Defence League, for example, which Jewish Communists controlled from its founding in 1937, counted 7,500 members in June 1939, while the Jewish People's Council against Fascism and Anti-Semitism (see below), much of whose leadership was Communist, drew support from all segments of the East End Jewish population, including the synagogues. An even more important reason was that the Communists filled a political vacuum. The Labour Party was indifferent to Jewish fears about Black-shirt violence and the persecution of Jews abroad, while the institutions of middle-class Anglo-Jewry—the Board of Deputies, in particular—failed to hold the confidence of East End Jews. Not only did the Board pursue a low profile, nonconfrontational approach in regard to the BUF, but it also failed to defend the economic interests of Jews (shopkeepers, street traders, and hairdressers) hit by new Sunday trading laws in the 1930s. The willingness of Communists to oppose the BUF from the start, to confront the Blackshirts head on, in the streets and in meeting halls, won them a mass following in working-class Jewish districts. When Jewish voters in the Spitalfields East ward elected the Communist activist Phil Piratin (1907–95) to the Stepney Borough Council in 1937 and, then, in the Mile End division elected him to Parliament in 1945, they were not so much voting for the CPGB's collectivist program as for its antifascist activism.

Piratin's victory in 1945 was the high-water mark of Anglo-Jewish support for Communism. The alliance, it turned out, was both short-term and limited to working-class districts—with a few well-born West End exceptions, of course, like Jack Gaster (b. 1907), son of Haham Gaster, and Ivor Montagu (1904–1984), third son of the second Lord Swaythling. The defeat of Nazism and the breakup of Jewish working-class districts as result of enemy bombing, war-time evacuation, and postwar economic success undermined the foundations of the alliance. In the late 1940s and early 1950s, Jewish Communism melted away. The handful who remained loyal members were mainly intellectuals, and most of them left the CPGB in 1956, following Nikita Khrushchev's revelations about Stalinism and the Soviet invasion of Hungary.

The disagreement between the Board and the East End about responding to the BUF belonged to a larger debate about Jewish politics in the interwar period. Old-line communal leaders were confused and frightened by growing hostility to Jews. They believed in a distinctive British tradition of toleration and fair play, attributing to it their fortunate exemption from the persecution that was the lot of Jews elsewhere. When confronted with evidence to the contrary, they fell back on two explanations. One, they attributed the rise in Jew baiting to the importation and manipulation of foreign, un-English doctrines. The barrister Neville Laski (1890–1969), president of the Board of Deputies from 1933 to 1939, traced the spread of racial antisemitism to Mosley and his followers, whom he accused of introducing "a new and strange element" (Nazism) into English public life. Its influence had created a "Jewish Question." Two, they also attributed antisemitism to undisciplined, vulgar, and illicit Jewish behavior. (That the two explanations were at odds with each other did not trouble those who invoked them.) This interpretation, in vogue since at least the late-nineteenth century, assumed that there was a link between what Jews did and what Jew baiters said about them, that Jews themselves contributed to antisemitism by misbehaving, that is, by overdressing, engaging in sharp practices, propagating unpatriotic doctrines, and breaking the law. The president of the Council of Manchester and Salford Jews, Samuel Finburgh (1867–1935), a cotton manufacturer and former Conservative MP, for example, told the council in 1934 that the cause of antisemitism, in both Germany and England, was "the one pernicious fault" of the Jews—"ostentation." Basil Henriques wrote in his club newsletter during the war that Jews who "do a lot of low-down things" were "very largely the cause of anti-Semitism." At times faith in the link between Jewish behavior and antisemitism had ludicrous consequences. In 1936, for example, the Jewish Lads' Brigade withdrew temporarily from the Prince of Wales Boxing Shield competition, which it had won repeatedly since its inception in the early 1920s, because it did not wish to provoke gentile envy. A similar motive led the *Jewish Chronicle* in 1937 to consider, in all seriousness, whether the community should voluntarily restrict the entry of young Jews into medicine, law, and accountancy.[51]

Before the appearance of the BUF, domestic antisemitism did not alarm the Board of Deputies. Its defense policy, to the extent it had one, was to rely on the press committee it had established in 1920 to respond to anti-Jewish slurs in newspapers and periodicals. By the mid-1930s, however, it was clear that more energetic steps were needed, but there was disagreement about what they should be. The Board's leaders, who were more anxious about antisemitism than their public rhetoric suggested, were opposed to direct confrontation and urged Jews to keep away from BUF meetings. They did not want to provoke further violence and feared that a *Jewish* response would backfire. It would give the BUF the publicity it was seeking and would cast the fight against fascism as a Jewish rather than a British issue, further separating the Jewish community from the rest of the country. In Laski's words, "If Jews wish to fight Fascism in this country, they must fight it as citizens and not as Jews."[52] In summer 1936, however, with BUF terror mounting, the Board decided to establish a defense committee with a mandate to take new measures.

The defense committee instituted two new programs. It launched a large-scale public relations campaign to counter anti-Jewish accusations and highlight Jewish contributions to British life. In the naive belief that ignorance about Jews and Judaism fostered antisemitism, it produced and distributed books, pamphlets, and leaflets, supplied the press and the BBC with information on the community, wrote letters to the editor, using the names of Jewish and non-Jewish backers, and dispatched volunteer speakers to open-air meetings. Armed with notes that the committee supplied, the speakers were prepared to answer questions about "The Jews and Bolshevism," "The Kol Nidrei Prayer," and "Chain Stores" or hold forth on "The Jew as Sportsman," "Jewish Pioneers of Empire," and "The Jewish Contribution to English Literature." The committee claimed, in 1943, that this kind of work kept antisemitism "within bounds," without substantiating its claim, which was, in the nature of things, unverifiable.[53] The second, more novel initiative was the establishment of "vigilance" committees in London and the provinces, which, along with tracking local outbreaks of antisemitism, monitored Jewish misdeeds, particularly in business. The assumption, again, was that the activities of unscrupulous Jews fed the fires of Jew-hatred. The committees investigated charges about price-cutting, conditions of employment, fraudulent bankruptcies, commercial swindles, and, during World War II, black marketeering, and, when they were found to have merit, tried to pressure the offenders to alter their conduct. In 1940, these committees merged into a body independent from but linked to the Board, the Trades Advisory Council, which, at the start of the twenty-first century, remains active, aiming to eliminate friction between Jews and non-Jews in economic life.

To Jewish nationalists and left-wing activists, as well as those who bore the brunt of Blackshirt attacks, the response of the communal establishment was pusillanimous.[54] In summer 1936, at a time when the Board was beginning to overcome its reluctance to act, a coalition of Jewish groups who wanted a vigorous response—trade unions, East End synagogues, the Workers' Circle, friendly societies, Zionist organizations, ex-servicemen's groups—created the Jewish People's Council against Fascism and Anti-Semitism (JPC). With local Communists taking the lead, it organized mass meetings, distributed leaflets, visited mayors, lobbied the Home Secretary to ban uniformed marches and racial incitement, and cooperated with other, mostly left-wing, antifascist organizations. Above all, it confronted Blackshirt gangs in the streets—until the government banned the BUF and jailed its leaders in 1940. On 4 October 1936, when the BUF tried to march through the East End, the JPC and its allies mobilized one hundred thousand people to stop them. (The Board of Deputies called for restraint and urged Jews to stay at home.) The antifascist crowd forced the police to divert the march from its planned route, and, in trying to remove barriers erected by the crowd to block the BUF, the police clashed with antifascist demonstrators, a confrontation known as "The Battle of Cable Street." In response to the escalation of violence, the government pushed through the Public Order Act, which, in effect, outlawed uniformed processions. However, the law did not ban BUF meetings or stop BUF gangs from harassing Jews.

The JPC's militant independence and left-wing complexion infuriated the Board's old-line leaders. They denounced its tactics and its view of the problem, which it framed—in explicitly political terms—as opposition to fascism rather than antisemitism alone. Laski and other communal notables believed that British Jews had no collective political interests of their own. They put their faith in Britain's liberal tradition, trusted in the state's goodwill, and relied on its representatives to protect their persons and property. In addition, they were outraged by the JPC's independence, which challenged their own long-standing claim to speak for British Jewry. Despite the Zionist assault on their authority earlier in the century, they still saw themselves as the legitimate representatives of the community, believing that they alone had the right to treat with the government in regard to Jewish matters. Their arrogance, alienation from the fears and concerns of second-generation Jews, and failure to act boldly cost them the confidence of their "followers" and further eroded their influence.

The response of the communal establishment to the rise of Nazism also aroused criticism and for similar reasons.[55] In March 1933, following Hitler's first anti-Jewish measures, the call arose in Jewish communities in Britain and America to organize a boycott of German goods and services. In Britain, boycott committees were formed and protests were staged, including a thirty-thousand-person march from the East End to Hyde Park on 20 July 1933. These activities enjoyed the support of all sections of the community, except for the old elite. In September, with the Board of Deputies and the even less representative Anglo-Jewish Association unwilling to back the boycott or public protests, a broad coalition of groups established a coordinating committee, the Jewish Representative Council for the Boycott of German Goods and Services (JRC), headed by Morris Davis (1894–1985), president of the Federation of Synagogues, Labour politician, and Zionist. The Board's leaders withheld their support for two reasons: first, they were uncomfortable with popular, collective Jewish politics and, second, the boycott would embarrass the government, whose policy was to appease Germany, and thus suggest that Jewish interests were different from those of other citizens. (Britain and its empire were Germany's biggest trading partner in the 1930s.) Over 350 Jewish organizations, with a total membership of 170,000, belonged to the JRC. The vitality of the boycott campaign fluctuated in the six years before the war and, even when most active, was of course unable to weaken the Nazi regime. It was important, however, for what it did for its backers; it allowed them to voice their outrage and overcome their sense of helplessness, thus restoring to them a measure of self-respect. In general, until late 1938, the Board's leaders opposed Jewish protest meetings against Nazi persecution, not wishing to take a public stand in opposition to the Chamberlain government's hopes for rapprochement with Germany. Their low-profile strategy, needless to say, provoked anger and dismay in broad segments of the community. Even Neville Laski's father Nathan (1863–1941), the leader of the Manchester community, took his son to task for the Board's lack of action.

The tide of refugees fleeing Nazi persecution also challenged the communal elite's understanding of Jewishness and the place of Jews in the British state. Jews began leaving Germany soon after Hitler became chancellor in January 1933. As their situation deteriorated, especially after Kristallnacht (9–10 November 1938), when even the most die-hard assimilationists realized that there was no future for Jews in Germany, they became ever more desperate to emigrate. It was their misfortune — and that of the Jews of Austria and Czechoslovakia after the German annexations of March 1938 and March 1939 respectively — that in the 1930s the liberal states of the West were unwilling to open their doors to Jewish immigrants as widely as they had before World War I. In both the United States and Great Britain, high unemployment, xenophobia, indifference to Jewish suffering, and overt antisemitism created an atmosphere that was hostile to large-scale Jewish immigration. To compound the problem, British officials also refused to open Palestine's doors, fearing that a mass influx of Jews would antagonize Arab nationalists throughout the Middle East, driving them into the German and Italian camps, and outrage Muslims in India, as well, where British rule was also threatened.[56]

The communal notables were ambivalent about Britain becoming a sanctuary for German-Jewish refugees. To some extent, they shared the view of government ministers and officials that a dramatic increase in the size of the community would create more antisemitism and thus saddle Britain (and themselves) with a German-style "Jewish Question." (In the 1930s, of course, neither they nor their counterparts elsewhere were able to foresee the horrors the future would bring.) Moreover, even to the extent that they felt that the official perception was incorrect, they lacked the confidence to challenge it and mobilize political support for a more humanitarian approach. They were frightened by the rise of domestic antisemitism, unaccustomed to popular politics and the mobilization of public opinion, and reluctant to fight for Jewish interests if doing so could be labeled as disloyal. As in the fight against the BUF, they believed that Jews must put the interests of the nation, *as officialdom defined them*, before their own "parochial" concerns. Yet, however timid or unimaginative they were in dealing with Westminster and Whitehall, Laski and his associates were not insensitive to the plight of Jews under Nazi rule. They felt bound to them by ties of peoplehood, fate, and history. Indifference or inaction would have been unthinkable. When disaster struck Germany's Jews in the 1930s, they responded with unflagging energy but in a manner that was, at the same time, consistent with their understanding of correct, effective political behavior.

Until the outbreak of the war, the cornerstone of communal refugee policy was an unusual agreement reached in April 1933 between the government and four leading Jewish figures—Laski; Otto M. Schiff (1875–1952), a German-born merchant banker, president of the Jews' Temporary Shelter, and founder of the Jewish Refugees Committee; Leonard G. Montefiore (1889–1961), Claude Goldsmid Montefiore's only child and president of the Anglo-Jewish Association; and Lionel L. Cohen (1888–1973), a barrister and chairman of the Board of Deputies' Law, Parliamentary, and General Purposes Committee. The government agreed to relax the legal requirement, dating back to 1919 and 1920, that immigrants needed to demonstrate their ability to support themselves in Britain. In return, the four men pledged that the Jewish community would not allow any refugee to become a charge on public funds. They assumed, and assured the government in good faith, that the total number of refugees would be small and that those who came would eventually re-emigrate to countries that were better suited, in their view, to receive immigrants. It was also understood that the Jewish community would control the influx, limiting the number who came and selecting those who would be the least troublesome and the most likely to re-emigrate. To this end, Schiff met regularly with officials at the Home Office to discuss individual cases and to help determine which categories of immigrants were to be admitted. Meanwhile, a host of organizations, some newly created, took charge of the refugees on their arrival, providing them with housing and food, helping them to obtain work, allowing them to continue their education, and the like. The most important were the Jews' Temporary Shelter, which had been founded in 1884 to assist East European immigrants and now took care of the immediate needs of the German refugees on their arrival; the Jewish Refugees Committee, which handled the admission of refugees and their maintenance, training, education, and re-emigration (when possible); and the Movement for the Care of Children from Germany, which was established in November 1938 to transport and care for unaccompanied children under age sixteen. These and other aid organizations were funded primarily by the Central British Fund for Jewish Relief and Rehabilitation, which was established in April 1933 and supported by both Zionists and non-Zionists. Before the outbreak of the war, British Jews contributed over £3 million to refugee relief work.[57]

The number of refugees admitted before November 1938 was modest — about eleven thousand — and, while a challenge to the community's organizational and fiscal resources, did not overwhelm them. However, after Kristallnacht and the Nazi takeover of Austria and Czechoslovakia, the situation became more desperate. In July 1938, the Home Office adopted a more liberal attitude in the matter of admissions, cutting red tape and accelerating the migration process. This resulted in the arrival of another forty-four thousand refugees between November 1938 and the start of the war in September 1939. This shift, however, met with resistance from Schiff and other refugee workers, who wished to tighten admissions, since their organizations, not the government, were responsible for the settlement and maintenance of the new arrivals. Overwhelmed by paperwork and decision making about admissions and alarmed at the cost of caring for tens of thousands of new dependents, few of whom had realistic chances of re-emigrating, they continued to advocate a policy of selective admissions. The government, however, overrode their resistance. By the start of the war, Britain had admitted more refugees, relative to the size of its population, than the United States, whose absorptive capacity was far greater.

British Jews gave the German-speaking newcomers a mixed welcome.[58] Some threw themselves into refugee work, helping the refugees find employment, easing their way into the life of the community, taking in children who arrived on the *Kindertransporte*. But there were those, as well, who remained indifferent and did not respond to appeals for funds and, more importantly, for homes for unaccompanied children, one-third of whom, as a result, were placed in Christian homes.[59] (This undoubtedly contributed to the high rate of radical assimilation among German Jews in Britain after the war.) Communal bodies and leaders were often insensitive to the feelings and needs of the newcomers. Even while working to admit and settle refugees, they feared that their presence would exacerbate antisemitism and thus admonished them to behave—to maintain a low profile and avoid calling attention to themselves. The Board of Deputies prepared a booklet, *While You Are in England* (1939), which all refugees received on arrival, containing a list of "do's" and "don't's" that reflected this fear. It advised the refugees to avoid speaking German and reading German newspapers in public, talking loudly, dressing conspicuously, taking part in politics, and, above all, commenting on how much better things were done in Germany. Social contact between refugees and English Jews was limited. What little contact there was—largely at the institutional level—left the new arrivals feeling humiliated, patronized, even resented. British Jews tended to view them as arrogant, "too assimilated" ("more German than Jewish" was a common observation), and deserving of their fate for having shed their Jewishness.

The rise of Nazism also contributed to shifting the balance between Zionism and anti-Zionism in communal politics.[60] By confirming the Zionist claim that emancipation (at least in Central Europe) was a failure, events in Germany broadened its appeal and strengthened its hand in communal politics. The issuance of the Balfour Declaration in 1917 and then, in 1920, the announcement of Britain's mandate for Palestine and the appointment of Herbert Samuel as high commissioner had captured the imagination of large numbers of British Jews. From 1917 to 1921, membership in various Zionist groups in Britain rose from about four thousand to thirty thousand; the number of societies affiliated to the English Zionist Federation rose from 61 to 234. From 1916 to 1918, the amounts contributed to various funds jumped from just over £500 to just under £120,000.[61] But this initial euphoria did not last, and in the 1920s interest in Zionism waned. Whereas in 1918–19, about twenty thousand persons purchased the shekel (that is, paid two shillings to belong to the World Zionist Federation and vote in its elections), in 1928–29, little more than nine thousand made this minimal commitment.[62] In the old immigrant neighborhoods, interest in Zionism remained alive among those who had been born abroad and remained attached to religious tradition. For them, the idea that Jews were a discrete nation whose fate was tied to the Land of Israel was neither outlandish nor threatening. Their children, on the other hand, were more inclined to seek salvation elsewhere, and, to the extent they embraced political activism, leaned leftward—to trade unionism, communism, the

Workers' Circle, and the Labour Party. Zionist officials voiced concern throughout the interwar period that Communism in particular attracted the best and the brightest among young Jewish workers.[63]

In the new suburbs, however, among middle-class Jews, Zionism struck deeper roots. In London, the strongest Zionist societies were in Cricklewood and Brondesbury in the northwest and Notting Hill in the west rather than in the East End. This does not mean that suburban Jews who attended Zionist meetings intended to pack their bags and set sail for the East, like the eponymous hero of George Eliot's proto-Zionist novel *Daniel Deronda*. Like other western Zionists, few accepted — and acted on — the classic Zionist doctrine that antisemitism was ineradicable, making Diaspora Jewish life everywhere untenable. Before 1948, no more than a few thousand British Zionists made *aliyyah* (settled in Israel). Rather, Zionism appealed to acculturated, middle-class, suburban Jews of East European background because it gave them a way to express their sense of Jewishness in secular, ethnic terms. It allowed them, in David Cesarani's formulation, to renegotiate their Jewish identity to fit the new social circumstances in which they found themselves, providing them with an ethnic rather than an exclusively observance-based identity. Moreover, at a time when Jew baiting at home and persecution abroad were on the rise, it allowed them to assert their identity in activist rather than apologetic terms. It became a vehicle for the expression of collective pride and solidarity, a way of shoring up a much battered self-esteem, thus permitting them to remain in Britain without succumbing to feelings of despair or helplessness.[64]

After declining in the 1920s, the number of Jews who paid the shekel rose — to almost eighteen thousand in 1932–33 and more than twenty-three thousand in 1938–39.[65] More critically, during the interwar years, Zionist activists intensified their efforts to "conquer" communal institutions, efforts that met with considerable success. Increasingly, communal bodies took on a Zionist coloration. Beginning in 1921, the Zionist faction on the council of the United Synagogue (US) battled with Sir Robert Waley Cohen (1877–1952), vice president of the US, over the issue of support for Keren Ha-Yesod, one of the two principal fund-raising arms of the Zionist movement. In 1926, at the urging of representatives of suburban synagogues (Hampstead, Hammersmith, Golders Green, etc.), where Zionism flourished, the US voted to collect funds for Keren Ha-Yesod, although Waley Cohen was able to delay the start of the fund-raising for two years by legal maneuvers. From the 1920s, other important bodies — the Federation of Synagogues, the Association of Jewish Friendly Societies, and B'nai B'rith—elected Zionists as presidents or identified unofficially with the Zionist movement. Even before the war, in 1913, Joseph Hertz, a Zionist since the 1890s, replaced Hermann Adler, a vocal anti-Zionist, as chief rabbi.[66]

At the Board of Deputies, Zionist deputies encountered intense resistance, for the stakes were higher there than in other forums, given the Board's role in articulating Jewish opinion to the government.[67] To recapitulate what I wrote above: the Zionist victory at the Board on 17 June 1917, when it condemned the anti-Zionism of the old elite, was the beginning, not the end, of the struggle for control. The presidents of the Board in the interwar period—Sir Stuart Samuel, H. S. Q. Henriques (1866–1925), Osmond Elim d'Avigdor-Goldsmid (1877–1940), and Neville Laski—were not Zionists; Laski, indeed, was fiercely anti-Zionist. But the membership of the Board was changing, as Zionists won election as representatives of friendly societies and of suburban, East End, and provincial synagogues, while the views of other deputies shifted or moderated in response to escalating anti-Jewish activity. In the late 1930s, when the British government in effect repudiated the Balfour Declaration, the Zionists, who were a clear majority on the Board's Palestine Committee, clashed time and again with Laski and his vice presidents, Robert Waley Cohen and Lionel Cohen. Repeatedly, the officers frustrated the Board's directives to protest the repudiation of the Balfour Declaration. Moreover, Laski, Waley Cohen, and others contacted Whitehall officials to make known their own views, without authorization from the Board and behind its back. This, along with Laski's guarded response to Nazism and the BUF, drove an enormous wedge between the old guard and the Board's rank and file. In January 1938, when the Board voted to support the creation of a Jewish Dominion within the British Empire, there were only seven negative votes. Afterward, Lionel Cohen resigned as vice president. In the election to replace him, Dr. Israel Feldman (1888–1981), the pro-Zionist chair of the Palestine Committee, defeated Otto Schiff, an ally of Laski. When Laski resigned in 1939—for personal as much as political reasons—his replacement was the Russian-born, East End–bred Selig Brodetsky (1888–1954), a professor of applied mathematics at Leeds and president of the Zionist Federation of Great Britain. The final stage in the conquest of the Board came in July 1943, following the Biltmore Declaration of May 1942, which called for the immediate establishment of a "Jewish Commonwealth" in Palestine after the war. In a campaign organized by Lavy Bakstansky (1904–71), general secretary of the English Zionist Federation, who represented a small synagogue on the Board, Zionist majorities were elected to all the Board's committees and the Board ended its partnership with the non-Zionist Anglo-Jewish Association on the Conjoint Foreign Committee.

Because Britain held the mandate for Palestine until 1948, London was the hub of World Zionist Organization diplomacy. British Jews were well represented in its headquarters in Great Russell Street and among those who promoted its cause in public forums. The barrister Leonard Stein (1887–1973) and the historian Lewis Namier (1888–1960), who otherwise had no links to Anglo-Jewry, served in turn as political secretary to the Jewish Agency, which represented Zionist interests in mandatory Palestine. British Jews were also prominent in the Palestine administration and in the Zionist civil service in Palestine. Norman Bentwich was attorney general from 1920 to 1931; Albert Hyamson (1875–1974), director of immigration and controller of labor from 1921 to 1938; Cyril Henriques (1880–1976), engineer to the Palestine Zionist Executive from 1925 to 1928; and Colonel Frederick Kisch (1888–1943), chair of its political department from 1922 to 1931. Herbert Samuel's son Edwin (1898–1978) served in half a dozen posts in the Palestine administration between 1920 and 1948. This dimension of the Anglo-Jewish experience, however, belongs more correctly to the history of Zionism, as does the diplomatic work of East European–born Zionist officials, like Chaim Weizmann, Nahum Sokolow (1861–1936), and Moshe Shertok (1894–1965), who lived in London between the wars but neither saw themselves nor were viewed as British Jews.[68]

Britain's assumption of the mandate was not irrelevant, however, to the fate of Zionism within the Anglo-Jewish community. The overlap between British and Zionist interests worked to mute opposition to Jewish nationalism in integrationist circles by deflating the charge that Zionism undermined Jewish loyalty to Britain. After all, how could Jewish support for a government-sponsored project be unpatriotic? Because of this convergence of interests, the anti-Zionist camp in Britain was weaker and less shrill than in other Western states. The League of British Jews, for example, was moribund by the mid-1920s. The mandate, moreover, allowed Jews who opposed the creation of an independent Jewish state to participate in the revival of Palestinian Jewish life through economic investment and philanthropic aid. Waley Cohen established the Palestine Corporation, which developed a host of industrial, agricultural, and financial enterprises, including the King David Hotel, Nesher Cement, the Union Bank, the Palestine Salt Company, and the Ihud

Insurance Agencies. Rufus Isaacs, first Marquess of Reading, became chairman of the board of directors of the Palestine Electric Corporation. In fact, the old elite, with some notable exceptions, was more non-Zionist than anti-Zionist. Unwilling to endorse political Zionism and its ultimate aim of creating a Jewish state, they were eager nonetheless to support what they called "practical" Zionism — the creation of a Jewish center in a British-controlled Palestine that would offer refuge to Jews from less tolerant lands.[69]

Issues of religious authority also divided Anglo-Jewry during this period, at times overlapping with and reinforcing political divisions within the community.[70] Nontraditional forms of Judaism (Reform and Liberal Judaism) expanded their following, largely at the expense of mainstream Orthodoxy. New Reform congregations were established in Golders Green (1933), Glasgow (1933), Edgware (1935), and Leeds (1944), and new Liberal synagogues in North London (1921), South London (1927), West Central London (1928), Liverpool (1928), Belsize Square (1939), and Ealing (1943). In addition, Basil Henriques opened a synagogue in 1919 in his St. George's Settlement in the East End, backed by both the Reform and Liberal movements. Altogether, then, there were fifteen nontraditional synagogues by the end of World War II. The expansion of non-Orthodox Jewish movements reflected the increasing anglicization and embourgeoisement of East European Jews, as well as declining levels of observance and piety in both the old and new communities. They attracted prosperous Jews, from both the old and the new communities, who wanted to retain ties to Judaism but were dissatisfied with the all-Hebrew, multi-hour, sex-segregated services of the United Synagogue (most of whose congregants were not themselves fully observant in any case). The arrival of refugees from Germany, where Reform had triumphed in the nineteenth century, also contributed to the expansion of non-Orthodox Judaism, both in London and the provinces. Of critical importance for this trend, which became even more marked after the war, was the arrival of German Reform rabbis, who transformed the Reform and Liberal movements overnight, providing them for the first time with experienced, well-trained rabbinical leadership.

Fissures within Orthodox Judaism that emerged in the period of mass migration also expanded during the interwar years. East European Jews who moved to middle- and upper-middle-class suburbs tended to join synagogues belonging to the United Synagogue (if in London) or accepting the authority of the chief rabbi (if in the provinces). The less

upwardly mobile continued to belong to smaller, less anglicized congregations. These included London congregations that were affiliated
with the Federation of Synagogues or that joined the separatist Union
of Orthodox Hebrew Congregations (which the Hungarian-born Rabbi
Victor Schonfeld [1880–1930], head of the Adat Yisrael community in
North London, established in 1926), as well as provincial synagogues
that did not recognize the chief rabbi and held the communal establishment at arm's length. The best known case of the latter was the separatist
East European community in Gateshead, near Newcastle, which in the
late 1920s established its own yeshivah — over the objections of Chief
Rabbi Hertz, who tried, but failed, to block the immigration of the
Polish rabbi whom the community invited to head the new institution.
Hertz and the officers of the United Synagogue, most of whom were
not observant, clashed repeatedly with these communities. Their rabbis
objected to Hertz's quasi-official status (especially his legal authority to
decide which congregations were allowed to appoint a marriage secretary), his live-and-let-live attitude toward Liberal and Reform congregations, and his desire to monopolize the supervision of shehitah and
kashrut.

Intertwined with these religious concerns were social and economic
resentments. The chief rabbi and the United Synagogue represented the
wealthiest, most acculturated wing of that section of Anglo-Jewry identifying itself as Orthodox, while those in the separatist camp were immigrants or the children of immigrants, with little social or economic
standing. At the Federation of Synagogues, which Samuel Montagu had
created in 1887 to promote immigrant acculturation, these resentments
erupted in a rank-and-file revolt against the West End leadership of the
Federation. In 1925, the Federation's Board of Delegates forced the resignation of its president, Louis Montagu, the second Lord Swaythling,
who had "inherited" the office from his father, and its executive secretary, who was loyal to him. Montagu was a nonobservant, anti-Zionist,
moneyed West End notable; the man who engineered his removal and
succeeded him in 1928 was the East End Zionist and Labour politician
Morrie Davis.[71] Davis's victory was part of the larger transformation in
communal leadership that took place in the interwar years. In the triumphalist words of the Federation's historian, his rise "bore witness to the
self-confidence and assertiveness of the immigrants and their children,"
putting the old communal establishment on notice "that its unfettered
discretion to order the affairs of British Jewry was at an end."[72]

The outbreak of war in September 1939 ushered in six years of havoc and loss, accelerating changes in Anglo-Jewish life that were already under way.[73] To start, there was the toll taken by German bombing, which began in September 1940 and did not end until March 1945, when the last V-2 rocket hit London. The East End, with its docks, warehouses, railroad termini and sidings, was a prime target. Waves of German bombers rained destruction on homes, workshops, businesses, synagogues, schools, clubs, and communal offices, taking lives, spreading fear, disrupting the provision of communal services. On 11 May 1941, German bombs started a fire that consumed the Great Synagogue in Duke's Place, the eighteenth-century "cathedral" synagogue of the Ashkenazi community. Thousands of children and parents from London and other cities were evacuated to safe areas in the countryside. Most of those who left the old immigrant districts during the war did not rebuild their lives there afterward. The Jewish population of the borough of Stepney fell from about sixty thousand in 1940 to not more than thirty thousand in 1945. The war also took another kind of toll. For six years, it shattered the routines of Anglo-Jewish life and, in particular, made the observance of Judaism, both domestic ritual and public worship and the regime of religious education that sustains it, haphazard. The social and cultural horizons of the sixty-two thousand men and women in the armed forces, most of whom did not have extensive social ties with non-Jews beforehand, broadened. Dispersed in units around the world and thus isolated as Jews, with little contact with the few Jewish chaplains in the armed forces, they were very much on their own. Most encountered prejudice, due as much to ignorance as malice, often from soldiers who had never before known Jews.[74] For some, the encounter with antisemitism reinforced their sense of Jewishness; for others, it suggested that it was a liability, an uncomfortable burden to be set aside. Although the long-term impact of military service on Jewish identity must remain a matter of speculation, it is hard to believe that the experience was irrelevant, leaving no permanent imprint at all.[75]

Civilian evacuees in country towns and villages also found themselves in unfamiliar surroundings. While safe from enemy fire, they, like Jews in the military, faced hostility and incomprehension. Country folk viewed them at best as exotics and outsiders and at worst as loud, overdressed, black marketeers, who aggravated housing, gasoline, and food shortages. For Christians who saw them through the lens of traditional religious doctrine, they were blasphemers and deicides. When the evacuees were also German refugees, the antisemitism took on an extra edge, for they were enemy aliens as well as urban Jews. However, the enmity

The Great Synagogue, Duke's Place, London.
Destroyed by German bombs, 11 May 1941. From a
private collection.

toward them and other evacuees was mainly verbal and rarely descended
into violence. Evacuees also had to cope with the limited availability of
kosher food and facilities for worship and religious instruction. Some
of them — the young in particular — did not find their absence a hardship
and, indeed, welcomed the chance to become more "English" (that is,
less observant). In any case, Jewish practice suffered, at home as well as
among the troops, as did Jewish education. In the long-term, the up-
rooting and dispersion of thousands of Jews during the war contributed
to the decline of religious practice and in all likelihood to the dilution
of Jewish commitments that characterized the second half of the century.

For Jewish refugees from Nazism, the war meant further humiliation
and suffering.[76] At its start, the government established a system of local
tribunals to assign enemy aliens, most of whom were German and Aus-

trian Jews, to one of three categories (A, doubtful loyalty; B, uncertain loyalty; C, unquestionable loyalty) and interned those in category A immediately (about five hundred of the sixty-two thousand persons interviewed). The tribunals were usually sympathetic to the refugees, almost all of whom were placed in category C. However, in early 1940, the right-wing press began to clamor for mass internment, branding the refugees a threat to British security—a nest of spies and saboteurs, a potential fifth column. When the so-called phony war gave way to the Blitzkrieg, and Denmark, Norway, Holland, Belgium, and France fell to the Germans, the mood of the country darkened, and liberal opposition to wholesale alien internment evaporated. In May and June, yielding to war hysteria and pressure from military and intelligence units, the government ordered the internment of all those in categories B and C, except for women in category C. By mid-summer, thirty thousand enemy aliens, the majority of whom were Jewish refugees from Nazism, were being held in makeshift detention camps throughout the country, the largest of which was on the Isle of Man in the Irish Sea. Furthermore, fearing (believe it or not) that the internees would come to the aid of German troops in the case of an invasion, the government started deporting them, mainly to Australia and Canada. When news about British and Canadian soldiers robbing and mistreating the deportees and a German submarine sinking the Canada-bound *Arandora Star* reached Britain, public opinion turned against both deportation and mass internment. Under pressure in Parliament, the government retreated and in late summer began releasing Jewish and other category B and C internees. By August 1941, only two internment camps remained, holding about thirteen hundred refugees.

The anti-refugee hysteria that led to internment in the first place was linked to the continued vitality of domestic antisemitism during the war years. While the banning of the BUF and the detainment of its leaders in May and June 1940 curtailed its public activities, other forms of antisemitism did not diminish. The hardships of the war years—especially the rationing, the blitz, and the absence of loved ones—created a climate that worked against the moderation of old fears and hatreds. Ugly rumors and charges surfaced in the press, survey research, and government reports: East End Jews were panicking in the air raid shelters; Jewish traders were making fortunes on the black market; Jewish homemakers were evading rationing; Jewish evacuees were corrupting the countryside; Jewish men were shirking national service; Jewish women were awash in chocolates, hot-house flowers, silk stockings, diamonds, and fur coats. Above all, as before the war, the chief complaint was that Jews were not English. They were alien, exclusive, clannish, and unassimila-ble. Indeed, they themselves were to blame for creating antisemitism by maintaining their distinctiveness and refusing integration into English society. Why, one letter writer angrily asked the publisher and left-wing publicist Victor Gollancz (1893–1967) in June 1945, do "the Jews stress their religion so much, instead of trying to become assimilated in the countries where they live?" After all, "one does not find Scots all over the globe referring to themselves as Presbyterians, or the Welsh as Wes-leyans, and expecting material favours because of it."[77]

The persistence of antisemitism heightened the unease of communal leaders and thus inhibited their defense of Jewish interests.[78] Fearing they would be accused of championing "Jewish" over "English" inter-ests, they were cautious in challenging wartime policies that discrimi-nated against Jews or that ignored their suffering. They feared that as-sertive, public demonstrations would not only achieve little but would, indeed, aggravate antisemitism — fears that led Lewis Namier to dub them "The Order of Trembling Israelites."[79] For example, when the government interned Jewish refugees in 1940, neither the Board of Dep-uties nor the refugee aid organizations protested. Four years later, when the issue of antisemitism in Polish army units on British soil came to a head, the Board of Deputies refused to participate in a public protest campaign because it did not want to embarrass the government, prefer-ring instead to negotiate behind the scenes with the War Office. In regard to the great life-or-death issue of the time — convincing the gov-ernment to rescue Jews facing death at German hands, whether by open-ing Palestine or Britain to those able to flee the continent or by taking even more dramatic steps — most communal leaders were also cautious. They were aware that an unprecedented tragedy was unfolding but were crippled by their caution and preoccupation with challenges at home. The Board of Deputies was distracted as well by the acrimonious debate between Zionists and anti-Zionists that dominated its meetings during the war years. It also resented the efforts of outsiders, like the anti-Zionist, ultra-Orthodox leader Solomon Schonfeld (1912–84), rabbi of the Adat Yisrael community in North London (and son of its founder), who tried on their own to mobilize support in Parliament for rescue work. For all these reasons, there were no mass demonstrations or other public measures to influence the government to take active steps to res-cue Jews.

This is not to say, however, that the fate of European Jewry would have been different if Anglo-Jewry had been more assertive. It is doubtful whether the cabinet would have responded favorably to Jewish demands to rescue Jews (especially since most rescue schemes included the admission of refugees to Palestine) and that, if it had, it would have been able to save significant numbers of Jewish lives *once the Germans occupied most of Europe*. (Both Great Britain and the United States could have saved several hundred thousand Jewish lives, at a minimum, if they had opened their doors more widely to refugees before the winter of 1941–42.) Acknowledging that the fate of the Jews was in the hands of the Germans and not the Allies is a different matter, however, than understanding the concerns that determined the behavior of Jewish leaders in wartime Britain. What is clear is that the antisemitic climate of the period and the fears it engendered shaped Anglo-Jewish responses to the destruction of European Jewry. Retrospective attacks on the behavior of communal leaders reveal, in the end, more about the historians making them and *their* concerns than they do about the agonizing days of World War II and the unprecedented challenges it presented.

Federation of Zionist Youth on a "gap" year program in Israel. From a private collection.

CHAPTER 6

The Fracturing of Anglo-Jewry
(1945–2000)

In the five decades after World War II, the landscape of British Jewry was transformed in ways both familiar and unfamiliar. Economic mobility and suburbanization, already under way in the interwar years, accelerated. Jews, women as well as men now, entered the professions and the new service industries in increasingly large numbers. By the end of the century, little remained of an inner-city Jewish working class. Antisemitism declined—fitfully and unevenly, to be sure—and Jews were appointed to high-profile positions in government, the universities, and public life. Indifference to ritual and worship, ignorance of Jewish learning and lore, and radical assimilation worried religious and lay leaders as never before, threatening, for the first time, the demographic health of the community. Ideological opposition to Zionism disappeared, except among the ultra-Orthodox and the hard left, while support for the State of Israel, along with memorialization of the Holocaust, became a pillar of Anglo-Jewish identity. What was unexpected, however, was the new vitality and numerical expansion of strict Orthodoxy and its disproportionate influence. Once confined to the margins of Anglo-Jewry, it introduced novel—and polarizing—concerns and standards into the conduct of communal business. By the end of the century, the religious life of Anglo-Jewry was more diverse, fractured, and contentious than in any previous period.

World War II took a heavy toll on Anglo-Jewry. German bombs and rockets flattened synagogues, including the historic Great Synagogue in the City of London, as well as schools, libraries, old-age homes, offices, and cemeteries. The last German rocket to hit London—in March

1945—destroyed a tenement house in Vallance Road in Whitechapel, killing 130 persons, all but 28 of whom were Jews. The blitz and its aftermath also accelerated flight from the East End, the Jewish population of Stepney falling from about sixty thousand to about thirty thousand between 1940 and 1945. Returning servicemen and evacuees, finding their homes and workshops in ruins, sought new lives elsewhere. They moved north to Hackney, which had the largest and densest Jewish population in the 1950s, northwest to Golders Green, Edgware, Finchley, Hendon, and even more distant suburbs, and east to Ilford and Woodford, which had begun to attract Jews in the 1930s. The eastern suburbs in particular experienced extraordinary growth, drawing upwardly mobile Jews not only from the East End but also from North London (Hackney and Stamford Hill). By the end of the century, the borough of Redbridge housed 9 percent of London's Jews. Those who remained in the East End were those who did not have the wherewithal to move—the aged, the poor, the misfortunate. As early as 1948, Rabbi Immanuel Jakobovits (1921–99) remarked on the exodus of persons between the ages of twenty and fifty and the absence of young married couples.[1] The offices of communal bodies, such as the Board of Guardians and the Federation of Synagogues, moved as well. The Jews' Free School, destroyed by bombs in 1941, reopened in Camden Town in 1958. By the 1960s, at the latest, the Jewish East End was in irreversible decline; by the 1990s, no more than four or five thousand Jews remained. The Jewish Soup Kitchen in Brune Street, which was still feeding over fifteen hundred families in the 1950s, closed in 1992.[2] When Bloom's in Whitechapel High Street, the self-declared "most famous kosher restaurant in Great Britain," shut its doors in 1996, the history of the Jewish East End came to a symbolic end.

The large provincial communities—Manchester, Leeds, Glasgow—also became overwhelmingly suburban in the second half of the century. In Glasgow, the immigrant district in the Gorbals disappeared, as did the Gorbals themselves, the result of massive urban renewal in the 1960s. In Manchester, the old Jewish quarter disappeared in the 1950s and 1960s, as Jewish settlement pushed even further into northern and southern suburbs. At the end of the century, one-third of Manchester's Jews lived in the northern districts of Whitefield and Prestwich. The more startling demographic shift in the second half of the century was the dwindling of the provincial communities themselves. During the war, as a result of evacuations, the number of Jews living in the provinces soared, but this growth was temporary. The lure of London was irresistible, especially to the young. There were more opportunities to do well and to make a good match. With few exceptions, provincial communities shrank dramatically in the decades after World War II. Liverpool's Jewish population, for example, which reached seventy-five hundred in the late-1930s, fell to six thousand in the early 1980s and even further, to a little over three thousand, in the mid-1990s (half were age sixty or over), and even though more than 90 percent of Liverpool's Jewish children attended its highly-ranked King David primary and secondary schools, they were in a minority in those schools. The Leeds community shrank almost as dramatically—from about eighteen thousand in the mid-1950s to ten thousand in 1995. As Jewish life outside London waned and became less vital, those families to whom vibrant communal institutions were critical moved as well. As a result, London's demographic importance in Anglo-Jewish life was more marked at the end of the century than ever before. Whereas in 1950, 58 percent of Britain's Jews lived in the capital, by 1995 the proportion was 72 percent. The only other communities with ten thousand or more Jews at the end of the century were Manchester and Leeds, both of which were losing rather than gaining Jewish families.[3]

A further demographic consequence of the war was the permanent settlement of fifty to sixty thousand Central European Jews in Britain. In the long term, however, they did not strengthen the community demographically. Coming from a milieu in which drift, defection, and indifference were advanced, many of them took advantage of British tolerance to shed the minimal Jewish ties and interests they retained. To a greater extent than British-born Jews, they kept their distance from communal bodies and gave their children little Jewish upbringing. On the other hand, their contribution to the cultural and scientific life of Britain was immense, dwarfing that of earlier generations. In the last decades of the century, refugees were awarded the Order of Merit and the Nobel Prize, elected Fellows of the Royal Society, and appointed heads of Oxbridge colleges in record numbers, an indication of the emphasis on intellectual achievement in German Jewish families (and the lack of emphasis in British Jewish ones).[4] It is doubtful, however, whether their achievements benefited the collective life of Anglo-Jewry, for most German- and Austrian-born scholars and researchers were indifferent, at best, to Judaism and Jewish culture. Still, however unrepresentative, there were synagogue-going Jews among the refugees, whose arrival invigorated pockets of Anglo-Judaism. Liberal Jews established a thriving congregation in Belsize Square in northwest London, which featured, for a time, German-language sermons and the *Einheits-gebetbuch* of German Reform. The arrival of several dozen university-educated Reform rabbis, including the theologian Leo Baeck (1873–1956), the head of German Jewry in its final days, enabled the Reform and Liberal movements to expand in the postwar period and to begin training their own rabbis. At the other end of the liturgical spectrum, Orthodox refugees, followers of the separatist, or secessionist, Judaism of S. R. Hirsch, established their own independent congregation, also in northwest London, the Golders Green Beth Hamedrash. In the 1950s, two to three thousand Jews from former British colonies — India, Iraq, and Egypt — arrived, swelling the small non-Ashkenazi population, and in 1967 a small community of Adeni Jews settled in London, following Yemen's declaration of independence. As a result, membership in the Spanish and Portuguese Congregation increased 75 percent between the end of the war and the start of 1959.[5]

Despite the defeat of Nazism abroad, fascism and antisemitism at home continued to plague British Jews in the immediate postwar period. Fascists, some of whom had been interned during the war, regrouped, renewing their attacks on Jews even before V-E Day.[6] From 1946 to 1950, a dozen or so fascist groups operated in London and, to a lesser extent, in the provinces. They sold papers outside tube stations, harangued passersby at outdoor meetings, especially in areas with large Jewish populations (Hackney, Stamford Hill, Edgware), opened bookstores, daubed walls with graffiti, plastered buildings with posters and stickers, and on at least three occasions attacked synagogues. The largest and most active group was the British League of Ex-Servicemen and Women, headed by Jeffrey Hamm, a pre-war follower of Oswald Mosley; in the late 1940s it staged fifteen outdoor meetings a week in London. The fascists exploited postwar privations, as well as resentments generated by Jewish attacks on British soldiers in Palestine, but they were even less successful than before the war in creating a mass movement.

Outraged by the renewal of provocative street-corner antisemitism, recently demobilized Jewish servicemen in London countered with violent reprisals and covert activities of their own.[7] Known as the 43 Group (after the forty-three persons present at the founding meeting in March 1946), the organization counted over five hundred ex-servicemen members by the end of September 1946. Its "commandos" assaulted fascist speakers and stewards, broke up outdoor meetings, destroyed the stock of antisemitic bookshops, and infiltrated fascist groups. Riots, arrests, and free-for-alls followed, which alarmed the Board of Deputies, whose own response to the renewal of fascist antisemitism was much the same as it had been before the war: literature, speakers, and deputations to government officials. The Board's leaders deplored the illegal tactics of the 43 Group and resented its challenge to their claim to represent communal opinion. They also feared that its militancy would enflame popular feelings about attacks on British soldiers and officials in Palestine. Meanwhile, the 43 Group's campaign began to show results. The number of fascist meetings dwindled, their tactics became less provocative and confrontational. Convinced that it had served its purpose, the 43 Group disbanded in April 1950. When British fascism revived, in a minor way, in later decades, it was less interested in Jews than in recent immigrants from Africa, the Caribbean, South Asia, and the Middle East, whose "difference" — in fascist eyes — was more marked than that of Jews.[8]

The rapid deterioration in relations between the British government and the Yishuv (the Jewish community in Palestine) at the end of the war disturbed British Jewish life as much as the revival of domestic fascism. During the war, there had been, in effect, a "cease-fire" between the government of the British mandate and the political mainstream of the Yishuv. However, as the war wore on and news of the destruction of European Jewry reached the West, the Zionist movement became less conciliatory and, at an emergency conference at the Biltmore Hotel in New York City in April 1942, called for the establishment of an independent Jewish state in Palestine after the war (the Biltmore Program), a step it had not taken previously to avoid antagonizing British and Arab opinion. When the Labour Party, which had championed Zionism in the past, triumphed in the general election of July 1945, Zionists everywhere were hopeful that the new government would honor Britain's earlier commitments. They were quickly and bitterly disappointed, however. By late summer 1945, it was clear that the new prime minister, Clement Atlee, and his foreign secretary, Ernest Bevin, intended to court Arab favor in order to protect British oil interests and contain the Soviet Union. This meant that Palestine's doors were to remain shut to the hundreds of thousands of Jewish survivors of Nazism — in Eastern Europe, the Balkans, and displaced persons camps in Germany — who were desperate to settle there.

The announcement of the newly elected government's position ended any hope of avoiding bloodshed in Palestine. Zionist underground groups, on both the left and the right, mounted a campaign of violence, sabotaging railways and oil facilities, bombing government buildings, mining roads, blowing up bridges, and assassinating officials. As British casualties mounted in Palestine (338 British citizens were killed between 1945 and 1948)[9], hostility to Jews at home rose, encouraged, seemingly, by Bevin's own crude, incendiary remarks. Two incidents in particular outraged public opinion. In July 1946, the Irgun, the right-wing underground, exploded bombs that destroyed the wing of the King David Hotel in Jerusalem that housed offices of the Palestine administration. Ninety-one persons were killed, twenty-eight of whom were British. One year later Irgun operatives hanged two British sergeants—in retaliation for the hanging of three Irgun men one day earlier—and then booby-trapped their bodies, causing injury to the officer who cut them down. The last incident, which antisemites exploited for decades afterward, sparked anti-Jewish violence in British cities. Mobs in Liverpool, Glasgow, Manchester, and London attacked synagogues and looted Jewish shops.[10]

The loss of British lives at Jewish hands dismayed Anglo-Jewry—it was, in one sense, its worst nightmare come true—but it did not erode support for the creation of a Jewish state. In the United Kingdom, as elsewhere in the West, Hitler's war on the Jews and the Yishuv's subsequent struggle for independence transformed most Jews into supporters of the idea of a Jewish state.[11] Vocal opposition in the postwar years came almost exclusively from well-born notables whose hold on communal life was eroding rapidly. During the war, when Zionism triumphed at the Board of Deputies, they retreated to the Anglo-Jewish Association, but even this avowedly undemocratic institution, while insisting on its right to articulate Jewish opinion on Palestine, was moving toward a pro-Zionist position. In 1944, diehard antinationalists, fearing that the community as a whole was being tarred with the Zionist label, launched the Jewish Fellowship in order to propagate the view that Jews were a religious, not a national, group. Its leading figures—the club leader Basil Henriques, the American-born Reform rabbi Israel Mattuck, and the former Conservative MP Louis Gluckstein (1897–1979) — were all members of the Liberal congregation in London. It attracted few followers and folded in 1948 after Israel's establishment.

In the second half of the twentieth century, devotion to Israel's welfare became a central concern of British Jews and a pillar of their self-identification. However, this did not represent a victory for classical Zionism. Few Jews, either before or after 1948, accepted the East European–rooted Zionist analysis of the condition of Diaspora Jewry.

They did not believe that emancipation in Britain was a failure and antisemitism an ineradicable threat to their security or that an authentic, fully Jewish life was possible only in the Jewish homeland. Evidence for this is the fact that few made aliyyah. From 1948 to the end of the century, between forty and fifty thousand Jews emigrated to Israel—about 3–4 percent of the community. (However small, the proportion making aliyyah was much greater than in the United States, where the equivalent figure was less than 1 percent.)[12] Nor was the Anglo-Jewish embrace of Zionism an immediate response to the establishment of the state. While the dramatic events of 1948 inspired widespread pride and made Zionism less marginal than it had been, it was not a central component of Anglo-Jewish identity in the 1950s. The statistician Hannah Neustatter noted that while there was "a sense of pride and an emotional attachment to the new state," it did not operate "as a focus of Jewish loyalty in the same way as religion in earlier generations."[13]

The Suez crisis of 1956 once again made the State of Israel headline news, but this time most of Anglo-Jewry was in agreement with the policy of the now Conservative government, headed by Anthony Eden, whose aim was to retain control of the Suez Canal. On the other hand, most of the seventeen Jewish Labour MPs, including Barnett Janner (1892–1982), president of both the Board of Deputies and the English Zionist Federation, followed their party's line and voted to condemn the government—to the distress of much of Anglo-Jewry. On balance, however, the Suez crisis was more a landmark in the British retreat from empire and in the loosening of Jewish ties to Labour than it was in the crystallization of Zionism's centrality in Anglo-Jewish consciousness. Only in the late 1960s, after the Six Day War in June 1967, when the existence of the state and the lives of its Jewish citizens seemed to hang in the balance, did concern for and identification with Israel's fate become central to what it meant to be a Jew in Britain. It then became the most potent force for keeping Jews within the communal fold, as well as for bringing back the estranged and the apathetic. Toward the end of the century, however, this identification weakened somewhat. Jews who came of age in the 1970s and 1980s did not themselves live through the Nazi years or experience the dramatic events of Israel's creation. In addition, the election of right-wing governments in Israel after 1977 diminished the enthusiasm of liberals and socialists. Still, even Likud's obduracy failed to destroy Israel's centrality in Anglo-Jewish consciousness. Survey research in the 1990s found that 43 percent of British Jews felt "strong" attachment toward Israel while a further 38 percent felt "moderate" attachment. These feelings of attachment, not unexpectedly, were stronger among older age groups than among younger ones.[14]

This revolution in Jewish self-consciousness manifested itself in diverse ways. Most obvious was the centrality of fund-raising for Israel in communal life. Professional fund-raisers, working with networks of arm-twisting volunteers, penetrated into every nook and cranny of Anglo-Jewry. In the early 1980s, when donations to Anglo-Jewish charities totaled £40 million a year, almost 60 percent of that amount—£23.7 million—went to Israel-related agencies. The pattern in the early 1990s was the same: Israel received 63 percent—more than £30 million—of the £50 million raised annually. While most of these funds came from a small number of large donors, it was estimated that between 25 and 30 percent of households made regular donations to Israel. However, in the late 1990s, as the centrality of Israel in Anglo-Jewish consciousness began to slip and as communal leaders became more anxious about the health of their own community (an issue to be discussed below), there was a shift in the allocation of donations. In 1996, 49 percent of Anglo-Jewish donations went to Israel-related charities, down from 57 percent in the previous year. Significantly, 60 percent of those who gave to Israel were age 50 or over; indeed, few Jews under age 50—only 21 percent—donated at all to Israel-related charities, even though 85 percent of them were donors to other charities, both Jewish and non-Jewish.[15]

Defending Israel in the media and in political forums also became a priority. Individually and through spokesmen, Jews attacked pro-Arab bias in Whitehall, Westminster, and Fleet Street with novel boldness. Even the previously fainthearted Board of Deputies was combative in Israel's defense, a departure from its prewar low-profile posture. Anglo-Jewry's new assertiveness was due to the departure of the old families from the arena of communal governance and the weakening of antisemitism. It also reflected a profound, if vicarious, sense of identification with the fate of Israel. A further manifestation of the penetration of Zionist sentiment was the growth of Zionist-sponsored day schools. In 1956, the Zionist Federation opened a day school in Edgware and within a few years was funding a network of eight schools in London, attracting students who otherwise would not have attended Jewish schools. By the 1970s Zionist-funded schools were educating almost one-quarter of all children attending Jewish schools. In addition, identification with Israel became a staple of Jewish religious education, except in ultra-Orthodox schools, where the idea of a secular, nonmessianic Jewish state was heretical. Ironically, educators saw the introduction of Israel into the curriculum as a stimulus to Jewish survival in the very Diaspora that Zionism aimed initially to dissolve. One further indicator of the prominence of Israel in Anglo-Jewish consciousness was the large number of Jews who visited the Jewish state. Survey research in the 1990s found that 78 percent of British Jews had visited Israel at some time in their lives and 28 percent had visited four or more times.[16]

Anglo-Jewish devotion to the welfare of Israel in the second half of the twentieth century was remarkable. Not only was it a rejection of the once regnant anti-Zionist fear that the creation of a Jewish state would imperil the status of Jews who wished to remain loyal Britons, but it linked Jewish identity and fate in Britain to events unfolding two thousand miles away, events that were, on the face of it, unlikely to influence the material or legal well-being of Anglo-Jewry. The explanation for this linkage, as well as its intensity, is to be found in the long-term impact of the Holocaust. Like other Western communities, Anglo-Jewry did not come to terms with the destruction of European Jewry until two or three decades after the war.[17] The horror was too overwhelming, too shattering, to be assimilated immediately, as is often the case with traumatic events. In the 1960s, this began to change. The dramatic arrest of the Nazi war criminal Adolf Eichmann in Argentina in 1960, his trial in Jerusalem in 1961, and subsequent execution initiated a process that brought the Holocaust to the surface of public consciousness.

In June 1967, when war broke out between Israel and the Arab states and it seemed, for a few days, that Jews once again faced mass destruction, the Jews of Britain, like their counterparts in France and the United States, experienced what one historian called "a collective trauma" and were overtaken by "by half-buried fears of 'a second Auschwitz' and suspicions of the intentions of non-Jews."[18] This time, however, they reacted with unprecedented vigor, Reform and Liberal Jews, traditionalists and secularists alike. An emergency appeal collected £11 million. Ten thousand persons attended a mass rally of support at the Albert Hall. Eight thousand young people volunteered to fly to Israel to fill jobs left vacant by workers serving in the military—and over seventeen hundred actually went, the largest contingent from any country. Even "non-Jewish" Jews, like the writers Harold Pinter (b. 1930) and A. Alvarez (b. 1929), signed public letters, defending Israel's right to exist.[19]

The passionate attachment to the survival of Israel that Jews showed then and for several decades afterward was linked to their belief that the Holocaust was a turning point, an orienting event, in Jewish history. Perhaps they also felt that they and their parents had been insufficiently active in rescuing Jews in the 1930s and 1940s, feelings that would have fueled a commitment to pro-Israel activism. At the same time, the establishment of the state and its remarkable achievements, military and otherwise, acted as an emotional counterweight to the Holocaust, offering consolation, instilling pride, and restoring confidence that life was not as bleak—or Jews as powerless—as the Holocaust suggested.

It was not the Holocaust alone, however, that made Israel central to Jewish life. The ground was prepared by the steady advance of secularization. In the interwar period, as I noted earlier, Zionism provided a secular, ethnic alternative to a synagogue-based Jewish identity. It flourished, above all, among second-generation, middle-class, East European suburban Jews who associated traditional ritual, worship, and belief with the poverty and Old World habits of their parents and grandparents. In the second half of the century, as Anglo-Jewry became overwhelmingly middle-class and suburban, religious indifference and disbelief became even more widespread. For those Jews who "felt" Jewish but lacked religious belief, identification with and support for Israel provided a means of and rationale for being Jewish. It was, moreover, a way of being Jewish that was neither time-consuming nor socially burdensome. It even allowed Jews who married outside the fold to retain ties to the Jewish community. For wealthy families like the Rothschilds and the Markses and Sieffs, the founders of the Marks and Spencer retail empire, political and philanthropic support for Israel was often their chief link to the Jewish world. Anthony Blond (b. 1928), a nephew of Simon Marks (1888–1964), observed that the Markses and Sieffs "associated davening [praying] with poverty. Their religion wasn't Judaism at all—it was Zionism."[20]

The campaign for Soviet Jewry in the 1970s and 1980s functioned in the same way. In the hope of pressuring the Kremlin to allow Jewish emigration, London Jews picketed public functions and athletic and cultural events, demonstrated outside the Soviet embassy and trade and airline offices, sent endless cables and letters to the Soviet ambassador, and signed countless petitions. These activities, like those on behalf of Israel, provided meaning and direction for Jews whose Jewishness was more ethnic than religious. The Labour MP and communal leader Greville Janner (b. 1928), noting the vitality of the campaign, remarked that "Soviet Jewry was doing infinitely more for our Anglo-Jewish community that we are doing for them."[21] Here too the impact of the Holocaust was felt, for an oft-repeated theme in the campaign was the refusal to remain silent and inactive in the face of Jewish persecution.

The decline of religious observance was a prominent feature of the postwar decades. To be sure, synagogue affiliation rose after the war (from 35 percent in 1933 to 61 percent in 1961, according to one estimate),[22] but this was a function of suburbanization rather than religious commitment. When Jews moved from inner-city, heavily Jewish districts, where their lives were largely Jewish in environmental and sociological terms, to suburbs, where Jewish settlement was less dense, they were forced to become more self-conscious about expressing their Jewishness. Joining a synagogue was one way of doing this.[23] (An additional incentive was that burial privileges were attached to synagogue membership and fees.) But affiliation, while a guide to ethnic cohesion, is not the same as attendance and observance. Second- and third-generation Jews were, on the whole, not as observant as the immigrants, who, for their part, were not as pious as memory painted them. A survey of Jewish university students in the academic year 1949–50, for example, found that 40 percent were indifferent to religion and that 66 percent who came from "very Orthodox" or "Orthodox" homes considered themselves less Orthodox than their parents. At a conference on Jewish life in modern Britain in 1962, Norman Cohen observed that the most fundamental fact of religious life was that "the great bulk of the community" had "only the slightest concern with Judaism." Behind "an impressive facade of institutional religion" lurked widespread apathy.[24]

There was little overall slackening in this trend in later decades. Survey research in the mid-1990s found that 25 percent of those raised in mainstream Orthodox synagogues were currently unaffiliated and that 15 percent were members of Reform and Liberal congregations. (Only 3 percent had moved to the right, joining ultra-Orthodox congregations.) In terms of attendance, 47 percent of adults reported that they attended synagogue once or twice a year or "on occasions" while 26 percent of adults said they never attended. This last group overlapped, in the main, with Jews who were unaffiliated, although 7 percent of synagogue members also fell into this category. In terms of self-definition, 20 percent categorized themselves as "secular" (nonpracticing) while another 23 percent preferred to describe themselves as "just Jewish" (as opposed to "progressive," "traditional," or "strictly Orthodox"). When the Reform movement surveyed young people in the 18-to-35-year-old group in 1995, it found that only 1 percent were attracted by conventional synagogue services, whereas 39 percent were attracted by social, cultural, and artistic activities.[25] For most British Jews, as for most non-Jews, religion at the end of the twentieth century was a marginal activity, "a tenuous association that does not break the rhythms of a life whose pulse is elsewhere," in the words of Chief Rabbi Jonathan Sacks (b. 1948).[26]

The postwar decline in religious observance was not accompanied immediately by a decline in ethnic cohesion. In most families of East European background, communal attachments remained intact for two or three decades. The children and grandchildren of the immigrants continued to feel that Jewishness was an important part of their identity, that they were members of an ancient, much beleaguered community, linked by ties of kinship, ethnicity, and history. Their closest friends and, more importantly, their marriage partners came from families similar to their own, and thus they perpetuated the collective character of Anglo-Jewry, even while moving away from its religious rites. But among families whose roots in England predated the East European immigration, and especially among those who governed Anglo-Jewry before the war, disaffiliation—intermarriage and, on occasion, conversion to the Church of England—made rapid strides. In the 1940s and 1950s, drift and defection weakened the hold of the old families on communal institutions as much as did the challenge mounted by new men of East European background. On the basis of wedding announcements in the London press, Harold Soref concluded in 1953 that it was becoming increasingly rare "for Jews of a certain social class to marry within the faith"—in contrast to a half century earlier, when "such marriages were few and excited comment" when they did occur. One corollary of intermarriage at this social level was the shrinkage—even possible extinction—of the Jewish peerage. Of the twenty-three Jewish hereditary titles at the time, Soref expected eight at most to remain Jewish in the next generation.[27] Yet, since the old elite were few in number relative to the whole community, their exodus created little stir. Soon, however, powerful social and political forces—economic mobility, occupational diversification, and growing toleration, in particular—began to weaken the ethnic cohesion of those of East European background as well, even though their full impact was not felt until the end of the century.

During the second half of the twentieth century, Anglo-Jewry, like other Western Jewish communities, became overwhelmingly middle-class. In the 1950s and 1960s, there were still significant pockets of Jewish poverty. In Stepney and Hackney, Jewish tailors, market traders, taxi drivers, hairdressers, and clerical workers lived in low-status council estates and industrial dwellings. But Jewish trade unionism was nearly extinct, a sure sign of economic mobility. While the number of Jewish trade unions had averaged twenty-two in the years of the first decade of the century, there were only four in the ten years before World War II and only one in the immediate postwar years, the small bakers union, with fewer than one hundred members.[28] An analysis of the social structure of Anglo-Jewry in 1961 found that 44 percent of British Jews belonged to the upper two social ranks (professional and intermediate) while only 10 percent belonged to the two lowest ranks (partly skilled and unskilled). (The respective figures for the British population as a whole were 19 percent and 27 percent.) By the end of the century, few Jews remained impoverished. Among economically active Jews age 18 to 64, only 6 percent of men and 2 percent of women were manual workers. By contrast, 86 percent of men and 76 percent of women were in semiprofessional, managerial, and professional occupations.[29] In comparison to the population as a whole, Jews were markedly more affluent: 60 percent earned over £20,000 annually (in comparison to 26 percent nationally); 24 percent earned over £40,000 (in comparison to 3 percent nationally).[30]

One mark of Anglo-Jewry's new affluence was a shift rightward in politics.[31] In the interwar period, the Conservative Party attracted few Jewish voters and even fewer aspiring Jewish politicians. The reasons are obvious: it represented antisemitism, anti-Zionism, social privilege, and inherited wealth. This combination, especially hostility at the local, or constituency, level, continued to repel Jews even after the war. Among the twenty-eight Jews elected to Parliament in 1945, twenty-six were members of the Labour Party, one a Communist (Phil Piratin), and one an Independent Conservative (Daniel Lipson [1886–1963]), who had defeated the official candidate of the local Conservative Association. Between 1955 and 1970, there were only two Jewish Tories in the Commons—Henry d'Avigdor-Goldsmid (1909–76) and Keith Joseph (1918–94), wealthy, Harrow- and Oxford-educated baronets, who were, in no sense, representative of Anglo-Jewry. But then, in the 1970s and 1980s, many Jews abandoned Labour, in part because it no longer represented their economic interests and in part because its left wing embraced a rabid anti-Zionism that at times veered into antisemitism. At the same time, Margaret Thatcher, whose own constituency, Finchley, included large numbers of Jewish voters, was refashioning the Conservative Party, making it more attractive to Jews. She preferred clever businessmen to well-born grandees and championed the Victorian middle-class values of independence, self-help, and hard work. Perhaps, "as an ambitious, aggrieved outsider in search of acceptance and success, it was natural for her to see Jews as kindred spirits . . . to admire those who triumphed over adversity through intelligence and determination as she herself did."[32] She surrounded herself with Jewish advisers and ministers—at one time there were five Jews in her cabinet—while the number of Jewish Tory MPs rose from twelve in the February 1974 general election to sixteen in 1987 (only seven Jewish Labour MPs were returned that year). In northwest London, the Anglo-Jewish heartland, middle-class Jews voters consistently voted Tory more heavily than other middle-class voters.

The upward mobility of Anglo-Jewry in this period continued a trend that stretched back to the previous century. What was different in the second half of the century was the diversification of the routes Jews took as they moved upward. Before the war light manufacturing and retail trade were the most common paths to prosperity. While Jews continued to achieve success in these areas in the postwar decades, they now made their mark in other areas as well, especially in property development, the entertainment and leisure industries, the professions, and the media. The property market in particular proved to be fertile ground for Jewish entrepreneurial dash, allowing legendary figures like Jack Cotton (1903–64), Charles Clore (1904–79), Harry Hyams (b. 1928), and Harold Samuel (1912–87), at one time the largest property owner in the world, to amass enormous fortunes. Of the 108 people who made over £1 million each in property deals between 1945 and 1965, 70 were Jewish.[33] The common thread running through these areas of economic activity was self-employment. As before the war, Jews preferred striking out on their own to rising diligently in the hierarchical structure of a large corporation or the civil service. In Redbridge, for example, 35 percent of economically active Jews in 1978 were self-employed—many as taxi drivers; in more affluent Edgware in 1971, the figure for all male Jews was 66 percent (in contrast to 7.4 percent of all economically active Britons that year).[34]

Anglo-Jewish affluence in the postwar period was made possible by two simultaneous developments: the expansion of the secondary and tertiary educational systems and the decline of social and occupational discrimination. Before the war, formal education played little role in the economic transformation of Anglo-Jewry. Full-time education beyond the official school-leaving age of fourteen was restricted to a small number of children, mainly boys—those who either competed successfully for scholarship places or had parents able and willing to pay school fees. This began to change at the end of the war. The Education Act of 1944 abolished secondary school fees, and then in the years after the war the "redbrick," or "civic," universities expanded their intake, while local education authorities became increasingly willing to support anyone who gained a place at university. The opening of new universities in the 1960s went even further in making formal education a critical factor in Anglo-Jewish mobility. The number of Jews attending university rose dramatically—from about three thousand in 1950 to six to seven thousand in the mid-1970s. By the end of the century, one-half of British Jews age eighteen to twenty-nine were completing or had completed a university degree—in contrast to the previous generation (age fifty-five to sixty-four), in which less than one-third had obtained a university degree.[35] As a result, large numbers of Jews entered the professions (law, medicine, dentistry, accountancy, industrial chemistry, architecture, engineering, university teaching), the media, and, to a lesser extent, higher levels of the civil service. This trend was already pronounced in the early 1960s, according to a survey of Edgware Jewry, which discovered that about one in six respondents was a professional (one in four among their children). At the end of the century, it was even more marked: among persons in paid employment age eighteen to sixty-four, 54 percent of men and 50 percent of women were in professional occupations.[36] This was a radical departure from earlier periods, when trade (in all its varieties) and light manufacturing dominated the Anglo-Jewish occupational profile.

At the same time that educational opportunities improved, hostility to Jews weakened, especially toward the end of the century. Quotas at public schools, much discussed in the early 1970s, were no longer an issue by the 1980s and 1990s. At the ancient universities, Jewish dons and even heads of colleges multiplied. At Oxford, the intellectual historian and social theorist Isaiah Berlin (1909–97), the most avowedly Jewish figure in postwar British intellectual life, made a brilliant career. He was elected a fellow of All Souls at age twenty-three—the first Jew to be elected there and only the third to hold a college fellowship at any Oxford college—and served as Chichele Professor of Social and Political Philosophy from 1957 to 1965. The following year he became founding president of Wolfson College, which was established with a gift of £1.5 million from Sir Isaac Wolfson, head of Great Universal Stores. In the last three decades of the century, at least a dozen colleges elected Jewish masters. Jews also rose to the highest ranks in the civil service and the media. In national politics, Jews entered the inner circles of both parties—as cabinet ministers, backstairs strategists, and media consultants.

Between 1945 and 1995, fourteen Jews held cabinet rank. The number of life peerages that successive governments awarded Jews also reveals the weakening of old prejudices. Between 1958, when life peerages were introduced, and 1989, fifty-six Jews were ennobled, almost 10 percent of the total.[37] Among them were entertainment moguls (Sidney Bernstein [1899–1993] and the brothers Lew Grade [1906–98] and Bernard Delfont [1909–94]), communal leaders (Barnett Janner and Samuel Fisher [1905–79]), retail magnates (Simon Marks and Israel Sieff [1889–1972]), public intellectuals (Solly Zuckerman [1904–93] and Max Beloff [1913–99]), industrialists and manufacturers (Arnold Weinstock [b. 1924] and Joseph Kagan [1919–95]), solicitors (Arnold Goodman [1913–94] and Victor Mishcon [b. 1915]) and, revealingly, Chief Rabbi Immanuel Jakobovits, whose conservative views on self-help and welfare endeared him to Margaret Thatcher.[38]

One further sign of the waning of public antisemitism was its marginal role in newspaper coverage of Jewish businessmen who were convicted of crimes or viewed as too aggressively enterprising. The activities of the slumlord Peter Rachman (1919–62), which came to light in the wake of the Profumo affair in 1963 and contributed the term *Rachmanism* (exploitation of slum tenants by unscrupulous landlords) to the English language; the high-profile property developments of Charles Clore and Jack Cotton in the 1960s and, especially, Clore's unfriendly takeover of the venerable department store Selfridge's in 1965; Arnold Weinstock's successful bid for Associated Electrical Industries in 1967; the Guinness scandal in the late 1980s, in which several Jewish businessmen and brokers illegally supported the share price of Guinness stock during its takeover bid for the Distillers group; and the mysterious drowning of the financially besieged media mogul Robert Maxwell (1923–90) — all made Jews anxious, encouraging them to fear the worst.[39] But their fears, while not baseless, were in the end exaggerated. While the media did not ignore the Jewishness of Jewish businessmen who made headlines, they did not exploit it either. In comparison to the antisemitism that swirled around the Marconi and Indian silver scandals of 1912–13, the Jewish dimension of the Guinness affair was muted. Upmarket newspapers avoided mentioning the Jewishness of the accused (the tabloids, naturally, were less restrained). A former editor of the *Jewish Chronicle* claimed that most Gentiles did not know that many of the accused were Jews and, if they did, did not think it important.[40]

Still, it would be misleading to suggest that toleration was triumphant in late-twentieth-century Britain. No taboo on public expressions of antisemitism emerged, as was the case in the United States. Journalists, newscasters, and politicians continued to remark on the Jewishness of Jewish malefactors, even if they did not harp on it. Snobbish upper-crust antisemitism remained a pervasive irritant. In winebars, restaurants, common rooms, and city and country clubs, snide remarks and knowing looks communicated distaste for Jewish drive, separatism, and success. In the company of Jews, the writer Lesley Hazleton noted, this distaste was usually not expressed openly but, rather, insinuated, "with the intent in the intonation rather than the words used, in the sneering impatience with those who point it out, in the use of a phrase like 'you people,' or the condescending smile and lingering emphases on the last word of 'Oh, you're Jewish? How . . . uh, *interesting.*'" Among the well-brought-up, it was expressed with "a slight sneer, a curl of the lip," with otherwise innocuous words that took on "a twist and a snap."[41] In business and financial circles, firms doing business in the Middle East were receptive to the Arab boycott of Israel. Some caved in to Arab demands to sever ties with Jewish banks and businesses and to fire Jewish employees. In a blaze of publicity in 1963, the second Lord Mancroft (1914–87), whose background was Jewish (the family name was Samuel until 1925), left the board of the Norwich Union Insurance Society when the Arab League's boycott office demanded his removal due to his business ties to Sir Isaac Wolfson, whose support for Israel was well known. The following year the Arab states blacklisted Global Tours (a subsidiary of Wolfson's Great Universal Stores), of which Mancroft was chairman, and pressured the London Chamber of Commerce to deny him its presidency, which he was slated to hold in 1965.[42]

In public forums the animal welfare movement exploited hoary notions of Jewish blood-lust and cruelty in its anti-shehitah campaign, as it had for over a century, while Israel's stunning victory in 1967 energized anti-Zionism, which drew on bitterness dating back to the 1940s. While opposition to Israeli occupation of the captured territories was not ipso facto antisemitic, it frequently provided a cover for the expression of hostility to Jews qua Jews on the socialist and humanitarian left, which often was more comfortable with Jews as victims than victors, as well as among Arabists and die-hard imperialists, who resented Britain's ouster from the Middle East between 1948 and the Suez crisis of 1956. In the universities in the 1980s and 1990s, militant Islamic groups mounted anti-Zionist campaigns that were blatantly anti-Jewish, and, on occasion, pro-Palestinian terrorists struck at Anglo-Jewish targets, most notably in 1973, when a gunman broke into the house of J. Edward

Sieff (1905–82), president of Marks and Spencer and a well-known supporter of Israel, and seriously wounded him. At the other end of the
social ladder, yobbish antisemitism erupted in more crude forms—
daubing swastikas on synagogue walls, desecrating Jewish gravestones,
chanting antisemitic jibes at football matches. In a three-year period in
the mid-1960s, there was a wave of fascist-inspired violence: sixteen synagogues in London and the provinces were set on fire or attacked by
petrol bombs, including one, the Brondesbury Synagogue in northwest
London, that burned to the ground in March 1965.[43]

In the long term, however, violent antisemitism did less damage to
Anglo-Jewry than ethnocentrism, cultural narrow-mindedness, and polite contempt. While Britain became a more diverse society after the
war—with more than one million Muslim residents by the end of the
century, for example—Britons were slow to accept, let alone welcome,
this change. By the 1990s, to be sure, there was some recognition that
definitions of citizenship and nationality, Britishness and Englishness,
required rethinking. But Britain was not yet a society that celebrated or
embraced its religious, ethnic, and racial diversity in the way that Canada
or the United States did. With a few exceptions here and there, it remained hostile or indifferent to expressions of cultural difference. It did
not recognize that its insistence on cultural homogeneity was, in the
words of Philip Roth's alter ego Nathan Zuckerman, "a not very subtle
form of *English* tribalism," but continued to insist in multifarious ways,
both overt and subtle, that Jews cease "clinging to an identity just for
the sake of it."[44] To be sure, the growing visibility of Third World newcomers deflected attention from Jews. But validation of cultural difference, in general, and understanding of Jewish needs, in particular, were
rare in the postwar period and even at the end of the century were often
little more than cosmetic. Most Englishmen continued to prefer a uni-
tary, homogeneous nation to "a variegated array of local communities,
local dialects, local ways of playing the game," each wishing to define
its own distinctive values and norms.[45] Most still believed that there was
one authentic way of being English. Thus, in the 1990s, when Orthodox
Jews in northwest London proposed the demarcation of a six-mile
square *eruv* (a legal fiction that, by extending the symbolic boundaries
of Jewish homes, allows the carrying of objects in public places on the
Sabbath and festivals), many Gentiles expressed outrage. The eruv, it
was charged, was an affront to Christianity, "a piece of impertinence"
(Lord Soper). It would foist Jewish religious symbols on a Christian
country, attract more Jews to the district, and promote Jewish tribalism.

Its opponents also claimed that the eruv's several dozen wire-strung wooden poles would deface the environment and endanger the lives of birds. As Ned Temko (b. 1951), American-born editor of the *Jewish Chronicle*, observed, while England was *becoming* a multi-ethnic society, it was still "deeply, fundamentally, uni-ethnic."[46]

Britain's genteel intolerance exacted a toll, not by blocking Jewish mobility, but by preventing Jews who were mobile from embracing their Jewishness unreservedly. It encouraged them to mute their Jewishness, rather than accept it naturally or even revel in it. It caused them to tolerate slights and avoid rocking the boat and making a fuss. For Jews whose communal and religious attachments were weak, it was a constant reminder that Jews were viewed as "English" only when they ceased to be "too Jewish." Britain's "mild-as-milk, matter-of-fact" antisemitism (Leslie Fiedler's apt formulation)[47] thus further loosened already weakened ties.

Nonetheless, kid-glove ethnocentrism was not an obstacle to integration and mobility. Gentile Britons were more willing to hire, promote, and reward Jews, to mix with them in formal and informal social settings, and even to marry them than ever before. For their part, upwardly mobile Jews—especially those working in non-Jewish environments—were no less eager to broaden their social horizons. For them, maintaining communal boundaries was not a priority, especially since Jewishness was still burdened with negative associations. The course of least resistance was to drift further, to choose friends and partners as they presented themselves. As a result, intermarriage and disaffiliation rose—to the point that they threatened the demographic well-being of Anglo-Jewry for the first time in its history. Beginning in the 1970s, the number of religious marriages began to decline, falling from about eighteen hundred per year in the late 1960s to about eleven hundred per year in the 1980s and then to nine hundred per year in the mid- and late 1990s. (Not all the decline was due to intermarriage; some was due to increasing numbers of young Jews cohabiting, with other Jews and with Gentiles, without marrying.) By the early 1990s, for every three Jews reaching marriageable age, only one married in a synagogue. At the end of the century, among Jewish men who were married or in a steady relationship, 44 percent of those under age forty had non-Jewish partners, while among those under age thirty the figure was, not unexpectedly, higher—50 percent.[48]

The rise in intermarriage, along with a fall in the birth rate (a national trend), led to a decline in the absolute size of Anglo-Jewry in the second

half of the century. After peaking at mid-century at about 430,000 persons, the British Jewish population began to decline steadily thereafter.
In the late 1970s, there were about 336,000 Jews in Britain; in the mid-
1980s, about 308,000; in the mid-1990s, about 285,000. At that point,
British Jewry was one-third smaller than it had been in 1950.[49] Although
the roots of its decline—intermarriage and indifference—were already
evident early in the period, there was little sense of alarm until the 1980s.
When social scientists at a communal "stocktaking" conference in 1962
presented statistical evidence pointing to a drop in numerical strength,
the reaction was muted. At a follow-up conference fifteen years later, in
1977, the issue received more attention, but there was certainly no sense
of crisis.[50] When, in the 1980s and 1990s, demographic research clarified
how much the community was shrinking, communal leaders often responded along party lines. Progressive Jews blamed the Orthodox,
charging them with obscurantism and rigidity, with driving away the
less observant, while the Orthodox blamed Reform and Liberal Jews,
for their secularism, lack of standards, and ignorance of tradition, for
providing a way station for Jews on the road out. A more constructive
response was increased funding for Jewish education, in general, and
Jewish day schools, in particular. Between 1975 and 1996, the number
of children attending day schools rose from about eleven thousand to
eighteen thousand. At the same time, the number of children receiving
no Jewish education, either day school or supplementary school, shrank
from about twenty-six thousand to fourteen thousand.[51] (Some of this
shrinkage, it should be remembered, was due to a decrease in the number of school-age children.) In 1993, Chief Rabbi Jonathan Sacks
launched a well-funded, innovative education and outreach scheme—
appropriately named Continuity—to stem the tide of demographic decline. However, the bulk of its funds went to projects in the Orthodox
community rather than to outreach projects targeting those who were
most likely to leave the fold, and soon it too was engulfed in partisan
squabbling.[52]

Although quick to apportion blame, neither Liberal and Reform Judaism, on the one hand, nor mainstream Orthodoxy, on the other, was
spared losses. In the twenty years between 1975 and 1994, the annual
number of mainstream Orthodox Ashkenazi marriages fell by 45 percent
(the small number of Sephardi marriages remained constant) while the
number of Reform and Liberal marriages fell by 24 percent, although
in absolute terms the former continued to outnumber the latter by a
ratio of more than three to one. Only the ultra-Orthodox resisted the

trend. In the same period, the annual number of marriages in congregations belonging to the right-wing Union of Orthodox Hebrew Congregations (see below) increased 42 percent, lifting their share of all synagogue marriages from 7 percent in 1974 to 21 percent in 1996.[53] This increase resulted from a combination of early marriage, a high birth rate, and an absence of social ties with persons outside their own subcommunity.

In the immediate aftermath of World War II, no one foresaw the growth of strict Orthodoxy. Historically, Jewish tradition did not fare well in Britain (however better it did in comparison to other Western countries). The historical record shows that observance became more relaxed with the passage of each generation and that, while most Jews continued to belong to nominally Orthodox congregations, they were not themselves Orthodox either in practice or in belief. In time, some transferred their allegiance to Reform or Liberal Judaism while still others passed out of the community altogether. The expansion of right-wing Orthodoxy in the second half of the century was thus unprecedented and surprising.

Ultra-Orthodoxy first took root in Britain during the late nineteenth century. Strictly observant immigrants from both Central and Eastern Europe, dismayed by the tolerant, easy-going traditionalism of the United Synagogue, created separatist congregations that refused to acknowledge the authority of the Adlers and their successors; the largest of these congregations were Mahzikei Ha-Dat and the North London Beth Hamedrash. In 1926, these congregations, at the initiative of Victor Schonfeld, rabbi of the Adat Yisrael synagogue in North London, formed a loose alliance, the Union of Orthodox Hebrew Congregations (UOHC), known popularly as the Adat. In the 1930s and 1940s, the ultra-Orthodox subcommunity began to outgrow its marginal status with the arrival of thousands of observant refugees and survivors, many of them Hasidim. In the following decade pious Jews fleeing Communist regimes in Eastern Europe, Hungary in particular, augmented their numbers. Meanwhile, the leaders of strict Orthodoxy were taking steps to insure its survival in Britain, thereby paving the way for its disproportionate influence in communal affairs at the end of the century. They created day schools and yeshivot, most famously the Gateshead yeshivah, which opened in 1929 and after the war became the largest Orthodox educational complex in Europe. In 1931 and 1932, they blocked Chief Rabbi Hertz's attempt to monopolize the licensing of shohetim and in 1935 gained a voice on the London bet din, when Hertz appointed

Rabbi Yehezkel Abramsky (1886–1976), a renowned talmudist, who had escaped from the Soviet Union in 1932, as a dayyan — despite opposition from the United Synagogue, whose leaders recognized that Abramsky's fundamentalism was out of step with mainstream Anglo-Jewish practice. Abramsky, by force of his learning and personality, moved the bet din in a conservative direction, asserting himself in particular during Hertz's long, last illness and the two-year interregnum before the appointment of his successor, Israel Brodie, in May 1948.[54]

The number of strictly Orthodox Jews in Britain multiplied in the postwar period. Initially this was due to immigration, later to larger than average families. The ultra-Orthodox created tightly knit, geographically concentrated communities of their own — in London (Stoke Newington, Tottenham, and Stamford Hill in the north and Hendon and Golders Green in the northwest), Manchester, and Gateshead — in which they cultivated a distinctive way of life without concern for gentile opinion.[55] Most provided their children with a minimal secular education while shielding them from the influence of both popular and high culture. Their fervor, unwillingness to compromise, and lack of concern with gentile approval were novel elements in Anglo-Jewish history. Most English Jews looked askance at this development, viewing it as a throwback to Old World fundamentalism and ignorance, although there were a few who found its discipline, coherence, fervor, and self-confidence attractive and who embraced its discipline.

Although right-wing Orthodoxy grew dramatically in this period — membership (male heads of family) in UOHC synagogues went from about three thousand in the mid-1950s to about sixty-six hundred in the mid-1990s — it remained a minority phenomenon, dwarfed by the combined membership of other synagogue bodies (about eighty-seven thousand in 1996). At most, the strictly Orthodox were 10 percent of the total Jewish population.[56] Their influence, however, was greater than their numbers suggest. First, because their commitment to Judaism was intense — while that of most Jews was not — they constituted a disproportionate number of those Jews who actively practiced their religion and made known their religious views. Second, there was a shortage of university-educated, modern Orthodox rabbis in the postwar decades, for, with rabbinic salaries low and rabbinic independence circumscribed because of the structure of the United Synagogue, Jews College was not attracting enough students to meet the community's needs. As a result, centrist Orthodox congregations began to employ rabbis whose outlook was closer to that of the yeshivah world and separatist Orthodoxy than

of the United Synagogue. By the mid-1990s, Lubavitcher rabbis occupied half of the United Synagogue's pulpits.[57] Educational and social
welfare institutions found themselves in a similar position. Thus, at the
end of the century, mainstream organizations were staffed, in part, by
persons who were unsympathetic to the latitudinarianism that was characteristic of Anglo-Jewry during much of its history. Most members of
the London bet din, for example, whose inflexibility was legendary,
came from subcommunities that rejected the authority of the chief rabbi,
who, ironically, appointed them![58] Third, moderate Orthodox rabbis,
not wishing to be outflanked by more conservative colleagues, moved
to the right themselves, becoming less flexible in their understanding of
what Jewish law required. Since they lacked the extensive yeshivah training of the strict Orthodox, they deferred to them in halakhic matters.
Authenticity in Orthodoxy became synonymous with standards and
modes of observance for which there were few precedents. Fourth, families accustomed to the tolerance of the past became less influential in
the governance of centrist Orthodox institutions. Some drifted out of
Judaism altogether; others moved to the Reform and Liberal camps. In
both cases, the void was filled by more observant Jews who were willing
to defer to an increasingly conservative rabbinical leadership.

The decline of mainstream Orthodoxy, which was rooted in prewar
trends, was viewed as a crisis only in the 1990s. A report by the research
unit of the Board of Deputies in 1991 revealed the extent to which the
right and the left were eroding the predominance of the center: between
1983 and 1990, the United Synagogue lost over four thousand male
members. The following year a major review of the United Synagogue,
headed by the chairman of the Dixons Group, Sir Stanley Kalms (b.
1931), made public the financial side of the crisis. Due to membership
losses, a top-heavy centralized bureaucracy, and financial mismanage-
ment, the United Synagogue was £9 million in debt.[59] In the wake of
the Kalms report, the elected officers resigned and financial belt-
tightening was imposed, but little was done to address the root of the
United Synagogue's decline — its drift toward the right. The chief rabbi,
the Cambridge-educated Jonathan Sacks, remained immobilized by a
rabbinate and a bet din whose Orthodoxy was more rigorous than that
to which most English Jews were accustomed. Whatever his true inclinations, he repeatedly deferred to the ultra-Orthodox, most notably
when he refused to attend the funeral of the nationally respected Reform
rabbi Hugo Gryn (1930–97) and then apologized to the UOHC for later
attending a nonreligious memorial meeting for Gryn — after the latter

declared his presence there a desecration of God's name (*hillul ha-shem*).[60]

The polarization of Anglo-Jewish religious life took both trivial and not-so-trivial forms. Orthodox rabbis refused to appear on platforms with Reform and Liberal rabbis or to participate in cultural and educational programs whose sponsors included non-Orthodox groups. Thus, when Anglo-Jewry marked its tercentenary in 1956 with a service at Bevis Marks, the leaders of the UOHC and some members of the bet din absented themselves because of the official presence of Liberal and Reform Jews. From at least the 1940s, the London bet din required potential converts to adopt standards of observance to which most English Jews did not adhere, as a result of which few Gentiles were converted under Orthodox auspices.[61] Chief Rabbis Brodie, Jakobovits, and Sachs, despite professions of "inclusivism" and denunciations of fractious behavior, attacked liberal forms of Judaism in terms that encouraged polarization. Nor was this hardening of attitudes only a London phenomenon. In 1960, the Manchester bet din requested the synagogues under its authority to ban mixed dancing at social events. In Cardiff, the self-styled "Rav of Cardiff and South Wales," Ber Rogosnitsky (1909–87), refused to allow the city's kosher caterer, whom he supervised, to cater weddings that were celebrated in the town's Reform synagogue. He also refused to allow Reform Jews to be called to the Torah, a ruling that resulted in a public scandal in 1994 when a member of the Reform congregation was refused an aliyyah at his grandson's bar mitzvah, which took place in the Orthodox synagogue. In Manchester the following year, four young children, two of them sons of the rabbi of a centrist Orthodox congregation, were expelled from an Orthodox day school because their parents attended a lecture by Shlomo Riskin, an American-born, modern Orthodox rabbi.[62] That so much feeling was invested in these matters reveals the depth and strength of Orthodox sectarian sentiment in the second half of the century.

The landmark event in the decline of the old Anglo-Judaism was the Jacobs affair of the early 1960s, an event whose impact continued to be felt decades afterward.[63] The affair began, without fanfare, in 1957 when Louis Jacobs (b. 1920), the yeshivah-trained, scholarly assistant rabbi of the New West End Synagogue, published a book on religious questions his congregants had asked him, *We Have Reason to Believe*. Among other matters, he expressed doubt about the traditional doctrine that God dictated the entire Pentateuch to Moses word for word (*torah min ha-shamayyim*). He did not, however, deny the binding character of the mitsvot. The book caused no stir at the time it was published, although it sold a very respectable one thousand copies. Two years later Jacobs left the New West End to teach at Jews' College, with the hope, encouraged by members of its governing council, that he would replace its then principal Isidore Epstein (1894–1962) when he retired, which he did in 1961. But Chief Rabbi Brodie, whose English bearing and speech outweighed his learning and who thus was easily influenced by his dayyanim, refused to promote Jacobs, in part because he and the right-wing feared that Jacobs would use the principalship as a springboard to the chief rabbinate, from which Brodie was due to retire in 1965. Although not dismissed from his lectureship, Jacobs felt compelled to resign from the college. When the lay officers of the college, headed by the High Court judge Sir Alan Mocatta (1907–90), a representative of the old notability, were unable to persuade Brodie to reconsider, they too resigned. By this point, the affair was attracting attention in the national press. To provide Jacobs with both a platform and an income, his supporters established the Society for the Study of Jewish Theology, under whose aegis he addressed meetings throughout the country.

The affair entered its second stage in 1964, when Jacobs's successor at the New West End left to take a Conservative pulpit in New York City and the officers of the congregation resolved to reappoint Jacobs to succeed him. However, the chief rabbi was able to block the appointment by refusing to certify Jacobs as fit to occupy the post. This was unprecedented: previous chief rabbis never imposed an ideological test in certifying congregational appointments. The congregation, in which remnants of the old communal elite, who valued civility and toleration over theological rectitude, were strong, tried to defy the chief rabbi but were blocked, since the United Synagogue was the legal owner of the synagogue premises. The council of the United Synagogue dismissed the New West End's officers and replaced them with persons who would do its bidding. Very soon thereafter over three hundred members quit the New West End and established an independent congregation, the New London Synagogue, with Jacobs as its rabbi. In the next three decades, Jacobs and his congregation became the center of a new movement, the Assembly of Masorti [traditional] Synagogues, a loose union of like-minded congregations. The Masorti movement, with six congregations and about fourteen hundred families in Greater London and St. Albans by the mid-1990s,[64] embodied the moderate traditionalism of the prewar United Synagogue, while opposing the fundamentalism that increasingly dominated formerly centrist institutions. While not identical to Conservative Judaism in the United States, it was similar enough to affiliate itself to the worldwide Conservative movement.

The Masorti movement better captured the outlook of mainstream British Jewry than did the Judaism of the chief rabbi and his bet din. Nonetheless, most synagogue-affiliated Jews remained members of congregations that acknowledged his authority—that is, congregations that did not represent their own personal religious outlook. The reason for this anomalous situation, so different from that in the United States, was that convenience, habit, family tradition, and indifference (as well as the wish to hold on to accumulated burial rights and to be buried near family) were stronger than religious consistency. Overall, however, the number of Jews who moved formally to the religious left increased in the postwar period, and, for the first time in their history, Liberal and Reform Judaism spread throughout the country. In 1956, Leo Baeck College, a seminary for training non-Orthodox rabbis, was established in London, and by the mid-1990s, there were sixty-nine Reform and Liberal synagogues, representing over twenty-five thousand families, about 27 percent of all affiliated families (the figure is 29 percent if the members of Masorti congregations are included.)[65] A small part of this growth was due to the immigration of Reform Jews from Germany in the 1930s, but most can be traced to native-born discontent with centrist Orthodoxy.

There was a further dimension to the fracturing of Anglo-Jewry. Before World War II, the central institutions of British Jewry, while not monopolistic, exerted immense influence. Their traditionalism, which was rooted both in Orthodoxy and in social conservatism, discouraged innovation—in religious practice, of course, but in education, philanthropy, youth work, and communal defense as well. When centrist Orthodoxy started to lose members and influence, space for innovation and individual initiative opened up. In the last quarter of the century, independent institutions, both religious and secular, emerged across the communal spectrum, often with the aim of energizing religious and cultural life and halting the tide of drift and indifference. On the religious front, independent minyanim and synagogues multiplied. Some were established to provide an informal, intimate, *shtiebel*-like alternative to the stuffiness of mainstream congregations. Others were created to attract the unaffiliated, the untutored, and the disaffected. Chief among the latter were the synagogue attached to the Yakar Study Centre in Hendon, which was established by the maverick Orthodox rabbi Michael Rosen in 1978, and the Saatchi Synagogue in Maida Vale, which

Advertisement for the Saatchi Synagogue, *Jewish Chronicle*, 5 May 2000.

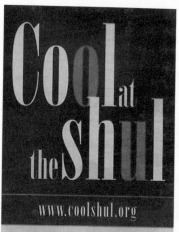

opened in 1998 with a flurry of eye-catching advertisements. (Its chief backers were the advertising moguls Charles [b. 1943] and Maurice Saatchi [b. 1946].) Still others met the needs of Orthodox women, lesbians and gays, and men and women wishing to pray in a traditional but egalitarian setting. Cultural life was enriched by lectures, courses, seminars, and concerts offered by Yakar and the Spiro Institute for the Study of Jewish History and Culture in West Hampstead, which was established in 1978. Major academic centers for Jewish studies emerged at Oxford, Southampton, and University College, London, while the study of Anglo-Jewish history flourished—outside, rather than within, the framework of the century-old Jewish Historical Society of England. At Oxford in the 1990s, the outreach events of the L'Chaim Society, a project of the unconventional, outspoken, American-born Lubavitch rabbi Shmuley Boteach (b. 1966), attracted hundreds of students.

Whether these initiatives, and others like them, will reinvigorate Anglo-Jewry and reverse its demographic decline is best left to those foolish enough to believe they can predict the future. But whether the initiatives succeed or fail, their significance is beyond doubt. They mark a break with the institutional conservatism of the past, a conservatism that rested, in the end, on the influence of an Anglo-Jewish establishment as powerful in its own way as the English establishment. The retreat of the old notability and the spread of religious indifference allowed the strictly observant, previously marginalized and powerless, to win a larger say in communal affairs. Their ascendance, in turn, stimulated secular and liberal Jews, more secure in their Jewishness due to the decline of antisemitism, to strike out in new directions. At the end of the twentieth century, despite its declining numbers, Anglo-Jewry exhibited greater liveliness, self-confidence, and diversity than at any time before. Its fracturing encouraged the contradictions and paradoxes—fervor *and* indifference, piety *and* godlessness, renewal *and* decline—that were its hallmark at the end of the twentieth century.

Conclusion

For earlier generations of historians, Anglo-Jewish history was a success story, a tale of toleration and achievement, to be proudly celebrated. Cecil Roth, it will be recalled, declared that "in this happy land" Jews "attained a measure of freedom . . . which has been the case in scarcely any other." Roth's upbeat appraisal is no mere historical curiosity, the artifact of a more confident, naive age. At the end of the century the British historian William Rubinstein echoed Roth, claiming that "the story of the Jewish people throughout the English-speaking world has almost always been a success story, a success story without parallel in the post-exilic history of the Jewish people."[1] Rubinstein's assessment, like Roth's, is not altogether misguided. Historical judgments are almost always relative in nature. Historians conclude that one outcome or solution was a "success" on the basis of their knowledge of other outcomes and solutions. In comparison to the histories of Jews in other European lands, the Anglo-Jewish experience was remarkable by virtue of its freedom from overt persecution. At any point between the mid-eighteenth and mid-twentieth centuries, it was easier to be a Jew in Britain than elsewhere in Europe. There was little violence. The "Jewish Question" was not high on the public agenda. Social and occupational discrimination, while not absent, was neither systematic nor pervasive, and there was no resulting flow of Jews into the arms of the Christian church, as was the case in much of Central Europe. Few in Britain obsessed about Jews or assigned them a villainous role in national affairs.

In economic terms, Anglo-Jewish history is even more a success story. Most Jews who settled in Britain in the modern period were poor, in flight from limited opportunities in Central and Eastern Europe. They started life in their new home in low-status, often disreputable occupations, as street and market traders and, in the case of the East Europeans, as sweated laborers, but their descendants did not remain poor for more than a generation or two. They assumed that mobility, not stasis, was "natural." At the end of the nineteenth century, those who traced their origins to immigration in the Georgian period were, for the most part, middle class; at the end of the twentieth century, the same was true of those who traced their origins to immigration in the Victorian period. While poverty was a characteristic feature of the community at various points in its history, it was not a permanent feature. The Jewish poor in 1900 were not the descendants of the Jewish poor in 1800 but, rather, recent arrivals. Eventually, most Jewish families emerged from poverty and moved upward, if not in one generation then in another. This was most un-English behavior. Group economic mobility is not a theme of British history, certainly in comparison to the United States, where the rags-to-riches notion is a feature of the national myth. However, it is a characteristic feature of the history of Western Jewish communities. In material terms, then, Britain's Jews were successful, but no more so than those in France or prewar Germany and certainly less so than those in the United States.

The record of social and political integration was more remarkable. Before the removal of legal disabilities in the mid-Victorian years, Jews were unable to participate as Jews (that is, without converting) in exclusive spheres of British life—the legislature, the bar, the magistrature, the ancient universities. Nonetheless, they mixed to an unprecedented degree with non-Jews, well-born and common, in informal and formal social settings, including learned societies, Masonic lodges, and other voluntary associations. In the first half of the eighteenth century, long before Moses Mendelssohn and the maskilim made their appearance in Berlin, Jews who had made their fortunes in the City were entertaining—and being entertained by—their Christian neighbors in the country. Sephardi savants like the conchologist and mineralogist Emanuel Mendes da Costa (1717–91) and the physician Jacob de Castro Sarmento (1691–1762) were elected Fellows of the Royal Society and made welcome at the homes of learned Christians with scientific interests. The hat maker David Levi, who defended Judaism against attacks from Joseph Priestly and Tom Paine, and the engraver Solomon Bennett (1761–1838), a critic of the communal establishment, met regularly with other minor literati for conversation and refreshment, while Isaac D'Israeli moved largely in non-Jewish circles. None bought his entry into society with baptism. This was remarkable in light of circumstances elsewhere in Europe at this time.

After emancipation, Jews enjoyed even more access to positions of influence and honor in British society. Within a decade of their admission to parliament, eight unconverted Jews sat in the Commons. Three Jews—Herbert Samuel, Rufus Isaacs, and Edwin Montagu—were members of Liberal cabinets in the early twentieth century. From 1945 to 1955, there were fourteen Jewish cabinet ministers and at least another nine Jews who held ministerial rank but did not sit in the cabinet. By World War I there were more than two dozen Jewish peers, baronets, and knights. Almost 10 percent of the life peerages created between 1958, when they were first introduced, and 1989 went to Jews.[2] The clubs of St. James, bastions of male establishment privilege, admitted Jews in sufficient numbers to obviate the need for Jews to establish their own, as happened in the United States. Again, there are few parallels to this in European Jewish history. France alone rivaled Britain in its willingness to admit unconverted Jews to exclusive social, political, and administrative circles. (After unification Italy was almost as receptive.) Moreover, Jews who became Christians in Britain—and their children even more so—faced no obstacles to their ascent. Before emancipation, five ex-Jews—Menassah Masseh Lopes, Ralph Franco (1788–1854), Ralph Bernal (1783–1854), David Ricardo (1772–1823), and Benjamin Disraeli—sat in the House of Commons while Disraeli, of course, climbed to the very top of the greasy pole. To be sure, their opponents threw their Jewishness in their faces in the heat of political battle, but it was not an insurmountable obstacle, barring advancement altogether, as it so often was in Central Europe. Those who remained outside the limelight were even more successful in neutralizing their background. Who today remembers (or ever knew) that Antony Armstrong-Jones, first Earl of Snowdon and husband of Princess Margaret from 1960 to 1978, was a descendant, on his mother's side, of the German-born Jewish stockbroker Ludwig Messel (1847–1915) or that the first husband of Wallis Warfield Simpson, who married the Duke of Windsor in 1937, was the son of a Jewish father, whose original name was Salaman, not Simpson?[3]

Yet this is not the whole story. While testifying to an unusual level of toleration in pre–World War II Europe, these examples do not respond to the question of whether Jews who remained Jews nonetheless suppressed, toned down, or reconfigured their Jewishness in response to social and cultural pressures to conform. They do not speak to the question of whether there was a price (short of baptism) to be paid for inclusion and acceptance, even if it was paid willingly. At the same time, examples like these avoid questions about the impact of British circumstances on the long-term maintenance of Jewish identity, affiliation, and observance. It is not enough to know that professing Jews who wished to make their mark in society and politics were able to do so. The "Jewish" fate of their descendants—whether they too identified themselves as Jews and participated in communal activities—is also a critical element in appraising how Anglo-Jewry fared. Biological and cultural continuity, the transmission of Jewishness from one generation to the next, is central to the telling of Jewish history. Thus it is essential to ask how successful Britain's Jews have been in perpetuating themselves.

Viewing Anglo-Jewish history with these considerations in mind problematizes any one-dimensional conclusion. While Britain was more hospitable to Jews than most European states, its acceptance of Jews *as* Jews was never absolute. Yes, notions of religious toleration were more firmly rooted in Britain than elsewhere, a consequence of both the fracturing of Christian unity in the sixteenth and seventeenth centuries and the diffusion of liberal political values in the eighteenth and nineteenth centuries. However, the toleration of religious difference is not the same as the toleration of ethnic and cultural difference, let alone its endorsement. Jews were at one and the same time a religious, ethnic, and national minority; they did not fit comfortably into the categories into which other minorities fit. British officials, statesmen, and opinion makers seemed to sense this. In any case, they never demanded that Jews define their group character in formal, abstract terms, explaining how their collective identity intersected with that of the English nation and the British state. The absence of an on-going, long-festering "Jewish Question" and of a protracted battle for civil rights spared everyone the task of thinking hard and long about the collective character of the Jews.

Still, Jews experienced pressure to become more "English," pressure that was no less powerful because it was subtle and diffuse. It could not have been otherwise. Before the arrival of large numbers of immigrants from Africa, Asia, the Caribbean, and the Middle East in the decades after World War II, the makeup of Britain's population was remarkably homogeneous. There was little ethnic or racial diversity, since the United Kingdom exported rather than imported people. (More than a million Britons departed for Canada in the early twentieth century, for example.)[4] To its citizens—and its historians—the presence of Christian and Celtic minorities, as well as the divisive character of its class system, suggested that the British demographic landscape was a mix of peoples. But heterogeneity and homogeneity are not absolute but relative states. To Jews—and historians of the Jews—Britons were remarkably alike. Whatever national and religious diversity existed was a pale version of the diversity that Jews had known or were to encounter elsewhere. England's elites, especially those whom Jews encountered in the metropolis, shared a common culture, a culture that was ruthlessly genteel, monolithic, arrogant, and exclusive. There was one, and only one, way of being authentically English. Men and women of property and education, whatever their politics, saw little value in the survival of Judaism and Jewish culture, even if they took no active measures to encourage its disappearance. Upwardly mobile Jews in search of approval and acceptance outside the Jewish community were aware of this. They knew that they were cultural outsiders, that Jews were absent in English narratives of the building of the nation. Thus, they modified their behavior, as all outsiders who wanted to become insiders did. Neither state nor society demanded that they become Christians, as happened elsewhere, but circumstances conspired to make them less Jewish in their sentiments and affiliations. This occurred everywhere in the West, of course. What was different in Britain and other liberal states was that the pressure to conform was more social and cultural than political in character and thus less obvious and more diffuse. But it was there nonetheless.

Over time this pressure had a disintegrative effect on the maintenance of Jewish identity. At any point in Anglo-Jewish history, Jews with Jewish commitments were able to find friends and fame outside their own community if they so wished. The descendants of these Jews, however, rarely felt the same level of Jewish commitments as their ancestors. Their education, friendships, recreations, and cultural interests drew them away from the Jewish community. This process of disengagement usually extended over several generations. In fact, because of the ease of Jewish integration in Britain, the dissolution of communal ties in upper-middle-class families proceeded more slowly than elsewhere. Between the late eighteenth and early twentieth centuries, there was less drift and defection within the London elite than within its counterparts in Paris, Berlin, Amsterdam, or New York. Nonetheless, after several generations, material comfort, acculturation, and integration more often than not ended in full absorption, not usually through conversion but through intermarriage. For once Jews forged intensive social ties with non-Jews, interfaith romance and marriage were inevitable. To a great extent, then, it was toleration that underwrote Anglo-Jewish disintegration, since it was toleration that encouraged social intercourse between Jews and Gentiles.

Toleration, however, is never absolute. In the British case, as I stressed, formal toleration was qualified by a lack of respect for Jewish concerns and Jewish difference. In addition, Jewishness remained a stigmatized quality at all times. The secularization of feeling and thought that accompanied the birth of the modern world did much to weaken theological notions about the damnation of the Jews, but it did not uproot notions of Jewish difference. These sentiments were too deeply embedded in Western culture, in its ways of thinking, feeling, and imagining, to be easily swept away. Long after Britons ceased to view Jews as Christ-killers and stiff-necked blasphemers, they continued to think of them as different in kind from other persons of similar wealth, education, and rank. In general, these feelings did not find expression in overt discrimination or in theory-driven comparisons of Jewishness and Englishness, as was common in Central Europe. They surfaced, rather, in humorous asides and off-hand comments and in representations of "the Jew" in literature and the media and on the stage—what the poet, essayist, and civil servant Humbert Wolfe (1886–1940) referred to as "exclusion from garden-parties, refusal of certain cherished intimacies, and occasional light-hearted sneers."[5] While it would be easy to dismiss the importance of "light-hearted sneers"—and they do seem unimportant, even inconsequential, when set next to pogroms, boycotts, and show trials—they were painful to those who were their victims. This was especially true in the case of Jews like Wolfe who were alienated from Judaism and integrated into English society and wanted to be English rather than Jewish. Jews like these eventually came to view their Jewishness as burdensome or unessential and were content to allow it to wither.

Over the centuries, casual "garden-party" antisemitism, in tandem with social integration and the aversion of English elites to cultural difference, ate away at the foundations of Jewish collective identity. Leakage from the community occurred in every period. At times, the demographic losses were barely noticeable and evoked little comment, as in the late-Victorian period, when the number of Jews pouring into Britain from Eastern Europe masked whatever losses the native community was experiencing. At other times, the losses were massive, threatening the demographic health of the community and causing panic and alarm, as in the second half of the twentieth century, when the size of

Anglo-Jewry declined from 410,000 to less than 300,000. At the end of the twentieth century, the number of Jews in England who trace their roots to families who settled there between the Resettlement and the start of East European immigration shrinks every year. Most descendants of the Sephardim who rose to prominence in the late seventeenth and eighteenth centuries are Christians, not Jews. Whether this makes Anglo-Jewish history a success story will depend on one's values and commitments. To those who cherish cultural pluralism in general and the perpetuation of the Jews and Judaism in particular, it is difficult to view this as a desirable outcome.

The toleration that Jews encountered in Britain also worked indirectly to weaken their communal life. Readers of this history will have noticed the relative absence of Jewish men of letters — religious thinkers; Hebraists and Yiddishists; poets, novelists, and essayists; and practitioners of Wissenschaft des Judentums (the critical study of Jewish history and culture). The reason for this is simple. There were few of them, relative to their numbers in Central and Eastern Europe or the United States, and those few were neither pioneers of new currents in Jewish thought, scholarship, or belles lettres nor, in most cases, communal activists, seeking to shape the Jewish future. From the late nineteenth century, but not before, there were, of course, Jews who were well known figures in the literary world — the Shakespeare scholar and editor of the *Dictionary of National Biography* Sidney Lee (1859–1926), the essayist Leonard Woolf, the poet and critic Humbert Wolfe, the novelists Israel Zangwill, Gilbert Frankau (1884–1952), G. B. Stern (1890–1973), Muriel Spark (b. 1918), and Anita Brookner (b. 1938), the playwrights Alfred Sutro (1863–1933), Peter Shaffer (b. 1926), Harold Pinter, and Tom Stoppard (b. 1937), the critic Queenie Leavis (1906–81). But, with one or two exceptions, they were not "Jewish" writers or intellectuals in the sense of exploring Jewish concerns and themes in their work and identifying themselves with Anglo-Jewry. Indeed, Wolfe, Frankau, Stern, and Spark were converts, the latter two to Roman Catholicism. There were also dozens of eminent Jewish academics and intellectuals, born and trained elsewhere, who found refuge and achieved distinction in Britain — the historians Lewis Namier, Eric Hobsbawm (b. 1917), and Geoffrey Elton (1921–94), the art historians Nikolaus Pevsner (1902–83) and Ernst Gombrich (b. 1909), the classicists Arnaldo Momigliano (1908–87) and M. I. Finley (1912–86), the historian of ideas Isaiah Berlin, the critic George Steiner (b. 1929), the novelist and essayist Arthur Koestler (1905–83) and several score physicists, chemists, biologists, and the like. However, none of these figures was the product of an Anglo-Jewish milieu, and most took no interest in Jewish life or letters. (Berlin, Steiner, and Momigliano hovered on the margins.) Even Namier, an outspoken Zionist and close associate of Chaim Weizmann in the 1920s and 1930s, was contemptuous of Anglo-Jewry and took no part in its collective life.[6]

Jewish scholarship in Britain was also very much a foreign import.[7] In the nineteenth and early twentieth centuries, the outstanding figures—Emanuel Deutsch at the British Museum; Adolf Neubauer at the Bodleian; Solomon Schechter (1847–1915), reader in rabbinics at Cambridge and later head of the Jewish Theological Seminary in New York—were Central or East Europeans. Before World War II, none of the administrators and few of the lecturers at Jews' College were English. Its most eminent scholar, the Second Temple historian Adolf Büchler (1867–1939), who served as principal from 1907 to 1939, was trained in Leipzig and taught at the rabbinic seminary in Vienna before coming to London. At the end of the twentieth century, less than half the staff of the two most important centers for Judaic research in England—the Department of Hebrew and Jewish Studies, University College, London, and the Oxford Centre for Hebrew and Jewish Studies—were British-born and British-educated. No English Jews rank among the giants of modern Jewish scholarship. The few whose work continues to be read—Israel Abrahams, who succeeded Schechter at Cambridge; Herbert Loewe (1882–1940), who taught at Oxford and then followed Abrahams at Cambridge; and Cecil Roth, the first reader in Jewish studies at Oxford—were not Olympian figures. English Jews were also absent in the ranks of thinkers and publicists who helped to shape modern Jewish consciousness and the ideological foundations of modern Jewish life. It is possible to teach a course in modern Jewish thought, for example, without mentioning one British Jew (as distinct from East European Jews, like Ahad Ha-Am and Rav Kook, who lived temporarily in London).

The intellectual poverty of Anglo-Jewry is an old lament. Complaints about communal indifference to the life of the mind begin in the mid-nineteenth century and continue uninterrupted to the present. Reproducing them here would serve no purpose. It is sufficient to note that those who commented on the low level of intellectual engagement in Anglo-Jewry included both those who were firmly attached to its welfare and those who were equally indifferent to and alienated from its collective concerns. The novelist Eva Figes (b. 1932), who belongs to the latter camp, summed up a century and a half of criticism when she told an interviewer, "When I think of English Jewry I think of Golders Green, of suburbia, and accountants, people who are very comfortable and liberal and quietly feathering their own nest—but not interested in ideas."[8]

The most frequently invoked explanation for the intellectual poverty of Anglo-Jewry is the philistinism of the English themselves. This theory holds that English men and women of property, the reference group for upwardly mobile Jews, never valued the life of the mind nor felt it was proper or necessary to talk seriously about intellectual matters. Cleverness was bad form. Eton limited its intake of Jewish students after World War II, according to a former headmaster, because they were "too clever" or "clever in the wrong way." Being clever meant being a "swot" or an admirer of the "bloody Bloomsbury set, modern art, and rubbish like that."[9] It is no coincidence that British, not American, speakers of English use the phrase "too clever by half." Jews seeking respectability and acceptance sensed that it was better to pretend to know very little— and that only in an amateurish way—than to speak as an intellectual, with passion, conviction, intensity, and concern. The cult of the amateur, contempt for abstract ideas, the devaluation of ideas for their own sake—these attributes of English respectability produced what the American Jewish novelist Philip Roth described as "a generally tame and unremarkable society of Jews."[10]

There are also less speculative explanations for the cultural barrenness of the Anglo-Jewish landscape. Before the 1960s, few Jews attended university and thus few were exposed to the world of ideas. While exclusion from the ancient universities before the emancipation era and later their overtly Christian atmosphere explain, in part, this absence, there is more to the story than this. After all, University College, London, welcomed Jews from its founding, but few chose to attend. The major reason for Anglo-Jewish indifference to higher education is that the universities were not conduits for Jewish social and economic mobility before the late twentieth century. Jewish integration before then rested on the accumulation of wealth—in commerce, finance, and overseas trade—and for this a university degree was unnecessary. The pursuit of wealth, while not as honorable as the inheritance of wealth, was not considered degrading either, an insurmountable bar to social respect and advancement. Ambitious, enterprising Jews did not turn their backs on the City and family business houses, seeking employment in the civil service, the academy, the arts, and the free professions, at least until the late twentieth century. Similarly, the acquisition of a university degree was irrelevant to demonstrating Jewish fitness for inclusion in state and society. It did not confer measurable status nor demonstrate, as in German-speaking Europe, Jewish devotion to the culture and science of the land; such devotion was not an issue in Britain, where emancipation was unconditional and enhanced rather than fundamentally altered Jewish legal status.

There is also the matter of numbers. At its peak, in the mid-twentieth century, the Anglo-Jewish population numbered little more than four hundred thousand persons. To compare its cultural life with that of the Jews of the United States, whose community numbered more than five million at mid-century, is unfair and will always work to Anglo-Jewry's disadvantage. Even in the mid- and late nineteenth centuries, the Jewish population of Britain was small in comparison to that of Central Europe, whose hundreds of thousands of German-speakers formed one unified cultural community. While size alone is an insufficient explanation for the lack of brilliance in Anglo-Jewish cultural and intellectual life, it cannot be ignored. At a certain point, numbers counted. For example, Anglo-Jewry, with its limited demographic base, was unable to support a broad array of cultural and educational institutions, particularly in a manner that made them attractive to other than their hard-core supporters. It was also unable to provide a substantial audience for the work of its artists, writers, and thinkers.

Numbers counted in another way as well. The smallness of Anglo-Jewry (relative to other Jewish communities), in combination with England's stigmatization of Jewishness and its monochromatic definition of Englishness, made the doings of the Jewish community appear insular and uninteresting to talented Jews. In the nineteenth and twentieth centuries, creative, ambitious individuals repeatedly looked outward to be challenged, find excitement, and win recognition. Life outside the tribal "duck pond" (Julia Frankau's phrase) seemed more exhilarating and rewarding (in every sense) than life within. There was thus a steady loss of Jewish talent, a constant centrifugal flow of the best and the brightest. In 1928, Selig Brodetsky lamented that "the majority of the best intellects we produce and nurture leave us, often in sorrow or disgust, but oftenest unconsciously and without any sense of struggle or feeling of loss."[11] Most Jews who contributed to English cultural and intellectual life cut their ties to the community or were indifferent to its concerns and took no part in its activities. Most believed that being Jewish was irrelevant to their work and wrote out references to their Jewishness, as in the case of Harold Pinter, or masked them, as in the case of Anita Brookner.

They did so because they were made to feel "distinctly uncomfortable with their Jewishness." Were they to explore their own background or Anglo-Jewish society, they risked being viewed as self-serving and parochial.[12] This is why Israel Zangwill, who owed his reputation to his "Jewish" writing (*Children of the Ghetto, The King of Schnorrers, The Melting Pot*), avoided Jewish themes in his late work. He did not want to be "shut up in the ghetto" and resented critics saying that his best work was his "Jewish" work (even if it was true!). He did not want to be remembered as a "Jewish" writer but as an "English" one.[13]

This same combination—small numbers and English disdain for cultural difference—also influenced how the Anglo-Jewish establishment defended communal interests and responded to antisemitism in the late nineteenth and twentieth centuries. The heads of Anglo-Jewry's central institutions were attentive, on the whole, to public measures that endangered Jewish observance and blocked Jewish integration. They also responded, but with less vigor and consistency, to cultural and social antisemitism and right-wing demagoguery. Their policies were cautious and measured. They preferred to work outside the limelight, relying on their own standing, respectability, and links to the British establishment to set matters right. They tended to play by the rules, to trust in human reason and England's fabled sense of fair play. Above all, they did not want to make a fuss, drawing attention to the Jews and their problems— not because they were spineless or timid, or ashamed of being Jewish, but because they believed that such tactics would backfire, fueling the fires of antisemitism, and because, like other men of property, they feared the mass politics of the streets. Their caution was prompted as well by their awareness that Jews were a negligible force in electoral politics, for there were never more than one or two boroughs in which Jewish voters made a difference in parliamentary elections. Moreover, even in these districts, mainstream communal leaders were reluctant to acknowledge the existence of a "Jewish vote," since in their view the term suggested that Jews as a group had political interests that set them apart from other Britons.

In contrast to its record in the cultural sphere, the institutional framework that British Jewry created for its collective needs was impressive. Although it was constituted on a voluntary basis, like its North American offshoots, its institutions were highly centralized and, in the case of the rabbinate, hierarchical. Their inspiration was both the Church of England and the state-imposed Gemeinde and Landesrabbiner of Central Europe, institutions with which the Anglo-Jewish leadership was familiar. The elaborate network of religious and charitable institutions that British Jews erected and supported voluntarily was one of the great successes of the Anglo-Jewish experience. There were, of course, needs that went unmet—this was true everywhere—but Anglo-Jewish charitable and religious institutions were certainly the equal of those in countries where the state imposed and collected taxes for the benefit of the community. In comparison to the record of other Western Jewries before World War II, middle-class British Jews (especially in the nineteenth and early twentieth centuries) were equally, if not more, charitable and committed to the welfare of their fellow Jews.

The strength and reputation of Anglo-Jewish institutions, especially the Board of Deputies, along with the wealth and standing of the City notables who headed the community before World War I, allowed Anglo-Jewry to take the lead in Jewish diplomatic efforts to help oppressed Jews in North Africa, the Middle East, and Eastern Europe. From the 1840s to the 1920s, the Board of Deputies and the Rothschild bank were the preeminent addresses to which Jewish communities in distress turned. However, with the decline of British power and the eclipse of Jewish financial houses in the City in the twentieth century, this role shifted to the Jewish community of the United States.

British Jews also distinguished themselves, in comparison to other Western Jews, by their loyalty to Jewish worship and ritual. For most of the nineteenth and early twentieth centuries, middle-class British Jews, especially those in its upper reaches, were more likely to observe the Sabbath and festivals and keep the dietary laws, in one fashion or another, than their counterparts in Paris, Berlin, Vienna, or New York. Whether this was due to the voluntary character of the community or to the centrality of religion to Victorian notions of middle-class respectability or to the low level of pressure to abandon Jewish religious distinctiveness is a matter of speculation. Very likely it is due to some combination of all three.

There was, however, a downside to Anglo-Jewish centralization. The near monopoly of religious life that the institutions of central Orthodoxy enjoyed until after World War II inhibited the search for new forms of worship, thought, and organization and thus contributed to the cultural poverty of Anglo-Jewish life. The chief rabbinate, backed by the lay leadership of the United Synagogue, was averse to free trade in religion and labored to prevent the emergence of competing institutions and to delegitimize those that succeeded in establishing themselves. It was never completely successful and from the end of the nineteenth century fought a losing battle against groups on both the left and the right of the religious spectrum. But the damage was already done. The intellectual ferment and experimentation that characterized nineteenth-century communities in Central Europe and the United States were absent. Of course, the Gemeinden of Central Europe, in which membership was compulsory, monopolized public religious worship as well, but there external pressure on Jews to transform Judaism (in the form of opposition to emancipation and acceptance) was a powerful stimulant to creativity. The illiberalism of Central Europe, in other words, energized Jewish life while the liberalism of Britain operated in a contrary fashion. Moreover, although left- and right-wing alternatives to centrist Orthodoxy gained strength from the 1930s on, the weight of tradition, history, and habit were on the side of the well-entrenched institutions of the latter. As a result, only at the very end of the twentieth century did British Jewry begin to display some of the cultural liveliness that characterized the American and German Jewish communities a century or more earlier.

In sum, the history of the Jews in Britain is not the success story that Roth claimed. Nor, however, is it the opposite, a sorry or unenviable tale of failure, betrayal, decline, and enervation. Stark, one-sided characterizations of the Anglo-Jewish past like these, which see the proverbial glass as either half-full or half-empty, are not enlightening. Historians who celebrate the good fortune of Anglo-Jewry, as well as those who dwell on its shortcomings, fail to confront the messiness of its past. They paint a picture that is at once too tidy and too unidimensional, largely, I suspect, because they bring to their task agendas and commitments fueled by still simmering communal and political tensions. It has been my hope to restore balance and complexity to Anglo-Jewish history by forswearing the urge to pronounce it a success or a failure. The danger, of course, is that abandoning the master narrative of success or failure may leave little more than a formless antiquarian tale. But this is a risk worth entertaining.

Notes

The following abbreviations are used in the notes:

JC   *Jewish Chronicle*, London
MJHSE   *Miscellanies of the Jewish Historical Society of England*
TJHSE   *Transactions of the Jewish Historical Society of England*

Introduction

1. Cecil Roth, "Why Anglo-Jewish History?," *TJHSE* 22 (1970): 22, 24, 25.

2. David Cannadine, "Cousinhood," *London Review of Books*, 27 July 1989, 10–12. Cannadine dismissed Anglo-Jewish history as "little more than a bland and lukewarm chronicle . . . neither very interesting nor very exciting [and] in the context of British history . . . not all that important." In his view, a history whose hallmarks are "sustained economic progress and successful political assimilation," rather than orchestrated outbursts of antisemitism, lacks excitement. As a "successful minority"—assimilated, free from persecution, materially comfortable—British Jews and their past offer little to stimulate the imagination. Two inferences can be made from his comments. The first is that Jews merit attention only when they appear as victims, as objects of persecution. The second is that historians should concern themselves with explaining failure, not success. The first strikes me as condescending, if not hostile; the second as ludicrous.

3. Jacob Katz, *Out of the Ghetto: The Social Background of Jewish Emancipation, 1770–1870* (Cambridge, Mass., 1973), 38–40. By the same token, historians of British Jewry tend to avoid descriptive concepts and categories from the continental Jewish experience in their work. None, for example, characterizes the second half of the eighteenth century as the age of *haskalah* or the first half of the next century as the age of religious conflict between tradition and reform.

The one exception is Cecil Roth, who claimed there was a haskalah in England, citing as evidence the presence of a few individuals who shared some of the ideas of the German haskalah and a few learned persons who wrote in a modernized Hebrew style, at times on themes of general cultural interest. But he failed to show there was an ideological movement to modernize traditional Jewish life, which was the hallmark of Jewish Enlightenment everywhere. See his article "The Haskalah in England," in *Essays Presented to Chief Rabbi Israel Brodie on the Occasion of His Seventieth Birthday,* ed. H. J. Zimmels et al. (London, 1967), 1: 365–76.

4. Raphael Mahler, *Divrei yemei yisrael: dorot ahronim* [A history of the Jews in modern times], 6 vols. (Tel Aviv, 1952–76); Salo W. Baron, "The Modern Age," in *Great Ages and Ideas of the Jewish People,* ed. Leo W. Schwarz (New York, 1956), 313–484; Shmuel Ettinger, "The Modern Period," in *A History of the Jewish People,* ed. Haim Hillel Ben-Sasson (Cambridge, Mass., 1975); Howard Morley Sachar, *The Course of Modern Jewish History,* rev. ed. (New York, 1977); Robert M. Seltzer, *Jewish People, Jewish Thought: The Jewish Experience in History* (New York, 1980), pt. 4. Also see the syllabi collected in Jack Wertheimer, ed., *The Modern Jewish Experience: A Reader's Guide* (New York, 1993), 331–78. David Vital, *A People Apart: The Jews in Europe, 1789–1939* (Oxford, 1999) is marginally more expansive in its treatment of Anglo-Jewry.

5. Stanley Waterman and Barry Kosmin, *British Jewry in the Eighties: A Statistical and Geographical Study* (London, 1986), 7; Paul R. Mendes-Flohr and Jehudah Reinharz, eds., *The Jew in the Modern World: A Documentary History* (New York, 1980), table 18.

6. Cecil Roth, *A History of the Jews in England,* 3rd ed. (Oxford, 1964), 270. A half-century earlier Max Nordau made the same point in his address to the first Zionist Congress. See the excerpt in *The Zionist Idea: A Historical Analysis and Reader,* ed. Arthur Hertzberg (New York, 1966), 237.

7. See, for example, Todd M. Endelman, "The Englishness of Jewish Modernity in England," in *Toward Modernity: The European Jewish Model,* ed. Jacob Katz (New Brunswick, N.J., 1987), 225–46; idem, "The Social and Political Context of Conversion in Germany and England, 1870–1914," in *Jewish Apostasy in the Modern World,* ed. Todd M. Endelman (New York, 1987), 83–107.

8. I include Cecil Roth in this group, since despite his Oxford credentials he wrote in the same apologetic vein as the amateurs of the Jewish Historical Society of England. Before the 1970s, the only academic historian to take up English Jewish history was the American-born and-trained Lloyd Gartner, who was a doctoral student of Salo Baron at Columbia University in the 1950s and whose pioneering book *The Jewish Immigrant in England, 1870–1914* appeared in 1960. Gartner has written broadly about East European immigration and settlement and not just about immigration to Great Britain. For a critique of the amateur school, see David Cesarani, "Dual Heritage or Duel of Heritages? Englishness and Jewishness in the Heritage Industry," and Tony Kushner, "The End of the 'Anglo-Jewish Progress Show': Representations of the Jewish East End, 1887–1987," in *The Jewish Heritage in British History: Englishness and Jewishness,* ed. Tony Kushner (London, 1992), 29–41, 78–105.

9. Gerald Newman, *The Rise of English Nationalism: A Cultural History, 1740–1830* (New York, 1987); Linda Colley, *Britons: Forging the Nation, 1707–1837* (New Haven, Conn., 1992). For examples in the medieval and Tudor-Stuart periods, see Colin Richmond, "Englishness and Medieval Anglo-Jewry," and David S. Katz, "The Marginalization of Early Modern Anglo-Jewish History," in *The Jewish Heritage in British History*, ed. Kushner, 42–77.

10. Beverly Lemire, "Consumerism in Preindustrial and Early Industrial England: The Trade in Secondhand Clothes," *Journal of British Studies* 27 (1988): 1–24; idem, *Fashion's Favourite: The Cotton Trade and the Consumer in Britain, 1660–1800* (Oxford, 1992).

11. One exception is Paul Smith, "Disraeli's Politics," *Transactions of the Royal Historical Society*, 5th ser., 37 (1987): 65–85. Awareness of the importance of Disraeli's Jewishness informs the following work: Stanley Weintraub, *Disraeli: A Biography* (New York, 1993); David Feldman, *Englishmen and Jews: Social Relations and Political Culture, 1840–1914* (New Haven, Conn., 1994), chap. 4; Paul Smith and Charles Richmond, eds., *The Self-Fashioning of Disraeli, 1818–1851* (Cambridge, 1998); Todd M. Endelman and Tony Kushner, eds., *Disraeli's Jewishness* (London, 2002).

12. Richmond, "Englishness and Medieval Anglo-Jewry."

13. For example, see Jerry White, *Rothschild Buildings: Life in an East End Tenement Block, 1887–1920* (London, 1980), 148; Joseph Buckman, *Immigrants and the Class Struggle: The Jewish Immigrant in Leeds, 1880–1914* (Manchester, 1983), 145.

14. The books that laid to rest Roth's view include, in order of date of publication: Colin Holmes, *Anti-Semitism in British Society, 1876–1939* (New York, 1979); Todd M. Endelman, *The Jews of Georgian England, 1714–1830: Tradition and Change in a Liberal Society* (Philadelphia, 1979); Tony Kushner, *The Persistence of Prejudice: Antisemitism in British Society during the Second World War* (Manchester, 1989); Tony Kushner and Kenneth Lunn, eds., *Traditions of Intolerance: Historical Perspectives on Fascism and Race Discourse in Britain* (Manchester, 1989); David Cesarani, ed., *The Making of Modern Anglo-Jewry* (Oxford, 1990); Todd M. Endelman, *Radical Assimilation in English Jewish History* (Bloomington, Ind., 1990); Feldman, *Englishmen and Jews* (1994).

15. The most extreme statement of this view is William D. Rubinstein, *A History of the Jews in the English-Speaking World: Great Britain* (London, 1996).

16. This, however, is the implication of the work of the Jerusalem school of historians (Ben Zion Dinur, Yitzhak Baer, Shmuel Ettinger, Jacob Katz, and their students), with its emphasis on self-conscious shifts in ideological orientation as the key markers of historical change.

17. Todd M. Endelman, "The Checkered Career of 'Jew' King: A Study in Anglo-Jewish Social History," *AJS Review* 7–8 (1982–83): 69–100, reprinted in *Profiles in Diversity: Jews in a Changing Europe, 1750–1870*, ed. Frances Malino and David Sorkin (Detroit, 1998), 151–81.

18. V. D. Lipman's *Social History of the Jews in England, 1850–1950* (London, 1954) was pioneering in its emphases. Bill Williams's *The Making of Manchester Jewry, 1740–1875* (Manchester, 1976) is still the most rigorous, intellectually chal-

lenging social history of a medium-sized Jewish community in Europe or America in any language.

19. For critical accounts of the new school, see Lloyd P. Gartner, "Mehagrim yehudim mi-mizrah eiropah be-angliyah: esrim ve-hameish shenot historiyografiyah" [Jewish immigrants from Eastern Europe in England: Twenty-five years of historiography], in *Temurot be-historiyah ha-yehudit he-hadashah: kovets maamarim shai le-Shmuel Ettinger* [Transformation and change in modern Jewish history: Essays presented in honor of Shmuel Ettinger], ed. Shmuel Almog et al. (Jerusalem, 1987), 527–42; Todd M. Endelman, "English Jewish History," *Modern Judaism* 11 (1991): 91–109; idem, "Jews, Aliens and Other Outsiders in British History," *The Historical Journal* 37 (1994): 959–69.

20. Feldman, *Englishmen and Jews*, 388.

1. The Resettlement (1656–1700)

1. Cecil Roth, *A History of the Jews in England*, 3rd ed. (Oxford, 1964), 91.

2. On the expulsion, see Robert C. Stacey, "Yahadut angliyah be-meah ha-shelosh-esrei u-vaayat ha-gerush" [Thirteenth century Anglo-Jewry and the problem of the expulsion], in *Gerush ve-shivah: yahadut angliyah be-hilufei ha-zemanim* [Banishment and return], ed. Yosef Kaplan and David Katz (Jerusalem, 1992), 9–25; and Robin R. Mundill, *England's Jewish Solution: Experiment and Expulsion, 1262–1290* (Cambridge, 1999), chap. 8.

3. V. D. Lipman, "The Anatomy of Medieval Anglo-Jewry," *TJHSE* 21 (1968): 65.

4. For this and other examples of Jews who visited England during the so-called middle period, see Roth, *History of the Jews in England*, chap. 6.

5. The word *marrano*, which was never used by the conversos themselves, was initially a pejorative term, probably derived from the Spanish word meaning swine, and is best avoided.

6. The best account of the origins of the converso group and the ambiguities of converso identity is Yosef Hayim Yerushalmi, *From Spanish Court to Italian Ghetto—Isaac Cardoso: A Study in Seventeenth-Century Marranism and Jewish Apologetics* (New York, 1971), chap. 1.

7. Lucien Wolf, "Jews in Tudor England," in *Essays in Jewish History*, ed. Cecil Roth (London, 1934), 73–90; Roth, *History of the Jews in England*, 136–44; David S. Katz, *The Jews in the History of England, 1485–1850* (Oxford, 1994), chap. 2.

8. Wolf, "Jews in Tudor England," 81, 87–89.

9. Wolf, "Jews in Tudor England," 89.

10. See, for example, the description of Jewish practices encountered by the Lisbon New Christian merchant Vicente Furtado on his visit to London in 1605, in Edgar R. Samuel, "Passover in Shakespeare's London," *TJHSE* 26 (1979): 117–18.

11. It is not clear whether merchants who had lived previously as practicing

Jews in Amsterdam and Hamburg felt they had to hide their origins and attend mass in Catholic chapels in London. According to Albert Hyamson, Simon de Caceres, who was born a Jew in Amsterdam, not only refused to conceal his Judaism but boasted of it and tried to convince the New Christians he met to embrace it publicly. Unfortunately, Hyamson fails to provide a source for this anecdote. *The Sephardim of England: A History of the Spanish and Portuguese Jewish Community, 1492–1951* (London, 1951), 12.

12. James Howell to R. Lewis, 3 January 1655, *Epistolae Ho-Elianae: The Familiar Letters of James Howell*, ed. Joseph Jacobs, 2 vols. (London, 1892), 2: 617.

13. The standard accounts of the resettlement are H. S. Q. Henriques, *The Return of the Jews to England, Being a Chapter in the History of English Law* (London, 1905); Mordecai Wilensky, *Shivat ha-yehudim le-angliyah ba-meah ha-sheva esreh* [The return of the Jews to England in the seventeenth century] (Jerusalem, 1943); Roth, *History of the Jews in England*, chap. 7; David S. Katz, *Philo-Semitism and the Readmission of the Jews to England, 1603–1655* (Oxford, 1982).

14. B. S. Capp's statistical survey of works by ministers supporting Parliament in the period 1640–53 found that just under 70 percent of his sample could be identified as millenarians, only 3.5 percent as antimillenarians. *The Fifth Monarchy Men: A Study in Seventeenth Century English Millenarianism* (London, 1972), 38–39.

15. Katz, *Philo-Semitism and the Readmission of the Jews*, 177.

16. The only biography is Cecil Roth, *A Life of Menasseh ben Israel—Rabbi, Printer, and Diplomat* (Philadelphia, 1934). This should be supplemented by Henry Mechoulan and Gerard Nahon, "Introduction," Menasseh ben Israel, *The Hope of Israel—The English Translation by Moses Wall, 1652* (Oxford, 1987); and Yosef Kaplan, Henry Mechoulan, and Richard H. Popkin, eds., *Menasseh ben Israel and His World* (Leiden, 1989).

17. Mechoulan and Nahon, "Introduction," 41.

18. Jonathan I. Israel, "Menasseh ben Israel and the Dutch Sephardic Colonization Movement of the Mid-Seventeenth Century (1645–1657)," in *Menasseh ben Israel and His World*, ed. Kaplan, Mechoulan, and Popkin, 139–63.

19. Menasseh ben Israel, *The Hope of Israel*, 100. On Menasseh's messianism, see Rivka Schatz, "Emdato shel Menasheh ben Yisrael kelapei ha-meshihiyyut ba-maarakh ha-yehudi-notsri" [Menasseh ben Israel's approach to messianism in the Jewish-Christian context], *Bar-Ilan* 22–23 (1987): 429–47.

20. Wilbur Cortez Abbott, ed., *The Writings and Speeches of Oliver Cromwell*, 4 vols. (Cambridge, Mass., 1937–47), 3: 64, 65.

21. Israel, "Menasseh ben Israel and the Dutch Sephardic Colonization Movement," 156–60.

22. Quoted in Katz, *Philo-Semitism and the Readmission of the Jews to England*, 194. I have modernized the spelling and punctuation of the original.

23. Christopher Hill, *God's Englishman: Oliver Cromwell and the English Revolution*, Pelican Books ed. (Harmondsworth, Eng., 1973), 139. In *The Jews of Georgian England, 1714–1830: Tradition and Change in a Liberal Society* (Philadelphia, 1979), 17, I wrote that "Cromwell's interest in the readmission of the Jews

was of a practical nature, untinged by doctrinaire or visionary concerns of any kind"—a view to which I no longer subscribe. I imagine that when I wrote that I was unduly influenced by the writings of Cecil Roth, who denied Cromwell's millenarianism. See, for example, his comments in *Menasseh ben Israel*, 215.

24. Lucien Wolf, "Cromwell's Jewish Intelligencers," in *Essays in Jewish History*, ed. Cecil Roth, 93–114.

25. Jonathan Israel suggests that Cromwell's preoccupation at the time with furthering English power in the Caribbean, where Jewish trading interests were strong, inclined him to favor Jewish readmission. *European Jewry in the Age of Mercantilism, 1550–1750* (Oxford, 1985), 159.

26. The text of the letter is published in translation in Roth, *Menasseh ben Israel*, 226–27, and in Roth, ed., *Anglo-Jewish Letters (1158–1917)* (London, 1938), 47–48.

27. Quoted in Roth, *Menasseh ben Israel*, 269.

28. The standard accounts for the reigns of Charles II, James II, and William and Mary are Edgar R. Samuel, "The First Fifty Years," in *Three Centuries of Anglo-Jewish History*, ed. Vivian D. Lipman (London, 1961), 27–44; Roth, *History of the Jews in England*, chap. 8; A. S. Diamond, "The Community of the Resettlement, 1656–1684: A Social Survey," *TJHSE* 24 (1975): 134–50; David S. Katz, "The Jews of England and 1688," in *From Persecution to Toleration: The Glorious Revolution and Religion in England*, ed. Ole Peter Orell, Jonathan I. Israel, and Nicholas Tyacke (Oxford, 1991), 217–49.

29. For an alternative account, which detects Stuart perfidy behind this attempt to harass the Jews, see R. A. Routledge, "The Legal Status of the Jews in England, 1190–1790," *The Journal of Legal History* 3 (1982): 108–10.

30. Isaiah Tishbi, "Yediot hadashot al kehilat ha-anusim be-London al pi iggerot Sasportas bi-shenat 5425 (1664–5)" [New information on the converso community in London according to letters of Sasportas from 1664–5], in *Galut ahar golah: mehkarim be-toldot am yisrael mugashim le-professor Haim Beinart limlot lo shivim shanah* [Exile after exile: Essays in Jewish history presented to Professor Haim Beinart on his seventieth birthday], ed. Aharon Mirsky et al. (Jerusalem, 1988), 488.

31. Oskar K. Rabinowicz, *Sir Solomon de Medina* (London, 1974).

32. On the estimate for 1660, see Samuel, "The First Fifty Years," 41, n. 6; on the Zagache list, see Lionel D. Barnett, ed., *Bevis Marks Records, Being Contributions to the History of the Spanish and Portuguese Congregation of London*, vol. 1, *The Early History of the Congregation from the Beginning until 1800* (Oxford, 1940), 16–20; on the figure for 1695, see Robert Cohen, "'La-vo im mishpehoteyhem . . . u-lehityashev kan': yahadut London ha-sefardit be-mahatsit ha-sheniyah shel ha-meah ha-sheva-esreh" ["To come with their families . . . and dwell here": London Sephardi Jewry in the second half of the seventeenth century], in *Gerush ve-shiva*, ed. Kaplan and Katz, 147–57.

33. Population figures for Jewish communities in early modern Europe are notoriously unreliable. According to Miriam Bodian, a specialist in the history of the western Sephardi Diaspora, the best estimates we have indicate that in the second half of the seventeenth century there were about 5,000 Sephardim

in Venice, 3,000 in Livorno, 2,500 in Amsterdam, and 600 in Hamburg. Personal communication.

34. Maurice Woolf, "Foreign Trade of London Jews in the Seventeenth Century," *TJHSE* 24 (1975): 38–58.

35. Woolf, "Foreign Trade of London Jews," 51; Diamond, "The Community of the Resettlement," 147–79.

36. In theory, Jews could not engage in retail trade. This was because retail trade was limited to freemen of the City of London, a status closed to Jews because they could not take the required christological oath. In practice, the authorities turned a blind eye and de facto permitted Jews to sell retail.

37. The governance of the new community is described in Hyamson, *The Sephardim of England*, 27–33.

38. Tishbi, "Kehilat ha-anusim be-London," 479–82.

39. David S. Katz, "The Abendana Brothers and the Christian Hebraists of Seventeenth-Century England," *The Journal of Ecclesiastical History* 40 (1989): 28–52.

40. Matt Goldish, "Jews, Christians and Conversos: Rabbi Solomon Aailion's Struggles in the Portuguese Community of London," *Journal of Jewish Studies* 45 (1994): 227–57.

41. Michael McKeon, "Sabbatai Sevi in England," *AJS Review* 2 (1977): 131–69. In his magisterial account of the Sabbatean movement during the lifetime of Shabbetai Zevi, Gershom Scholem does not mention any instances of penitential awakening or messianic enthusiasm among the Sephardim of London. *Sabbatai Sevi: The Mystical Messiah*, trans. R. J. Zwi Werblowsky (Princeton, N.J., 1973).

42. Barnett, *Bevis Marks Records*, 1: 27–8.

43. Yosef Hayim Yerushalmi, "Professing Jews in Post-Expulsion Spain," in *Salo Wittmayer Baron Jubilee Volume*, ed. Saul Lieberman and Arthur Hyman, 3 vols. (Jerusalem, 1974), 2: 1023–58; idem, "Anusim ha-hozrim le-yahadut be-meah ha-shevah-esreh: haskalatam ha-yehudit ve-hachsharatam ha-nafshit" [Conversos returning to Judaism in the seventeenth century: Their Jewish knowledge and psychological preparation], *Proceedings of the Fifth World Congress of Jewish Studies*, 5 vols. (Jerusalem, 1972), 2: 201–9; idem, *From Spanish Court to Italian Ghetto*, 276–99.

44. Yosef Hayim Yerushalmi, *The Re-education of Marranos in the Seventeenth Century*, Rabbi Louis Feinberg Memorial Lecture in Judaic Studies, no. 3 (Cincinnati, Ohio, 1980), 7.

45. Yerushalmi, *The Re-education of Marranos;* idem, *From Spanish Court to Italian Ghetto*, 197–206.

46. Katz, *Philo-Semitism and the Readmission of the Jews*, 3.

47. For these and other examples of conversos who refused to join the Jewish community or who stumbled while trying to do so, see Todd M. Endelman, *Radical Assimilation in English Jewish History, 1656–1945* (Bloomington, Ind., 1990), chap. 1.

48. Lucien Wolf, ed. and trans., *Jews in the Canary Islands, Being a Calendar of Jewish Cases Extracted from the Records of the Canariote Inquisition in the Collec-*

tion of the Marquess of Bute (London, 1926), 205; Tishbi, "Yediot hadashot al kehilat ha-anusim be-London," 483–84.

49. Tishbi, "Yediot hadashot al kehilat ha-anusim be-London," 483.

50. This is also the conclusion of Yosef Kaplan. See his important article "The Jewish Profile of the Spanish-Portuguese Community of London during the Seventeenth Century," *Judaism* 41 (1992): 229–40.

51. Endelman, *Radical Assimilation*, 14–15.

52. Much recent research on this topic is summarized in Yirmiyahu Yovel, *Spinoza and Other Heretics,* vol. 1, *The Marrano of Reason* (Princeton, N.J., 1989), chap. 3.

53. This point is discussed at greater length in Todd M. Endelman, "Jewish Communal Structure in Britain from the Resettlement to the Present," in *Studien zur jüdischen Geschichte und Soziologie: Festschrift Julius Carlebach,* ed. Ursula Beitz et al. (Heidelberg, 1992), 1–16. On the rejudaisation of conversos in Amsterdam, see Miriam Bodian, *Hebrews of the Portuguese Nation: Conversos and Community in Early Modern Amsterdam* (Bloomington, Ind., 1997).

54. Yerushalmi, *From Spanish Court to Italian Ghetto,* 44.

55. Endelman, *Radical Assimilation,* chap. 1.

56. See the many examples in H. S. Q. Henriques, *The Jews and the English Law* (London, 1908).

57. Roth, *History of the Jews in England,* 187; Henriques, *The Jews and the English Law,* 164–66; Katz, "The Jews of England and 1688," 236–46.

58. Routledge, "The Legal Status of the Jews," 110–16; Norma Perry, "Anglo-Jewry, the Law, Religious Conviction, and Self-Interest (1655–1753)," *European Studies* 14 (1984): 7–11.

59. J. M. Ross, "Naturalisation of Jews in England," *TJHSE* 24 (1975): 59–72.

60. Routledge, "The Legal Status of the Jews," 116.

61. Samuel Pepys, *The Diary of Samuel Pepys,* Everyman's Library ed., 2 vols. (London, 1906), 1: 414; Greenhaigh quoted in Elliot Horowitz, "'A Different Mode of Civility': Lancelot Addison on the Jews of Barbary," *Studies in Church History* 29 (1992): 312. On the identification of Jews with barbarism, see Horowitz's discussion, 310–13.

62. On the persistence of traditional Christian attitudes toward Jews, see Bernard Glassman, *Anti-Semitic Stereotypes without Jews: Images of the Jews in England, 1290–1700* (Detroit, 1975), 139–46.

63. Hyamson, *The Sephardim of England,* 46–48; Cecil Roth, "The Lord Mayor's Salvers," in *Essays and Portraits in Anglo-Jewish History* (Philadelphia, 1962), 108–12.

2. Bankers and Brokers, Peddlers and Pickpockets (1700–1800)

1. These figures are, of course, estimates. For a fuller discussion, see Todd M. Endelman, *The Jews of Georgian England, 1714–1830: Tradition and Change in*

a Liberal Society (Philadelphia, 1979), 171–72. The Catholic statistics are in A. D. Gilbert, *Religion and Society in Industrial England: Church, Chapel and Social Change, 1740–1914* (London, 1976), 46, table 2.8.

2. V. D. Lipman, "Sephardi and Other Jewish Immigrants in England in the Eighteenth Century," in *Migration and Settlement: Proceedings of the Anglo-American Jewish Historical Conference . . . July 1970* (London, 1971), 38.

3. Endelman, *The Jews of Georgian England*, 174–75.

4. Moses A. Shulvass, *From East to West: The Westward Migration of Jews from Eastern Europe during the Seventeenth and Eighteenth Century* (Detroit, 1971), 109.

5. A. S. Diamond, "Problems of the London Sephardi Community, 1720–1733 — Philip Carteret Webb's Notebooks," *TJHSE* 21 (1968): 40, 60; Lipman, "Sephardi and Other Jewish Immigrants," 44; Richard D. Barnett, "Dr. Samuel Nunes Ribeiro and the Settlement of Georgia," in *Migration and Settlement*, 79–80; idem, *Bevis Marks Records*, vol. 4, *The Circumcision Register of Isaac and Abraham de Paiba (1715–1775)* (London, 1991), 3–5.

6. The 1803 aliens register from the Bevis Marks congregation indicates the origins of the poorer Sephardim who arrived in the second half of the eighteenth century. A transcription of the register appears as Appendix A in Lipman, "Sephardi and Other Jewish Immigrants."

7. Robert Cohen, *Jews in Another Environment: Surinam in the Second Half of the Eighteenth Century* (Leiden, 1991), 22. See also Zosa Szajkowski, "Population Problems of Marranos and Sephardim in France from the 16th to the 18th Centuries," *Proceedings of the American Academy for Jewish Research* 27 (1958): 14.

8. The peddlers, hawkers, and old clothes men of this period are discussed at length in Endelman, *The Jews of Georgian England*, chap. 5.

9. *Old Bailey Sessions Papers* 23 (1783): 743–47.

10. On the secondhand clothing trade, see Madeleine Ginsburg, "Rags to Riches: The Second-Hand Clothes Trade, 1700–1978," *Costume* 14 (1980): 121–35; Beverly Lemire, "Consumerism in Preindustrial and Early Industrial England: The Trade in Secondhand Clothes," *Journal of British Studies* 27 (1988): 1–24; idem, *Fashion's Favourite: The Cotton Trade and the Consumer in Britain, 1660–1800* (Oxford, 1992).

11. Robert Southey, *Letters from England*, 2nd ed., 3 vols. (London, 1808), 3: 151–52; Henry Mayhew, *London Labour and the London Poor*, 3 vols. (London, 1851), 2: 130; Benjamin Silliman, *A Journal of Travels in England, Holland, and Scotland*, 3rd ed., 3 vols. (New Haven, 1820), 1: 270–71.

12. Henry Fielding, "An Enquiry into the Causes of the Late Increase of Robbers," *The Works of Henry Fielding*, 10 vols. (London, 1806), 10: 412; Patrick Colquhoun, *A Treatise on the Commerce and Police of the River Thames* (London, 1800), 196–97.

13. *The Times*, 30 July 1795. On Jewish involvement in the manufacture and distribution of counterfeit coins, see Endelman, *The Jews of Georgian England*, 206–8.

14. Jewish crime — its character and incidence and reactions to it — is treated at length in Endelman, *The Jews of Georgian England*, chap. 6. The problem was

not confined to England alone, although it may have flourished in London more than in other European capitals. For a comparative perspective, see Rudolf Glanz, *Geschichte des niederen jüdischen Volkes in Deutschland: eine Studie über historisches Gaunertum, Bettelwesen und Vagantentum* (New York, 1968); Richard Cobb, "Dinah Jacob and the *Bande Juive*," in *Paris and Its Provinces, 1792–1802* (London, 1975), 142–93; Florike Egmond, "Crime in Context: Jewish Involvement in Organized Crime in the Dutch Republic," *Jewish History*, 4, 1 (spring 1989): 75–100; Otto Ulbricht, "Criminality and Punishment of the Jews in the Early Modern Period," in *In and Out of the Ghetto: Jewish-Gentile Relations in Late Medieval and Early Modern Germany*, ed. R. Po-Chia Hsia and Hartmut Liehmann (Cambridge, 1995), 49–70.

15. Endelman, *The Jews of Georgian England*, 136–37, 270–71; John M. Shaftesley, "Jews in English Regular Freemasonry, 1717–1860," *TJHSE* 25 (1977): 153–54, 162–63.

16. Neil McKendrick, John Brewer, and J. H. Plumb, *The Birth of a Consumer Society: The Commercialization of Eighteenth-Century England* (Bloomington, Ind., 1982), 9.

17. On Prager and his family's activities, see Gedalia Yogev, *Diamonds and Coral: Anglo-Dutch Jews and Eighteenth-Century Trade* (Leicester, Eng., 1978). The literature on the Rothschild family is enormous, and much of it is untrustworthy. The most useful account of the early years of the family in England is Niall Ferguson, *The House of Rothschild: Money's Prophets, 1798–1848* (New York, 1998).

18. John Brewer, *The Sinews of Power: War, Money and the English State, 1688–1783* (New York, 1988). For Gideon's financial activities, see Lucy S. Sutherland, "Samson Gideon: Eighteenth Century Jewish Financier," *TJHSE* 17 (1953): 79–90.

19. Cecil Roth, *The Great Synagogue, London, 1690–1940* (London, 1950), 154.

20. Arthur Barnett, *The Western Synagogue through Two Centuries (1761–1961)* (London, 1961), chap. 1; M. Rosenbaum, *The History of the Borough Synagogue* (London, 1917), 5.

21. Cecil Roth, *The Rise of Provincial Jewry: The Early History of the Jewish Communities in the English Countryside, 1740–1840* (London, 1950), 24. Roth's account is dated and should be supplemented by V. D. Lipman, "The Origins of Provincial Anglo-Jewry," in *Provincial Jewry in Victorian Britain*, ed. Aubrey Newman (London, 1975); and Harold Pollins, *Economic History of the Jews in England* (Rutherford, N.J., 1982), chap. 4.

22. Bill Williams, *The Making of Manchester Jewry, 1740–1875* (Manchester, 1976), 10–12.

23. Geoffrey L. Green, *The Royal Navy and Anglo-Jewry, 1740–1820: Traders and Those Who Served* (London, 1989). The terms used to describe the occupations of eighteenth-century Jewish traders should not be taken too literally. Most did not limit their activity to one specialized branch of commerce but acted in a variety of capacities, regardless of how they styled themselves or were described by others.

24. Israel J. Solomon, *Records of My Family* (New York, 1887).

25. The best source for the early history of the Ashkenazi community is still Roth, *The Great Synagogue*, chaps. 1–5.

26. See, for example, Cecil Roth, "The Chief Rabbinate of England," in *Essays and Portraits in Anglo-Jewish History* (Philadelphia, 1962).

27. Roth, *The Great Synagogue*, chaps. 4, 9; David Kaufmann, "Rabbi Zvi Ashkenazi and His Family in London," *TJHSE* 3 (1899): 102–25.

28. Roth, *The Great Synagogue*, 120–21; A. Barnett, *The Western Synagogue*, chap. 1.

29. Cecil Roth, "The Lesser Synagogues of the Eighteenth Century," *MJHSE* 3 (1937): 1–7; New Synagogue, minute book F, 1820–24, entry for 17 February 1822, Archives of the United Synagogue, London Metropolitan Archives; MS rules of Hevrat Margoa la-Nefesh, Society for Administering Pecuniary Comforts, 1797/98, FS 1/408B, Public Record Office, London.

30. Charles Duschinsky, *The Rabbinate of the Great Synagogue, London, from 1756–1842* (London, 1921), 74–78; Roth, *The Great Synagogue*, 125–30; idem, "The Chief Rabbinate of England," 253–55.

31. Leo Hershkowitz and Isidore S. Meyer, eds., *The Lee Max Friedman Collection of American Jewish Colonial Correspondence: Letters of the Franks Family (1733–1748)* (Waltham, Mass., 1968), 7–8; Duschinsky, *The Rabbinate of the Great Synagogue*, 15–16; *The Times*, 28 October 1802.

32. Meyer Schomberg, "Emunat omen" [True faith], trans. Harold Levy, *TJHSE* 20 (1964): 102; An English Israelite, *A Letter to the Parisian Sanhedrin* (London, 1808), 35–36; New Synagogue, minute book G, 1824–32, entry for 31 October 1830; Hambro Synagogue, minute book, committee, 1794–1809, entry for 22 November 1807, Archives of the United Synagogue, London Metropolitan Archives.

33. Endelman, *The Jews of Georgian England*, 123, 128–31.

34. Endelman, *The Jews of Georgian England*, chap. 4.

35. Endelman, *The Jews of Georgian England*, 126–8; idem, *Radical Assimilation in English Jewish History, 1656–1945*, (Bloomington, Ind., 1990), 11–13, 35–40.

36. Levi Alexander [and Henry Lemoine], *Memoirs of the Life and Commercial Connections of the late Benjamin Goldsmid, Esq., of Roehampton* (London, 1808), 51.

37. Endelman, *The Jews of Georgian England*, 131, 198–201, 223–34.

38. Endelman, *The Jews of Georgian England*, 215–23. In the Old Price Riots of 1809 (discussed later in this chapter), the management of the Covent Garden Theatre hired Jewish toughs to intimidate demonstrators. See Marc Baer, *Theatre and Disorder in Late Georgian London* (Oxford, 1992).

39. The most eloquent spokesman for this view of the origins of Jewish modernity was Jacob Katz, whose words are quoted here. See his *Out of the Ghetto: The Social Background of Jewish Emancipation, 1770–1870* (Cambridge, Mass., 1973), esp. 34–36. For a critique of this position, see Todd M. Endelman, "The Englishness of Jewish Modernity in England," in *Toward Modernity: The European Jewish Model*, ed. Jacob Katz (New Brunswick, N.J., 1986), 225–46;

and the preface to the second, corrected edition of *The Jews of Georgian England* (Ann Arbor, Mich., 1999).

40. Arthur Barnett, "Eliakim ben Abraham (Jacob Hart): An Anglo-Jewish Scholar of the Eighteenth Century," *TJHSE* 14 (1940): 207–20; Cecil Roth, "The Haskalah in England," in *Essays Presented to Chief Rabbi Israel Brodie on the Occasion of His Seventieth Birthday*, ed. H. J. Zimmels et al., 2 vols. (London, 1967), 1: 365–76; S. B. Leperer, "Abraham ben Naphtali Tang—A Precursor of the Anglo-Jewish Haskalah," *TJHSE* 24 (1975): 82–88; Jefim Schirmann, *Le-toldot ha-shirah ve-ha-dramah ha-ivrit* [Toward a history of Hebrew poetry and drama], 2 vols. (Jerusalem, 1979), 1: 184–93; David B. Ruderman, *Jewish Thought and Scientific Discovery in Early Modern Europe* (New Haven, Conn., 1995), chaps. 11 and 12; idem, *Jewish Enlightenment in an English Key: Anglo-Jewry's Construction of Modern Jewish Thought* (Princeton, N.J., 2000); Richard H. Popkin, "David Levi, Anglo-Jewish Theologian," *Jewish Quarterly Review* 87 (1996–97): 79–101.

41. Siegfried Stein, "*Sefer Giddul Banim:* An Anonymous Judaeo-German Tract on the Education of Children, Printed in London in 1771," in *Remember the Days: Essays on Anglo-Jewish History Presented to Cecil Roth*, ed. John M. Shaftesley (London, 1966), 145–79.

42. D'Israeli's views are discussed in Endelman, *The Jews of Georgian England*, 152–54; and idem, "Disraeli's Jewishness Reconsidered," *Modern Judaism* 5 (1985): 110–11.

43. Duschinsky, *The Rabbinate of the Great Synagogue*, 21–23, 94.

44. On Nieto, see Israel Solomons, "David Nieto and Some of His Contemporaries," *TJHSE* 12 (1931): 1–101; Cecil Roth, "Haham David Nieto," in *Essays and Portraits in Anglo-Jewish History;* Jakob J. Petukowski, *The Theology of Haham David Nieto: An Eighteenth-Century Defense of the Jewish Tradition*, rev. ed. (New York, 1970); Raphael Loewe, "The Spanish Supplement to Nieto's *Esh Dath,*" *Proceedings of the American Academy for Jewish Research* 48 (1981): 267–96; Ruderman, *Jewish Thought and Scientific Discovery*, chap. 11.

45. Nina Salaman, "Ephraim Luzzatto (1729–1792)," *TJHSE* 9 (1922): 85–102; Schirmann, *Le-toldot ha-shirah ve-ha-dramah ha-ivrit*, 1: 217–38.

46. Very little work has been done on Jewish education in eighteenth-century Britain. Some information about schools can be found in Roth, *The Great Synagogue;* Hyamson, *The Sephardim of England;* P. L. S. Quinn, "The Jewish Schooling Systems of London, 1656–1956" (Ph.D. diss., University of London, 1958).

47. Duschinsky, *The Rabbinate of the Great Synagogue*, 23.

48. Johanan Holleschau, *Maaseh rav* [A great occurrence or the tale of a rabbi] (London, 1707), in Simha Assaf, *Mekorot le-toldot ha-hinukh be-yisrael: mitehilat yemei ha-beinayyim ad tekufat ha-haskalah* [Sources for the history of Jewish education: From the beginning of the Middle Ages to the Age of Enlightenment], 4 vols. in 2 (Tel Aviv, 1925), 1: 185.

49. Horace Walpole, *The Yale Edition of Horace Walpole's Correspondence*, ed. W. S. Lewis, vol. 33, *Horace Walpole's Correspondence with the Countess of Upper*

Ossory, pt. 2, ed. W. S. Lewis and A. Dayle Wallace (New Haven, Conn., 1965), 182–83.

50. Endelman, *Radical Assimilation,* chaps. 1 and 2.

51. Endelman, *The Jews of Georgian England,* 267–69.

52. Nathaniel Wraxall, *The Historical and the Posthumous Memoirs of Sir Nathaniel William Wraxall, 1772–1784,* ed. Henry B. Wheatley, 5 vols. (London, 1884), 5: 121; *The Annual Register for 1806* (London, 1807), 458.

53. *Westminster Journal,* 7 July 1753, quoted in *A Collection of the Best Pieces in Prose and Verse against the Naturalization of the Jews* (London, 1753), 59. On anti-Jewish sentiment, both religious and secular, in the eighteenth century, see Endelman, *The Jews of Georgian England,* chap. 3; Frank Felsenstein, *Anti-Semitic Stereotypes: A Paradigm of Otherness in English Popular Culture, 1660–1830* (Baltimore, Md., 1995); Bernard Glassman, *Protean Prejudice: Anti-Semitism in England's Age of Reason* (Atlanta, Ga., 1998).

54. Quoted in Roy Porter, *English Society in the Eighteenth Century,* The Penguin Social History of Britain, rev. ed. (London, 1990), 170.

55. *An Address to the Friends of Great Britain* (London, 1753), 7; *A Looking-Glass for the Jews, or, The Credulous Unbelievers* (London, 1753), i-v.

56. Quoted in Porter, *English Society in the Eighteenth Century,* 279.

57. On conversionist philosemitism in the eighteenth century, see Endelman, *The Jews of Georgian England,* chap. 2; N. I. Matar, "The Controversy over the Restoration of the Jews: From 1754 until the London Society for Promoting Christianity among the Jews," *Durham University Journal,* January 1990, 29–44.

58. Thomas Winstanley, *A Sermon Preached at the Parish Church of St. George, Hanover Square, Sunday, October 28, 1753* (London, 1753), 12–14.

59. *An Address to the Friends of Great Britain,* 17.

60. Thomas Witherby, *An Attempt to Remove Prejudices Concerning the Jewish Nation by Way of Dialogue* (London, 1803), 2; *Reasons Offered to the Consideration of Parliament for Preventing the Growth of Judaism* (London, n.d.), 8–9. Although the copy of the latter work in the library of the Jewish Theological Seminary, New York, is undated, Cecil Roth, *Magna Bibliotheca Anglo-Judaica,* new ed. (London, 1937), 214, lists editions from 1738 and 1753.

61. Patrick Colquhoun, *A Treatise on the Police of the Metropolis,* 5th ed. (London, 1797), 159–60.

62. The engraving is reproduced in Endelman, *The Jews of Georgian England,* between 182 and 183; reaction to *Family Quarrels* is presented on 217–18.

63. Quoted in Harold Perkin, *Origins of Modern English Society,* Routledge Paperback ed. (London, 1991), 93.

64. Endelman, *The Jews of Georgian England,* 196–98, 201–2.

65. Endelman, *The Jews of Georgian England,* 229–31.

66. Porter, *English Society in the Eighteenth Century,* 178–79.

67. The standard account is Thomas W. Perry, *Public Opinion, Propaganda, and Politics in Eighteenth-Century England: A Study of the Jew Bill of 1753* (Cambridge, Mass., 1962), which should be supplemented by Endelman, *The Jews of Georgian England,* 59–60, 88–91; Robert Liberles, "The Jews and Their Bill:

Jewish Motivations in the Controversy of 1753," *Jewish History*, 2, 2 (fall 1987): 29–36; and Alan H. Singer, "Aliens and Citizens: Jewish and Protestant Naturalization in the Making of the Modern British Nation" (Ph.D. diss., University of Missouri, Columbia, 1999).

68. Linda Colley, *Britons: Forging the Nation, 1707–1837* (New Haven, Conn., 1992). Colley, it should be added, ignores the Jew Bill clamor. For an application of Colley's approach to the 1753 events, see Singer, "Aliens and Citizens."

69. Quoted in Baer, *Theatre and Disorder*, 215.

3. Poverty to Prosperity (1800–1870)

1. These are rough estimates. Vivian D. Lipman discusses various ways of calculating the size of the Jewish community in his "Survey of Anglo-Jewry in 1851," *TJHSE* 17 (1953): 173–74, 177–78. Lipman's estimates, it seems to me, do not give adequate weight to unaffiliated Jews and are probably on the low side.

2. Of the 501 native-born Jews in Manchester in 1851, 298 were born elsewhere in England. More remarkably, of the 47 Jews in Glasgow in 1831, 10 came from Sheerness. Bill Williams, *The Making of Manchester Jewry, 1740–1875* (Manchester, 1976), 176; Abraham Levy, "The Origins of Scottish Jewry," *TJHSE* 19 (1960): 155.

3. Geoffrey Alderman, *Modern British Jewry* (Oxford, 1992), 21; Williams, *The Making of Manchester Jewry*, 356; Birmingham Jewish History Research Group, *Birmingham Jewry*, 2 vols. (Birmingham, 1980), vol. 1, *1749–1914*, 36.

4. Lipman, "A Survey of Anglo-Jewry in 1851," 187–88.

5. It is impossible even to estimate how many German Jews settled in Britain during the Victorian period. At best, one can say that the number was several thousand but certainly no more than ten thousand.

6. See, in general, Todd M. Endelman, "German-Jewish Settlement in Victorian England," in *Second Chance: Two Centuries of German-Speaking Jews in the United Kingdom*, ed. Werner E. Mosse et al. (Tübingen, 1991), 37–56.

7. Williams, *The Making of Manchester Jewry*, 270; Birmingham Jewish History Research Group, *Birmingham Jewry*, 1: 37; *JC*, 30 October 1846, 3 March 1854.

8. V. D. Lipman, "The Structure of London Jewry in the Mid-Nineteenth Century," in *Essays Presented to Chief Rabbi Israel Brodie on the Occasion of His Seventieth Birthday*, ed. H. J. Zimmels et al., 2 vols. (London, 1967), 1: 255–58; Moses and Judith Montefiore, *Diaries of Sir Moses and Lady Montefiore*, ed. Louis Loewe, 2 vols. (Chicago, 1890), 1: 75; Birmingham Jewish History Research Group, *Birmingham Jewry*, 1: 38.

9. Todd M. Endelman, *The Jews of Georgian England, 1714–1830: Tradition and Change in a Liberal Society* (Philadelphia, 1979), 299; J. J. Tobias, *Prince of Fences: The Life and Crimes of Ikey Solomons* (London, 1974).

10. The evidence for Jewish participation in socially marginal and criminal occupations in the mid-nineteenth century is scattered. For the 1830s, see the references in Endelman, *The Jews of Georgian England*, chaps. 5 and 6, and, for

later decades, Birmingham Jewish History Research Group, *Birmingham Jewry*, vol. 1, chap. 4; James Ewing Ritchie, *The Night Side of London* (London, 1857), 37–38; John Blackmore, *The London by Moonlight Mission, Being An Account of Midnight Cruises on the Streets of London during the Last Thirteen Years* (London, 1860), 58–59. William Makepeace Thackeray's fiction and journalism are also a good source for Jews in low-status occupations; see the references in S. S. Prawer, *Israel at Vanity Fair: Jews and Judaism in the Writings of W. M. Thackeray* (Leiden, 1992).

11. Flora Tristan, *Flora Tristan's London Journal: A Survey of London Life in the 1830s*, trans. Dennis Palmer and Giselle Pincetl (London, 1980), 144.

12. Charles Dickens, "Meditations in Monmouth Street," in *Sketches by Boz;* Thomas Carlyle, *Sartor Resartus*, bk. 3, chap. 6; John Mills, *The British Jews* (London, 1853), 270.

13. The organization of poor relief before the establishment of the Jewish Board of Guardians in 1859 is described in V. D. Lipman, *A Century of Social Service, 1859–1959: The Jewish Board of Guardians* (London, 1959), 14–20.

14. Solomon Hirschell to Lionel de Rothschild, 11 November 1840, RAL 109/39/22/XI/109/45, Rothschild Archives, London.

15. This and other efforts to reform the manners and morals of the Jewish poor in the late eighteenth and early nineteenth centuries are discussed in Endelman, *The Jews of Georgian England*, chap. 7.

16. The enrollment figures for 1870 and Angel's testimony are in Lloyd P. Gartner, *The Jewish Immigrant in England, 1870–1914*, 2nd ed. (London, 1973), 222–23. For the history of the JFS, see Gerry Black, *J.F.S.: The History of the Jews' Free School, London, since 1732* (London, 1998).

17. Arthur Barnett, *The Western Synagogue through Two Centuries (1761–1961)* (London, 1961), chap. 10.

18. Quoted in Williams, *The Making of Manchester Jewry*, 94.

19. On missionary activity in the nineteenth century, see Endelman, *The Jews of Georgian England*, 70–79; idem, *Radical Assimilation in English Jewish History, 1656–1945* (Bloomington, Ind., 1990), chap. 5; R. H. Martin, "United Conversionist Activities among the Jews in Great Britain, 1795–1815: Pan-Evangelicalism and the London Society for Promoting Christianity amongst the Jews," *Church History* 46 (1977): 437–52; Robert Michael Smith, "The London Jews' Society and Patterns of Jewish Conversion in England, 1801–1859," *Jewish Social Studies* 43 (1981): 275–90; Michael D. Sherman, "Christian Missions to the Jews in East London, 1870–1914" (Master's thesis, Yeshiva University, 1983).

20. Endelman, *The Jews of Georgian England*, 242–43; Eugene C. Black, *The Social Politics of Anglo-Jewry, 1880–1920* (Oxford, 1988), 111; Williams, *The Making of Manchester Jewry*, 90–91.

21. Arthur Barnett, "Sussex Hall—The First Anglo-Jewish Venture in Popular Education," *TJHSE* 19 (1960): 65–79; *Fifth Annual Report of the Jewish Association for the Diffusion of Religious Knowledge* (London, 1865), 6–8. The British Library has a bound volume with tracts from 1860 to 1879, from which these quotes have been taken.

22. The standard history is Lipman, *A Century of Social Service*, which should

be supplemented with the more critical account in E. C. Black, *The Social Politics of Anglo-Jewry*, chap. 3.

23. Williams, *The Making of Manchester Jewry*, 279–97; N. Kokosalakis, *Ethnic Identity and Religion: Tradition and Change in Liverpool Jewry* (Washington, D.C., 1982), 92–98; Birmingham Jewish History Research Group, *Birmingham Jewry* (Birmingham, 1984), vol. 2: *More Aspects, 1740–1930*, 98–99; Rainer Liedtke, *Jewish Welfare in Hamburg and Manchester, c. 1850–1914* (Oxford, 1998), 71–76, 84–87.

24. Lipman, *A Century of Social Service*, 18.

25. Gerry Black, *Lender to the Lords, Giver to the Poor* (London, 1992).

26. B. A. Fersht, "Chebrah Rodphea Sholom—Notes upon the First Jewish Friendly Society in England," *MJHSE* 2 (1935): 90–98; MS rules of Hevrat Margoa la-Nefesh, Society for Administering Pecuniary Comforts, 1797/98, FS 1/408B; MS rules of Path of Rectitude Benefit Society, filed at the Guildhall, 27 October 1817, FS 1/417; *Rules of a Friendly Society called the United Israelites* (London, 1835), FS 1/486A; MS rules of the Guardians of Faith [ca. 1832], FS 1/443; all rules in Public Record Office, London.

27. Patrick Colquhoun, *A Treatise on the Police of the Metropolis*, 5th ed. (London, 1797), vii; Henry Mayhew, *London Labour and the London Poor*, 3 vols. (London, 1851), 1: 106–7, 2: 121; Harold Pollins, *Economic History of the Jews in England* (Rutherford, N.J., 1982), 126–27.

28. Birmingham Jewish History Research Group, *Birmingham Jewry*, 1: 54; Joseph Harris, *Random Notes and Reflections* (Liverpool, 1912).

29. Pollins, *Economic History of the Jews in England*, 120–22.

30. The economic transformation of nineteenth-century English Jewry before mass migration from Eastern Europe is still in need of study. Some evidence can be found in Williams, *The Making of Manchester Jewry*; Birmingham Jewish History Research Group, *Birmingham Jewry*; V. D. Lipman, *Social History of the Jews in England, 1850–1950* (London, 1954); Pollins, *Economic History of the Jews in England*.

31. Mills, *The British Jews*, 264–69, 271–72; Pollins, *Economic History of the Jews in England*, 99–102; Beverly Lemire, "Consumerism in Preindustrial and Early Industrial England: The Trade in Secondhand Clothes," *Journal of British Studies* 27 (1988): 15–21; S. D. Chapman, "The Innovating Entrepreneurs in the British Ready-Made Clothing Industry," *Textile History* 24 (1993): 5–25; Pamela Sharpe, "'Cheapness and Economy': Manufacturing and Retailing Ready-Made Clothing in London and Essex, 1830–50," *Textile History* 26: 2 (1995): 203–13. Pawnbroking was a particularly important avenue for mobility in the provinces. See, for example, Ursula Henriques, "The Jewish Community of Cardiff, 1813–1914," *Welsh History Review* 14 (1988): 278–80.

32. Lipman, "The Structure of London Jewry," 255–58; idem, *Social History of the Jews in England*, 76–78; Pollins, *Economic History of the Jews in England*, 90; Harold Perkins, *The Rise of Professional Society—England since 1880* (London, 1990), 30, table 2.2. Pollins believes that Jacobs overestimated the number of London Jews in the middle class but does not explain why he thinks

so, aside from the cryptic comment that Jacobs "thought that those in the upper groups . . . approximated to the membership of synagogues in the wealthy districts."

33. The communal elite of the Victorian period and beyond—sometimes referred to as "the Cousinhood"—has received a disproportionate amount of attention. The scholarly literature includes E. C. Black, *The Social Politics of Anglo-Jewry*, chap. 1; Endelman, *Radical Assimilation*, chap. 3; and more specifically, Richard Davis, *The English Rothschilds* (Chapel Hill, N.C., 1983); Moshe Samet, *Moshe Montefiore: metsiyut ve-aggadah* [Moses Montefiore: Reality and legend] (Jerusalem, 1989). The estimate of two hundred households is in Lipman, "The Structure of London Jewry," 257.

34. Williams, *The Making of Manchester Jewry*.

35. In general, see Phyllis S. Lachs, "A Study of a Professional Elite: Anglo-Jewish Barristers in the Nineteenth Century," *Jewish Social Studies* 44 (1982): 125–34.

36. Asher Tropp, *Jews in the Professions in Great Britain, 1891–1991* (London, 1991), 5.

37. Donald J. Olsen, *The Growth of Victorian London*, Penguin Books ed. (Harmondsworth, Eng., 1979), 18.

38. Endelman, *The Jews of Georgian England*, 128; Lipman, *Social History of the Jews in England*, 17; idem, "Social Topography of a London Congregation: The Bayswater Synagogue, 1862–1963," *Jewish Journal of Sociology* 6 (1964): 69–74; idem, "The Rise of Jewish Suburbia," *TJHSE* 21 (1968): 78–103. A similar middle-class exodus occurred in Manchester, beginning in the 1830s. See Williams, *The Making of Manchester Jewry*, 73–74, 85–86, 125–26.

39. Leonard Hyman, "Hyman Hurwitz: The First Anglo-Jewish Professor," *TJHSE* 21 (1968): 232–42; *JC*, 16 April 1875; Raphael Loewe, "Louis Loewe: Aide and Confidant," in *The Century of Moses Montefiore*, ed. Sonia Lipman and V. D. Lipman (Oxford, 1985), 104–17; Jeffrey Baum and Barbara Baum, *A Light unto My Path: The Story of H. N. Solomon of Edmonton* (Edmonton, Eng., 1981); E. Lawrence Levy, *The Autobiography of an Athlete* (Birmingham [ca. 1913]), 2; Albert M. Hyamson, *The Sephardim of England: A History of the Spanish and Portuguese Jewish Community, 1492–1951* (London, 1951), 262; Williams, *The Making of Manchester Jewry*, 206.

40. *JC*, 31 August 1855; Margery Bentwich and Norman Bentwich, *Herbert Bentwich: The Pilgrim Father* (Jerusalem, [ca. 1940]), 31–32; album of newspaper clippings, 1872–93, A100/57, Herbert Bentwich Collection, Central Zionist Archives, Jerusalem.

41. Steven Singer, "Jewish Education in the Mid-Nineteenth Century: A Study of the Early Victorian London Community," *Jewish Quarterly Review* 77 (1986–87): 163–78; University College School, London, *Alphabetical and Chronological Register for 1831–1891* (London, n.d.); Williams, *The Making of Manchester Jewry*, 25, 36, 336, 405; Birmingham Jewish History Research Group, *Birmingham Jewry*, 1: 22; E. C. Black, *The Social Politics of Anglo-Jewry*, 117; H. E. Chetwynd-Stapylton, ed., *Eton School Lists, 1853–1892*, 2nd ser. (Eton, 1900); J. H.

Stogdon, ed., *The Harrow School Register, 1845–1925,* 2nd ser., 2 vols. (London, 1925).

42. Davis, *The English Rothschilds,* 56–57, 105–7; Lucy Cohen, *Arthur Cohen: A Memoir by His Daughter for His Descendants* (London, 1919), 13; *JC,* 6 November 1914; Cecil Roth, "The Vicissitudes of the First Oxford Jewish Graduate," *The Oxford Magazine,* n.s., 3 (1962–63): 230–32.

43. On this theme, see Ian Baucom, *Out of Place: Englishness, Empire, and the Locations of Identity* (Princeton, N.J., 1999).

44. Alan Haig, *The Victorian Clergy* (London, 1984), 30–31.

45. Richard Price, *British Society, 1660–1880: Dynamism, Containment and Change* (Cambridge, 1999), 195.

46. For Manchester, see the examples in Williams, *The Making of Manchester Jewry,* 82, 86–87, 199, 256, 336.

47. Davis, *The English Rothschilds,* 92–100; Endelman, *Radical Assimilation,* 75; Niall Ferguson, *The House of Rothschild: Money's Prophets, 1798–1848* (New York, 1998), 331–33, 336–43.

48. The account appeared in a two-penny newssheet, *The Town,* which Thackeray quoted in a review in *Fraser's Magazine* in March 1838. Prawer, *Israel at Vanity Fair,* 38–40.

49. Isaac Lyon Goldsmid, *The British Jew to His Fellow Countrymen* (London, 1853), 28–29.

50. The standard accounts are Abraham Gilam, *The Emancipation of the Jews in England, 1830–1860* (New York, 1982); M. C. N. Salbstein, *The Emancipation of the Jews in Britain: The Question of the Admission of the Jews to Parliament, 1828–1860* (Rutherford, N.J., 1982); and David Feldman, *Englishmen and Jews: Social Relations and Political Culture, 1840–1914* (New Haven, Conn., 1994).

51. Endelman, *The Jews of Georgian England,* 78–82.

52. Israel Finestein, "Religious Disabilities at Oxford and Cambridge and the Movements for Abolition, 1771–1871," in *Anglo-Jewry in Changing Times: Studies in Diversity, 1840–1914* (London, 1999), 102–39.

53. Quoted in Salbstein, *The Emancipation of the Jews in Britain,* 235. For further evidence of public indifference, see the comments of other political figures cited by Salbstein, 234–35.

54. Harry Stone, "Dickens and the Jews," *Victorian Studies* 2 (1959): 223–53.

55. New York *Asmonean,* 10 January 1850, quoted in Salo W. Baron, "The Modern Age," in *Great Ages and Ideas of the Jewish People,* ed. Leo W. Schwarz (New York, 1956), 322; Mayhew, *London Labour and the London Poor,* 2: 141. See also Israel Finestein, "Anglo-Jewish Opinion during the Struggle for Emancipation," *TJHSE* 20 (1964): 133–34.

56. *The Mirror of Parliament* 2 (1830): 1423.

57. Montefiore and Montefiore, *Diaries of Sir Moses and Lady Montefiore,* 1: 108–9, 111; Israel Finestein, "The Uneasy Victorian: Montefiore as Communal Leader," in *The Century of Moses Montefiore,* ed. Lipman and Lipman, 45–70.

58. Endelman, *The Jews of Georgian England,* 279–80.

59. For the history of the Board in the pre-emancipation period, see Charles

H. L. Emanuel, *A Century and a Half of Jewish History Extracted from the Minute Books of the London Committee of Deputies of the British Jews* (London, 1910), 1–15. The name was inspired by that of a similar Protestant body, the London Board of Dissenting Deputies, which was founded in 1732.

60. Geoffrey Alderman, *The Jewish Community in British Politics* (Oxford, 1983), 24.

61. To describe this association as "proletarian," as Gilam does, is incorrect. *The Emancipation of the Jews*, 62. Its members were more likely traders, shop-keepers, and artisans.

62. David Cesarani, *The "Jewish Chronicle" and Anglo-Jewry, 1841–1991* (Cambridge, 1994).

63. Lloyd P. Gartner, "Urban History and the Pattern of Provincial Jewish Settlement in Victorian England," *Jewish Journal of Sociology* 23 (1981): 43–47.

64. Israel Finestein, "Jewish Emancipationists in Victorian England: Self-Imposed Limits to Assimilation," in *Assimilation and Community in Nineteenth-Century Europe*, ed. Jonathan Frankel and Steven J. Zipperstein (Cambridge, 1992), 39.

65. Thomas Babington Macaulay, *Critical and Historical Essays Contributed to the Edinburgh Review*, 2 vols. (London, 1854), 1: 142–44.

66. The history of religious reform before the creation of an independent Reform synagogue is traced in Endelman, *The Jews of Georgian England*, 159–65. The introduction of canonicals probably owed as much to Sephardi practice as to Anglican. Sephardi rabbis in Holland and England wore clerical gowns and white collar bands from the end of the seventeenth century.

67. On Reform Judaism in Victorian Britain, see Robert Liberles, "The Origins of the Jewish Reform Movement in England," *AJS Review* 1 (1976): 121–50; Williams, *The Making of Manchester Jewry*, 100–110, 191–204, 240–65; Michael A. Meyer, *Response to Modernity: A History of the Reform Movement in Judaism* (New York, 1988), 171–80; Anne J. Kershen and Jonathan A. Romain, *Tradition and Change: A History of Reform Judaism in Britain, 1840–1995* (London, 1995).

68. Quoted in Endelman, *The Jews of Georgian England*, 162.

69. In 1822, a group of pious North African Jews who occasionally worshipped in a private house one mile from Bevis Marks were put in herem for transgressing ascama one. Meir Benayahu, "Vikuhim ba-kehillah ha-sefaradit ve-ha-portugezit be-London ve-teshuvot ha-hakham rabbi Raphael Meldola" [Disputes in the Spanish and Portuguese Community of London and the responsa of Rabbi Raphael Meldola], *Michael: On the History of the Jews in the Diaspora* 10 (1986): 15–19.

70. Quoted in Kershen and Romaine, *Tradition and Change*, 3.

71. The seceding members of the Spanish and Portuguese Synagogue to the Elders, 24 August 1841, in Cecil Roth, ed., *Anglo-Jewish Letters, 1158–1917* (London, 1938), 285.

72. This interpretation was first propounded in Liberles, "The Origins of the Jewish Reform Movement in England." It is incorporated uncritically in Alder-

man, *Modern British Jewry*, 57. For critiques of this view, see Todd M. Endelman, "The Englishness of Jewish Modernity in England," in *Toward Modernity: The European Jewish Model*, ed. Jacob Katz (New Brunswick, N.J., 1987), 225–46; and Kershen and Romaine, *Tradition and Change*, 13–14.

73. Montefiore and Montefiore, *Diaries of Sir Moses and Lady Montefiore*, 1: 82–83; *JC*, 21 March 1845.

74. Jacob Katz, "Ha-haganah ha-ortodoksit al yom tov sheni galuyot" [The orthodox defense of observance of the second day of festivals in the Diaspora], *Tarbits* 57 (1988): 406–10.

75. Quoted in Kershen and Romaine, *Tradition and Change*, 28.

76. Steven Singer, "Jewish Religious Observance in Early Victorian London, 1840–1860," *Jewish Journal of Sociology* 28 (1986): 117–37.

77. On the traditionalists and their conflict with centrist Orthodoxy in London, see Steven Singer, "Orthodox Judaism in Early Victorian London, 1840–1858" (Ph.D. diss., Yeshiva University, 1981).

78. Although in no sense Orthodox, the wealthiest families tended to be more observant in the Victorian period than those in the middle ranks of the community. Endelman, *Radical Assimilation in English Jewish History*, 80–97.

79. On Nathan Adler and the development of the chief rabbinate during his tenure, see Aubrey Newman, "The Chief Rabbinate and the Provinces, 1840–1914," in *Tradition and Transition: Essays Presented to Chief Rabbi Sir Immanuel Jakobovits to Celebrate Twenty Years in Office*, ed. Jonathan Sacks (London, 1986), 217–25; Eugene C. Black, "The Anglicization of Orthodoxy: The Adlers, Father and Son," in *Profiles in Diversity: Jews in a Changing Europe, 1750–1870*, ed. Frances Malino and David Sorkin (Detroit, 1998), 295–325; Alderman, *Modern British Jewry*, 40–44.

80. Williams, *The Making of Manchester Jewry*, 182–88, 191–96, 209–32, 234–67.

81. Aubrey Newman, *The United Synagogue, 1870–1970* (London, 1977), 14; Israel Finestein, "The Lay Leadership of the United Synagogue since 1870," in *A Century of Anglo-Jewish Life, 1870–1970*, ed. Salmond S. Levin (London, n.d.), 32.

82. Nathan M. Adler, *Sermon Delivered at the Great Synagogue on the Occasion of His Installation into Office as Chief Rabbi of Great Britain* (London, 1845), 11.

83. Barnett, *The Western Synagogue*, 179–87.

84. S. Singer, "Orthodox Judaism in Early Victorian London," 143–65; *Bayswater Synagogue, 1863–1938* (London, 1938), 7.

85. Michael Goulston, "The Status of the Anglo-Jewish Rabbinate, 1840–1914," *Jewish Journal of Sociology* 10 (1968): 55–82; Steven Singer, "The Anglo-Jewish Ministry in Early Victorian London," *Modern Judaism* 5 (1985): 279–99.

86. *JC*, 8 July 1861, 25 August 1854, 1 September 1854.

87. Isaak Markus Jost, quoted in C. C. Aronsfeld, "German Jews in Victorian England," *Leo Baeck Institute Year Book* 7 (1962): 323; *JC*, 19 October 1849. See also Israel Finestein, "The Uneasy Victorian," 60–63; Julius Carlebach, "The Impact of German Jews on Anglo-Jewry—Orthodoxy, 1850–1950," in *Second*

Chance, ed. Mosse et al. (Tübingen, 1991), 406–8; David G. Dalin, "America-Bound: *Wissenschaft* in England," in *The Jewish Legacy and the German Conscience: Essays in Memory of Rabbi Joseph Asher,* ed. Moses Rischin and Raphael Asher (Berkeley, Calif., 1991), 101–2.

88. *The Encyclopaedia Judaica,* s.v. "Zedner, Joseph," "Friedlaender, Michael," and "Neubauer, Adolf"; Beth-Zion Lask Abrahams, "Emanuel Deutsch of 'The Talmud' Fame," *TJHSE* 23 (1971): 53–63; Raphael Loewe, "The Contribution of German-Jewish Scholars to Jewish Studies in the United Kingdom," in *Second Chance,* ed. Mosse et al., 443–48.

89. In the absence of a history of the Board of Deputies, see Emanuel, *A Century and a Half of Jewish History,* which provides an overview of its activities from its founding to 1910.

90. Emanuel, *A Century and a Half of Jewish History,* 76, 110.

91. Ursula R. Q. Henriques, "Who Killed Father Thomas?," and Benjamin Jaffe, "Sir Moses Montefiore in Russia," in *Sir Moses Montefiore: A Symposium,* ed. V. D. Lipman (Oxford, 1982), 50–81; Tudor Parfitt, "'The Year of the Pride of Israel': Montefiore and the Blood Libel of 1840," David Littman, "Mission to Morocco," Ursula R. Q. Henriques, "Journey to Romania, 1867," and Chimen Abramsky, "The Visits to Russia," in *The Century of Moses Montefiore,* ed. Lipman and Lipman, 131–48, 171–265; Samet, *Moshe Montefiore;* Jonathan Frankel, *The Damascus Affair: "Ritual Murder," Politics, and the Jews in 1840* (Cambridge, 1997).

92. There is at present no definitive statement of the emancipation contract interpretation of English Jewish history, although it underpins much of the work of David Cesarani, Bill Williams, and Tony Kushner cited in this and later chapters.

4. Native Jews and Foreign Jews (1870–1914)

1. The best introduction to the immigrant period is still Lloyd P. Gartner, *The Jewish Immigrant in England, 1870–1914,* 2nd ed. (London, 1973). On the volume of immigration, see also V. D. Lipman, *Social History of the Jews in England, 1850–1950* (London, 1954), 87–90.

2. Bill Williams, *The Making of Manchester Jewry, 1740–1875* (Manchester, 1976),176, 202; idem, "'East and West': Class and Community in Manchester Jewry, 1850–1914," in *The Making of Modern Anglo-Jewry,* ed. David Cesarani (Oxford, 1990), 17; Joseph Jacobs, *Studies in Jewish Statistics: Social, Vital and Anthropomorphic* (London, 1891), 20; V. D. Lipman, *A History of the Jews in Britain since 1858* (New York, 1990), 45–46.

3. Lloyd P. Gartner, "Jewish Migrants en route from Europe to America: Traditions and Realities," *Jewish History* 1, 2 (fall 1986): 50.

4. Hans Rogger, *Jewish Policies and Right-Wing Politics in Imperial Russia* (Berkeley, Calif., 1964), chaps. 2 and 4.

5. Gartner, "Jewish Migrants," 51.

6. Murray Freedman, *Leeds Jewry: The First Hundred Years* (Leeds, 1992), 22–23.

7. Anthony Glaser and Ursula R. Q. Henriques, "The Valley Communities," in *The Jews of South Wales: Historical Studies,* ed. Ursula R. Q. Henriques (Cardiff, 1993), 47–49; Daphne Gerlis and Leon Gerlis, *The Story of the Grimsby Jewish Community* (Hull, Eng., 1986); Lewis Olsover, *The Jewish Communities of North-East England* (Gateshead, Eng., 1980).

8. Kenneth E. Collins, *Second City Jewry: The Jews of Glasgow in the Age of Expansion, 1790–1919* (Glasgow, 1990), 223, table 6. In Liverpool, which had no substantial manufacturing sector, Jewish peddling "intensified in the 1880s and 1890s, was still going strong in the late 20s and continued until the Second World War." N. Kokosalakis, *Ethnic Identity and Religion: Tradition and Change in Liverpool Jewry* (Washington, D.C., 1982), 125.

9. Goronwy Rees, *St Michael: A History of Marks and Spencer,* rev. ed. (London, 1973), chap. 1; Maurice Levine, *Cheetham to Cordova: A Manchester Man of the Thirties* (Manchester, 1984), 6; Monty Dobkin, *Tales of Manchester Jewry and Manchester in the Thirties* (Manchester, 1986), 38; Kokosalakis, *Ethnic Identity and Religion,* 125–27. In his charming memoir of growing up Jewish in Edinburgh in the 1920s, David Daiches described immigrants who were still working as itinerant salesmen in the Fife coast towns, to which they traveled daily by train from Edinburgh. *Two Worlds: A Jewish Childhood in Edinburgh* (New York, 1956), 150–53.

10. Lipman, *Social History of the Jews in England,* 107; Freedman, *Leeds Jewry,* 29; Collins, *Second City Jewry,* 223, table 6.

11. See, in general, Rickie Burman, "The Jewish Woman as the Breadwinner," *Oral History Journal* 10, 2 (autumn 1982): 27–39; idem, "Jewish Women and the Household Economy in Manchester, c. 1890–1920," in *The Making of Modern Anglo-Jewry,* ed. Cesarani, 55–75; Jerry White, *Rothschild Buildings: Life in an East End Tenement Block, 1887–1920* (London, 1980), chap. 6. See also the programmatic essay of Lara V. Marks, "Carers and Servers of the Jewish Community: The Marginalized Heritage of Jewish Women in Britain," in *The Jewish Heritage in British History: Englishness and Jewishness,* ed. Tony Kushner (London, 1992), 106–27.

12. White, *Rothschild Buildings,* 222, 228–29; Gartner, *The Jewish Immigrant in England,* 74.

13. Arcadius Kahan, "The Impact of Industrialization in Tsarist Russia on the Socioeconomic Conditions of the Jewish Population," in *Essays in Jewish Social and Economic History,* ed. Roger Weiss (Chicago, 1986), 8.

14. Gartner, *The Jewish Immigrant in England,* 57–58.

15. Harold Pollins, *Economic History of the Jews in England* (Rutherford, N.J., 1982), 97–102, 120–29; Williams, *The Making of Manchester Jewry,* 273–76.

16. *JC,* 13 June 1851; V. D. Lipman, *A Century of Social Service, 1859–1959: The Jewish Board of Guardians* (London, 1959): 67–69.

17. Ernest Krausz, *Leeds Jewry: Its History and Social Structure* (Cambridge, 1964), 21; Pollins, *Economic History of the Jews in England,* 145.

18. James A. Schmiechen, *Sweated Industries and Sweated Labor: The London*

Clothing Trades, 1860–1914 (Urbana, Ill., 1984), chap. 1; David Feldman, *Englishmen and Jews: Social Relations and Political Culture, 1840–1914* (New Haven, Conn., 1994), chap. 8; Andrew Godley, "Immigrant Entrepreneurs and the Emergence of London's East End as an Industrial District," *London Journal* 21 (1996): 38–45.

19. Gartner, *The Jewish Immigrant in England*, 87; Lipman, *Social History of the Jews in England*, 108–9.

20. On the immigrant economy in Leeds, see Joseph Buckman, *Immigrants and the Class Struggle: The Jewish Immigrant in Leeds, 1880–1914* (Manchester, 1983).

21. Buckman, *Immigrants and the Class Struggle*, 49–50. On conditions in the garment trade, see also Robert Stephen Wechsler, "The Jewish Garment Trade in East London, 1875–1914: A Study of Conditions and Responses" (Ph.D. diss., Columbia University, 1979), chap. 3.

22. Quoted in Gartner, *The Jewish Immigrant in England*, 160.

23. Pollins, *Economic History of the Jews in England*, 147; Lipman, *A Century of Social Service*, 129–35.

24. Wechsler, "The Jewish Garment Trade in East London," chap. 5; Schmiechen, *Sweated Industries and Sweated Labor*, chap. 6.

25. The account of pre–World War I radical politics and trade union activity that follows is based on William J. Fishman, *East End Jewish Radicals, 1875–1914* (London, 1975); Bill Williams, "The Beginnings of Jewish Trade Unionism in Manchester, 1889–1891," in *Hosts, Immigrants and Minorities: Historical Responses to Newcomers in British Society, 1870–1914*, ed. Kenneth Lunn (London, 1980), 263–307; Pollins, *Economic History of the Jews in England*, chap. 10; Buckman, *Immigrants and the Class Struggle*; Feldman, *Englishmen and Jews*, chap. 9; Anne J. Kershen, *Uniting the Tailors: Trade Unionism amongst the Tailoring Workers of London and Leeds, 1870–1939* (London, 1995).

26. Pollins, *Economic History of the Jews in England*, 123–24.

27. The best account of Liberman's political ideas is Jonathan Frankel, *Prophecy and Politics: Socialism, Nationalism, and the Russian Jews, 1862–1917* (Cambridge, 1981), 28–47. Fishman, *East End Jewish Radicals*, seems unaware that Liberman was a haskalah activist, accomplished Hebrew writer, and proto-nationalist.

28. On antisemitism in pre–World War I socialism, see Edmund Silberner, "British Socialism and the Jews," *Historia Judaica* 14 (1952): 27–52; Yosef Gorni, "Beatrice Webb's Views on Judaism and Zionism," *Jewish Social Studies* 40 (1978): 95–116; Bryan Cheyette, "H. G. Wells and the Jews: Antisemitism, Socialism and English Culture," *Patterns of Prejudice* 22, 3 (winter 1988): 22–35. On Beatrice Webb, see also David Englander, "Booth's Jews: The Presentation of Jews and Judaism in *Life and Labour of the People in London*," *Victorian Studies* 32 (1989): 556–58.

29. Frankel, *Prophecy and Politics*, 119.

30. See Rocker's memoir, *The London Years* (London, 1956) and that of his son, Fermin Rocker, *The East End Years: A Stepney Childhood* (London, 1998).

31. Eric Hobsbawm, *Worlds of Labour* (London, 1984), 142; Anne J. Kershen,

"Trade Unionism amongst the Jewish Tailoring Workers of London and Leeds, 1872–1915," in *The Making of Modern Anglo-Jewry,* ed. Cesarani, 36.

32. See, for example, Buckman, *Immigrants and the Class Struggle,* and White, *Rothschild Buildings.* For an alternative approach, see Feldman, *Englishmen and Jews,* chap. 10.

33. This immigrant petite bourgeoisie is discussed in Williams, "'East and West,'" and Rainer Liedtke, *Jewish Welfare in Hamburg and Manchester, c. 1850–1914* (Oxford, 1998), 222–28.

34. *JC,* 5 October 1908.

35. Andrew Godley, "Jewish Soft Loan Societies in New York and London and Immigrant Entrepreneurship, 1880–1914," *Business History* 38, 3 (1997): 101–16.

36. Gartner, *The Jewish Immigrant in England,* 141.

37. If the immigrants were "made" into a working class during this period, it was a fragile, impermanent construction, hardly worthy of the name, for it started to decay even before it was fully formed, with the beginnings of upward mobility. This, of course, poses the question of how supposedly working-class Jews acquired middle-class aspirations and habits and, in most cases, were able to enter the middle ranks of British society by the middle third of the twentieth century.

38. White, *Rothschild Buildings,* 245–49; Burman, "Jewish Women and the Household Economy."

39. In Liverpool, this was definitely the case. Kokosalakis, *Ethnic Identity and Religion,* 126–27.

40. V. D. Lipman, "The Rise of Jewish Suburbia," *TJHSE* 21 (1968): 87–88; idem, *A History of the Jews in Britain,* 53; Henry Shaw, *Notting Hill Synagogue, Diamond Jubilee, 1900–1960: A History* (London, 1960), 8–9. See also Israel Zangwill's evocation of an immigrant home in Dalston in the title story of his collection *They That Walk in Darkness: Ghetto Tragedies* (Philadelphia, 1899), 2–3.

41. Williams, "'East and West,'" 20; Krausz, *Leeds Jewry,* 21–22.

42. [Robert Blatchford], *Julie: A Study of a Girl* (London, 1900?), 33.

43. On immigrant attitudes toward anglicized synagogues, see Chaim Lewis, *A Soho Address* (London, 1965), 57–60.

44. The enrollment figures for the East End are in Suzanne Kirsch Greenberg, "Compromise and Conflict: The Education of Jewish Immigrant Children in London in the Aftermath of Emancipation, 1881–1905" (Ph.D. diss., Stanford University, 1985), 168; the remainder are in Gartner, *The Jewish Immigrant in England,* 234–36. The director of the Liverpool Hebrew Higher Grade School, the Hebraist J. S. Fuchs (1868–1938), wrote a stinging critique of the character of English Judaism, *Merkaz ivri: hashkafah klalit al ha-yahadut ha-anglit u-mahsorah* [A Hebrew center: A general view of English Judaism and its poverty] (London [1909]).

45. Julius Carlebach, "The Impact of German Jews on Anglo-Jewry— Orthodoxy, 1850–1950," in *Second Chance: Two Centuries of German-Speaking*

Jews in the United Kingdom, ed. Werner E. Mosse et al. (Tübingen, 1991), 421, n. 61.

46. Charles Liebman, "Religion, Class and Culture in American Jewish History," *Jewish Journal of Sociology* 9 (1967): 227–41.

47. An open-air hiring market in the Whitechapel Road in the East End, known popularly as the *hazer mark,* or pig market, was busiest on Saturdays. Gartner, *The Jewish Immigrant in England,* 71. See also Kokosalakis, *Ethnic Identity and Religion,* 120–22.

48. Maurice Samuel, *The Gentleman and the Jew: Twenty-Five Centuries of Conflict in Manners and Morals* (New York, 1977), 14–15; idem, *Little Did I Know: Recollections and Reflections* (New York, 1963), 66; Gartner, *The Jewish Immigrant in England,* 197; Solomon Fisch, *Yeriot Shlomoh: pirkei hayyim, divrei hagut, derashot, ve-hidushei torah* [The pages of Solomon: Memoirs, studies, addresses, novellae] (Jerusalem, 1983), 13–14. Further evidence regarding the halachic selectivity of the immigrants can be found in Gartner, *The Jewish Immigrant in England,* 192–97, and White, *Rothschild Buildings,* 85–91.

49. Eugene C. Black, *The Social Politics of Anglo-Jewry, 1880–1920* (Oxford, 1988), 195–200.

50. Williams, "'East and West,'" 23–25; Liedtke, *Jewish Welfare in Hamburg and Manchester,* 214–27.

51. Jacob Hodess, "Tsu der geshikhete fun der english-yidisher presse" [The Jewish press in England], and S. J. Harendorf, "Yidish teater in england" [The Yiddish theatre in England], in *YIVO Bleter* 43 (1966): 40–71, 225–48; Leonard Prager, *Yiddish Culture in Britain: A Guide* (Frankfurt am Main, 1990); David Mazower, *Yiddish Theatre in London,* 2nd ed. (London, 1996).

52. There is no historical literature on the popular culture of the immigrant community before World War I. Some insights can be gained from M. Samuel, *Little Did I Know;* Lewis, *A Soho Address;* White, *Rothschild Buildings;* John Harding, *Jack Kid Berg: The Whitechapel Windmill* (London, 1987).

53. Greenberg, "Compromise and Conflict," 134.

54. Bernard Homa, *Footprints on the Sands of Time* (Gateshead, 1990), 8.

55. Harold Rosen, quoted in Venetia Murray, ed., *Echoes of the East End* (London, 1989), 141–42; Ena Abrahams, quoted in Jewish Women in London Group, *Generations of Memories: Voices of Jewish Women* (London, 1989), 86.

56. See, for example, G. I. T. Machin, *The Catholic Question in English Politics, 1820–1830* (Oxford, 1964); G. F. A. Best, "Popular Protestantism in Victorian Britain," in *Ideas and Institutions of Victorian Britain: Essays in Honour of George Kitson Clark,* ed. Robert Robson (New York, 1967), 115–42; E. R. Norman, *Anti-Catholicism in Victorian England* (New York, 1968); Walter L. Arnstein, *Protestant versus Catholic in Mid-Victorian England: Mr. Newdegate and the Nuns* (Columbia, Mo., 1982); Gerald Newman, *The Rise of English Nationalism: A Cultural History, 1740–1830* (New York, 1987); Linda Colley, *Britons: Forging the Nation, 1707–1837* (New Haven, Conn., 1992).

57. Feldman, *Englishmen and Jews.* In what follows I am much indebted to Feldman's original treatment of Jewish emancipation and the linkage between

definitions of the English collectivity and constructions of the Jew. Where I differ from him is in the weight I assign to this discourse in shaping the process of social integration.

58. Feldman, *Englishmen and Jews,* 54–55.

59. The literature on representations of the Jew in Victorian culture is vast and of uneven quality. The most helpful studies are Harry Stone, "Dickens and the Jews," *Victorian Studies* 2 (1959): 223–53; Edgar Rosenberg, *From Shylock to Svengali: Jewish Stereotypes in English Fiction* (Stanford, Calif., 1960); S. S. Prawer, *Israel at Vanity Fair: Jews and Judaism in the Writings of W. M. Thackeray* (Leiden, 1992); Bryan Cheyette, *Constructions of "The Jew" in English Literature and Society: Racial Representations, 1875–1945* (Cambridge, 1993); Michael Ragussis, *Figures of Conversion: "The Jewish Question" and English National Identity* (Durham, N.C., 1995). While of little analytical worth, Anne Cowen and Roger Cowen, *Victorian Jews through British Eyes* (Oxford, 1986), is a treasure trove of representations of Jews in illustrated magazines.

60. *JC,* 15 December 1876.

61. On Anglo-Jewish writing before the 1880s, see Michael Galchinsky, *The Origin of the Modern Jewish Writer: Romance and Reform in Victorian England* (Detroit, 1996).

62. *The Times,* 3 September 1852. The Hebraist and journalist Marcus H. Bresslau (d. 1864) protested the article with a short pamphlet, *The Reopening of the Great Synagogue: A Few Observations in Reply to the Times Report of Friday, Sept. 3, 1852* (London, [1852]).

63. Feldman, *Englishmen and Jews,* chap. 4; Anthony S. Wohl, "'Dizzi-Ben-Dizzi': Disraeli as Alien," *Journal of British Studies* 34 (1995): 375–411; Edgar J. Feuchtwanger, "'Jew Feelings' and *Realpolitik:* Disraeli as a Maker of Foreign and Imperial Policies," in *Disraeli's Jewishness,* ed. Todd M. Endelman and Tony Kushner (London, 2002).

64. Colin Holmes, *Anti-Semitism in British Society, 1876–1939* (New York, 1979), 66–70; Claire Hirshfield, "The Anglo-Boer War and the Issue of Jewish Culpability," *Journal of Contemporary History* 15 (1980): 619–31; idem, "Labouchere, *Truth* and the Uses of Antisemitism," *Victorian Periodicals Review* 26 (1993): 134–42; John Allett, "New Liberalism, Old Prejudices: J. A. Hobson and the 'Jewish Question,'" *Jewish Social Studies* 49 (1987): 99–114.

65. Frances Donaldson, *The Marconi Scandal* (London, 1962); G. R. Searle, *Corruption in British Politics, 1895–1930* (Oxford, 1987), chaps. 8–9; Bernard Wasserstein, *Herbert Samuel: A Political Life* (Oxford, 1992), 129–46.

66. William D. Rubinstein, "Jews among Top British Wealth Holders, 1857–1969: Decline of the Golden Age," *Jewish Social Studies* 34 (1972): 77.

67. The social ascent of rich Jews in this period is discussed in Todd M. Endelman, *Radical Assimilation in English Jewish History, 1656–1945* (Bloomington, Ind., 1990), 74–80.

68. Cecil Roth, "The Court Jews of Edwardian England," in *Essays and Portraits in Anglo-Jewish History* (Philadelphia, 1962), 282–94; Anthony Allfrey, *Edward VII and His Jewish Court* (London, 1991).

69. John Vincent, ed., *The Crawford Papers: The Journals of David Lindsay, Twenty-Seventh Earl of Crawford and Tenth Earl of Balcarres, 1871–1940, during the Years 1892–1940* (Manchester, 1984), 268.

70. Gareth Stedman Jones, *Outcast London: A Study in the Relationship between Classes in Victorian Society,* Penguin Books ed. (London, 1992).

71. Bernard Gainer, *The Alien Invasion: The Origins of the Aliens Act of 1905* (New York, 1972), 166.

72. On the debate over Jewish immigration, see John A. Garrard, *The English and Immigration: A Comparative Study of the Jewish Influx, 1880–1910* (London, 1971); Gainer, *The Alien Invasion;* Holmes, *Anti-Semitism in British Society,* part 1; David Feldman, "The Importance of Being English: Jewish Immigration and the Decay of Liberal England," in *Metropolis—London: Histories and Representations since 1800,* ed. David Feldman and Gareth Stedman Jones (London, 1989), 56–84.

73. Royal Commission on Alien Immigration, 1903, II, Minutes of Evidence, Cd. 1742, quoted in Gainer, *The Alien Invasion,* 42; *East London Observer,* 18 January 1902; Henry Walker, *East London: Sketches of Christian Work and Workers* (London, 1896), 17.

74. Feldman, *Englishmen and Jews,* 172–84.

75. A. S. Barnett, "Introduction," C. Russell and H. S. Lewis, *The Jew in London: A Study of Racial Character and Present-Day Conditions* (London, 1901), xxv.

76. Martin L. Friedland, *The Trials of Israel Lipski: A True Story of a Victorian Murder in the East End of London* (New York, 1984); Judith R. Walkowitz, *City of Dreadful Delight: Narratives of Sexual Danger in Late-Victorian London* (Chicago, 1992), chap. 7; Chaim Bermant, *Point of Arrival: A Study of London's East End* (London, 1975), chap. 9; Fishman, *East End Jewish Radicals,* 287–93; Donald Rumbelow, *The Siege of Sidney Street* (New York, 1973); Colin Holmes, "East End Crime and the Jewish Community," in *The Jewish East End, 1840–1939,* ed. Aubrey Newman (London, 1981), 109–23; Edward J. Bristow, *Prostitution and Prejudice: The Jewish Fight against White Slavery, 1870–1939* (New York, 1983); Lloyd P. Gartner, "Anglo-Jewry and the Jewish International Traffic in Prostitution, 1885–1914," *AJS Review* 7–8 (1982–83): 129–78. Those responsible for the Tottenham robbery and the Houndsditch burglary were Lithuanians, not Jews, but they lived and worked in the midst of Russian Jews and were frequent visitors to the Jewish radical club in Berner Street. In addition, several of them took Russian Jewish women as lovers.

77. On the politics of anti-aliens legislation, see Garrard, *The English and Immigration;* Gainer, *The Alien Invasion;* Feldman, *Englishmen and Jews,* chap. 11.

78. On the administration of the Aliens Act, see Jill Pellew, "The Home Office and the Aliens Act, 1905," *The Historical Journal* 32 (1989): 369–85; E. C. Black, *The Social Politics of Anglo-Jewry,* 309–16.

79. Lipman, *History of the Jews in Britain,* 45, 73; Feldman, "The Importance of Being English," 76.

80. Matthew Arnold, *Culture and Anarchy*, ed. J. Dover Wilson (Cambridge, 1963), 75.

81. Feldman, "The Importance of Being English," 57, 79.

82. Hermann Adler, quoted in A. L. Shane, "The Dreyfus Affair: Could It Have Happened in England?," *TJHSE* 30 (1989): 143; Friedland, *The Trials of Israel Lipski*, 170–71.

83. On violence against immigrants, see Holmes, *Anti-Semitism in British Society*, 93, 96–101; Alan Lee, "Aspects of the Working-Class Response to the Jews in Britain, 1880–1914," in *Hosts, Immigrants and Minorities*, ed. Lunn, 120–21; Stephen Humphries, *Hooligans or Rebels? An Oral History of Working-Class Childhood and Youth, 1889–1939* (Oxford, 1981), 188–90, 192, 196–98; White, *Rothschild Buildings*, 133–38; Robert Roberts, *The Classic Slum: Salford Life in the First Quarter of the Century*, Pelican Books ed. (Harmondsworth, Eng., 1973), 171–73; Murray, *Echoes of the East End*, 174; Anthony Glaser, "The Tredegar Riots of August 1911," in *The Jews of South Wales*, 151–76; William D. Rubinstein, "The Anti-Jewish Riots of 1911 in South Wales: A Re-examination," *The Welsh History Review* 18 (1997): 667–99.

84. Nigel Nicolson, ed., *The Letters of Virginia Woolf*, 6 vols. (London, 1975–79), 1: 184, 496, 500, 501, 3: 269–70, 4: 195–96; Frederic Spotts, ed. *Letters of Leonard Woolf* (London, 1989), 470; Maren Tova Linett, "Figuring the Modern: Jews as Metaphors in Modernist British Fiction" (Ph.D. diss., University of Michigan, 1999), chap. 3.

85. E. Lawrence Levy, *The Autobiography of an Athlete* (Birmingham [ca. 1913]), 37–38; Morris Joseph, "Anti-Semitic Tendencies in England," *JC*, 4 July 1913; Nachum T. Gidal, "Jews in Photography," *Leo Baeck Institute Year Book* 32 (1987): 443–44.

86. The best account of Jewish participation in national political life is Geoffrey Alderman, *The Jewish Community in British Politics* (Oxford, 1983).

87. Michael Jolles, *A Directory of Distinguished British Jews, 1830–1930* (London, 1999) lists all Jews, practicing, converted, and otherwise, who were the recipients of honors.

88. See the statements of Lowther and Evans-Gordon quoted in Garrard, *The English and Immigration*, 63.

89. For details, see Asher Tropp, *Jews in the Professions in Great Britain, 1891–1991* (London, 1991), 5–6; Pollins, *Economic History of the Jews in England*, 114–15, 179–82.

90. Endelman, *Radical Assimilation*, 77–80.

91. Alderman, *The Jewish Community in British Politics*, 36–46.

92. Stephen Sharot, "Religious Change in Native Orthodoxy in London, 1870–1914: The Synagogue Service," *Jewish Journal of Sociology* 15 (1973): 57–78; Raymond Apple, *The Hampstead Synagogue, 1892–1967* (London, 1967), 10–18; *Higher Broughton Hebrew Congregation—The First Fifty Years, 1907–1957* ([Manchester, 1957]), 9.

93. Sharot, "Religious Change in Native Orthodoxy," 65–68.

94. The account of Liberal Judaism that follows is based on Stephen Sharot,

"Reform and Liberal Judaism in London, 1840–1940," *Jewish Social Studies* 41 (1979): 211–28; Steven Bayme, "Claude Montefiore, Lily Montagu and the Origins of the Jewish Religious Union," *TJHSE* 27 (1982): 61–71; Michael A. Meyer, *Response to Modernity: A History of the Reform Movement in Judaism* (New York, 1988), 212–21; Anne Kershen, ed., *150 Years of Progressive Judaism* (London, 1990).

95. Ellen Umansky, *Lily Montagu and the Advancement of Liberal Judaism: From Vision to Vocation* (New York, 1983).

96. C. G. Montefiore, *Judaism, Unitarianism and Theism,* Papers for Jewish People, no. 4 (London, 1908), quoted in Meyer, *Response to Modernity,* 216.

97. Todd M. Endelman, "The Frankaus of London: A Study in Radical Assimilation, 1837–1967," *Jewish History* 8, 1–2 (winter 1994): 1–38. See also idem, "Jewish Self-Hatred in Britain and Germany," in *Two Nations: The Historical Experiences of British and German Jews in Comparative Perspective,* ed. Michael Brenner, Rainer Liedtke, and David Rechter (Tübingen, 1999), 331–63.

98. Evidence for this reading of Zangwill can be found in Joseph H. Udelson, *Dreamer of the Ghetto: The Life and Works of Israel Zangwill* (Tuscaloosa, Ala., 1990); and Meri-Jane Rochelson, "Language, Gender, and Ethnic Anxiety: Zangwill's *Children of the Ghetto,*" *English Literature in Transition* 31 (1988): 399–412.

99. Spotts, *Letters of Leonard Woolf,* (London, 1989), 102; Leonard Woolf, *The Wise Virgins: A Story of Words, Opinions and a Few Emotions* (London, 1979); Naomi B. Levine, *Politics, Religion and Love: The Story of H. H. Asquith, Venetia Stanley and Edwin Montagu, Based on the Life and Letters of Edwin Samuel Montagu* (New York, 1991), 173; H. H. Munro [Saki], *The Unbearable Bessington* (New York, 1927), 74–75.

100. Steven Bayme, "Jewish Leadership and Anti-Semitism in Britain, 1898–1918" (Ph.D. diss., Columbia University, 1976), chap. 8; David Cesarani, *Reporting Anti-Semitism: The "Jewish Chronicle," 1879–1979,* The Parkes Lecture, 1993 (Southampton, Eng., 1994); *JC,* 2 June 1893, 18 March 1898.

101. *JC,* 7 August 1891.

102. The most extensive account of the response of communal leaders to the immigrant influx is E. C. Black, *The Social Politics of Anglo-Jewry,* chaps. 3–11. See also the following, more specialized studies: Lipman, *A Century of Social Service,* chaps. 3–4; Stephen Sharot, "Native Jewry and the Religious Anglicization of Immigrants in London, 1870–1905," *Jewish Journal of Sociology* 16 (1974), 39–56; Richard A. Voeltz, "'. . . A Good Jew and a Good Englishman': The Jewish Lads' Brigade, 1894–1922," *Journal of Contemporary History* 23 (1988): 119–27; Suzanne Kirsch Greenberg, "Anglicization and the Education of Jewish Immigrant Children in the East End of London," in *Jewish History: Essays in Honour of Chimen Abramsky,* ed. Ada Rapoport-Albert and Steven J. Zipperstein (London, 1988), 111–26; Daniel Gutwein, *The Divided Elite: Economics, Politics and Anglo-Jewry, 1882–1917* (Leiden, 1992), part 2; Judy Glasman, "Assimilation by Design: London Synagogues in the Nineteenth Century," in *The Jewish Heritage in British History: Englishness and Jewishness,* ed. Tony Kushner (London, 1992),

171–209; Feldman, *Englishmen and Jews,* chap. 12; Sharman Kadish, *"A Good Jew and a Good Englishman": The Jewish Lads' and Girls' Brigade, 1895–1995* (London, 1995).

103. Lipman, *A Century of Social Service,* 94.

104. *JC,* 26 February 1886.

105. *JC,* 24 January 1902.

106. The best introduction to this network of charities is E. C. Black, *The Social Politics of Anglo-Jewry,* chaps. 3–6.

107. Lara V. Marks, *Model Mothers: Jewish Mothers and Maternity Provision in East London, 1870–1939* (Oxford, 1994).

108. Endelman, *Radical Assimilation,* 167–72.

109. Gartner, *The Jewish Immigrant in England,* 224.

110. *JC,* 7 July 1905. See also Gerry Black, *J.F.S.: The History of the Jews' Free School, London, since 1732* (London, 1998), 123–33.

111. Voeltz, "' . . . A Good Jew and a Good Englishman'"; Kadish, *"A Good Jew and a Good Englishman."*

112. Basil Henriques, *The Indiscretions of a Warden* (London, 1937); Lionel Louis Loewe, *Basil Henriques: A Portrait Based On His Diaries, Letters and Speeches, as Collated by His Widow, Rose Henriques* (London, 1976); Raphael Loewe, "The Bernhard Baron Settlement and Oxford & St. George's Club," in *The Jewish East End,* ed. Newman, 143–46.

113. M. Samuel, *The Gentleman and the Jew,* 17–18.

114. Sidney Bunt, *Jewish Youth Work in Britain: Past, Present, and Future* (London, 1975), 47.

115. Russell and Lewis, *The Jew in London,* 97.

116. Royal Commission on Alien Immigration, 1903, II, Minutes of Evidence, Cd. 1742, Min. 16772.

117. Geoffrey Alderman, *The Federation of Synagogues, 1887–1987* (London, 1987).

118. *JC,* 3 August 1888.

119. The most extensive discussion of the conflict between Rothschild and Montagu and the struggle over the East End Scheme is in Gutwein, *The Divided Elite,* part 2.

120. David Englander, *"Stille Huppah* (Quiet Marriage) among Jewish Immigrants in Britain," *The Jewish Journal of Sociology* 34 (1992): 85–109; Charles Tucker, "Jewish Marriages and Divorces in England until 1940," *The Genealogists' Magazine,* part 1, September 1992, cols. 173–85; part 2, December 1992, cols. 277–86.

121. Bernard Homa, *Orthodoxy in Anglo-Jewry, 1880–1940* (London, 1969); idem, *Footprints on the Sands of Time;* Geoffrey Alderman, "Power, Authority and Status in British Jewry: The Chief Rabbinate and Shechita," in *Outsiders and Outcasts: Essays in Honour of William J. Fishman,* ed. Geoffrey Alderman and Colin Holmes (London, 1993), 12–31.

122. *JC,* 5 June 1911.

5. The Great War to the Holocaust (1914–1945)

1. *JC*, 7 August 1914; Michael Adler, "The Story of British Jewry in the War," *American Jewish Year Book* 21 (1919): 99; Sidney Salomon, *The Jews of Britain*, 2nd ed. (London, 1938), 48.

2. C. C. Aronsfeld, "Jewish Enemy Aliens in England during the First World War," *Jewish Social Studies* 18 (1956): 275–83; Colin Holmes, *Anti-Semitism in British Society, 1876–1939* (New York, 1979), chap. 8; David Cesarani, "An Embattled Minority: The Jews in Britain during the First World War," *Immigrants and Minorities* 8 (1989): 61–81; Mark Levene, *War, Jews, and the New Europe: The Diplomacy of Lucien Wolf, 1914–1919* (Oxford, 1992), chap. 1.

3. Holmes, *Anti-Semitism in British Society*, 126–37; Julia Bush, *Behind the Lines: East London Labour, 1914–1919* (London, 1984), chap. 6; Bernard Wasserstein, *Herbert Samuel: A Political Life* (Oxford, 1992), 126–37; C. C. Aronsfeld, "Anti-Jewish Outbreaks in Modern Britain," *The Gates of Zion* 6, 4 (July 1952): 15–18, 21.

4. David Cesarani's claim that Jewish status was "savagely eroded" is overstated. "An Embattled Minority," 75.

5. On this theme, see Barbara W. Tuchman, *Bible and Sword: England and Palestine from the Bronze Age to Balfour* (New York, 1956); Franz Kobler, *The Vision Was There: A History of the British Movement for the Restoration of the Jews to Palestine* (London, 1956); Israel Finestein, "Early and Middle Nineteenth Century British Opinion on the Restoration of the Jews: Contrasts with America," and Lionel E. Kochan, "Jewish Restoration to Zion: Christian Attitudes in Britain in the Late 19th and Early 20th Centuries," in *With Eyes Toward Zion*, vol. 2, ed. Moshe Davis (New York, 1986), 72–121; Sybil M. Jack, "No Heavenly Jerusalem: The Anglican Bishopric, 1841–83," *The Journal of Religious History* 19 (1995): 181–203.

6. The literature on Montefiore is enormous. See Ruth P. Goldschmidt-Lehmann, *Sir Moses Montefiore: A Bibliography* (Jerusalem, 1984). Among recent works, the most helpful are V. D. Lipman, ed., *Sir Moses Montefiore: A Symposium* (Oxford, 1982); Sonia Lipman and V. D. Lipman, eds., *The Century of Moses Montefiore* (Oxford, 1985); and Moshe Samet's iconoclastic (and entertaining) *Moshe Montefiore: Metsiyut ve-aggadah* [Moses Montefiore: Reality and myth] (Jerusalem, 1989).

7. Norman Bentwich and John M. Shaftesley, "Forerunners of Zionism in the Victorian Era," in *Remember the Days: Essays on Anglo-Jewish History Presented to Cecil Roth*, ed. John M. Shaftesley (London, 1966), 207–39.

8. Elhanan Oren, *Hibbat tsiyyon be-britanyah, 1878–1898* [The Love of Zion movement in Britain] (Tel Aviv, 1974).

9. Paul Goodman, *Zionism in England, 1899–1949: A Jubilee Record* (London, 1949), 25.

10. For the history of British Zionism (as distinct from the history of Zionist diplomacy in Britain) from its origins through the Balfour Declaration, see Stuart A. Cohen, *English Zionists and British Jews: The Communal Politics of Anglo-*

Jewry, 1895–1920 (Princeton, N.J., 1982); Virginia Herzog Hein, "The British Followers of Theodor Herzl: English Zionist Leaders, 1896–1904" (Ph.D. diss., Georgia State University, 1978).

11. Steven Bayme, "Jewish Leadership and Anti-Semitism in Britain, 1898–1918" (Ph.D. diss., Columbia University, 1976), chap. 7; S. Cohen, *English Zionists and British Jews*, 64–72; Paul Goodman, *B'nai B'rith: The First Lodge of England, 1910–1935* (London, 1936).

12. S. Cohen, *English Zionists and British Jews*, chaps. 4 and 5 and p. 282; Gideon Shimoni, "Poale Zion: A Zionist Transplant in Britain (1905–1945)," *Studies in Contemporary Jewry* 2 (1986): 228–32.

13. For Weizmann's career in England from his arrival to 1922, see Jehuda Reinharz, *Chaim Weizmann*, vol. 1, *The Making of a Zionist Leader*, and vol. 2, *The Making of a Statesman* (New York, 1985 and 1993).

14. There is a large and contentious literature on the tangle of negotiations and intrigues that led to the issuance of the Balfour Declaration. The most useful accounts are Leonard Stein, *The Balfour Declaration* (New York, 1961); Isaiah Friedman, *The Question of Palestine, 1914–1918: British-Jewish-Arab Relations* (London, 1973); S. Cohen, *English Zionists and British Jews;* Levene, *War, Jews, and the New Europe;* Reinharz, *Weizmann*, vol. 2.

15. On the origins of the Judaeans, see David Vital, *Zionism: The Crucial Phase* (Oxford, 1987), 144–50, 228–32.

16. Quoted in Reinharz, *Weizmann*, 2: 26–27.

17. S. Cohen, *English Zionists and British Jews*, 262–63.

18. Bill Williams, *The Making of Manchester Jewry, 1740–1875* (Manchester, 1976), chaps. 8–10.

19. Bayme, "Jewish Leadership and Anti-Semitism in Britain," chap. 7; S. Cohen, *English Zionists and British Jews*, 130–43.

20. Goodman, *B'nai B'rith.*

21. David Cesarani, *The "Jewish Chronicle" and Anglo-Jewry, 1841–1991* (Cambridge, 1994), chap. 4.

22. Andrew Godley, "Leaving the East End: Regional Mobility among East European Jews in London, 1880–1914," in *London—The Promised Land? The Migrant Experience in a Capital City*, ed. Anne J. Kershen (Aldershot, Eng., 1997), 59.

23. Charles Landstone, *Blue Tiger Yard* (London, 1927), 8, 9, 65, 67.

24. Harold Pollins, *Economic History of the Jews in England* (Rutherford, N.J., 1982), 186–89.

25. V. D. Lipman, "Jewish Settlement in the East End, 1840–1940" and "The Booth and New London Surveys as Source Material for East London Jewry (1880–1930)," in *The Jewish East End, 1840–1939*, ed. Aubrey Newman (London, 1981), 37, 47; idem, *A History of the Jews in Britain since 1858* (New York, 1990), 207; Aubrey Newman, *The United Synagogue, 1870–1970* (London, 1976), 216, 218; Henrietta Adler, "Jewish Life and Labour in East London," in *The New Survey of London Life and Labour*, ed. H. Llewellyn Smith, 9 vols. (1930–35), 6: 269–71.

26. Monty Dobkin, *Tales of Manchester Jewry and Manchester in the Thirties* (Manchester, 1986), 33–34.

27. Pollins, *Economic History of the Jews in England*, 189; Hannah Neustatter, "Demographic and Other Statistical Aspects of Anglo-Jewry," in *A Minority in Britain: Social Studies of the Anglo-Jewish Community*, ed. Maurice Freedman (London, 1955), 132; W. Victor Sefton, "Growing Up Jewish in London, 1920–1950: A Perspective from 1973," in *Studies in the Cultural Life of the Jews in England*, ed. Dov Noy and Issachar Ben-Ami (Jerusalem, 1975), 321.

28. Geoffrey D. M. Blok and Harry C. Schwab, *A Survey of Jewish Students at the British Universities* (London, 1938), 3, 6–7, 8–9, 11.

29. Horace Thorogood, *East of Aldgate* (London, 1935), 84–85.

30. For a more detailed treatment, see Geoffrey Alderman, *London Jewry and London Politics, 1889–1986* (London, 1989), 65–68; Todd M. Endelman, *Radical Assimilation in English Jewish History, 1656–1945* (Bloomington, Ind., 1990), 194–96.

31. Ena Abrahams, quoted in Jewish Women in London Group, *Generations of Memories: Voices of Jewish Women* (London, 1989), 101; M. S. Holzman to R. N. Salaman, 6 February 1927, box 1, Salaman Papers, CUL Add. MS 8171, Cambridge University Library.

32. There is a much larger literature on these forms of interwar antisemitism. See, e.g., Gisela C. Lebzelter, *Political Anti-Semitism in England, 1918–1939* (New York, 1978); Holmes, *Anti-Semitism in British Society*, part 3; Tony Kushner and Kenneth Lunn, eds., *Traditions of Intolerance: Historical Perspectives on Fascism and Race Discourse in Britain* (Manchester, 1989); Andrea Freud Loewenstein, *Loathsome Jews and Engulfing Women: Metaphors of Projection in the Works of Wyndham Lewis, Charles Williams, and Graham Greene* (New York, 1993); Anthony Julius, *T. S. Eliot, Anti-Semitism, and Literary Form* (Cambridge, 1995).

33. George Sacks, *The Intelligent Man's Guide to Jew-Baiting* (London, 1935), 12–13; Thorogood, *East of Aldgate*, 83–84. The card game is found in the collection of the Manchester Jewish Museum.

34. Betty Miller, *Farewell Leicester Square*, Persephone Books ed. (London, 2000), 142–44; Ralph Glasser, *Gorbals Boy at Oxford*, Pan Books ed. (London, 1990), 25.

35. Saul Friedländer, *Nazi Germany and the Jews*, vol. 1, *The Years of Persecution, 1933–1939* (New York, 1997), chap. 3.

36. Israel Zangwill to R. N. Salaman, 4 April 1920, A120/68/1; Nina Salaman to Israel Zangwill, 9 July 1920, A120/85/1, Israel Zangwill Papers, Central Zionist Archives, Jerusalem.

37. There is a large literature on the history of the BUF. See, for example, Robert J. Benewick, *The Fascist Movement in Britain* (London, 1972); Robert Skidelsky, *Oswald Mosley* (London, 1975); Kenneth Lunn and Richard C. Thurlow, eds., *British Fascism* (London, 1980); D. S. Lewis, *Illusions of Grandeur: Mosley, Fascism and British Society, 1931–81* (Manchester, 1987); Richard Thurlow, *Fascism in Britain: A History, 1918–1985* (Oxford, 1987); Thomas P. Linehan, *East London for Mosley: The British Union of Fascists in East London and South-West*

Essex, 1933–1940 (London, 1996). Of particular interest is *Jewish History and Culture* 1, 2 (winter 1998), which is devoted to "Cable Street: Fascism and Anti-Fascism in British Society."

38. See, for example, William D. Rubenstein, *A History of the Jews in the English-Speaking World: Great Britain* (London, 1996), 313–18.

39. Maurice Levine, *Cheetham to Cordova: A Manchester Man of the Thirties* (Manchester, 1984), 26; Sharon Gewirtz, "Anti-Fascist Activity in Manchester's Jewish Community in the 1930s," *Manchester Region History Review* 4, 1 (spring-summer 1990): 22–23; Sacks, *Guide to Jew-Baiting*, 12.

40. For a firsthand description of the emotional impact of Blackshirt terror, see Morris Beckman, *The Hackney Crucible* (London, 1996).

41. *The Times*, 27 and 28 November 1924.

42. William Goldman, "A Blighted Romance," in *"In England and in English": A Collection of Modern Stories by Jewish Writers*, ed. William Goldman (London, 1947), 45. For similar comments, see Levine, *Cheetham to Cordova*, 12.

43. H. Llewellyn Smith, "Introduction," *New Survey of London Life and Labour*, 6: 22.

44. Elaine Smith, "East End Jews in Politics, 1918–1939: A Study in Class and Ethnicity" (Ph.D. diss., University of Leicester, 1990), chap. 1; Endelman, *Radical Assimilation*, 176–79; David Cesarani, "The East London of Simon Blumenfeld's *Jew Boy*," *London Journal* 13 (1987–88): 46–53; Jewish Women in London Group, *Generations of Memories*, 89. In 1924, a reporter was astonished "to see lads in dress clothes and very well turned out young women emerging from the most unpromising-looking alleys on their way to a dancing hall" in the East End. *The Times*, 28 November 1924.

45. Jack Solomons, *Jack Solomons Tells All* (London, 1951); John Harding, *Jack Kid Berg: The Whitechapel Windmill* (London, 1987); Robert Murphy, *Smash and Grab: Gangsters in the London Underworld, 1920–1960* (London, 1993), chap. 3; Raphael Samuel, ed., *East End Underworld: Chapters in the Life of Arthur Harding* (London, 1981); Sidney Theodore Felstead, *The Underworld of London* (New York, 1923), 106–19.

46. John Vincent, ed., *The Crawford Papers: The Journals of David Lindsay, Twenty-Seventh Earl of Crawford and Tenth Earl of Balcarres, 1871–1940, during the Years 1892–1940* (Manchester, 1984), 596; *The Times*, 28, 29, and 30 July 1936; Murphy, *Smash and Grab*, 30–34.

47. Lily H. Montagu, *My Club and I: The Story of the West Central Jewish Club* (London, 1954); Lionel Lewis Loewe, ed., *Basil Henriques: A Portrait Based on His Diaries, Letters, and Speeches, as Collated by His Widow, Rose Henriques* (London, 1976); Sharman Kadish, *"A Good Jew and a Good Englishman": The Jewish Lads' and Girls' Brigade, 1895–1995* (London, 1995).

48. E. Smith, "East End Jews in Politics," chap. 4; Stephan Wendehorst, "British Jewry, Zionism and the Jewish State, 1936–1956" (D. Phil. diss., University of Oxford, 1997), 281; Tony Kushner, "Jewish Communists in Twentieth-Century Britain: The Zaidman Collection," *Labour History Review* 55, 2 (1990): 68–69; Charles Poulsen, *Scenes from a Stepney Youth* (London, 1988), 92–95; Ralph Glasser, *Growing Up in the Gorbals*, Pan Books ed. (London, 1987), 7.

49. On British Jews and Communism, see E. Smith, "East End Jews in Politics," chap. 4; Levine, *Cheetham to Cordova;* Alderman, *London Jewry and London Politics,* chap. 4; Gewirtz, "Anti-Fascist Activity in Manchester's Jewish Community"; Kushner, "Jewish Communists in Twentieth-Century Britain"; Henry Felix Srebrnik, *London Jews and British Communism, 1935–1945* (London, 1995). Phil Piratin's memoir *Our Flag Stays Red,* 2nd ed. (London, 1978) and Joe Jacobs's autobiography *Out of the Ghetto,* 2nd ed. (London 1991) are also helpful.

50. Raphael Samuel, "The Lost World of British Communism," *New Left Review* 154 (1985): 11.

51. Neville J. Laski, *Jewish Rights and Jewish Wrongs* (London, 1939), 115–18; *JC,* 2 February 1934; Basil L. Q. Henriques, *Fratres: Club Boys in Uniform* (London, 1951), 119; Kadish, "*A Good Jew and a Good Englishman,*" 126; David Cesarani, *Reporting Anti-Semitism: The "Jewish Chronicle," 1879–1979,* The Parkes Lecture 1993 (Southampton, Eng., 1994), 5, 11, 15, 19, 28.

52. Laski, *Jewish Rights and Jewish Wrongs,* 136.

53. Jewish Defence Committee, *The Problem and Meaning of Jewish Defence* (London, [ca. 1943]), 3, 4–5, 7.

54. Opposition to the Board's response to the BUF is discussed in Lebzelter, *Political Anti-Semitism in England,* chap. 7; David Rosenberg, *Facing Up to Anti-semitism: How Jews in Britain Countered the Threats of the 1930s* (London, 1985), 46–60; Elaine R. Smith, "Jewish Responses to Political Antisemitism and Fascism in the East End of London, 1920–1939," in *Traditions of Intolerance: Historical Perspectives on Fascism and Race Discourse in Britain,* ed. Tony Kushner and Kenneth Lunn (Manchester, 1989), 53–71.

55. A. J. Sherman, *Britain and Refugees from the Third Reich, 1933–1939* (London, 1973); Louise London, "Jewish Refugees, Anglo-Jewry and British Government Policy, 1930–1940," in *The Making of Modern Anglo-Jewry,* ed. David Cesarani (Oxford, 1990), 163–90; Sharon Gewirtz, "Anglo-Jewish Responses to Nazi Germany, 1933–39: The Anti-Nazi Boycott and the Board of Deputies of British Jews," *Journal of Contemporary History* 26 (1991): 255–76; V. D. Lipman, "Anglo-Jewish Attitudes to the Refugees from Central Europe, 1933–1939," in *Second Chance: Two Centuries of German-Speaking Jews in the United Kingdom,* ed. Werner E. Mosse et al. (Tübingen, 1991), 519–31; Ronald Stent, "Jewish Refugee Organisations," in *Second Chance,* 579–98.

56. The best account of British refugee policy is Louise London, *Whitehall and the Jews, 1933–1948: British Immigration Policy and the Holocaust* (Cambridge, 2000).

57. Norman Bentwich, *They Found Refuge* (London, 1956), 41–42.

58. On the experiences of the refugees and, in particular, their contacts with English Jews, see Marion Berghahn, *German-Jewish Refugees in England* (London, 1984); Zoë Josephs, *Survivors: Jewish Refugees in Birmingham, 1933–1945* (Birmingham, 1988); Elaine Blond, *Marks of Distinction: The Memoirs of Elaine Blond* (London, 1988), 58–94; Karen Gershon, *We Came as Children: A Collective Autobiography* (London, 1989); Lipman, "Anglo-Jewish Attitudes to the Refugees"; Tony Kushner, "An Alien Occupation—Jewish Refugees and Domestic Service

in Britain, 1933–1948," in *Second Chance,* ed. Mosse et al., 553–78. See also Lore Segal's moving autobiographical novel, *Other People's Houses,* Plume Books ed. (New York, 1973).

59. Blond, *Marks of Distinction,* 86.

60. The fullest accounts of Zionism in Britain after the Balfour Declaration are David Cesarani, "Zionism in England, 1917–1939" (D.Phil. diss., University of Oxford, 1986); and Wendehorst, "British Jewry, Zionism, and the Jewish State."

61. S. Cohen, *English Zionists and British Jews,* 282.

62. Geoffrey Alderman, *Modern British Jewry* (Oxford, 1992), 261; Lipman, *A History of the Jews in Britain,* 179.

63. Cesarani, "The East London of Simon Blumenfeld's *Jew Boy,*" 49–50; idem, "The Transformation of Communal Authority in Anglo-Jewry," in *The Making of Modern Anglo-Jewry,* ed. Cesarani (Oxford, 1990), 131; E. Smith, "East End Jews in Politics," chap. 4.

64. Cesarani develops this argument in his dissertation and in the articles cited above, as well as in "One Hundred Years of Zionism in England," *European Judaism* 25, 1 (spring 1992): 40–47, and "A Funny Thing Happened on the Way to the Suburbs: Social Change in Anglo-Jewry between the Wars, 1914–1945," *Jewish Culture and History* 1, 1 (1998): 5–26. This function of western Zionism was first put forward in Stephen M. Poppel, *Zionism in Germany, 1897–1933: The Shaping of a Jewish Identity* (Philadelphia, 1977).

65. Gideon Shimoni, "The Non-Zionists in Anglo-Jewry, 1937–1948," *Jewish Journal of Sociology* 28 (1986): 91.

66. Immanuel Jakobovits, *The Attitude to Zionism of Britain's Chief Rabbis as Reflected in Their Writings* (London, 1981).

67. On the Zionist "conquest" of the Board in the interwar years, see Cesarani, "The Transformation of Communal Authority in Anglo-Jewry."

68. Similarly, Asher Ginzberg (1856–1927), the Hebrew essayist and cultural Zionist better known by his pen name Ahad Ha-Am, lived in London from 1908 to 1921 (laboring unhappily in the office of the Wissotzsky tea firm), but he, even more than the Zionist officials, was in England but not of England. Indeed, his contempt for Anglo-Jewry was boundless. See Steven J. Zipperstein, *Elusive Prophet: Ahad Ha'am and the Origins of Zionism* (Berkeley, Calif., 1993), 277–82.

69. Gideon Shimoni, "From Anti-Zionism to Non-Zionism in Anglo-Jewry, 1917–1937," *Jewish Journal of Sociology* 28 (1986): 19–48; idem, "The Non-Zionists in Anglo-Jewry, 1937–1948"; Rubinstein, *Jews in the English-Speaking World,* 252–57.

70. See Bernard Homa, *Orthodoxy in Anglo-Jewry, 1880–1940* (London, 1969), idem, *Footprints on the Sands of Time* (Gateshead, 1990), part 3; Newman, *The United Synagogue,* part 3; Geoffrey Alderman, *The Federation of Synagogues* (London, 1987), chaps. 3–4; Anne J. Kershen and Jonathan A. Romain, *Tradition and Change: A History of Reform Judaism in Britain, 1840–1995* (London, 1995), chap. 5.

71. For more on this colorful figure, see Geoffrey Alderman, "M. H. Davis: The Rise and Fall of a Communal Upstart," *TJHSE* 31 (1990): 249–68.

72. Alderman, *Modern British Jewry,* 256.

73. On British Jewry during World War II, see Chaim Bermant, *Point of Arrival: A Study of London's East End* (London, 1975), chap. 15; Newman, *The United Synagogue,* chap. 12; Tony Kushner, *The Persistence of Prejudice: Antisemitism in British Society during the Second World War* (Manchester, 1989), chap. 2; Richard Bolchover, *British Jewry and the Holocaust* (Cambridge, 1993).

74. B. L. Q. Henriques, *Fratres,* 138–42.

75. For a suggestive discussion of the impact of military service on American Jews, see Deborah Dash Moore, *When Jews Were GIs: How World War II Changed a Generation and Remade American Jewry,* Fourth David W. Belin Lecture in American Jewish Affairs (Ann Arbor, Mich., 1994).

76. Bernard Wasserstein, *Britain and the Jews of Europe, 1939–1948* (Oxford, 1979), 83–108; Kushner, *The Persistence of Prejudice,* 142–50; idem, "Clubland, Cricket Tests and Alien Internment, 1939–40," in *The Internment of Aliens in Twentieth Century Britain,* ed. David Cesarani and Tony Kushner (London, 1993); Louise Burletson, "The State, Internment and Public Criticism in the Second World War," in *The Internment of Aliens,* 79–124.

77. Quoted in Todd M. Endelman, "Anti-Semitism in War-Time Britain: Evidence from the Victor Gollancz Collection," *Michael* 10 (1986): 92. See also A. L. Goldman, "The Resurgence of Antisemitism in Britain during World War II," *Jewish Social Studies* 46 (1984): 37–50.

78. The question of what British Jewish institutions did—or did not do—during the war to combat antisemitism, to rescue Jews under Nazi rule, and to open Palestine to Jewish immigration, is much contested. The chief contributions to the debate are Kushner, *The Persistence of Prejudice,* chap. 6; Bolchover, *British Jewry and the Holocaust;* Rubinstein, *A History of the Jews in the English-Speaking World,* chap. 6; Meier Sompolinsky, *The British Government and the Holocaust: The Failure of Anglo-Jewish Leadership?* (Brighton, Eng., 1999).

79. Norman Rose, *Lewis Namier and Zionism* (Oxford, 1980), 7.

6. The Fracturing of Anglo-Jewry (1945–2000)

1. Howard M. Brotz, "The Outlines of Jewish Society in London," in *A Minority in Britain: Social Studies of the Anglo-Jewish Community,* ed. Maurice Freedman (London, 1955), 142–47; Stephen Brook, *The Club: The Jews of Modern Britain* (London, 1989), chap. 19; Marlena Schmool and Frances Cohen, *A Profile of British Jewry: Patterns and Trends at the Turn of the Century* (London, 1998), 12, table 3; Immanuel Jakobovits, *The East End and the Anglo-Jewish Community,* The First Annual Dayan Julius Jakobovits Memorial Lecture (London, 1948), 10. For the physical destruction of the East End, see D. L. Munby, *Industry and Planning in Stepney: A Report Presented to the Stepney Reconstruction Group* (London, 1951).

2. *JC,* 26 July 1996.

3. Bill Williams, *Manchester Jewry: A Pictorial History, 1788–1988* (Manchester, 1988); N. Kokosalakis, *Ethnic Identity and Religion: Tradition and Change in*

Liverpool Jewry (Washington, D.C., 1982), 154; Mervyn Goodman, "The Jewish Community of Liverpool," *Jewish Journal of Sociology* 38 (1996): 90, 96; Ernest Krausz, *Leeds Jewry: Its History and Social Structure* (Cambridge, 1964), 6–9; Schmool and Cohen, *Profile of British Jewry*, 11, table 2.

4. The best guide to German-Jewish contributions is Werner E. Mosse et al., eds., *Second Chance: Two Centuries of German-Speaking Jews in the United Kingdom* (Tübingen, 1991). On the impact of the refugees on religious life, see also Anne J. Kershen and Jonathan A. Romain, *Tradition and Change: A History of Reform Judaism in Britain, 1840–1995* (London, 1995), 165–67. The only account of refugee acculturation and integration—Marion Berghahn, *German-Jewish Refugees in England: The Ambiguities of Assimilation* (London, 1984)—rests on a narrow and unrepresentative body of evidence.

5. Sefton D. Temkin, "Great Britain," *American Jewish Year Book* 61 (1960): 199.

6. On postwar fascism, see D. S. Lewis, *Illusions of Grandeur: Mosley, Fascism and British Society, 1931–81* (Manchester, 1987), 238–53; Richard Thurlow, *Fascism in Britain: A History, 1918–1985* (Oxford, 1987), chap. 10; Trevor Grundy, *Memoir of a Fascist Childhood: A Boy in Mosely's Britain* (London, 1998). James H. Robb, *Working-Class Anti-Semite: A Psychological Study in a London Borough* (London, 1954) is based on field research in Bethnal Green in 1947–49.

7. Morris Beckman, *The 43 Group* (London, 1992). See also a fictional account of 43 Group activities in Alexander Baron, *With Hope, Farewell* (London, 1952), in the "1948" section.

8. In a Gallup poll of 959 non-Jewish Britons in September 1993, Jews emerged as the least disliked ethnic minority in the United Kingdom. *JC*, 29 October 1993.

9. Donald Neff, *Warriors at Suez: Eisenhower Takes America into the Middle East* (New York, 1981), 206.

10. Tony Kushner, "Anti-Semitism and Austerity: The August 1947 Riots in Britain," in *Racial Violence in Britain, 1840–1950*, ed. Panikos Panayi (Leicester, Eng., 1993), 149–68.

11. The indispensable work on Zionism in postwar Britain is Stephan Wendehorst, "British Jewry, Zionism and the Jewish State, 1936–1956" (D. Phil. thesis, University of Oxford, 1998). William Frankel, later editor of the *Jewish Chronicle*, observed that the only institutional opposition to the creation of the state in the late 1940s came from the Jewish Fellowship and that in general British Jews were united in their opposition to the government's Palestine policy. "Great Britain," *American Jewish Year Book* 50 (1949): 283.

12. Figures on aliyyah from Britain are incomplete and not always in accord with each other. See the discussion in V. D. Lipman and Sonia Lipman, eds., *Jewish Life in Britain, 1962–1977* (New York, 1981), 46 n. 4, 67–68, 71. See also Schmool and Cohen, *Profile of British Jewry*, 31, table 10.

13. Hannah Neustatter, "Demographic and Other Statistical Aspects of Anglo-Jewry," in *A Minority in Britain*, ed. Freedman, 123–24. In the years immediately following the establishment of the State of Israel, the number of persons contributing to the Joint Palestine Appeal fell. The number of contributors

in 1948 was estimated at 33,000; in 1949 at 16,600; in 1950 at 18,250; in 1951 at 26,700; and in 1952 at 19,000. Barnet Litvinoff, "Great Britain," *American Jewish Year Book* 54 (1953): 239.

14. Schmool and Cohen, *Profile of British Jewry,* 29; *JC,* 7 November 1997.

15. Neustatter, "Demographic and Other Statistical Aspects," 122; Schmool and Cohen, *Profile of British Jewry,* 29; *JC,* 3 March 1995, 16 February 1996, 4 July 1997.

16. Jacob Braude, "Jewish Education in Britain Today," in *Jewish Life in Britain,* ed. Lipman and Lipman, 123; Chaim Bermant, *Troubled Eden: An Anatomy of British Jewry* (New York, 1970), 116–17; Schmool and Cohen, *Profile of British Jewry,* 29.

17. The best introduction to this topic in the English context is Tony Kushner's essay "Liberal Culture and the Post-War Confrontation with the Holocaust," in his collection *The Holocaust and the Liberal Imagination: A Social and Cultural History* (Oxford, 1994). See also Joanne Reilly, *Belsen: The Liberation of a Concentration Camp* (London, 1998), chap. 4.

18. Bernard Wasserstein, *Vanishing Diasporas: The Jews in Europe since 1945* (Cambridge, Mass., 1996), 97. The reactions of British Jews are summarized in Wasserstein and in Michael Leigh, "Great Britain," *American Jewish Year Book* 69 (1968): 440–41.

19. See, for example, the letter to the *Sunday Times,* 4 June 1967, signed by thirty-six writers.

20. Quoted in Brook, *The Club,* 356.

21. Quoted in Lionel and Miriam Kochan, "Great Britain," *American Jewish Year Book* 74 (1973): 386.

22. Immanuel Jakobovits, "An Analysis of Religious versus Secularist Trends in Anglo-Jewry, Especially during the Past Fifteen Years," in *Jewish Life in Britain,* ed. Lipman and Lipman, 35.

23. For this insight, I am indebted to Nathan Glazer, *American Judaism,* 2nd ed. (Chicago, 1972), 116–19. In 1948, Immanuel Jakobovits noted that Judaism fared worse in the East End than anywhere else in London. The proportion of children receiving no Hebrew education at all and of Jews unattached to a synagogue was higher there than elsewhere. He also noted that Talmud *shiurim* (study sessions) had all but disappeared, since "the new generation are considered scholars if they can read the Kaddish faultlessly." *The East End and the Anglo-Jewish Community,* 12, 14.

24. *JC,* 23 February 1951; Norman Cohen, "Trends in Anglo-Jewish Religious Life," in *Jewish Life in Modern Britain,* ed. Julius Gould and Shaul Esh (London, 1964), 42. For comments in a similar vein, see Joseph Leftwich, "Great Britain," *American Jewish Year Book 5707* 48 (1946–47): 270–71; Jacob Sonntag, "Introduction," *The Jewish Quarterly,* no. 1 (spring 1953).

25. Schmool and Cohen, *Profile of British Jewry,* 15, figs. 9 and 10; 20, fig. 16; *JC,* 2 June 1995.

26. Jonathan Sacks, *The Persistence of Faith: Religion, Morality and Society in a Secular Age* (London, 1991), 87.

27. Harold Soref, "Portrait of Anglo-Jewry," *Menorah Journal* 41, 1 (spring-

summer 1953): 78. See also Cecil Roth, "The Conversion Menace," *JC,* 12 January 1945; *JC,* 1 June 1945; Redcliffe N. Salaman, *Whither Lucien Wolf's Anglo-Jewish Community?* (London, 1954); Sefton Temkin, "Three Centuries of Jewish Life in England, 1656–1956," *American Jewish Year Book* 58 (1956): 42, 56–57; Todd M. Endelman, "The Decline of the Anglo-Jewish Notable," *The European Legacy—Toward New Paradigms* 4, 6 (1999): 58–71.

28. Ernest Krausz, "The Economic and Social Structure of Anglo-Jewry," in *Jewish Life in Modern Britain,* ed. Gould and Esh, 31.

29. J. W. Carrier, "A Jewish Proletariat," in *Explorations: An Annual on Jewish Themes,* ed. Murray Mindlin and Chaim Bermant (Chicago, 1967), 120–40; Harold Pollins, *Economic History of the Jews in England* (Rutherford, N.J., 1982), chap. 14; S. J. Prais and M. Schmool, "The Social-Class Structure of Anglo-Jewry," *Jewish Journal of Sociology* 17 (1975): 11; Schmool and Cohen, *Profile of British Jewry,* 26, fig. 25.

30. *JC,* 16 February 1996.

31. Geoffrey Alderman, *The Jewish Community in British Politics* (Oxford, 1983), chaps. 8–9; idem, *London Jewry and London Politics, 1889–1986* (London, 1989), 106–41; Brook, *The Club,* chap. 25.

32. Charles Dellheim, *The Disenchanted Isle: Mrs. Thatcher's Capitalist Revolution* (New York, 1995).

33. Oliver Marriot, *The Property Boom* (London, 1967), Appendix A. See also Charles Gordon, *The Two Tycoons: A Personal Memoir of Charles Clore and Jack Cotton* (London, 1984), and David Clutterbuck and Marion Devine, *Clore: The Man* (London, 1987).

34. Barry A. Kosmin and Caren Levy, *The Work and Employment of Suburban Jews: The Socio-Economic Findings of the 1978 Redbridge Jewish Survey* (London, 1981), 19.

35. *JC,* 16 February 1951; Michael Copeland, "Other Estimates of the Number of Jewish Students in Britain," in *Jewish Life in Britain,* ed. Lipman and Lipman, 159–61; Schmool and Cohen, *Profile of British Jewry,* 22.

36. Ernest Krausz, "The Edgware Survey: Occupation and Social Class," *Jewish Journal of Sociology* 11, 1 (1969): 84; Schmool and Cohen, *Profile of British Jewry,* 26, fig. 25. See also Asher Tropp, *Jews in the Professions in Great Britain, 1891–1991* (London, 1991).

37. William D. Rubinstein, *A History of the Jews in the English-Speaking World: Great Britain* (London, 1996), 403.

38. When Jakobovits took his seat in the House of Lords, the *New York Times,* 10 February 1988, reported: "Lord Jakobovits is widely regarded as Prime Minister Margaret Thatcher's favorite religious leader. . . . His firm pronouncements on the values of work, thrift, family solidarity, and personal morality fit nicely with Mrs. Thatcher's campaign to popularize what she thinks of as Victorian values. Mrs. Thatcher is known to regard the English bishops as a collection of soggy liberals, and the Chief Rabbi as the country's most authoritative spokesman for traditional virtues." A complete list of Jewish peers, baronets, and life peers may be found in Michael Jolles, *A Directory of Distinguished British Jews* (London, 1999), 37–52.

39. Norman Cohen observed that the extensive press coverage of Clore's and Cotton's activities, "however financially sound and economically respectable" they were, built up an impression of Jewish financial domination. "Great Britain," *American Jewish Year Book* 63 (1962): 299.

40. William Frankel, quoted in Brook, *The Club*, 387. See also David Cesarani, "Guiness Isn't Good for Us," *The Guardian*, 4 September 1990, and Douglas Davis, "The Guiness Affair: Four Fallen Jews," *The Jerusalem Post*, 2 September 1990.

41. Lesley Hazleton, *England, Bloody England: An Expatriate's Return* (New York, 1990), 50. Philip Roth captured the tone of this genteel antisemitism in his novel *The Counterlife* (New York, 1968).

42. Walter Henry Nelson and Terence C. F. Prittie, *The Economic War against the Jews* (New York, 1977), 60–63; Norman Cohen, "Great Britain," *American Jewish Year Book* 66 (1965): 365–66.

43. Bermant, *Troubled Eden*, 259–60; Jewish Aid Committee of Britain (JACOB), *With a Strong Hand: A Policy for Jewish Defence Submitted to the Jewish Community for Discussion, March 1966* ([London, 1966]).

44. Roth, *The Counterlife*, 301.

45. Ian Baucom, *Out of Place: Englishmen, Empire, and the Locations of Identity* (Princeton, N.J., 1999), 196.

46. *New York Times*, 22 February 1993; Calvin Trillin, "Drawing the Line," *The New Yorker*, 12 December 1994, 50–62; *JC*, 23 and 30 September 1994, 13 January 1995.

47. Leslie A. Fiedler, *To the Gentiles* (New York, 1972), 157.

48. Schmool and Cohen, *Profile of British Jewry*, 7, 34, table A4; *JC*, 13 July 1990, 16 February 1996. There are less reliable data for women. One estimate was that women were marrying out at a rate of 20 to 25 percent. *JC*, 16 February 1996.

49. Schmool and Cohen, *Profile of British Jewry*, 5, 32, table A1.

50. See, in particular, the records of the conference discussions in Gould and Esh, eds., *Jewish Life in Modern Britain*, and Lipman and Lipman, eds., *Jewish Life in Britain*.

51. Schmool and Cohen, *Profile of British Jewry*, 22, fig. 18.

52. A newspaper advertisement for Continuity carried the headline "For Decades, We've Supported Every Jewish Cause Except One: Our Future." The first paragraph stated that Anglo-Jewry was facing "a crisis of immense proportions"—half of young Jews were either not marrying, marrying out, or leaving the community in some other way. *JC*, 21 January 1994. On Continuity's failure, in the end, to address seriously the problem of demographic decline, see *JC*, 14 October 1994, 28 April 1995, 21 June 1996.

53. Schmool and Cohen, *Profile of British Jewry*, 8.

54. Lewis Olsover, *The Jewish Communities of North-East England, 1755–1980* (Gateshead, Eng., 1980), 221–50; Bernard Homa, *Orthodoxy in Anglo-Jewry, 1880–1940* (London, 1969), 28–36. For a description of the Gateshead yeshivah in the 1950s, see Louis Jacobs, *Helping with Inquiries: An Autobiography* (London, 1989). It was also said that in his later years Hertz himself became increasingly

sympathetic to ultra-Orthodoxy due to the influence of his son-in-law, Solomon Schonfeld (1912–84), who succeeded his father, Victor, as rabbi of the Adat Yisrael synagogue in North London.

55. Bermant, *Troubled Eden,* chap. 17; Brook, *The Club,* chaps. 4–6.

56. Maurice Freedman, "Jews in the Society of Britain," in *A Minority in Britain,* ed. Freedman, 230; Schmool and Cohen, *Profile of British Jewry,* 14, table 5; Stephen H. Miller, "The Structure and Determinants of Jewish Identity in the United Kingdom," in *Jewish Survival: The Identity Problem at the Close of the Twentieth Century,* ed. E. Krausz and G. Tulea (New Brunswick, N.J., 1998), 230.

57. It was clear that there were insufficient numbers of candidates for the rabbinate as early as the 1950s. Barnet Litvinoff, "Great Britain," *American Jewish Year Book* 55 (1954): 177–78; Geoffrey Alderman, "Anglo-Jewry and Its Present Discontents," *The Jewish Quarterly,* no. 158 (summer 1995), 23.

58. See, for example, Chaim Bermant, *Lord Jakobovits: The Authorized Biography of the Chief Rabbi* (London, 1990), 102–7.

59. *JC,* 21 July 1989, 11 October 1991, 18 September 1992, 26 March 1999.

60. *JC,* 31 January and 14 March 1997. See also the insightful column of Geoffrey Paul in the *JC,* 28 March 1997.

61. *JC,* 1 June 1945.

62. Norman Cohen, "Great Britain," *American Jewish Year Book* 63 (1962): 295; *JC,* 1 April 1994, 3 March 1995.

63. On the Jacobs affair, see Bermant, *Troubled Eden,* chap. 19; Aubrey Newman, *The United Synagogue, 1870–1970* (London, 1977), 183–87; Jacobs, *Helping with Inquiries,* chaps. 8–12.

64. Schmool and Cohen, *Profile of British Jewry,* 14, table 5.

65. Schmool and Cohen, *Profile of British Jewry,* 14, table 5. Also see Kershen and Romain, *Tradition and Change,* chaps. 6–8.

Conclusion

1. William D. Rubinstein, *A History of the Jews in the English-Speaking World: Great Britain* (London, 1996), 6.

2. Rubinstein, *A History of the Jews in the English-Speaking World,* 403.

3. Charles Castle, *Oliver Messel: A Biography* (London, 1986); *JC,* 28 July 1972.

4. Peter Clarke, *Hope and Glory: Britain, 1900–1990* (London, 1996), 18.

5. Humbert Wolfe, *Now a Stranger* (London, 1933), 125–26. See also Philip Bagguley, *Harlequin in Whitehall: A Life of Humbert Wolfe, Poet and Civil Servant, 1885–1940* (London, 1997).

6. In one area alone of twentieth-century British cultural life were Jews a conspicuous presence—painting and sculpture. The most important figures are William Rothenstein (1872–1942), Alfred Wolmark (1877–1961), Jacob Epstein (1880–1959), Isaac Rosenberg, now better known as a poet (1890–1918), David Bomberg (1890–1957), Mark Gertler (1891–1939), Bernard Meninsky (1891–

1950), Jacob Kramer (1892–1962), Lucien Freud (b. 1922), Anthony Caro (b. 1924), Leon Kossoff (b. 1926), Frank Auerbach (b. 1931), and R. B. Kitaj (b. 1932). Why they were prominent in this area of English cultural life is a still open question. (Kitaj was born in the United States but worked in England until the 1990s, when he returned to America, in part because he found England inhospitable to his growing interest in Jewish culture.)

7. Raphael Loewe, "The Contribution of German-Jewish Scholars to Jewish Studies in the United Kingdom," in *Second Chance: Two Centuries of German-Speaking Jews in the United Kingdom,* ed. Werner E. Mosse et al. (Tübingen, 1991), 437–62.

8. Figes, quoted in Stephen Brook, *The Club: The Jews of Modern Britain* (London, 1989), 323.

9. Ben Rogers, *A. J. Ayer: A Life* (London, 1999), 270–71; Charles Hannam, *Almost an Englishman* (London, 1979), 88. When the French Jewish art dealer René Gimpel (1881–1945) visited a nephew who was studying at Oxford before World War I, his nephew told him that he often heard the phrase there "We hate brain." Gimpel concluded from his visit that in Oxford's "peaceful, crenelated courts" its students learned that "all agitation is vain; that one of the secrets of a happy life is to watch it pass from one's window; that running won't help you go farther and that jostling is hateful." René Gimpel, *Diary of an Art Dealer,* trans. John Rosenberg (New York, 1966), 236.

10. Jonathan Brent, "What Facts? A Talk with Roth," *The New York Times Book Review,* 25 September 1988, 46.

11. Selig Brodetsky and Herbert Loewe, *The Intellectual Level of Anglo-Jewish Life* (London, 1928), 9.

12. Bryan Cheyette, "Moroseness and Jewishness: The Rise of British Jewish Literature," *The Jewish Quarterly,* no. 157 (spring 1995); 23.

13. See, for example, Edith Zangwill to Redcliffe Nathan Salaman, 24 May 1923, Add MS. 8171/61, Redcliffe Nathan Salaman Collection, Cambridge University Library.

Glossary of Hebrew
and Yiddish Words

aggadah (s.), *aggadot* (pl.)	Nonlegal materials in the Talmud and other rabbinic texts.
aliyyah (s.), *aliyyot* (pl.)	Lit., ascent, going up; (1) settling permanently in the Land of Israel; (2) the honor of being called to the reading of the Torah in the synagogue.
amidah	Lit., standing; the central section of all obligatory prayers, recited while standing.
ascama (s.), *ascamot* (pl.)	Communal rules and regulations in Sephardi congregations; from the Hebrew *haskamah,* agreement.
bet din (s.), *batei din* (pl.)	Court of law.
bet midrash (s.), *batei midrash* (pl.)	Hall or room for the study of the Talmud and other rabbinic texts, often served as communal library as well.
dayyan (s.), *dayyanim* (pl.)	Judge.
haham	Lit., wise one; the rabbinic head of the London Sephardi community.
halakhah	Jewish law.
haskalah	The Jewish enlightenment.
hazzan	Cantor.
heder (s.), *hadarim* (pl.)	One-room, ungraded, private elementary religious school, usually in the teacher's house.
herem	Ban that isolates an individual from the community for nonconformist behavior.

315

hevrah (s.), *hevrot* (pl.)	Society, fellowship.
ivrit-be-ivrit	The method of teaching Hebrew, in Hebrew, as a modern living language.
kaddish	Liturgical text in praise of God recited at the conclusion of each principal section of the service, best known as text recited by mourners.
kashrut	System of dietary laws and regulations.
kriyyat ha-torah	The public reading of the Torah in the synagogue.
maariv	Evening service.
maggid	Preacher.
mahamad	The board or governing council of a Western Sephardi community, from the Hebrew *maamad*, orig., the representatives of the people who assisted at the Temple sacrifices in antiquity.
maskil (s.), *maskilim* (pl.)	Adherent of the Jewish enlightenment.
matsah (s.), *matsot* (pl.)	Unleavened "bread" eaten at Passover.
melammed (s.), *melammedim* (pl.)	Low-status teacher in elementary religious school.
minyan (s.), *minyanim* (pl.)	Lit., number; (1) quorum of ten adult males required for public prayer; (2) small, informal, private congregation.
mi-she-berakh	Special prayer in honor of friends or relatives of person receiving an *aliyyah*.
mishnah	Earliest compilation of rabbinic teachings and discussions (ca. 200 C.E.), the foundational textual stratum of the Talmud.
mitsvah (s.), *mitsvot* (pl.)	Divine commandment.
mussaf	Additional service on Sabbaths and festivals.
parnas (s.), *parnasim* (pl.)	Member of communal governing board or council.
piyyut (s.), *piyyutim* (pl.)	Medieval liturgical poem added to the statutory prayers, often written in overblown, obscure, grammatically incorrect Hebrew.
rav	Rabbi, teacher, master.
shaharit	Morning service.
shehitah	Method of slaughtering that makes animals or birds fit for consumption by Jews.
shohet	Jewish male trained and certified to perform *shehitah*.

shtiebel	Yiddish term for a small, informal congregation that meets in a private residence or storefront.
shtille huppah	Yiddish term for marriage ceremony conducted by unauthorized persons, without the supervision of communal officials.
Simhat Torah	Lit., rejoicing of the Law; autumn festival marking the completion of the annual cycle of reading the Torah.
tallit	Prayer shawl.
talmud torah	Community-funded religious school; before the twentieth century, largely for the poor.
tefillin	Leather straps and boxes, containing biblical texts, worn by Jewish men age thirteen and over during weekday morning prayer.
tref	Not kosher.
yeshivah (s.), *yeshivot* (pl.)	Academy for the study of Jewish law.

Bibliography

Abrahams, Beth-Zion Lask. "Emanuel Deutsch of 'The Talmud' Fame." *Transactions of the Jewish Historical Society of England* 23 (1971): 53–63.

Adler, Henrietta. "Jewish Life and Labour in East London." In *The New Survey of London Life and Labour*, edited by H. Llewellyn Smith, vol. 6, 268–98. London, 1934.

Alderman, Geoffrey. "Anglo-Jewry and Its Present Discontents." *The Jewish Quarterly*, no. 158 (summer 1995): 21–25.

———. *The Federation of Synagogues, 1887–1987*. London, 1987.

———. *The Jewish Community in British Politics*. Oxford, 1983.

———. *London Jewry and London Politics, 1889–1986*. London, 1989.

———. "M. H. Davis: The Rise and Fall of a Communal Upstart." *Transactions of the Jewish Historical Society of England* 31 (1990): 249–68.

———. *Modern British Jewry*. Oxford, 1992.

———. "Power, Authority and Status in British Jewry: The Chief Rabbinate and Shechita." In *Outsiders and Outcasts: Essays in Honour of William J. Fishman*, edited by Geoffrey Alderman and Colin Holmes, 12–31. London, 1993.

Allett, John. "New Liberalism, Old Prejudices: J. A. Hobson and the 'Jewish Question.'" *Jewish Social Studies* 49 (1987): 99–114.

Allfrey, Anthony. *Edward VII and His Jewish Court*. London, 1991.

Apple, Raymond. *The Hampstead Synagogue, 1892–1967*. London, 1967.

Aris, Stephen. *But There Are No Jews in England*. New York, 1971.

Aronsfeld, C. C. "Anti-Jewish Outbreaks in Modern Britain." *The Gates of Zion* 6, 4 (July 1952): 15–18, 21.

———. "German Jews in Victorian England." *Leo Baeck Institute Year Book* 7 (1962): 312–29.

———. "Jewish Enemy Aliens in England during the First World War." *Jewish Social Studies* 18 (1956): 275–83.

Barnett, Arthur. "Eliakim ben Abraham (Jacob Hart): An Anglo-Jewish Scholar of the Eighteenth Century." *Transactions of the Jewish Historical Society of England* 14 (1940): 207–20.

———. "Sussex Hall—The First Anglo-Jewish Venture in Popular Education." *Transactions of the Jewish Historical Society of England* 19 (1960): 65–79.

———. *The Western Synagogue through Two Centuries (1761–1961).* London, 1961.

Barnett, Lionel D., ed. *Bevis Marks Records, Being Contributions to the History of the Spanish and Portuguese Congregation of London.* 2 vols. Oxford, 1940–49.

Barnett, Richard D. *Bevis Marks Records.* Vol. 4, *The Circumcision Register of Isaac and Abraham de Paiba (1715–1775).* London, 1991.

Baum, Jeffrey, and Barbara Baum. *A Light unto My Path: The Story of H. N. Solomon of Edmonton.* Edmonton, Eng. 1981.

Bayme, Steven. "Claude Montefiore, Lily Montagu and the Origins of the Jewish Religious Union." *Transactions of the Jewish Historical Society of England* 27 (1982): 61–71.

———. "Jewish Leadership and Anti-Semitism in Britain, 1898–1918." Ph.D. diss., Columbia University, 1976.

Beckman, Morris. *The 43 Group.* London, 1992.

———. *The Hackney Crucible.* London, 1996.

Benayahu, Meir. "Vikuhim ba-kehillah ha-sefaradit ve-ha-portugezit be-London ve-teshuvot ha-hakham rabbi Raphael Meldola [Disputes in the Spanish and Portuguese community of London and the responsa of Rabbi Raphael Meldola]." *Michael: On the History of the Jews in the Diaspora* 10 (1986): 9–77.

Bentwich, Norman. *They Found Refuge.* London, 1956.

Bentwich, Norman, and Margery Bentwich. *Herbert Bentwich: The Pilgrim Father.* Jerusalem, [ca. 1940].

Bentwich, Norman, and John M. Shaftesley. "Forerunners of Zionism in the Victorian Era." In *Remember the Days: Essays on Anglo-Jewish History Presented to Cecil Roth,* edited by John M. Shaftesley, 207–39. London, 1966.

Berghahn, Marion. *German-Jewish Refugees in England.* London, 1984.

Bermant, Chaim. *Lord Jakobovits: The Authorized Biography of the Chief Rabbi.* London, 1990.

———. *Point of Arrival: A Study of London's East End.* London, 1975.

———. *Troubled Eden: An Anatomy of British Jewry.* New York, 1970.

Birmingham Jewish History Research Group. *Birmingham Jewry.* 2 vols. Birmingham, 1980–84.

Black, Eugene C. "The Anglicization of Orthodoxy: The Adlers, Father and Son." In *Profiles in Diversity: Jews in a Changing Europe, 1750–1870,* edited by Frances Malino and David Sorkin, 295–325. Detroit, 1998.

———. *The Social Politics of Anglo-Jewry, 1880–1920.* Oxford, 1988.

Black, Gerry. *J.F.S.: A History of the Jews' Free School, since 1732.* London, 1998.

———. *Lender to the Lords, Giver to the Poor.* London, 1992.

Blok, Geoffrey D. M., and Harry C. Schwab. *A Survey of Jewish Students at the British Universities.* London, 1938.

Bolchover, Richard. *British Jewry and the Holocaust.* Cambridge, 1993.

Braude, Jacob. "Jewish Education in Britain Today." In *Jewish Life in Britain, 1962–1977*, edited by V. D. Lipman and Sonia Lipman, 119–29. New York, 1981.

Brenner, Michael, Rainer Liedtke, and David Rechter, eds. *Two Nations: The Historical Experiences of British and German Jews in Comparative Perspective.* Tübingen, 1999.

Bristow, Edward J. *Prostitution and Prejudice: The Jewish Fight against White Slavery, 1870–1939.* New York, 1983.

Brook, Stephen. *The Club: The Jews of Modern Britain.* London, 1989.

Brotz, Howard M. "The Outlines of Jewish Society in London." In *A Minority in Britain: Social Studies of the Anglo-Jewish Community,* edited by Maurice Freedman, 135–97. London, 1955.

Buckman, Joseph. *Immigrants and the Class Struggle: The Jewish Immigrant in Leeds, 1880–1914.* Manchester, 1983.

Bunt, Sidney. *Jewish Youth Work in Britain: Past, Present, and Future.* London, 1975.

Burletson, Louise. "The State, Internment and Public Criticism in the Second World War." In *The Internment of Aliens in Twentieth Century Britain,* edited by David Cesarani and Tony Kushner. London, 1993.

Burman, Rickie. "The Jewish Woman as the Breadwinner." *Oral History Journal* 10, 2 (autumn 1982): 27–39.

———. "Jewish Women and the Household Economy in Manchester, c. 1890–1920." In *The Making of Modern Anglo-Jewry,* edited by David Cesarani, 55–75. Oxford, 1990.

Carlebach, Julius. "The Impact of German Jews on Anglo-Jewry—Orthodoxy, 1850–1950." In *Second Chance: Two Centuries of German-Speaking Jews in the United Kingdom,* edited by Werner E. Mosse et al., 405–23. Tübingen, 1991.

Carrier, J. W. "A Jewish Proletariat." In *Explorations: An Annual on Jewish Themes,* edited by Murray Mindlin and Chaim Bermant, 120–40. Chicago, 1967.

Cesarani, David. "Dual Heritage or Duel of Heritages? Englishness and Jewishness in the Heritage Industry." In *The Jewish Heritage in British History: Englishness and Jewishness,* edited by Tony Kushner, 29–41. London, 1992.

———. "The East London of Simon Blumenfeld's *Jew Boy*." *London Journal* 13 (1987–88): 46–53.

———. "An Embattled Minority: The Jews in Britain during the First World War." *Immigrants and Minorities* 8 (1989): 61–81.

———. "A Funny Thing Happened on the Way to the Suburbs: Social Change in Anglo-Jewry between the Wars, 1914–1945." *Jewish Culture and History* 1, 1 (1998): 5–26.

———. *The "Jewish Chronicle" and Anglo-Jewry, 1841–1991.* Cambridge, 1994.

———. "One Hundred Years of Zionism in England." *European Judaism* 25, 1 (spring 1992): 40–47.

———. *Reporting Anti-Semitism: The "Jewish Chronicle," 1879–1979.* The Parkes Lecture, 1993. Southampton, Eng., 1994.

————. "The Transformation of Communal Authority in Anglo-Jewry." In *The Making of Modern Anglo-Jewry,* edited by David Cesarani. Oxford, 1990.

————. "Zionism in England, 1917–1939." D.Phil. diss., University of Oxford, 1986.

————, ed. *The Making of Modern Anglo-Jewry.* Oxford, 1990.

Cheyette, Bryan. *Constructions of 'The Jew' in English Literature and Society: Racial Representations, 1875–1945.* Cambridge, 1993.

————. "H. G. Wells and the Jews: Antisemitism, Socialism and English Culture." *Patterns of Prejudice* 22, 3 (winter 1988): 22–35.

————. "Moroseness and Jewishness: The Rise of British Jewish Literature." *The Jewish Quarterly,* no. 157 (spring 1995): 22–26.

Cohen, Lucy. *Arthur Cohen: A Memoir by His Daughter for His Descendants.* London, 1919.

Cohen, Norman. "Trends in Anglo-Jewish Religious Life." In *Jewish Life in Modern Britain,* edited by Julius Gould and Shaul Esh, 41–66. London, 1964.

Cohen, Robert. "'La-vo im mishpehoteyhem . . . u-lehityashev kan': yahadut London ha-sefardit be-mahatsit ha-sheniyah shel ha-meah ha-sheva-esreh." ["To come with their families . . . and dwell here": London Sephardi Jewry in the second half of the seventeenth century]. In *Gerush ve-shivah: yehudei angliyah be-hilufei ha-zemanim* [Exile and return: Anglo-Jewry through the ages], edited by Yosef Kaplan and David Katz, 147–58. Jerusalem, 1993.

Cohen, Stuart A. *English Zionists and British Jews: The Communal Politics of Anglo-Jewry, 1895–1920.* Princeton, N.J., 1982.

Collins, Kenneth. *Second City Jewry: The Jews of Glasgow in the Age of Expansion, 1790–1919.* Glasgow, 1990.

Cowen, Anne, and Roger Cowen. *Victorian Jews through British Eyes.* Oxford, 1986.

Daiches, David. *Two Worlds: A Jewish Childhood in Edinburgh.* New York, 1956.

Dalin, David G. "America-Bound: *Wissenschaft* in England." In *The Jewish Legacy and the German Conscience: Essays in Memory of Rabbi Joseph Asher,* edited by Moses Rischin and Raphael Asher, 99–114. Berkeley, Calif., 1991.

Davis, Richard. *The English Rothschilds.* Chapel Hill, N.C., 1983.

Diamond, A. S. "The Community of the Resettlement, 1656–1684: A Social Survey." *Transactions of the Jewish Historical Society of England* 24 (1975): 134–50.

————. "Problems of the London Sephardi Community, 1720–1733—Philip Carteret Webb's Notebooks." *Transactions of the Jewish Historical Society of England* 21 (1968): 39–63.

Dobkin, Monty. *Tales of Manchester Jewry and Manchester in the Thirties.* Manchester, 1986.

Donaldson, Frances. *The Marconi Scandal.* London, 1962.

Duschinsky, Charles. *The Rabbinate of the Great Synagogue, London, from 1756–1842.* London, 1921.

Emanuel, Charles H. L. *A Century and a Half of Jewish History Extracted from the Minute Books of the London Committee of Deputies of the British Jews.* London, 1910.

Endelman, Todd M. "Anti-Semitism in War-Time Britain: Evidence from the Victor Gollancz Collection." *Michael: On the History of the Jews in the Diaspora* 10 (1986): 75–95.

———. "Benjamin Disraeli and the Myth of Sephardi Superiority." *Jewish History* 10, 2 (fall 1996): 21–35.

———. "The Checkered Career of 'Jew' King: A Study in Anglo-Jewish Social History." *AJS Review* 7–8 (1982–83): 69–100. Reprinted in *Profiles in Diversity: Jews in a Changing Europe, 1750–1870*, edited by Frances Malino and David Sorkin, 151–81. Detroit, 1998.

———. "The Decline of the Anglo-Jewish Notable." *The European Legacy — Toward New Paradigms* 4, 6 (December 1999): 58–71.

———. "Disraeli's Jewishness Reconsidered." *Modern Judaism* 5 (1985): 109–23.

———. "English Jewish History." *Modern Judaism* 11 (1991): 91–109.

———. "The Englishness of Jewish Modernity in England." In *Toward Modernity: The European Jewish Model*, edited by Jacob Katz, 225–46. New Brunswick, N.J., 1987.

———. "The Frankaus of London: A Study in Radical Assimilation, 1837–1967." *Jewish History* 8, 1–2 (winter 1994): 1–38.

———. "German-Jewish Settlement in Victorian England." In *Second Chance: Two Centuries of German-Speaking Jews in the United Kingdom*, edited by Werner E. Mosse et al., 37–56. Tübingen, 1991.

———. "'A Hebrew to the End': The Emergence of Disraeli's Jewishness." In *The Self-Fashioning of Disraeli, 1818–1851*, edited by Charles Richmond and Paul Smith, 106–30. Cambridge, 1999.

———. "Jewish Self-Hatred in Britain and Germany." In *Two Nations: The Historical Experiences of British and German Jews in Comparative Perspective*, edited by Michael Brenner, Rainer Liedtke, and David Rechter. Tübingen, 1999.

———. "Jews, Aliens and Other Outsiders in British History." *The Historical Journal* 37 (1994): 959–69.

———. *The Jews of Georgian England, 1714–1830: Tradition and Change in a Liberal Society.* Philadelphia, 1979. 2nd ed., Ann Arbor, Mich., 1999.

———. *Radical Assimilation in English Jewish History, 1656–1945.* Bloomington, Ind., 1990.

Endelman, Todd M., and Tony Kushner, eds. *Disraeli's Jewishness.* London, 2002.

Englander, David. "Booth's Jews: The Presentation of Jews and Judaism in *Life and Labour of the People in London*." *Victorian Studies* 32 (1989): 551–72.

———. "*Stille Huppah* (Quiet Marriage) among Jewish Immigrants in Britain." *The Jewish Journal of Sociology* 34 (1992): 85–109.

Feldman, David. *Englishmen and Jews: Social Relations and Political Culture, 1840–1914.* New Haven, Conn., 1994.

———. "The Importance of Being English: Jewish Immigration and the Decay of Liberal England." In *Metropolis — London: Histories and Representations since*

1800, edited by David Feldman and Gareth Stedman Jones, 56–84. London, 1989.

Felsenstein, Frank. *Anti-Semitic Stereotypes: A Paradigm of Otherness in English Popular Culture, 1660–1830.* Baltimore, Md., 1995.

Ferguson, Niall. *The House of Rothschild: Money's Prophets, 1798–1848.* New York, 1998.

Fersht, B. A. "Chebrah Rodphea Sholom—Notes upon the First Jewish Friendly Society in England." *Miscellanies of the Jewish Historical Society of England* 2 (1935): 90–98.

Feuchtwanger, Edgar J. "'Jew Feelings' and *Realpolitik:* Disraeli as a Maker of Foreign and Imperial Policies." In *Disraeli's Jewishness,* edited by Todd M. Endelman and Tony Kushner. London, 2002.

Finestein, Israel. "Anglo-Jewish Opinion during the Struggle for Emancipation." *Transactions of the Jewish Historical Society of England* 20 (1964): 113–43.

———. *Anglo-Jewry in Changing Times: Studies in Diversity, 1840–1914.* London, 1999.

———. "Early and Middle Nineteenth Century British Opinion on the Restoration of the Jews: Contrasts with America." In *With Eyes Toward Zion,* edited by Moshe Davis, vol. 2, 72–101. New York, 1986.

———. "Jewish Emancipationists in Victorian England: Self-Imposed Limits to Assimilation." In *Assimilation and Community in Nineteenth-Century Europe,* edited by Jonathan Frankel and Steven J. Zipperstein, 38–56. Cambridge, 1992.

———. *Jewish Society in Victorian England: Collected Essays.* London, 1993.

———. "The Lay Leadership of the United Synagogue since 1870." In *A Century of Anglo-Jewish Life, 1870–1970,* edited by Salmond S. Levin, 29–41. London, n.d.

———. "The Uneasy Victorian: Montefiore as Communal Leader." In *The Century of Moses Montefiore,* edited by Sonia Lipman and V. D. Lipman, 45–70. Oxford, 1985.

Fisch, Solomon. *Yeriot Shlomoh: pirkei hayyim, divrei hagut, derashot, ve-hidushei torah* [The pages of Solomon: Memoirs, studies, addresses, novellae]. Jerusalem, 1983.

Fishman, William J. *East End Jewish Radicals, 1875–1914.* London, 1975.

Freedman, Maurice. "Jews in the Society of Britain." In *A Minority in Britain: Social Studies of the Anglo-Jewish Community,* edited by Maurice Freedman, 199–242. London, 1995.

Freedman, Murray. *Leeds Jewry: The First Hundred Years.* Leeds, 1992.

Friedland, Martin L. *The Trials of Israel Lipski: A True Story of a Victorian Murder in the East End of London.* New York, 1984.

Friedman, Isaiah. *The Question of Palestine, 1914–1918: British-Jewish-Arab Relations.* London, 1973.

Gainer, Bernard. *The Alien Invasion: The Origins of the Aliens Act of 1905.* New York, 1972.

Galchinsky, Michael. *The Origin of the Modern Jewish Writer: Romance and Reform in Victorian England*. Detroit, 1996.

Garrard, John A. *The English and Immigration: A Comparative Study of the Jewish Influx, 1880–1910*. London, 1971.

Gartner, Lloyd P. "Anglo-Jewry and the Jewish International Traffic in Prostitution, 1885–1914." *AJS Review* 7–8 (1982–93): 129–78.

———. *The Jewish Immigrant in England, 1870–1914*. 2nd ed. London, 1973.

———. "Jewish Migrants en route from Europe to America: Traditions and Realities." *Jewish History* 1, 2 (fall 1986): 49–66.

———. "Mehagrim yehudim mi-mizrah eiropah be-angliyah: esrim ve-hameish shenot historiyografiyah." [Jewish immigrants from Eastern Europe in England: Twenty-five years of historiography]. In *Temurot be-historiyah ha-yehudit he-hadashah: kovets maamarim shai le Shmuel Ettinger* [Transformation and change in modern Jewish history: Essays presented in honour of Shmuel Ettinger], edited by Shmuel Almog et al., 527–42. Jerusalem, 1987.

———. "Urban History and the Pattern of Provincial Jewish Settlement in Victorian England." *Jewish Journal of Sociology* 23 (1981): 37–55.

Gerlis, Daphne, and Leon Gerlis. *The Story of the Grimsby Jewish Community*. Hull, 1986.

Gershon, Karen. *We Came as Children: A Collective Autobiography*. London, 1989.

Gewirtz, Sharon. "Anglo-Jewish Responses to Nazi Germany, 1933–39: The Anti-Nazi Boycott and the Board of Deputies of British Jews." *Journal of Contemporary History* 26 (1991): 255–76.

———. "Anti-Fascist Activity in Manchester's Jewish Community in the 1930s." *Manchester Region History Review* 4, 1 (spring–summer 1990): 17–27.

Gilam, Abraham. *The Emancipation of the Jews in England, 1830–1860*. New York, 1982.

Glaser, Anthony. "The Tredegar Riots of August 1911." In *The Jews of South Wales: Historical Studies*, edited by Ursula R. Q. Henriques, 151–76. Cardiff, 1993.

Glaser, Anthony, and Ursula R. Q. Henriques. "The Valley Communities." In *The Jews of South Wales: Historical Studies*, edited by Ursula R. Q. Henriques, 45–67. Cardiff, 1993.

Glasman, Judy. "Assimilation by Design: London Synagogues in the Nineteenth Century." In *The Jewish Heritage in British History: Englishness and Jewishness*, edited by Tony Kushner, 171–209. London, 1992.

Glassman, Bernard. *Anti-Semitic Stereotypes without Jews: Images of the Jews in England, 1290–1700*. Detroit, 1975.

———. *Protean Prejudice: Anti-Semitism in England's Age of Reason*. Atlanta, Ga., 1998.

Godley, Andrew. "Immigrant Entrepreneurs and the Emergence of London's East End as an Industrial District." *London Journal* 21 (1996): 38–45.

———. "Jewish Soft Loan Societies in New York and London and Immigrant Entrepreneurship, 1880–1914." *Business History* 38, 3 (1997): 101–16.

———. "Leaving the East End: Regional Mobility among East European Jews in London, 1880–1914." In *London — The Promised Land? The Migrant Experience in a Capital City,* edited by Anne J. Kershen, 50–65. Aldershot, Eng., 1997.

Goldish, Matt. "Jews, Christians and Conversos: Rabbi Solomon Aailion's Struggles in the Portuguese Community of London." *Journal of Jewish Studies* 45 (1994): 227–57.

Goldman, A. L. "The Resurgence of Antisemitism in Britain during World War II." *Jewish Social Studies* 46 (1984): 37–50.

Goodman, Mervyn. "The Jewish Community of Liverpool." *Jewish Journal of Sociology* 38 (1996): 89–104.

Goodman, Paul. *B'nai B'rith: The First Lodge of England, 1910–1935.* London, 1936.

———. *Zionism in England, 1899–1949: A Jubilee Record.* London, 1949.

Gorni, Yosef. "Beatrice Webb's Views on Judaism and Zionism." *Jewish Social Studies* 40 (1978): 95–116.

Gould, Julius, and Shaul Esh, eds. *Jewish Life in Modern Britain.* London, 1964.

Goulston, Michael. "The Status of the Anglo-Jewish Rabbinate, 1840–1914." *Jewish Journal of Sociology* 10 (1968): 55–82.

Green, Geoffrey L. *The Royal Navy and Anglo-Jewry, 1740–1820: Traders and Those Who Served.* London, 1989.

Greenberg, Suzanne Kirsch. "Anglicization and the Education of Jewish Immigrant Children in the East End of London." In *Jewish History: Essays in Honour of Chimen Abramsky,* edited by Ada Rapoport-Albert and Steven J. Zipperstein, 11–26. London, 1988.

———. "Compromise and Conflict: The Education of Jewish Immigrant Children in London in the Aftermath of Emancipation, 1881–1905." Ph.D. diss., Stanford University, 1985.

Gutwein, Daniel. *The Divided Elite: Economics, Politics and Anglo-Jewry, 1882–1917.* Leiden, 1992.

Harding, John. *Jack Kid Berg: The Whitechapel Windmill.* London, 1987.

Hein, Virginia Herzog. "The British Followers of Theodor Herzl: English Zionist Leaders, 1896–1904." Ph.D. diss., Georgia State University, 1978.

Henriques, Basil L. Q. *Fratres: Club Boys in Uniform.* London, 1951.

———. *The Indiscretions of a Warden.* London, 1937.

Henriques, H. S. Q. *The Jews and the English Law.* London, 1908.

———. *The Return of the Jews to England, Being a Chapter in the History of English Law.* London, 1905.

Henriques, Ursula R. Q. "The Jewish Community of Cardiff, 1813–1914." *Welsh History Review* 14 (1988): 269–300.

Hirshfield, Claire. "The Anglo-Boer War and the Issue of Jewish Culpability." *Journal of Contemporary History* 15 (1980): 619–31.

———. "Labouchere, *Truth* and the Uses of Antisemitism." *Victorian Periodicals Review* 26 (1993): 134–42.

Holmes, Colin. *Anti-Semitism in British Society, 1876–1939.* New York, 1979.

———. "East End Crime and the Jewish Community." In *The Jewish East End, 1840–1939,* edited by Aubrey Newman, 109–23. London, 1981.

Homa, Bernard. *Footprints on the Sands of Time.* Gateshead, 1990.

———. *Orthodoxy in Anglo-Jewry, 1880–1940*. London, 1969.

Hyamson, Albert. *The Sephardim of England: A History of the Spanish and Portuguese Jewish Community, 1492–1951*. London, 1951.

Hyman, Leonard. "Hyman Hurwitz: The First Anglo-Jewish Professor." *Transactions of the Jewish Historical Society of England* 21 (1968): 232–42.

Israel, Jonathan I. "Menasseh ben Israel and the Dutch Sephardic Colonization Movement of the Mid-Seventeenth Century (1645–1657)." In *Menasseh ben Israel and His World*, edited by Yosef Kaplan, Henry Mechoulan, and Richard H. Popkin, 139–63. Leiden, 1989.

Jacobs, Joseph. *Studies in Jewish Statistics: Social, Vital, and Anthropomorphic*. London, 1891.

Jakobovits, Immanuel. "An Analysis of Religious versus Secularist Trends in Anglo-Jewry, Especially during the Past Fifteen Years." In *Jewish Life in Britain, 1962–1977*, edited by V. D. Lipman and Sonia Lipman, 33–48. New York, 1981.

———. *The Attitude to Zionism of Britain's Chief Rabbis as Reflected in their Writings*. London, 1981.

———. *The East End and the Anglo-Jewish Community*. The First Annual Dayan Julius Jakobovits Memorial Lecture. London, 1948.

Jolles, Michael. *A Directory of Distinguished British Jews, 1830–1930*. London, 1999.

Josephs, Zoë. *Survivors: Jewish Refugees in Birmingham, 1933–1945*. Birmingham, 1988.

Julius, Anthony. *T. S. Eliot, Anti-Semitism, and Literary Form*. Cambridge, 1995.

Kadish, Sharman. *"A Good Jew and a Good Englishman": The Jewish Lads' and Girls' Brigade, 1895–1995*. London, 1995.

Kaplan, Yosef. "The Jewish Profile of the Spanish-Portuguese Community of London during the Seventeenth Century." *Judaism* 41 (1992): 229–40.

Kaplan, Yosef, Henry Mechoulan, and Richard H. Popkin, eds. *Menasseh ben Israel and His World*. Leiden, 1989.

Katz, David S. "The Abendana Brothers and the Christian Hebraists of Seventeenth-Century England." *The Journal of Ecclesiastical History* 40 (1989): 28–52.

———. *The Jews in the History of England, 1485–1850*. Oxford, 1994.

———. "The Jews of England and 1688." In *From Persecution to Toleration: The Glorious Revolution and Religion in England*, edited by Ole Peter Orell, Jonathan I. Israel, and Nicholas Tyacke. Oxford, 1991.

———. "The Marginalization of Early Modern Anglo-Jewish History." In *The Jewish Heritage in British History: Englishness and Jewishness*, edited by Tony Kushner, 60–77. London, 1992.

———. *Philo-Semitism and the Readmission of the Jews to England, 1603–1655*. Oxford, 1982.

Kaufmann, David. "Rabbi Zvi Ashkenazi and His Family in London." *Transactions of the Jewish Historical Society of England* 3 (1899):102–25.

Kershen, Anne J. "Convenience or Ideology? The Origins of Reform Judaism in Britain." *The Jewish Quarterly*, no. 146 (summer 1992): 55–59.

———. *150 Years of Progressive Judaism*. London, 1990.

———. "Trade Unionism amongst the Jewish Tailoring Workers of London and Leeds, 1872–1915." In *The Making of Modern Anglo-Jewry,* edited by David Cesarani, 34–52. Oxford, 1990.

———. *Uniting the Tailors: Trade Unionism amongst the Tailoring Workers of London and Leeds, 1870–1939.* London, 1995.

Kershen, Anne J., and Jonathan A. Romain. *Tradition and Change: A History of Reform Judaism in Britain, 1840–1995.* London, 1995.

Kobler, Franz. *The Vision Was There: A History of the British Movement for the Restoration of the Jews to Palestine.* London, 1956.

Kochan, Lionel E. "Jewish Restoration to Zion: Christian Attitudes in Britain in the Late 19th and Early 20th Centuries." In *With Eyes Toward Zion,* edited by Moshe Davis, vol. 2, 102–21. New York, 1986.

Kokosalakis, N. *Ethnic Identity and Religion: Tradition and Change in Liverpool Jewry.* Washington, D.C., 1982.

Kosmin, Barry A., and Caren Levy. *The Work and Employment of Suburban Jews: The Socio-Economic Findings of the 1978 Redbridge Jewish Survey.* London, 1981.

Krausz, Ernest. "The Economic and Social Structure of Anglo-Jewry." In *Jewish Life in Modern Britain,* edited by Julius Gould and Shaul Esh. London, 1964.

———. "The Edgware Survey: Occupation and Social Class." *Jewish Journal of Sociology* 11 (1969): 84.

———. *Leeds Jewry: Its History and Social Structure.* Cambridge, 1964.

Kushner, Tony. "An Alien Occupation—Jewish Refugees and Domestic Service in Britain, 1933–1948." In *Second Chance: Two Centuries of German-Speaking Jews in the United Kingdom,* edited by Werner E. Mosse et al., 553–78. Tübingen, 1991.

———. "Anti-Semitism and Austerity: The August 1947 Riots in Britain." In *Racial Violence in Britain, 1840–1950,* edited by Panikos Panayi. Leicester, Eng., 1993.

———. "Clubland, Cricket Tests and Alien Internment, 1939–40." In *The Internment of Aliens in Twentieth-Century Britain,* edited by David Cesarani and Tony Kushner. London, 1993.

———. "The End of the 'Anglo-Jewish Progress Show': Representations of the Jewish East End, 1887–1987." In *The Jewish Heritage in British History: Englishness and Jewishness,* edited by Tony Kushner, 78–105. London, 1992.

———. *The Holocaust and the Liberal Imagination: A Social and Cultural History.* Oxford, 1994.

———. "Jewish Communists in Twentieth-Century Britain: The Zaidman Collection." *Labour History Review* 55, 2 (1990): 66–75.

———. *The Persistence of Prejudice: Antisemitism in British Society during the Second World War.* Manchester, 1989.

———, ed. *The Jewish Heritage in British History: Englishness and Jewishness.* London, 1992.

Kushner, Tony, and Kenneth Lunn, eds. *Traditions of Intolerance: Historical Perspectives on Fascism and Race Discourse in Britain.* Manchester, 1989.

Lachs, Phyllis S. "A Study of a Professional Elite: Anglo-Jewish Barristers in the Nineteenth Century." *Jewish Social Studies* 44 (1982): 125–34.

Lebzelter, Gisela C. *Political Anti-Semitism in England, 1918–1939.* New York, 1978.

Lee, Alan. "Aspects of the Working-Class Response to the Jews in Britain, 1880–1914." In *Hosts, Immigrants and Minorities: Historical Responses to Newcomers in British Society, 1870–1914,* edited by Kenneth Lunn, 107–33. London, 1980.

Leperer, S. B. "Abraham ben Naphtali Tang—A Precursor of the Anglo-Jewish Haskalah." *Transactions of the Jewish Historical Society of England* 24 (1975): 82–88.

Levene, Mark. *War, Jews, and the New Europe: The Diplomacy of Lucien Wolf, 1914–1919.* Oxford, 1992.

Levine, Maurice. *Cheetham to Cordova: A Manchester Man of the Thirties.* Manchester, 1984.

Levine, Naomi B. *Politics, Religion and Love: The Story of H. H. Asquith, Venetia Stanley and Edwin Montagu, Based on the Life and Letters of Edwin Samuel Montagu.* New York, 1991.

Levy, Abraham. "The Origins of Scottish Jewry." *Transactions of the Jewish Historical Society of England* 19 (1960): 129–62.

Levy, E. Lawrence. *The Autobiography of an Athlete.* Birmingham, [ca. 1913].

Lewis, Chaim. *A Soho Address.* London, 1965.

Liberles, Robert. "The Jews and Their Bill: Jewish Motivations in the Controversy of 1753." *Jewish History* 2, 2 (fall 1987): 29–36.

———. "The Origins of the Jewish Reform Movement in England." *AJS Review* 1 (1976): 121–50.

Liedtke, Rainer. *Jewish Welfare in Hamburg and Manchester, c. 1850–1914.* Oxford, 1998.

Linett, Maren Tova. "Figuring the Modern: Jews as Metaphors in Modernist British Fiction." Ph.D. diss., University of Michigan, 1999.

Lipman, Sonia, and V. D. Lipman, eds. *The Century of Moses Montefiore.* Oxford, 1985.

Lipman, V. D. "The Anatomy of Medieval Anglo-Jewry." *Transactions of the Jewish Historical Society of England* 21 (1968): 65–77.

———. "Anglo-Jewish Attitudes to the Refugees from Central Europe, 1933–1939." In *Second Chance: Two Centuries of German-Speaking Jews in the United Kingdom,* edited by Werner E. Mosse et al., 519–31. Tübingen, 1991.

———. "The Booth and New London Surveys as Source Material for East London Jewry (1880–1930)." In *The Jewish East End, 1840–1939,* edited by Aubrey Newman. London, 1981.

———. *A Century of Social Service, 1859–1959: The Jewish Board of Guardians.* London, 1959.

———. *A History of the Jews in Britain since 1858.* New York, 1990.

———. "Jewish Settlement in the East End, 1840–1940." In *The Jewish East End, 1840–1939,* edited by Aubrey Newman. London, 1981.

———. "The Origins of Provincial Anglo-Jewry." In *Provincial Jewry in Victorian Britain,* edited by Aubrey Newman. London, 1975.

———. "The Rise of Jewish Suburbia." *Transactions of the Jewish Historical Society Of England* 21 (1968): 78–103.

———. "Sephardi and Other Jewish Immigrants in England in the Eighteenth Century." In *Migration and Settlement: Proceedings of the Anglo-American Jewish Historical Conference . . . July 1970*, 37–62. London, 1971.

———. *Social History of the Jews in England, 1850–1950*. London, 1954.

———. "Social Topography of a London Congregation: The Bayswater Synagogue, 1862–1963." *Jewish Journal of Sociology* 6 (1964): 69–74.

———. "The Structure of London Jewry in the Mid-Nineteenth Century." In *Essays Presented to Chief Rabbi Israel Brodie on the Occasion of His Seventieth Birthday*, edited by H. J. Zimmels, J. Rabinowitz, and Israel Finestein, 2 vols., 1: 253–73. London, 1967.

———. "A Survey of Anglo-Jewry in 1851." *Transactions of the Jewish Historical Society of England* 17 (1953): 171–88.

———, ed. *Sir Moses Montefiore: A Symposium*. Oxford, 1982.

Lipman, V. D., and Sonia Lipman, eds. *Jewish Life in Britain, 1962–1977*. New York, 1981.

Loewe, Lionel Louis, ed. *Basil Henriques: A Portrait Based on His Diaries, Letters and Speeches, as Collated by his Widow, Rose Henriques*. London, 1976.

Loewe, Raphael. "The Bernhard Baron Settlement and Oxford and St. George's Club." In *The Jewish East End, 1840–1939*, edited by Aubrey Newman, 143–46. London, 1981.

———. "The Contribution of German-Jewish Scholars to Jewish Studies in the United Kingdom." In *Second Chance: Two Centuries of German-Speaking Jews in the United Kingdom*, edited by Werner E. Mosse et al., 437–62. Tübingen, 1991.

Loewenstein, Andrea Freud. *Loathsome Jews and Engulfing Women: Metaphors of Projection in the Works of Wyndham Lewis, Charles Williams, and Graham Greene*. New York, 1993.

London, Louise. "Jewish Refugees, Anglo-Jewry and British Government Policy, 1930–1940." In *The Making of Modern Anglo-Jewry*, edited by David Cesarani, 163–90. Oxford, 1990.

———. *Whitehall and the Jews, 1933–1948: British Immigration Policy, Jewish Refugees and the Holocaust*. Cambridge, 2000.

McKeon, Michael. "Sabbatai Sevi in England." *AJS Review* 2 (1977): 131–69.

Marks, Lara V. "Carers and Servers of the Jewish Community: The Marginalized Heritage of Jewish Women in Britain." In *The Jewish Heritage in British History: Englishness and Jewishness*, edited by Tony Kushner, 106–27. London, 1992.

———. "'Dear Old Mother Levy's': The Jewish Maternity Home and Sick Room Helps Society, 1895–1939." *Social History of Medicine* 3 (1990): 61–87.

———. *Model Mothers: Jewish Mothers and Maternity Provision in East London, 1870–1939*. Oxford, 1994.

Martin, R. H. "United Conversionist Activities among the Jews in Great Britain, 1795–1815: Pan-Evangelicalism and the London Society for Promoting Christianity amongst the Jews." *Church History* 46 (1977): 437–52.

Matar, N. I. "The Controversy over the Restoration of the Jews: From 1754 until the London Society for Promoting Christianity among the Jews." *Durham University Journal*, January 1990, 29–44.

Mazower, David. *Yiddish Theatre in London*, 2nd ed. London, 1996.

Mechoulan, Henry, and Gerard Nahon. "Introduction" to Menasseh ben Israel, *The Hope of Israel—The English Translation by Moses Wall, 1652*. Oxford, 1987.

Menasseh ben Israel. *The Hope of Israel—The English Translation by Moses Wall, 1652*. Oxford, 1987.

Miller, Stephen H. "The Structure and Determinants of Jewish Identity in the United Kingdom." In *Jewish Survival: The Identity Problem at the Close of the Twentieth Century*, edited by E. Krausz and G. Tulea, 227–39. New Brunswick, N.J., 1998.

Mills, John. *The British Jews*. London, 1853.

Montagu, Lily H. *My Club and I: The Story of the West Central Jewish Club*. London, 1954.

Mosse, Werner E., Julius Carlebach, Gerhard Hirschfeld, Aubrey Newman, Arnold Paucker, and Peter Pulzer, eds. *Second Chance: Two Centuries of German-Speaking Jews in the United Kingdom*. Tübingen, 1991.

Mundill, Robin R. *England's Jewish Solution: Experiment and Expulsion, 1262–1290*. Cambridge, 1999.

Neustatter, Hannah. "Demographic and Other Statistical Aspects of Anglo-Jewry." In *A Minority in Britain: Social Studies of the Anglo-Jewish Community*, edited by Maurice Freedman, 55–133. London, 1955.

Newman, Aubrey. "The Chief Rabbinate and the Provinces, 1840–1914." In *Tradition and Transition: Essays Presented to Chief Rabbi Sir Immanuel Jakobovits to Celebrate Twenty Years in Office*, edited by Jonathan Sacks, 217–25. London, 1986.

———. *The United Synagogue, 1870–1970*. London, 1977.

———, ed. *The Jewish East End, 1840–1939*. London, 1981.

Olsover, Lewis. *The Jewish Communities of North-East England*. Gateshead, Eng., 1980.

Oren, Elhanan. *Hibbat tsiyyon be-britanyah, 1878–1898* [The Love of Zion movement in Britain]. Tel Aviv, 1974.

Pellew, Jill. "The Home Office and the Aliens Act, 1905." *The Historical Journal* 32 (1989): 369–85.

Perry, Norma. "Anglo-Jewry, the Law, Religious Conviction, and Self-Interest (1655–1753)." *Journal of European Studies* 14 (1984): 1–23.

Perry, Thomas W. *Public Opinion, Propaganda, and Politics in Eighteenth-Century England: A Study of the Jew Bill of 1753*. Cambridge, Mass., 1962.

Petukowski, Jacob J. *The Theology of Haham David Nieto: An Eighteenth-Century Defense of the Jewish Tradition*. Rev. ed. New York, 1970.

Pollins, Harold. *Economic History of the Jews in England*. Rutherford, N.J., 1982.

Popkin, Richard H. "David Levi, Anglo-Jewish Theologian." *Jewish Quarterly Review* 87 (1996–97): 79–101.

Prager, Leonard. *Yiddish Culture in Britain: A Guide*. Frankfurt am Main, 1990.

Prais, S. J., and M. Schmool. "The Social-Class Structure of Anglo-Jewry." *Jewish Journal of Sociology* 17 (1975): 5–15.

Prawer, S. S. *Israel at Vanity Fair: Jews and Judaism in the Writings of W. M. Thackeray.* Leiden, 1992.

Quinn, P. L. S. "The Jewish Schooling Systems of London, 1656–1956." Ph.D. diss., University of London, 1958.

Rabinowicz, Oskar K. *Sir Solomon de Medina.* London, 1974.

Ragussis, Michael. *Figures of Conversion: "The Jewish Question" and English National Identity.* Durham, N.C., 1995.

Rees, Goronwy. *St Michael: A History of Marks and Spencer.* Rev. ed. London, 1973.

Reilly, Joanne. *Belsen: The Liberation of a Concentration Camp.* London, 1998.

Richmond, Colin. "Englishness and Medieval Anglo-Jewry." In *The Jewish Heritage in British History: Englishness and Jewishness,* edited by Tony Kushner, 42–59. London, 1992.

Rochelson, Meri-Jane. "Language, Gender, and Ethnic Anxiety: Zangwill's *Children of the Ghetto.*" *English Literature in Transition* 31 (1988): 399–412.

Rose, Norman. *Lewis Namier and Zionism.* Oxford, 1980.

Rosenbaum, M. *The History of the Borough Synagogue.* London, 1917.

Rosenberg, Edgar. *From Shylock to Svengali: Jewish Stereotypes in English Fiction.* Stanford, Calif., 1960

Ross, J. M. "Naturalization of Jews in England." *Transactions of the Jewish Historical Society of England* 24 (1975): 59–72.

Roth, Cecil. "The Chief Rabbinate of England." In *Essays and Portraits in Anglo-Jewish History.* Philadelphia, 1962.

———. "The Court Jews of Edwardian England." In *Essays and Portraits in Anglo-Jewish History,* 282–94. Philadelphia, 1962.

———. *Essays and Portraits in Anglo-Jewish History.* Philadelphia, 1962.

———. *The Great Synagogue, London, 1690–1940.* London, 1950.

———. "The Haskalah in England." In *Essays Presented to Chief Rabbi Israel Brodie on the Occasion of His Seventieth Birthday,* edited by H. J. Zimmels, J. Rabinowitz, and Israel Finestein, 2 vols., 1: 365–76. London, 1967.

———. *A History of the Jews in England.* 3rd ed. Oxford, 1964.

———. "The Lesser Synagogues of the Eighteenth Century." *Miscellanies of the Jewish Historical Society of England* 3 (1937): 1–7.

———. *A Life of Menasseh ben Israel—Rabbi, Printer, and Diplomat.* Philadelphia, 1934.

———. "The Lord Mayor's Salvers." In *Essays and Portraits in Anglo-Jewish History,* 108–112. Philadelphia, 1962.

———. *The Rise of Provincial Jewry: The Early History of the Jewish Communities in the English Countryside, 1740–1840.* London, 1950.

———. "The Vicissitudes of the First Oxford Jewish Graduate." *The Oxford Magazine,* n.s., 3 (1962–63): 230–32.

———. "Why Anglo-Jewish History?" *Transactions of the Jewish Historical Society of England* 22 (1970): 21–29.

————, ed. *Anglo-Jewish Letters (1158–1917)*. London, 1938.

Routledge, R. A. "The Legal Status of the Jews in England, 1190–1790." *The Journal of Legal History* 3 (1982): 91–124.

Rubinstein, William D. "The Anti-Jewish Riots of 1911 in South Wales: A Re-examination. *The Welsh History Review* 18 (1997): 667–99.

————. *A History of the Jews in the English-Speaking World: Great Britain*. London, 1996.

————. "Jews among Top British Wealth Holders, 1857–1969: Decline of the Golden Age." *Jewish Social Studies* 34 (1972): 73–84.

————. "Recent Anglo-Jewish Historiography and the Myth of Jix's Antisemitism." *Australian Journal of Jewish Studies* 7 (1993): 41–70.

Ruderman, David B. *Jewish Enlightenment in an English Key: Anglo-Jewry's Construction of Modern Jewish Thought*. Princeton, N.J., 2000.

Rumbelow, Donald. *The Siege of Sidney Street*. New York, 1973.

Russell, C., and H. S. Lewis. *The Jew in London: A Study of Racial Character and Present-Day Conditions*. London, 1900.

Salaman, Redcliffe N. *Whither Lucien Wolf's Anglo-Jewish Community?* London, 1954.

Salbstein, M. C. N. *The Emancipation of the Jews in Britain: The Question of the Admission of the Jews to Parliament, 1828–1860*. Rutherford, N.J., 1982.

Salomon, Sidney. *The Jews of Britain*. 2nd ed. London, 1938.

Samet, Moshe. *Moshe Montefiore: metsiyut ve-aggadah* [Moses Montefiore: Reality and myth]. Jerusalem, 1989.

Samuel, Edgar R. "The First Fifty Years." In *Three Centuries of Anglo-Jewish History,* edited by V. D. Lipman, 27–44. London, 1961.

————. "Passover in Shakespeare's London." *Transactions of the Jewish Historical Society of England* 26 (1979): 117–18.

Schatz, Rivka. "Emdato shel Menasheh ben Yisrael kelapei ha-meshihiyyut ba-maarakh ha-yehudi-notsri" [Menasseh ben Israel's approach to messianism in the Jewish-Christian context]. *Bar-Ilan* 22–23 (1987): 429–47.

Schmiechen, James A. *Sweated Industries and Sweated Labor: The London Clothing Trades, 1860–1914*. Urbana, Ill., 1984.

Schmool, Marlena, and Frances Cohen. *A Profile of British Jewry: Patterns and Trends at the Turn of the Century*. London, 1998.

Searle, G. R. *Corruption in British Politics, 1895–1930*. Oxford, 1987.

Sefton, W. Victor. "Growing Up Jewish in London, 1920–1950: A Perspective from 1973." In *Studies in the Cultural Life of the Jews in England,* edited by Dov Noy and Issachar Ben-Ami, 311–330. Jerusalem, 1975.

Shaftesley, John M. "Jews in English Regular Freemasonry, 1717–1860." *Transactions of the Jewish Historical Society of England* 25 (1977): 150–209.

Shane, A. L. "The Dreyfus Affair: Could It Have Happened in England?" *Transactions of the Jewish Historical Society of England* 30 (1989): 135–48.

Shapiro, James. *Shakespeare and the Jews*. New York, 1996.

Sharot, Stephen. "Native Jewry and the Religious Anglicization of Immigrants in London, 1870–1905." *Jewish Journal of Sociology* 16 (1974): 39–56.

————. "Reform and Liberal Judaism in London, 1840–1940." *Jewish Social Studies* 41 (1979): 211–28.

————. "Religious Change in Native Orthodoxy in London, 1870–1914: The Rabbinate and Clergy." *Jewish Journal of Sociology* 15 (1973): 167–87.

————. "Religious Change in Native Orthodoxy in London, 1870–1914: The Synagogue Service." *Jewish Journal of Sociology* 15 (1973): 57–78.

Sherman, A. J. *Britain and Refugees from the Third Reich, 1933–1939.* London, 1973.

Sherman, Michael D. "Christian Missions to the Jews in East London, 1870–1914." Master's thesis, Yeshiva University, 1983.

Shimoni, Gideon. "From Anti-Zionism to Non-Zionism in Anglo-Jewry, 1917–1937." *Jewish Journal of Sociology* 28 (1986):19–48.

————. "The Non-Zionists in Anglo-Jewry, 1937–1948." *Jewish Journal of Sociology* 28 (1986): 89–115.

————. "Poale Zion: A Zionist Transplant in Britain (1905–1945)." *Studies in Contemporary Jewry* 2 (1986): 227–69.

————. "Selig Brodetsky and the Ascendancy of Zionism in Anglo-Jewry (1939–1945)." *Jewish Journal of Sociology* 22 (1980): 125–61.

Silberner, Edmund. "British Socialism and the Jews." *Historia Judaica* 14 (1952): 27–52.

Singer, Alan H. "Aliens and Citizens: Jewish and Protestant Naturalization in the Making of the Modern British Nation, 1689–1753." Ph.D. diss., University of Missouri, Columbia, 1999.

Singer, Steven. "The Anglo-Jewish Ministry in Early Victorian London." *Modern Judaism* 5 (1985): 279–99.

————. "Jewish Education in the Mid-Nineteenth Century: A Study of the Early Victorian London Community." *Jewish Quarterly Review* 77 (1986–87): 163–78.

————. "Jewish Religious Observance in Early Victorian London, 1840–1860." *Jewish Journal of Sociology* 28 (1986): 117–37.

————. "Orthodox Judaism in Early Victorian London, 1840–1858." Ph.D. diss., Yeshiva University, 1981.

Smith, Elaine R. "East End Jews in Politics, 1918–1939: A Study in Class and Ethnicity." Ph.D. diss., University of Leicester, 1990.

————. "Jewish Responses to Political Antisemitism and Fascism in the East End of London, 1920–1939." In *Traditions of Intolerance: Historical Perspectives on Fascism and Race Discourse in Britain,* edited by Tony Kushner and Kenneth Lunn, 53–71. Manchester, 1989.

Smith, Paul. "Disraeli's Politics." *Transactions of the Royal Historical Society,* 5th ser., 37 (1987): 65–85.

Smith, Paul, and Charles Richmond, eds. *The Self-Fashioning of Disraeli, 1818–1851.* Cambridge, 1998.

Smith, Robert Michael. "The London Jews' Society and Patterns of Jewish Conversion in England, 1801–1859." *Jewish Social Studies* 43 (1981): 275–90.

Solomons, Israel. "David Nieto and Some of His Contemporaries." *Transactions of the Jewish Historical Society of England* 12 (1931): 1–101.

Sompolinsky, Meier. *The British Government and the Holocaust: The Failure of Anglo-Jewish Leadership?* Brighton, Eng., 1999.

Srebrnik, Henry Felix. *London Jews and British Communism, 1935–1945.* London, 1995.

Stacey, Robert C. "Yahadut angliyah be-meah ha-shalosh-esrei u-vaayat ha-gerush" [Thirteenth century Anglo-Jewry and the problem of the expulsion]. In *Gerush ve-shiva: yahadut angliyah be-hilufei ha-zemanim* [Banishment and return], edited by Yosef Kaplan and David Katz, 9–25. Jerusalem, 1992.

Stein, Leonard. *The Balfour Declaration.* New York, 1961.

Stein, Siegfried. "*Sefer Giddul Banim:* An Anonymous Judaeo-German Tract on the Education of Children, Printed in London in 1771." In *Remember the Days: Essays on Anglo-Jewish History Presented to Cecil Roth,* edited by John M. Shaftesley, 145–79. London, 1966.

Stent, Ronald. "Jewish Refugee Organisations." In *Second Chance: Two Centuries of German-Speaking Jews in the United Kingdom,* edited by Werner E. Mosse et al., 579–98. Tübingen, 1991.

Stone, Harry. "Dickens and the Jews." *Victorian Studies* 2 (1959): 223–53.

Sutherland, Lucy S. "Samson Gideon: Eighteenth Century Jewish Financier." *Transactions of the Jewish Historical Society of England* 17 (1953): 79–90.

Tishbi, Isaiah. "Yediot hadashot al kehilat ha-anusim be-London al pi iggerot Sasportas bi-shenat 5425 (1664–5)." [New information on the converso community in London according to letters of Sasportas from 1664–65]. In *Galut ahar golah: mehkarim be-toldot am yisrael mugashim le-professor Haim Beinart limlot lo shivim shanah* [Exile after exile: Essays in Jewish history presented to Professor Haim Beinart on his seventieth birthday], edited by Aharon Mirsky, Avraham Grosman, and Yosef Kaplan, 470–96. Jerusalem, 1988.

Tobias, J. J. *Prince of Fences: The Life and Crimes of Ikey Solomons.* London, 1974.

Trillin, Calvin. "Drawing the Line." *The New Yorker,* 12 December 1994, 50–62.

Tropp, Asher. *Jews in the Professions in Great Britain, 1891–1991.* London, 1991.

Tuchman, Barbara W. *Bible and Sword: England and Palestine from the Bronze Age to Balfour.* New York, 1956.

Tucker, Charles. "Jewish Marriages and Divorces in England until 1940." *The Genealogists' Magazine,* part 1, September 1992, cols. 173–85; part 2, December 1992, cols. 277–86.

Udelson, Joseph H. *Dreamer of the Ghetto: The Life and Works of Israel Zangwill.* Tuscaloosa, Ala., 1990.

Umansky, Ellen. *Lily Montagu and the Advancement of Liberal Judaism: From Vision to Vocation.* New York, 1983.

Voeltz, Richard A. "' . . . A Good Jew and a Good Englishman': The Jewish Lads' Brigade, 1894–1922." *Journal of Contemporary History* 23 (1988): 119–27.

Wasserstein, Bernard. *Britain and the Jews of Europe, 1939–1948.* Oxford, 1979.

———. *Herbert Samuel: A Political Life.* Oxford, 1992.

Waterman, Stanley, and Barry Kosmin. *British Jewry in the Eighties: A Statistical and Geographical Study.* London, 1986.

Wechsler, Robert Stephen. "The Jewish Garment Trade in East London, 1875–1914: A Study of Conditions and Responses." Ph.D. diss., Columbia University, 1979.

Weintraub, Stanley. *Disraeli: A Biography.* New York, 1993.

Wendehorst, Stephan. "British Jewry, Zionism and the Jewish State, 1936–1956." D.Phil. diss., University of Oxford, 1997.

White, Jerry. *Rothschild Buildings: Life in an East End Tenement Block, 1887–1920.* London, 1980.

Wilensky, Mordecai. *Shivat ha-yehudim le-angliyah ba-meah ha-sheva-esreh* [The return of the Jews to England in the seventeenth century]. Jerusalem, 1943.

Williams, Bill. "The Beginnings of Jewish Trade Unionism in Manchester, 1889–1891." In *Hosts, Immigrants and Minorities: Historical Responses to Newcomers in British Society, 1870–1914,* edited by Kenneth Lunn, 263–307. London, 1980.

———. "'East and West': Class and Community in Manchester Jewry, 1850–1914." In *The Making of Modern Anglo-Jewry,* edited by David Cesarani, 15–33. Oxford, 1990.

———. *The Making of Manchester Jewry, 1740–1875.* Manchester, 1976.

———. *Manchester Jewry: A Pictorial History, 1788–1988.* Manchester, 1988.

Wohl, Anthony S. "'Dizzi-Ben-Dizzi': Disraeli as Alien." *Journal of British Studies* 34 (1995): 375–411.

Wolf, Lucien. "Cromwell's Jewish Intelligencers." In *Essays in Jewish History,* edited by Cecil Roth, 93–114. London, 1934.

———. "Jews in Tudor England." In *Essays in Jewish History,* edited by Cecil Roth, 73–90. London, 1934.

———, ed. and trans. *Jews in the Canary Islands, Being a Calendar of Jewish Cases Extracted from the Records of the Canariote Inquisition in the Collection of the Marquess of Bute.* London, 1926.

Woolf, Maurice. "Foreign Trade of London Jews in the Seventeenth Century." *Transactions of the Jewish Historical Society of England* 24 (1975): 38–58.

Yogev, Gedalia. *Diamonds and Coral: Anglo-Dutch Jews and Eighteenth-Century Trade.* Leicester, 1978.

Index

Compositor:	Binghamton Valley Composition
Text:	10/13 Galliard
Display:	Galliard
Printer and Binder:	Sheridan Books, Inc.